Learning to Write, Reading to Learn

D0209955

Equinox Textbooks and Surveys in Linguistics
Series Editor: Robin Fawcett, Cardiff University

Published

Analysing Casual Conversation
Suzanne Eggins and Diana Slade

Genre Relations: Mapping Culture
J.R. Martin and David Rose

Intonation in the Grammar of English
M.A.K. Halliday and William S. Greaves

An Introduction to Irish English
Carolina P. Amador Moreno

An Introduction to Linguistics and Language Studies
Anne McCabe

Invitation to Systemic Functional Linguistics through the Cardiff Grammar: An Extension and Simplification of Halliday's Systemic Functional Grammar. Third edition
Robin Fawcett

Language in Psychiatry: A Handbook of Clinical Practice
Jonathan Fine

Meaning-Centered Grammar: An Introductory Text
Craig Hancock

Multimodal Transcription and Text Analysis: A Multimodal Toolkit and Coursebook with Associated On-line Course
Anthony Baldry and Paul J. Thibault

The Power of Language: How Discourse Influences Society
Lynne Young and Brigid Fitzgerald

The Western Classical Tradition in Linguistics
Second edition
Keith Allan

Writing Readable Research: A Guide for Students of Social Science
Beverly A. Lewin

Forthcoming

Corpora and Meaning
Steven Jones and Howard Jackson

Functional Syntax Handbook: Analysing English at the Level of Form
Robin Fawcett

An Introduction to English Sentence Structure: Clauses, Markers, Missing Elements
Jon Jonz

Multimodal Corpus-Based Approaches to Website Analysis
Anthony Baldry and Kay O'Halloran

Text Linguistics: The How and Why of Meaning
M.A.K. Halliday and Jonathan Webster

Learning to Write, Reading to Learn

Genre, Knowledge and Pedagogy
in the Sydney School

David Rose and J.R. Martin

Published by Equinox Publishing Ltd.

UK: Unit S3, Kelham House, 3 Lancaster Street, Sheffield, South Yorkshire S3 8AF

USA:ISD, 70 Enterprise Drive, Bristol, CT 06010

www.equinoxpub.com

First published 2012

© David Rose and J.R. Martin 2012

All rights reserved. No part of this publication may be reproduced or transmitted in any form or by any means, electronic or mechanical, including photocopying, recording or any information storage or retrieval system, without prior permission in writing from the publishers.

ISBN   978-1-84553-143-0   (hardback)
          978-1-84553-144-7   (paperback)

British Library Cataloguing-in-Publication Data
A catalogue record for this book is available from the British Library.

Library of Congress Cataloging-in-Publication Data
Rose, David, 1955-
  Learning to write, reading to learn : genre, knowledge and pedagogy in the Sydney school / David Rose and J.R. Martin.
      p. cm. -- (Equinox Textbooks and Surveys in Linguistics)
  Includes bibliographical references and index.
  ISBN 978-1-84553-143-0 -- ISBN 978-1-84553-144-7 (pb) 1. Language and languages--Study and teaching--Australia. 2. Language and education--Australia. 3. Literacy programs--Australia. 4. Linguistics--Research--Australia. I. Martin, J. R., 1950- II. Title.
  P57.A9R67 2010
  306.44'994--dc22
                          2011016470

Typeset by Steve Barganski, Sheffield
Printed and bound in the UK by MPG Books Group

Nganyinytja
(1928–2007)
For your inspiration, love and tireless work for others

Contents

Acknowledgements

In this book we describe genre-based literacy programs as they have evolved in the 'Sydney School' through three phases of development over three decades. There are many people we can thank for making this development possible, only a few of whom we have room to name here.

In the first phase, beginning with the *Writing Project* and *Language as Social Power* project, key contributions came from Joan Rothery's expertise in engaging functional linguistic theory in classroom practice, Brian Gray's 'concentrated language encounter' program for Indigenous children in Alice Springs, Gunther Kress's interest in genre and the politics of literacy, and the collaboration with Bill Cope and Mary Kalantzis through LERN (Literacy and Education Research Network). Mike Callaghan and Sue Doran initiated and fostered an ongoing collaboration with the Disadvantaged Schools Program (DSP) in Sydney, and John Carr from the Queensland Department of Education led the way in implementing genre in a state English syllabus.

In the second phase, the *Write it Right project* involved an enterprising team of researchers in language and education, including Robert Veel, Mary Macken-Horarik, Sally Humphrey, Caroline Coffin, Susan Feez, Maree Stenglin, Jon Callow and Katina Zammit (working alongside Jim and Joan). The third *Reading to Learn* phase has been enabled by a network of teacher educators of exceptional commitment and vision, including Kate Mullin of the Association of Independent Schools in WA, Claire Acevedo and Sarah Culican at the Catholic Education Office Melbourne, and Lyndall Harrison and Cheryll Koop of the NSW Department of Education, among many others.

In addition to this school based work, Carolyn Webb, Janet Jones and Helen Drury developed genre-based pedagogy for academic literacy in the Learning Centre at the University of Sydney, and Helen Joyce and Sue Hood, from the NSW Adult Migrant English Service (AMES), developed genre-based pedagogy, curriculum and assessment in relation to their TESOL context. Over the years, invaluable support was given by Geoff Williams and Len Unsworth, based in Education at the University of Sydney, and by Bev Derewianka and Jenny Hammond, at the University of Wollongong and later UTS. More recently Ahmar Mahboob and Shooshi Dreyfus worked with Jim and Sally on the SLATE project (Scaffolding Literacy in Tertiary and Academic Environments) and Peter Freebody, Karl Maton and Erika Matruglio worked with Jim on the DISKS project (Disciplinarity, Knowledge and Schooling).

Illustrations from *Rosie's Walk* by Pat Hutchins, published by The Bodley Head, are reprinted by permission of The Random House Group Limited.

Anyone who knows our work will be aware of the incomparable intellectual debt we owe to two remarkable theorists – the linguist Michael Halliday and the sociologist Basil Bernstein. Finally we need to make special mention of Frances Christie, whose institutional leadership and intellectual engagement, from our beginnings in 1979, were fundamental to the success of our project – and continue to be so. It is with great respect that we thank you, Fran.

1 Contexts

This chapter introduces the work on genre-based literacy pedagogy that has developed in the Sydney School over the past three decades. It begins with the social and educational contexts in which the Sydney School project began, followed by an analysis of the contexts of schooling informed by educational sociology. We then sketch out a general model of pedagogic practice that can be applied to integrating literacy teaching with learning the curriculum, with the goal of overcoming the inequality of outcomes produced by the school. The chapter concludes with an outline of the model of language in social context that underpins genre pedagogy.

1.1 Genre, knowledge and pedagogy in the Sydney School

The term 'Sydney School' was first coined in 1994 (by Green and Lee), to refer to the work in language and education that had begun over a decade earlier at the University of Sydney in the Department of Linguistics, where Jim was based. By 1994 the research project it referred to had already expanded well beyond Sydney to universities and school systems across Australia. The work has since become an international movement, with centres in Singapore and Hong Kong, the UK, Scandinavia, China, Indonesia, South Africa, and South and North America. For better or worse, Green and Lee's christening was published in the US and has become the name by which our work is known internationally (e.g. Coe, Lingard and Teslenko 2002, Freedman and Medway 1994a, Hyon 1996, Lee 1996, Johns 2002, Martin 2000a, b, Rose 2008a, 2011e).

The initial aim of the Sydney School project was to design a writing pedagogy that could enable any student to succeed with the writing demands of the school. The project began with research into types of writing in the primary school, out of which grew the concept of genre as a 'staged goal-oriented social process'.

The teaching strategies that were designed to guide students to write the genres of schooling became known as 'genre-based pedagogy', but the term we will generally use in this book is simply **genre pedagogy**. The project has gone through three broad phases, beginning with the initial research in the 1980s with the *Writing Project* and *Language and Social Power* project (outlined in Chapter 2). The second phase extended this research in the 1990s to describe the genres that students are expected to read and write across the secondary school curriculum, known as the *Write it Right* project (Chapter 3). The third phase over the past decade has applied this work to design a methodology for integrating reading and writing with learning the curriculum in primary, secondary and tertiary education, known as *Reading to Learn* (Chapter 4).

The word *knowledge* in our title refers in part to the knowledge of the school curriculum that reading and writing affords access to, at least for the most literate students. To understand the relation between knowledge, pedagogy and schooling we have been indebted to the work of Basil Bernstein (1971, 1973, 1975, 1990, 1996/2000). But central to the Sydney School project is the principle that effective teaching involves providing learners with explicit knowledge about the language in which the curriculum is written and negotiated in the classroom. The knowledge about language that has accumulated throughout the research is a key thread in each chapter, culminating in Chapter 5. A second thread running through the chapters is the knowledge about pedagogy that has accumulated through the project, summed up in Chapter 6.

1.2   Why Australia?

Australia in the late twentieth century was a microcosm and in some ways a harbinger of changes that were under way around the world. For one thing it was a nation of immigrants – a handful of British convicts and early settlers were followed by multitudes of others as agricultural trade grew in the nineteenth and early twentieth centuries. Then as the nation industrialised after the Second World War, workers came from all over Europe and the Middle East to its factories and visionary state infrastructure projects. By the 1980s a third of Australians had been born overseas, many from non-English-speaking backgrounds and often from rural areas with relatively little formal education. At the same time the nation had unfinished business with its Indigenous peoples whom the British immigrants had dispossessed and oppressed for generations. The children of all these peoples came to public schools that had been built to train colonial Australia in basic reading, writing, arithmetic and general knowledge, and inculcate the values of obedience to authority and loyalty to the British monarchy. There were secondary schools for only half the population, as further education was not required for farm and factory labourers, and just 7% of the population held a university degree (Australian Bureau of Statistics 1994).

But changes were afoot, not least because the rapid growth in population required many more schools and teachers, and the expanding industrial economy required more qualified workers. Teaching up to this point had been treated more as a trade than a profession, consisting of well-tried procedures for delivering common curricula. Teachers were trained in apprenticeship programs, beginning with a technical college diploma, followed by the guidance of principals and subject masters when they began their classroom practice. Much of this was swept away as teaching became professionalised with university degree-level training in the 1960s and 1970s. In place of an apprenticeship into tried procedures, trainee teachers were enrolled in courses consisting of theories, and the most popular theory by far, which had been gestating in liberal Anglo-American education circles since the time of Rousseau, was progressivism. With its advocacy of individual creativity and opposition to traditional routines of direct instruction, progressivism was embraced with religious zeal in burgeoning education faculties and state education departments. Today the progressivist movement is as strong as ever, but is now widely known as constructivism.

The problem which arose for the Australian context was that constructivism was oriented to the interests of middle-class professional families. It was not designed to provide access to education for marginalised groups in the society. Teachers of immigrant and working-class children in the Australian cities, and Indigenous children in the outback, were finding that 'whole language' reading, 'process writing' from personal experience, and 'invented spelling' did not give their students sufficient support to read much more than basal picture books or to write more than a few lines of simple recounts or observations. Text [1.1] illustrates a common standard for many students in upper primary school, after four or five years of process writing (Gray 1987, Martin 1990a, Rose 1999, Rose, Gray and Cowey 1999).

[1.1] Process writing in upper primary

> Ob Oa Un the holiday or or
> I went to my day dads for theoo
> weaks an we went to ante Shihs hou
> for crismuse I got Lego and a humonic
> I was vere happy to se veu all
> fomke BLak

It was not that children writing such texts lacked the resources of spoken English, but that they could not use these resources as a basis for learning to read and write, as whole language and process writing expected them to. Nor did they completely lack direct literacy instruction, as teachers generally continued drills in the alphabet and sound–letter correspondences, despite the dominance of constructivism.

It was in this context that Joan Rothery approached Jim Martin at Sydney University in 1979 with the problem of teaching children to write in school. Beginning as an action research program with the Disadvantaged Schools Program in inner Sydney, genre writing emerged as an entirely original approach to explicit literacy teaching, which achieved outstanding results not just for children from less advantaged backgrounds, but for primary school students in general. The approach spread rapidly across NSW schools and in 1994 became part of the state primary school syllabus. The Sydney School's analysis of genres in the primary school was subsequently appropriated by education publishers and state departments of education under the name of 'text types', and sold to schools across Australia.

From 1990 to 1994 the Sydney School research expanded into the language demands of subjects in the secondary school curriculum and the relation between secondary school and workplace discourse in the *Write it Right* project, which focused on science industries, media and administration workplaces, alongside secondary science, English, geography, history and mathematics curricula. From the late 1990s the *Reading to Learn* program (*R2L*) drew together the genre-writing pedagogy and the research in language across the curriculum, with reading strategies developed at Canberra University, initially to address the needs of Indigenous Australian students (Rose, Gray and Cowey 1999). It has subsequently developed into a comprehensive methodology and training program for teachers in primary and secondary schools, and in tertiary education (Rose 2011a, b).

1.3   Learning in school

Genre-based literacy pedagogy has never been conceived as a set of strategies that teachers can simply add to their already crowded toolbox. It has always been a project with the ambitious goal of democratising the outcomes of education systems. The Sydney School project has involved researching the kinds of reading and writing that schools expect of students. But beyond this it has also involved researching the mechanisms through which schools enhance and constrain the opportunities of different groups of students. Our main inspiration for this work was the educational sociology of Basil Bernstein (1971, 1973, 1975, 1990, 1996), who had been a collaborator of Michael Halliday since the early 1960s in the UK. As a way in to our social perspective on the problem of literacy education in schools, we will outline a few key elements of Bernstein's model.

1.3.1   The pedagogic device

Bernstein describes the education system of a society as a 'pedagogic device', and interprets its workings on three levels – as sets of organising principles, or 'rules' in sociological terms. The first level he calls distributive rules, which refers in part to the distribution of knowledge to different groups of students. Distributive rules are related to the division of labour in the society, which needs people to be trained as engineers, accountants, doctors, carpenters, plumbers and so on. But, more generally, work is divided between jobs that require a professional degree from universities, those that require vocational training, and those that require no qualifications other than on-the-job training. While further education trains people for specific jobs at professional and vocational levels, the broader function of schools is to produce groups of students who will go into universities, into trades training, or neither. In developed economies like Australia, the proportions of people's qualifications are roughly 20% university, 30% trades training and 50% no further education (Australian Bureau of Statistics 1994, 2004). So, in this broadest sense, distributive rules in education create a hierarchy of school outcomes that is functional in an unequal economic system. One problem for this system today is that there are fewer and fewer jobs for people with no further education, and that the proportions of school outcomes have not changed as fast as the economy is changing. This is one reason why literacy and school effectiveness have recently become such large issues in education.

The second level Bernstein calls recontextualising rules. Recontextualisation is a key term in Bernstein's theory, and in our understanding of learning in schools. The basic principle is that knowledge produced in one context, such as theoretical physics or practical carpentry, is recontextualised in education as a different kind of knowledge, such as school science or woodwork classes. Recontextualising rules are shaped by the system's distributive rules, and in their turn shape the distribution of knowledge. For example, the ways that scientific knowledge is recontextualised for high-achieving secondary students can be quite different from the ways it is recontextualised for low-achieving students. The former may study textbooks containing dense technical information that builds in quantity and complexity into the senior secondary years, towards potential careers in science, engineering, medicine and other science-related fields. The latter may have textbooks containing brief texts with many bright pictures and concrete examples, or often just worksheets with summaries of topics and tasks, they may spend much of their class time on hands-on 'discovery learning' activities, and may not be expected to continue science beyond year 10.

The third level Bernstein terms evaluative rules. He reminds us that evaluation is central to education at all levels, that 'the key to pedagogic practice is continuous evaluation … evaluation condenses the meaning of the whole [pedagogic] device' (1996: 50). Formal evaluations determine whether students will matriculate to university, to vocational training, or neither. They determine if and when students are allowed to progress in school, which subjects they will be allowed to study, and which version of each subject. But regular evaluations through assessment tasks, and continual evaluations in classroom interactions, create hierarchies of success and failure in each class, and shape students' identities as more- or less-successful learners. The shaping of identities through evaluation serves a fundamental social function in that, for the student as well as the school, it locates the source of success or failure within the student. By this means the unequal distribution of knowledge that the school produces appears to be natural, and the inequality of opportunities in the society at large seems inevitable.

Genre pedagogy aims to make the distribution of knowledge in school more equitable. In this respect it is consistent with the professed education policies of most nations and of UNESCO (2010) for 'full and equal opportunities for education for all … to advance the ideal of equality of educational opportunity'. To this end it is designed to give teachers the tools they need to overcome the inequality of access, participation and outcomes in their classes. We have been strongly influenced in this goal by our work with less-advantaged groups, including immigrant and working-class children and their teachers in urban and rural schools, and Indigenous communities and schools that we have worked with around Australia (Martin 1990a, Rose 2004, 2005, 2006b, 2011d).

1.3.2   Learning activities in the school

Our observations of classrooms and ongoing discussions with teachers continually bear out the centrality of evaluation in schooling. Most of the activities that occur in classrooms contain some element of evaluation, and many have it as their primary purpose, including those that are often thought of as learning activities. But to put this into perspective we need first to ask what a learning activity consists of. One thing that we can generalise across pedagogic situations is that learning happens through doing tasks. The task may be a simple manual activity such as tying shoelaces, or a complex semiotic activity such as learning knowledge from a textbook. As far as we can see, this basic aspect of learning is assumed both in pedagogic theories and everyday learning activities, more or less implicitly.

The learning task is thus the core of any learning activity. If the learner were doing it alone, the task could constitute the whole of the activity – such as a child drawing a picture, a writer experimenting with a stylistic technique, or a researcher investigating a problem. This is the idealised image of learners in constructivist pedagogy, learning for themselves without teacher direction. Learning on your own does not of course preclude evaluation; it is still there, but delayed until the product of the independent learning task is shown to others. In school-based pedagogic situations the learning task is normally initiated by the teacher, perhaps as a command, 'Cut along here' or 'Start writing now', or a question, 'What were the causes of the Vietnam War?' or 'What did you do on your holidays?' At the scale of lessons and lesson sequences, Christie (1999, 2002) refers to this element as the 'lesson initiation' or 'curriculum initiation', and shows that it may involve considerable complexity in itself. As its broad function is to focus students' attention on the task to perform, we will use the simple term **Focus** for this phase of a learning activity; the Focus specifies the task for the learner.

The other core element of any learning activity is of course evaluation – assessing learners' performance of the task. It is often assumed that evaluation is necessary to guide learners towards success, by telling them what they are doing well as well as what they could do better. This is undoubtedly a component of teaching in many contexts. But positive and negative evaluations can have different effects. Most of us can probably remember experiences when negative evaluations of our efforts reduced our capacity for doing a task successfully, creating frustration and feelings of impotence or embarrassment, rather than motivating us to keep trying. Parents caring for young children often seem to be aware of this, as they continually praise children for almost everything they do (illustrated in §2.4, §3.3 and §4.2 below). Negative evaluations tend to be used to discourage children from unwanted behaviours, rather than to encourage desired ones.

In school, on the other hand, negative evaluations are a feature of most activities, even if we aren't aware of them as such. For example, writing activities may be assessed by the teacher, who provides feedback for students to attend to. Children who are better writers may receive strong praise as well as corrections and suggestions for improvement, and apply these to their next writing task. But children who are struggling writers are less likely to receive strong praise, and more likely to experience corrections as criticism. As a result, many children become loath to write anything they fear will be corrected; instead they make themselves a small target by producing brief recounts throughout primary school, using only words they know how to spell and sentence structures they are confident with (Gray 1986, Rose 1999). Examples include [1.1] above and texts [2.2], [2.3] and [2.14] in Chapter 2 below. This is one outcome for less-advantaged students of the 'process writing' activity advocated by constructivism. Similarly, short-answer questions and maths problems are daily activities that are assessed as correct or incorrect. The assumption is that students will learn from their mistakes and do better in the next activity. Students who get most of their questions and maths problems correct may benefit from this practice; but students who get more incorrect may have struggled to answer the questions in the first place and may struggle even more to comprehend why they are marked wrong.

At the level of classroom interactions, teachers continually evaluate what students' say in response to questions they ask of the class. In the terms we are developing here, the students' Task is to respond to the teacher's Focus question. A few students in any class consistently give responses that teachers can affirm and build on as a lesson unfolds; other students respond less often and are less likely to be affirmed; while others participate little in classroom discussion. The following exchange [1.2] is a very typical example (from Williams 1995: 501). The teacher is reading *Jack and the Beanstalk* to a Year 1 class and asks the children to tell her the meaning of 'widow'. The children's Task in this case is to propose a response from their own knowledge.

[1.2] Typical exchange in Shared Book Reading

	Teacher	[reads]	*Long ago in a far away land lived a widow and her son Jack.*
1		Focus	*What's a widow? It looks like a lady to me. What's a widow? Rhianna?*
	Child	Task	*An old woman.*
	Teacher	Evaluate	*Well she doesn't look too old.*
		Focus	*Is there a daddy there?*
	Children	Task	*No.*
2	Teacher	Focus	*What do you think has happened to the daddy?*
	Child	Task	*Looks like ... a cow.*
	Teacher	Focus	*David?*
	Child	Task	*It's it's it's a little cow.*
	Teacher	Evaluate	*No no.*
3		Focus	*When there's a widow, something's happened to daddy.*
	Child	Task	*He died? Miss, he died?*
	Teacher	Evaluate	*Yes that's right.*

Rhianna bases her response *An old woman* on a clue in the teacher's Focus *looks like a lady*, but is rejected. David completely misses the 'lady' clue, and instead bases his (belated) response on what he sees in the illustration *a cow*, as children are told to use clues in book illustrations to help them read, and is also rejected. Each time the teacher provides more clues, her Focus moves until one child gives the response she can affirm.

In school, as we suggested above, evaluation serves another function aside from guiding learning: that is, to create, maintain and naturalise the hierarchy of success and failure between students. In schools everywhere this hierarchy is naturalised in terms of students' 'ability'. Although the notion of ability is rarely defined explicitly, it is widely assumed to explain academic differences between students. Bernstein for one does not accept this explanation:

> The school must disconnect its own internal hierarchy of success and failure from ineffectiveness of teaching within the school and the external hierarchy of power relations between social groups outside the school. How do schools individualize failure and legitimize inequalities? The answer is clear: failure is attributed to inborn facilities (cognitive, affective) or to the cultural deficits relayed by the family which come to have the force of inborn facilities (1996: 5).

The effect of the school's hierarchy of success and failure is to create circles of inclusion and exclusion in the discourse of the classroom. From large-scale observational studies of classrooms Nuthall reports that:

> The teacher is largely cut off from information about what individual students are learning … They are sustained, however, by the commonly held belief that if students are engaged most of the time in appropriate activities, some kind of learning will be taking place … Teachers depend on the responses of a small number of students as indicators and remain ignorant of what most of the class knows and understands (2005: 919-20).

Top students who participate most consistently have the most direct relation with the teacher and thus with the content they interact about; others who participate less receive less benefit from the discussion; while those who rarely participate have little engagement with the content (Figure 1.1).

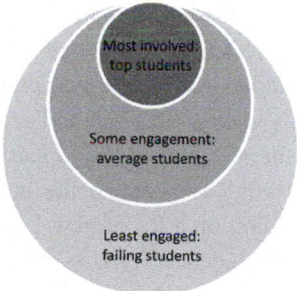

Figure 1.1: Circles of inclusion and exclusion in the classroom

Summing up to this point, the learner's Task is the central phase of a learning activity, flanked by Focus and Evaluation. These three phases form the nucleus of any learning activity, diagrammed in Figure 1.2.

Figure 1.2: Nucleus of a learning activity

While Task, Focus and Evaluation are inherent phases of a learning activity, what is less universally acknowledged is that to do a learning task successfully the learner must be prepared in some way by a teacher. With manual activities, the teacher preparation is often obvious, in the form of demonstrations and then guidance as the learner attempts the task. With more complex tasks, such as reading and writing, the preparation may be less visible. Some parts of these tasks are actually material, such as recognising and forming letters and relating them to sounds, with the result that these tasks are usually taught explicitly by demonstration and guidance. But other parts of these tasks are immaterial, such as comprehending and creating meanings in stories. The fact that some children can perform tasks like these without any apparent teacher preparation is one factor behind the constructivist notion that learning emerges from within the individual and should not be constrained by teacher instruction. What may not be visible in the classroom context is that many children have actually spent hundreds of hours reading with their parents, and discussing written ways of meaning as they read, before starting school (see §4.2.1 below). Their preparation for the reading and writing tasks in school has thus accumulated over time, as has older students' preparation for reading textbooks and writing assignments.

From the perspective of genre pedagogy, teaching means preparing learners for each learning task and then handing control to learners to do the task themselves. Providing effective preparation means understanding the nature of the learning task. This may be relatively straightforward with simple manual tasks, but becomes extremely complex when it comes to reading and writing, as language is the most complex system we know of. Partly because of this complexity, language is poorly understood, so explicit preparation tends to be limited to its simplest basic elements, such as forming and saying letters and memorising common words, and much the rest may be left to learners' intuitions. In contrast, the approach of genre pedagogy is to make the entire language-learning task explicit, and this means building up a lot of new knowledge about language (or KAL) for both teachers and students. KAL is built up throughout this book, beginning with §1.4 below.

For us, differences between students in their success with learning tasks indicate that some students are better prepared for the task than others. This perspective shifts the focus away from students' differences and onto designing preparations that all students need in order to do each task successfully. In this respect genre pedagogy includes positive aspects of traditional pedagogies, in which the teacher is an authoritative guide into school knowledge, and of progressive pedagogies, which emphasise affirmation for all students. This is achieved in genre pedagogy by deconstructing the learning tasks involved in reading and writing, and demonstrating them in a carefully designed sequence of activities. Detailed planning of learning interactions (described in Chapters 4 and 6 below) ensures that all students are continually successful at all points of a lesson, so that affirmation is equally distributed around the class. By these means all students are included in the learning community of the classroom, thus diminishing behavioural problems, and reshaping all children's identities as successful learners.

A fifth common element of learning activities, following evaluation, is elaboration. Successful accomplishment of a learning task, accompanied by praise from a teacher, provides a platform of understanding, and the motivation, for taking another step in learning. An elaboration could be the next step in the sequence of a manual activity, or it could be a deeper understanding of a concept under focus in the learning task. Elaborations can be seen frequently in parent–child interactions (see below §2.4, §3.3 and §4.2), in which parents take advantage of children's attention and positive emotion to expand their understanding. It is also a common feature of classroom interactions, in which teachers use students' responses as stepping stones to give the class an increment of knowledge in the topic they are studying (§4.2). In classroom learning activities, elaborations may involve discussion following a task such as reading or viewing a text, in order to deepen students' understanding of certain elements in the text. Elaborations are a key focus of many pedagogic theories that are concerned to extend students 'high order thinking', including neo-Vygotskyan theorists such as Gibbons (2002, 2006, 2009), Mercer (1995, 2000) and Wells (1999, 2002). One key area of difference with genre pedagogy is our strong focus on preparing all students to do each learning task successfully. Without such preparation only those students in the inner circle of Figure 1.1 benefit most from the elaboration.

Summing up, we can identify five common steps in learning activities, beginning with the preparation and focus provided by the teacher, followed by the learner's task, which is in turn evaluated, and often elaborated. The task is the central element and together with the focus and evaluation forms the nucleus of a learning activity. Preparations and elaborations are possible but not inherent elements in any activity, so they are more peripheral. This nuclear structuring of learning activities is diagrammed in Figure 1.3.

Figure 1.3: Five general elements of a learning activity

Preparations and elaborations also involve tasks for students, such as listening to the teacher's information in preparation phases, or participating in discussions in elaboration phases. Accordingly, preparations should be designed to build on understandings that are already shared between teachers and students, and elaborations should be designed to build on understandings gained from success with the central learning Task. For these reasons, the sequence of phases in a learning activity can also be modelled as a cycle, in which the elaboration of one cycle forms a basis for preparing the next, diagrammed in Figure 1.4.

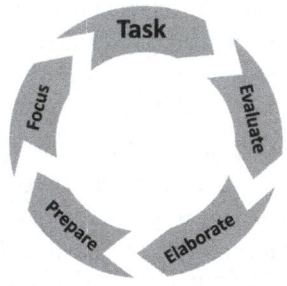

Figure 1.4: Learning activity cycle

This general structure can be used to analyse and plan learning activities at the levels of a whole lesson sequence (which Christie 2002 terms a 'curriculum macro-genre'), such as the teaching-learning cycle for genre writing described in Chapter 2, at the level of a single lesson activity within a lesson sequence, exemplified in Chapters 2 and 4, and at the level of teacher–learner exchanges within each lesson, exemplified in [1.2] above and discussed in detail in Chapter 4. Each element of this global structure can be expanded to include one or more microtasks, each of which may be prepared, focused, evaluated and elaborated. As each learning activity cycle builds on preceding cycles, teaching sequences take the form of a spiral curriculum, advocated by Bruner (1986). Each task is more challenging than the last, as students' skills and knowledge accumulate (Figure 1.5).

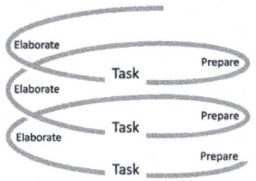

Figure 1.5: Spiral curriculum of learning cycles

1.3.3   Individual and guided practice

A common practice in both traditional and constructivist pedagogies is to give students tasks that are at or just beyond their independent competence. Their performance may then be evaluated, by observation or by a formative assessment task (such as answering questions or a short writing task). If students are successful, they may be deemed ready for a further learning task that is just beyond their new competence, and the cycle continues for that task. Thus learning progresses in incremental steps, from one learning task to the next, each extending slightly further than the last – towards a learning goal at the end of a curriculum unit. At this point, students may be given a formal assessment in which they must demonstrate what they have learnt by completing a major task, such as writing a whole text.

In Figure 1.6 below, such a learning sequence is modelled as development of skills over time. Each learning activity in the sequence is represented as a dot, and each successive activity is slightly higher than the preceding one.

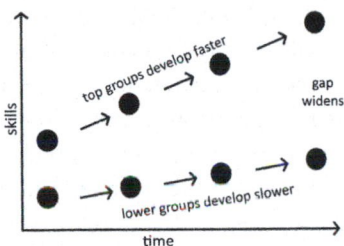

Figure 1.6: Incremental learning

The initial dots in Figure 1.6 represent different groups of students who start with different levels of skills. High-achieving students are given more difficult tasks at each step, and low-achieving students are given less difficult tasks. In addition, the pacing of the high group's learning may be faster, and the pacing of the lower group's learning slower. This is the approach of both traditional and constructivist pedagogies: traditional regimes 'stream' or 'track' students into different classes according to their assessed abilities, while constructivist classrooms are organised internally in a hierarchy of 'ability groups' and 'individual work plans' with different levels of tasks. Over time the gap in skills between the groups inexorably widens.

In his large-scale meta-analysis of the outcomes of teaching approaches, Hattie (2009: 89) reports that ability grouping is a very common practice in primary classes, but has very low benefits for the learning of any group ($d = 0.16$, where $d = 2.0$ is considered a small improvement). He also reported 'individualized instruction to be barely more effective than the traditional lecture approach ($d = 0.08$)' (2009: 198). For separating classes based on ability, he found that:

> tracking has minimal effects on learning outcomes and profound negative equity effects ... the effects on self-concept were close to zero ... The overall effects for the three major ability levels across the studies were $d = 0.14$ for high-tracked, $d = -0.03$ for middle-tracked, and $d = 0.09$ for low tracked students – no one profits (2009: 90).

Hattie quotes Oakes et al. (1993: 20), that tracking 'limits students' schooling opportunities, achievements and life chances' and in the US 'minority students were seven times more likely to be identified as low-ability than as high-ability students'. This finding is consistent with our own observations of the streaming of Indigenous students in Australian rural schools and immigrant students in metropolitan schools.

By contrast, genre pedagogy starts with the democratic principle that all learners in a class or grade need to accomplish the same level of task, and that teachers need strategies to support them equally. This is achieved in genre pedagogy by analysing the nature of each learning task and designing a sequence of learning activities that will enable all students to do each task successfully. Rather than limiting the learning demands to a point just above each learners' competence, genre pedagogy supports all learners in a class to do tasks that are challenging for all students and may be well beyond the independent skills of some. In Figure 1.7, open dots along the top represent the level of guided tasks, and the filled dots represent learners' independent levels.

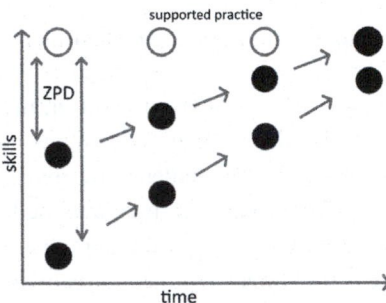

Figure 1.7: Narrowing the gap with supported practice

Practising at a higher level with the guidance of a teacher is a more effective method of acquiring skills than practising at a lower level. Of course, when students attempt a similar task on their own, they will not be able to attain quite the same level of achievement as they did with the teacher's support. This is precisely what Vygotsky (1962) meant by his 'zone of proximal development' (ZPD), namely the difference between what a learner can do with and without a teacher's support. The teacher's support is designed in genre pedagogy to enable all students in a class to do each task at the same time. This means that the zone of proximal development is larger for lower achieving students than it is for high achievers, as shown in Figure 1.7. For this reason, preparations are planned to enable the weakest students to do each task. Elaborations then build on this success to extend the competence of all students.

The next step in this type of learning sequence is to repeat the learning task at the same high level, once again with the teacher's guidance. This time, each learner's independent competence will be higher again, although for some it will be still below the guided level. If the task is then repeated a third time, all learners will be drawn closer to the intended level. At this point students may be ready for an independent task on which they can be assessed. Both high and lower achieving students will have improved at a faster rate than through a series of learning activities at their individual ability levels, and the gap between them will be narrowing.

The narrowing of the achievement gap between students, through repeated guided interaction, has been demonstrated again and again in genre pedagogy. Independent adjudication consistently finds an average of double the learning growth expected in any school year for all students from all backgrounds and ability levels: top students tend to grow at around 1.5 times expected learning rates, while the weakest students accelerate at up to 4 times their expected rates (see §6.2.2 below) (McCrae et al. 2000, Culican 2006, Rose 2011c, Rose et al. 2008).

1.3.4   Types of knowledge

A second relevant dimension of Bernstein's work is his theory of different types of knowledge that are associated with different modes of learning. He makes a primary distinction between the commonsense knowledge of everyday life with family and community and the knowledge structures of academic and institutional fields. Everyday knowledge he refers to as 'horizontal discourse' because it is learnt through sundry experiences in the contexts of everyday life, often through demonstration and practice, without necessarily naming what is being learnt. Academic knowledge he refers to as 'vertical discourse' because it is theoretically organised above and beyond the contexts in which it will be applied (i.e. contexts of technology and bureaucracy) and has to be learned by literate students in educational institutions.

Vertical discourses are of two types: (i) sciences are hierarchically structured bodies of knowledge, integrated in textbooks and accumulated through study; (ii) humanities are horizontally structured, for example as series of differently positioned interpretations of texts in literary studies or explanations of events in history. Whereas scientific knowledge is built up over generations, by contesting hypotheses and evolving consensus across an ever-expanding database, theories in humanities and social sciences tend to be displaced by new theories in successive generations, often with a change of focus on what needs to be interpreted or explained.

Both vertical and horizontal discourses are recontextualised as curriculum in school, but at opposite ends of the sequence of schooling. The curriculum subjects of the senior secondary school recontextualise the academic disciplines of the university, as school science, maths, history, English, other languages, and so on. These curriculum subjects were originally designed to prepare elite students for university study, and this remains their primary purpose. To this end, university disciplines have a relatively strong influence on the content and assessment of senior secondary subjects. In Bernstein's terms this is a strongly classified type of pedagogy, in which the criteria for assessment are visible and the focus is on explicit transmission of knowledge, skills and values.

At the other end of schooling, in the early years, the classroom is organised to resemble the context of the home, at least for children from middle-class families; for children from other backgrounds, there may be less that is familiar in the context of school. The focus of learning at this stage is primarily on children's personal development (cognitive, social, emotional), so the recontextualising rules here currently derive from psychology – particularly the developmental psychology of Piaget, who believed that all children go through biologically fixed stages of cognitive and emotional development.[1] As the focus is on development of the whole person, the curriculum is based around holistic 'themes' rather than distinct subjects. In Bernstein's terms this is a weakly classified type of pedagogy. As learning is supposed to emerge from within, the criteria for assessment are not visible to the child and the pedagogic focus is on implicit acquisition of cognitive and emotional dispositions.

Bernstein (1975: 119-20) classifies these approaches as visible and invisible pedagogies respectively:[2]

A **visible** pedagogy is created by:
(1) explicit hierarchy
(2) explicit sequencing rules
(3) explicit and specific criteria.
The underlying rule is: **'Things must be kept apart.'**

An **invisible** pedagogy is created by:
(1) implicit hierarchy;
(2) implicit sequencing rules;
(3) implicit criteria.
The underlying rule is: **'Things must be put together.'**

In these terms, constructivism sits firmly within the second, invisible type of pedagogy. Wedged between these opposing recontextualisation principles, the middle years of schooling are sites of struggle over knowledge and pedagogy. At

---

[1] Piaget, whose developmental psychology is a founding influence in constructivist learning theory, derived his hypothesis of individual learning in fixed biological stages from a series of laboratory experiments on children. He also observed children learning with their mothers, but apparently deleted the mothers' roles in his descriptions. He 'was originally a biologist, and began his work on the development of mind in the belief that as the digestive system processes and extracts what it needs from food, so the mind extracts and digests what it needs from experience' (Nuthall 2005: 14).

[2] For useful breakdowns of this opposition, see Alexander 2000: 548-9 and Brophy 2002: ix, both of whom argue for a judiciously inclusive pedagogy in place of crusading adversarialism.

one time the subjects taught in the junior secondary and upper primary years were much like the senior subjects, strongly bounded from each other and explicitly designed to be taught in a strict sequence. The entire curriculum was driven from the university down, and there was some continuity between the secondary and primary curricula. Today, however, the personal development approach of the early years has permeated the curriculum in primary school, so that subjects are typically learnt as part of weakly classified 'themes' drawing on a range of subject areas, which are less explicitly designed to prepare children for secondary subject learning. The boundaries between subjects are weaker with the result that the boundary between primary and secondary schooling is stronger. Partly because students are now arriving at secondary school with less explicit preparation, and partly because of the increasing influence of constructivism, curriculum subjects in the junior secondary are themselves becoming more weakly bounded, less demanding, less vertical and more like horizontal discourses. Alarmingly, this is especially true for less successful students. Once, many of these students would have been expected to leave after Year 9 or 10, and undertake apprenticeships or manual labour. But today in Australia almost all students are expected to stay until Year 12. Less successful students are now often streamed towards technology subjects in senior years, which prepare them for vocational training.

Genre pedagogy is designed to work across all these sectors. One aspect of the Sydney School project has been to design teaching strategies that can be applied at different grade levels in different subject areas: Chapter 2 describes the genre approach to writing that is used in primary, secondary and tertiary education; Chapter 4 describes different strategies for working with stories, factual texts and arguments in the primary and secondary school, and strategies for initiating children into reading and writing at the start of school. Each of these sets of strategies is designed to address the learning problems that students have at each stage of schooling. The strategies for junior primary years are designed to harmonise explicit teaching of school knowledge with the focus on children's home experience; the strategies for upper primary years are designed to prepare students with the skills in independent reading and writing across the curriculum that they will need in secondary school; the strategies for secondary subjects are designed to integrate teaching the curriculum with the skills that students need to read and write it. To this end, another aspect of the project has been to describe the types of knowledge that students learn across the curriculum, and the written genres through which this knowledge is learnt and demonstrated, from junior primary to senior secondary and beyond. Chapter 3 focuses on types of knowledge and details the variety of written genres in the school curriculum. Chapter 5 explores the knowledge about language that teachers can use to make their teaching explicit throughout the school.

1.4   The language learning task

Teaching literacy means teaching language; indeed all teaching involves language, whether or not we teach it consciously. Arguing for a 'language based theory of learning', Halliday makes this comment:

> When children learn language, they are not simply engaging in one kind of learning among many; rather, they are learning the foundation of learning itself. The distinctive characteristic of human learning is that it is a process of making meaning – a semiotic process; and the prototypical form of human semiotic is language. Hence the ontogenesis of language is at the same time the ontogenesis of learning (1993: 97).

Teaching any subject or skill involves teaching *through* language; but teaching literacy involves explicitly teaching *about* language as well. To teach language and literacy effectively we need a sound understanding of how language works, as well as a **metalanguage** to talk about it with our students. This is no small call, as language is such a complex system. Throughout this book, we will gradually build up a model of how language works, together with a metalanguage that can be used for discussing it in the classroom.

Genre pedagogy has grown from a theory of how speakers use language in social life (a functional theory of language), and more specifically out of the systemic functional linguistic (SFL) theory developed by MAK Halliday and colleagues over the past six decades. Halliday himself became interested in linguistics as a language teacher (of Chinese, English and Russian) and has always intended this model of language to be directly relevant to teachers, in part as a tool for showing learners how to use language effectively. SFL has evolved over time as an extensive description of language. The description we provide in this book, however, is much less detailed – sufficient for teachers to use with their students, but no more than is necessary. To begin with here, we introduce the functional model of language from four perspectives:

1. the twin functions of language – for speakers and writers and readers to interact with each other, and to represent their experience to each other;
2. the social contexts of language use, including relations between speakers, writers and readers and the activities they are involved in;
3. the organisation of language at the levels of text, sentence and word;
4. the relation between the language system and the actual texts we speak, read and write.

1.4.1   Two functions of language – interacting and construing experience

The first thing we need to recognise about language is that when we speak, read or write we are doing two things at the same time: we are interacting *with* one or more other people, and we are interacting *about* something; that is, we are both enacting a social relationship and saying something about our experience. These two functions of language are nicely illustrated in the following exchange [1.3] between two-year-old 'Hal' and his mother (from Painter 1986: 206). At this age Hal is still uncertain about colour names and ritually answers *that's blue* when asked to identify colours. He asks questions with a rising tone (shown by ´) and makes statements with a falling tone (`).

[1.3] Negotiating classification at age 2

Phase 1

Hal	Thats blùe. (pointing at blue peg)
Mother	Yes, that's blue.
Hal	Thats blùe. (pointing at another peg)
Mother	No.
Hal	Thats blúe? (pointing at another)
	Thats òrange.
Mother	That's orange. (affirming)

Phase 2

Hal	Thats blúe? (pointing at another)
Mother	No.
Hal	Thats blúe? (pointing at a blue peg)
Mother	Yes.
Hal	Thats blúe? (pointing at another)
Mother	No.
Hal	Thats òrange.
Mother	Yes.
Hal	Thats òrange.

In Phase 1 of this exchange, Hal initiates the conversation by demonstrating what he knows, pointing and naming the colour blue, which his mother affirms, repeating his words. Then he tries again with the same name (*blue*) for a different colour, which his mother negates (*No*). So then he changes the statement to a question (*Thats blúe?*), and answers himself with another statement (*Thats òrange*), which his mother affirms by repeating his words. Hal is practising two things at once here: distinguishing names for different colours, and distinguishing statements about colours from questions about them. By making a statement he adopts the role of 'knower', but his mother, in affirming or negating his statements, assumes greater authority; she is the 'primary knower', the teacher in this relationship. Hal experiments with these roles by asking a question and answering himself, which his mother again affirms as the primary knower.

In Phase 2, as the exchange continues, the roles of learner asking questions and teacher answering are clearly sorted, and Hal can concentrate on the task of classifying the colours. By asking the question (*Thats blúe?*) he explicitly adopts the role of knowledge seeker and positions his mother as the knowledge giver, who affirms or negates his questions. By the end of this exchange, he can confidently use two alternatives for classifying colours (*Thats blùe/Thats òrange*). Note that these colours do not come with labels already attached; it is language that gives them these names. Critically it is through language that speakers construe the world of experience, and Hal is discovering how the things that his senses experience are construed by his mother tongue. The categories are learned through negotiation with his mother and her evaluations assign positive and negative values to the categories, reinforcing the distinctions for him.

Hal is practising using two kinds of meanings here – interacting with his mother as he construes his world of experience. Meanings to do with interacting (e.g. asking for information and giving information, adopting the roles of knowledge seeker and knowledge giver, and evaluating) are known as **interpersonal** meanings. Meanings to do with representing experience (e.g. classifying the colours of pegs as blue or orange) are known as **ideational** meanings. Interpersonal and ideational meanings are woven together simultaneously as we speak and write. In terms of functional theory, we can say accordingly that language has two broad functions in social life, or **metafunctions**: an interpersonal metafunction (enacting our relationships) and an ideational metafunction (construing our experience). Alongside the interpersonal and ideational meanings he is making, Hal also relates what he is saying to the context of speaking, by pointing to each peg and saying *that*. These kinds of meanings, that here relate text to its situational context, are known as **textual** (Figure 1.8).

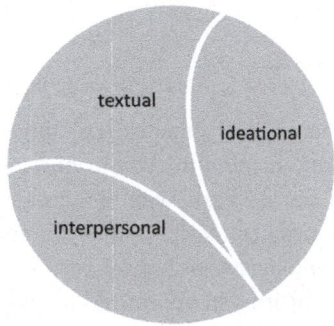

Figure 1.8: Metafunctions of language

1.4.2 Levels of language – discourse, grammar, phonology

Within language we need to distinguish three levels, or strata. Firstly, meanings come in the form of texts. The exchange between Hal and his mother above is an example of a text, and so is this book, so texts can be either spoken or written. We will refer to patterns of meaning across whole texts as **discourse**.

The spoken Text [1.3] is made up of smaller units such as Hal's *that's blue* and his mother's *yes, that's blue*. These smaller units are known as clauses. In written texts, clauses are traditionally seen as combining to form sentences (beginning with a capital and ending with a full stop) – a simple sentence consists of one clause, and a complex or compound sentence consists of two or more clauses (often with a comma or conjunction between them). Patterns of meaning within clauses are known as **grammar**.[3]

A text and a clause are units of different sizes (although a text can consist of a single clause, or even a single word like *Stop!*). But the relation between discourse and grammar is not simply one of size. Rather patterns of meaning in whole texts are expressed or 'realised' by patterns of wordings in clauses. For example, Hal is learning to classify colours in [1.3], which he does clause by clause as the exchange unfolds. So the classification is a discourse-level pattern. But the meaning of classification at the level of discourse is realised within each clause as the words *blue* and *orange*.

Each word is then realised as a pattern of sounds or letters, which are part of **phonology** (in speaking) and **graphology** (in writing). Phonology is more than just the patterns of sounds in words, but also includes patterns such as rising and falling tones, which Hal uses to distinguish questions and statements in [1.3]. Likewise, graphology is not just the patterns of letters in words, but includes patterns such as punctuation within and between sentences, and paragraphing.

So a text consists of patterns of patterns of patterns. Patterns of meaning at the level of the text are known as **discourse**, patterns of meaning at the level of the clause are known as **grammar**, and patterns of sounds or letters are known as **phonology** or **graphology**. The relation between these three levels is known as **realisation** – patterns of meaning in discourse are realised as patterns of meaning in grammar, which are realised as patterns of phonology or graphology. In Figure 1.9 below, this relation is represented by the line between each level.

Within each of these language strata are further layers of structure. For example, a text is not just a string of sentences, but involves intermediate phases of meaning that are expressed as paragraphs in writing – i.e. a paragraph expresses a phase of meaning. Likewise a clause is not just a string of words but involves intermediate elements of meaning, such as who it is about, what they are doing, where and when, that are expressed as groups of words. For example, the clause

---

[3] In SFL theory, grammar is referred to as lexicogrammar, as it includes both words and grammatical structures, and the technical term for discourse is discourse semantics.

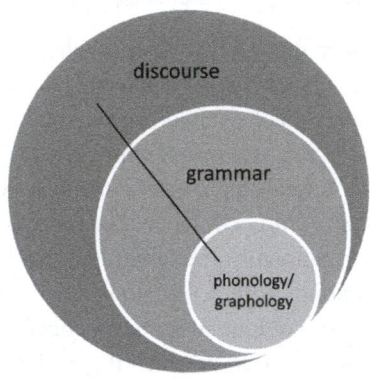

Figure 1.9: Levels within language

A frog was swimming in a pond after a rainstorm includes four groups of words, expressing the meanings of 'who' (*A frog*), 'what doing' (*was swimming*), 'where' (*in a pond*) and 'when' (*after a rainstorm*). There is no punctuation to distinguish these word groups and phrases, but any child will recognise them intuitively. Thirdly, a word is not just a string of letters or sounds, but involves intermediate patterns, including syllables and the Onset and Rhyme of each syllable; in writing the Onset is the initial consonant(s) and the Rhyme is the remainder of the syllable, such as Onset *st-* and Rhyme *-orm*.

As we speak, read or write, we are processing all of these patterns of patterns of patterns simultaneously and automatically – an immensely complex semiotic task. For these reasons, learning to speak, listen, read and write is the most complex learning task we will ever undertake.

1.4.3   Social contexts of language – register and genre

As language has three general functions because of the way it is used, so the social contexts of language use can be viewed from three perspectives: the relationships that are enacted by language, the experiences that are construed by it, and the role that language plays in the context. These three dimensions of social context are known as the **tenor** of social relations (who is involved), the **field** of experience (what they are involved in or speaking about), and the **mode** of communication, such as speaking or writing. Together, field, tenor and mode are known as the **register** of a text.

Beyond register is the global social purpose of a text, its **genre**. The particular social purpose of any text shapes the kind of text it is – narrating a complicating event produces a narrative, explaining a sequence of cause and effect makes an explanation, classifying and describing things makes a report, arguing for a point of view makes an exposition, and so on. Field, tenor and mode are woven together at the level of genre: for example, in an explanation genre the field may be a natural process such as a life cycle, or a social activity such as a global financial crisis; its mode may be spoken or written; and its tenor may be personal and entertaining or cool and objective (Figure 1.10).

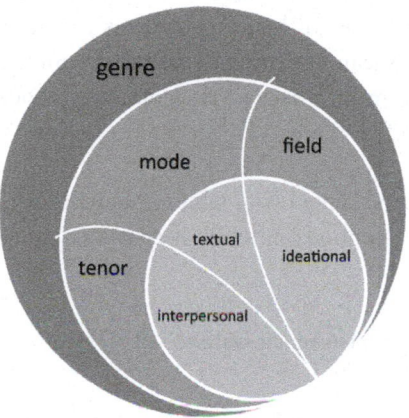

Figure 1.10: Genre as a configuration of tenor, field and mode

We can note at this point that the view of language we have been building up here is quite different from that of traditional school grammar. This is because traditional grammars were focused on the *forms* of words and sentences, rather than their meanings, and looked at grammar from below – from the forms of words (or morphology) up towards the clause. Where they do address meaning, it is usually the ideational meaning of words that is taken into account, rather than interpersonal or textual meaning, or the meanings of word groups and clauses. Similarly, formal grammars do not account for role of language in social interaction. As they are focused primarily on the formal arrangement of words and word groups in sentences, they have little to say about patterns of meanings in texts, and still less about the relation between texts and social contexts. In fact, genre pedagogy was only possible because it could build on the functional approach to language that Halliday designed (cf. Coffin et al. 2009, Martin 2004 for discussion).

1.4.4   Language systems and texts

The fourth perspective on language we need to introduce here is the relation between language systems and the actual texts that people speak, read and write. A system is a set of options that speakers select from as a text unfolds. Halliday defines systems in the context of infants first learning to communicate with caregivers through non-verbal symbols (simple sounds and gestures).

The child creates the symbols, using vocal and gestural resources in acting out the role of learner, and by the same token enabling the 'others' to act out their roles as teachers … These sets of symbolic acts develop into systems. An act of meaning implies a certain choice: If there is a meaning 'I want', then there can be a meaning 'I don't want', perhaps also 'I want very much', as alternatives. If there is a meaning 'I'm content', this can contrast with other states of being: 'I'm cross', 'I'm excited', and so on. Sets of alternative meanings of this kind form semiotic paradigms called 'systems': Each term in a system excludes, and hence presupposes, the other(s) (1993: 96).

Systems are often represented with tables or paradigms. A familiar example at the level of grammar is options in tense; here is a small segment of the English tense system (Table 1.1).

Table 1.1: Segment of English tense system

	simple	continuous
past	*did go/went*	*was going*
present	*goes*	*is going*
future	*will go*	*will be going*

Choices in systems are alternative, 'either/or', and additional, 'and'. So in Table 1.1, tenses are either past *or* present *or* future, *and* either simple *or* continuous. Each cell in the table combines two of these options, for example 'was going' is both past and continuous. Although we can present these options as a system like this, they only come into being as meanings in actual texts. The kinds of tense options that speakers and writers select as a text unfolds vary with the genre and field. For example, as stories recount past events, they tend to use past tenses; texts that generalise about phenomena such as explanations and reports tend to use simple present tense; texts that predict future events, such as weather reports, often use future tenses.

An example from the level of discourse is the system of 'speech function', which gives rise to the statements and questions that Hal was experimenting with above. Statements give information, whereas questions ask for it. Alongside exchanges of information are exchanges of goods or services, where we use commands to demand goods or services, and offers to give them. These four options make up the basic system of speech functions (Table 1.2).

Setting out the options for speech functions in this way enables us to see that the meanings of 'statement', 'question', 'command' and 'offer' lie not in the words themselves, but in two kinds of contrast: between converse roles in a social exchange (giving or demanding) and two kinds of commodities that speak-

Table 1.2: Basic speech functions

	information	goods-and-services
demanding	**question** *Is that blue?*	**command** *Give me a peg!*
giving	**statement** *That's blue.*	**offer** *Have a peg.*

ers exchange (information or goods-and-services). This is another key point: meanings do not reside within words, but arise from semantic contrasts, such as blue/orange, past/present/future, question/statement, and so on. Language systems consist of sets of these contrasts. Furthermore, the system of speech functions only makes sense in relation to the context of social interaction. It enables us to see that language, from an interpersonal perspective, is an exchange between speakers.

At the level of graphology, the alphabet is one system that is explicitly taught at the beginning of school. Children have to learn two sets of contrasts in this system, between lower and upper letter cases, and between the names for the 26 letters and the sounds they make. As the sounds that letters make in the context of real words is actually far more diverse, children also usually have to learn common letter combinations (e.g. *ou*, *th*), and the sounds they make. These systems of 'sound/letter correspondences' are the focus of phonics programs. However this is merely the lowest level of the spelling system as a whole. The ways that letters combine and the sounds they make depend on their position in the syllable and the word they are in (Henderson and Templeton 1986). In writing, the initial consonants in a syllable are known as the Onset and the remainder of the syllable is the Rhyme. For example, the letter combination /gh/ makes a different sound as the Onset of a syllable (*ghost*) or the Rhyme (*rough*), and the common Rhyme pattern /ough/ sounds different again in words like *through* or *bough*. Just as traditional school grammars tend to miss the role of word groups in constructing meanings in sentences (treating a sentence as a string of words), so phonics programs often miss the role of the syllable in the spelling and sound system (treating a word as string of letter patterns). These approaches leave it to learners' intuitions to recognise the intermediate layers of structure.

At the level of genre, we can organise systems along various lines. For example, genres can be grouped according to whether or not they are organised as a sequence of events, in Table 1.3.

While narratives and recounts are structured as a sequence of events, news stories in English broadsheet newspapers are not sequenced in time. They begin with a lead paragraph that gives the nub of the story, and then come back to it from different angles – so that they jump around in time. Many explanations are

Table 1.3: Simple genre system

	+ event structured	− event structured
recounting events	narrative	news story
generalising phenomena	explanation	report
proposing action	procedure	protocol

also sequences of events, linked by cause and effect. Reports, however, are concerned with describing things rather than events, so they are not time sequenced. Procedures consist of a series of steps, which are often expressed as a command (*Chop the vegetables. Place in a saucepan of boiling water* ...). But protocols include texts such as rules, which also consist of commands about what to do and not to do, but are simply listed rather than sequenced in time.

Tables of paradigms like those above illustrate the options that speakers and writers can choose between texts, and moment by moment as a text unfolds. Linguists use such paradigms to map out the sets of options available in a language. The number of such systems at the levels of phonology, grammar, discourse, register and genre is very large indeed, and describing them is a very challenging task. Halliday characterises the whole set of options for meaning in a language, and the relative frequencies in which they are used, as the 'semantic code' of its culture: 'Each language has its own semantic code, although languages that share a common culture tend to have codes that are closely related ... The context of culture determines the nature of the code' (1994: xxxi).

However, it is crucial for our understanding of language learning to recognise that language is not learnt by memorising contrasts in systems, but by experiencing contrasts in texts. Hal's mother did not design a language lesson in order to demonstrate the contrast between a question with rising tone and a statement with falling tone, nor to demonstrate the contrast between the colours blue and orange. Rather, Hal has come to recognise the distinctions between these semantic contrasts, from experiencing repeated instances of them in social discourse, with the guidance of his caregivers. Learning a language involves construing its systems out of repeated experiences of this kind. The learner's knowledge of language systems accumulates over time, largely unconsciously.

> As a language is manifested through its texts, a culture is manifested through its situations; so by attending to text-in-situation a child construes the code, and by using the code to interpret text s/he construes the culture. Thus for the individual, the code engenders the culture; and this gives a powerful inertia to the transmission process (Halliday 1994: xxxi).

The process of construing language systems intuitively is almost entirely unconscious, but becomes conscious at certain points. The exchange between Hal and his mother above is an example, as Hal consciously works with his mother's guidance, to state the contrast accurately between blue and orange that he has heard many times previously. It is this accumulated experience of language features in meaningful contexts that enables Hal to consciously recognise the contrast. As children grow older, this kind of guided language learning is enhanced by being able to name linguistic contrasts. For example, Painter recorded the following conversation [1.4] with her son Stephen about the terms *question* and *order*, in the year before he started school (1999: 124).

[1.4] age 4:6

Stephen	*Mummy, is a **question** that you don't eat porridge with your fingers? [pause] It's a **question** that you don't eat porridge with your fingers.*
Mother	*That's not a **question** it's an **order**.*
Stephen	*What's an **order**?*
Mother	*It's something that you tell somebody and they have to do.*
Stephen	*I meant an **order**.*

The terms *question* and *order* are words about language, or metalanguage. At age 2, Hal could attend consciously to contrasts between names for concrete things like pegs. At age 4, Stephen is thinking about names for linguistic categories, which are abstract things. He is not simply 'attending to text-in-situation', but is also attending to the language system, using names for its contrasts. But notice here that the metalanguage his mother gives him is not the same as that we introduced for speech functions in Table 1.2 above. There we used the technical terms for speech functions, **question**, **statement**, **command** and **offer**. Here Stephen's mother is using 'folk' metalanguage *order* to contrast with Stephen's *question*.

As Painter's data illustrates, language learning is often a conscious process, and metalanguage is a tool for making language systems conscious from an early age. But this does not mean that language teaching starts with language systems; rather, learning a language system is the endpoint of an extended process of experiencing its contrasts in meaningful contexts.

In spite of this, traditional language teaching does start with systems, including the rule systems of traditional school grammars, and of sound/letter systems in phonics. Typically, decontextualised fragments of language are used to exemplify each option in a system, and students are supposed to recognise and remember these isolated language features. A common activity for memorising them is to write and say each feature repeatedly in a series of examples. Later, students may put these fragments of language together into whole words, word groups, clauses and eventually texts. Or they may use them to parse the words, word groups and clauses in a text. These practices are recontextualised from the practices of linguists, who describe grammars as systems, usually using decontextualised examples of words, word groups and clauses.

At the other extreme, constructivist pedagogies such as whole language oppose explicit teaching of language systems, in the belief that learning emerges from within the child, and that language is osmotically absorbed from the child's environment, in a process that has been dubbed 'natural language learning' (Gray 1987). It is claimed that explicit language teaching constrains an individual's freedom to create their own meanings. These practices are recontextualised from several sources. One is Piaget's cognitive psychological hypothesis of individual learning; another is the notion of creative genius in the arts; and a third is the liberal humanist doctrine of individual freedom. The constructivist view is quite at odds with actual observations of language learning in the home, such as Painters' examples, which show how caregivers deliberately and explicitly guide children's language learning. Furthermore, the rejection of explicit language teaching forces teachers and students to rely on non-systematic, tacitly learnt folk metalanguage to discuss language in the classroom.

In a sense, genre pedagogy takes a middle road. That is it starts with meaningful whole texts, but the way they are explored is informed by systematic understandings of the way that language is organised, such as those outlined above. And as each text unfolds, its language features may be explicitly reviewed and named as opportunities arise. Furthermore, once students can recognise and comprehend meanings in the context of each text, these meanings can be further reviewed as systems of linguistic contrasts (Rose 2010b). This kind of extension activity is an example of an elaborating phase in a learning cycle, which follows successful completion of a learning task, and builds on understandings gained through the task. This principle can be applied to language systems from genres (§3.7) all the way down to sounds and letter patterns (§4.7).

The pedagogic principle of prepare–task–elaborate is also applied throughout this book. Each chapter begins with a discussion of its context (as this chapter also did). Then the body of each chapter unfolds as a series of reading tasks – more often than not short texts, spoken or written. Before each text, the reader is prepared with some brief information, which is elaborated in more detail after the text. By this means the book is made as easy to access as possible, but the knowledge that is shared between us and the reader builds in spirals, as in Figure 1.5 above. Towards the end of each chapter, and the later chapters of the book, the accumulated shared knowledge is reviewed as contrasts in systems, i.e. as theories of language and pedagogy.

2 Language and social power

This chapter focuses on writing in infants and primary school, describing the first phase of the Sydney School research, the *Writing Project* and *Language as Social Power* project. It first outlines the context in which our work began, outlining the kinds of writing we found in Australian primary schools at the time. The range of genres that primary students are expected to write are then described, and the model of genre that developed out of this work is introduced. We then outline the development of the pedagogy designed to apprentice students into control of these genres and illustrate the different kinds of teacher-student interaction this apprenticeship involves. The chapter concludes with examples of the kinds of writing that children have achieved by means of this pedagogy.

2.1 Beginnings: the *Writing Project*

In 1979 Michael Halliday organised a Language in Education conference at the University of Sydney, which brought together a group of educators interested in language with a group of linguists interested in education. It was through this conference that Jim first began working with Joan Rothery, who was studying student writing in school. This led to the first phase of Sydney School literacy research – the *Writing Project* (roughly 1980–1985).[1] This project undertook to build a classification of the kinds of writing done by students, focusing on infants and primary school (Years K–6 in the New South Wales system, with students aged 5–12 years). Cate Poynton played a key role in data collection and ethnographic analysis during this phase.

By the early 1980s Australian infants and primary school education had been strongly influenced by what was known at the time as progressive education

---

[1] The *Writing Project* research was funded by the University of Sydney and the Australian Research Council.

(now constructivism), with what was probably a stronger uptake than anywhere else in the world. This was reflected in its wholehearted adoption of progressive literacy programs which had been developed in America and imported under the banners of Process Writing (Graves, e.g. 1983) and Whole Language (Goodman, e.g. 1986). The writing we studied was by and large collected from classrooms enacting this writing curriculum and pedagogy. Poynton's collection in particular drew on a working-class/lower middle-class suburban school which had been in-serviced in this regard by one of New South Wales key literacy consultants under the auspices of a supportive principal.

Australian implementations of process writing/whole language programs (e.g. Turbill 1983, Walshe 1981) emphasised the importance of making time for writing, preferably every day. They encouraged students to work on whole texts, which they would re-draft through 'conferencing' with peers and their teacher, working towards a culminative 'publication' stage. Teachers were encouraged to let children write on topics of their own choice, in whatever form they chose, and to let spelling develop naturally, from invented spelling to mature standards (with an analogy drawn to the way in which children apparently develop the spoken 'accent' of their communities without direct instruction and error correction).

This pedagogy, as can be seen, places teachers in a non-authoritative facilitating role – a reaction to what was considered to be a more directive authoritarian traditional stance, which was read as inhibiting their ability to express themselves in writing. The idea was to build a supportive nurturing class-room environment for literacy development, apparently similar to that experi-enced by children during spoken-language development in the home. In our observation this change of teaching gears was successfully enacted by many classroom teachers, even if it meant biting one's tongue and slipping up from time to time. As Scott reports in one of the key process writing manuals, 'One of the greatest temptations was to tell children what and how to write. I had to literally bite my tongue and remember that children can think for themselves' (Scott 1983: 1). And as one of the Year 2 teachers Cate and Jim were observing apologised during a lesson: 'I know I'm not supposed to tell them anything, but after all, I **am** their teacher!' Halliday's apt term for progressive pedagogy of this kind is 'benevolent inertia'.

These ideas are alive and well today in many parts of the world, with the term 'constructivist' now generally used to refer to the approach. Alexander 2000, Brophy 2002 and Wells 1999 provide useful overviews from the turn of the millennium. Alexander, in his revealing study of primary school pedagogy around the world, notes the following piece of progressive philosophy (2000: 548), prominently displayed on the classroom wall of one of his Michigan, USA schools. Although posted almost two decades later, this teacher's issues capture perfectly the polarising ideological climate in which we undertook our 1980s Australian research.

Important issues to me -

Process orientation vs product orientation
Teaching students vs teaching programs
Teacher as facilitator vs teacher as manager
Developing a set of strategies vs mastering a set of skills
Celebrating approximation vs celebrating perfection
Promoting independence in learning vs dependence on teacher

In literacy classrooms of this kind, what kind of writing do we find? Our work with teachers (via interviews, discussions, classroom observations etc.) seemed to indicate that the answer to this question was a simple one: infants and primary school students write 'stories'. As linguists, however, this professional rhetoric, however practical for process writing and whole language classrooms, gave us pause. Concerned colleagues, for example, passed on to us Text [2.1] below, from their eight-year-old son.

[2.1] Ben's history of the planet

OUR PLANET

Earth's core is as hot as the furthest outer layer of the sun. They are both 6000c°.

Earth started as a ball of fire. Slowly it cooled. But it was still too hot for Life. Slowly water formed and then the first signs of life, microscopic cells. Then came trees. About seven thousand million years later came the first man.

Ben had a keen interest in science and had written what looked to us like a proto-scientific explanation of the history of the planet. This was assessed by his teacher as (i) incomplete (since his drawing of the planet was considered unfinished), (ii) poorly presented graphologically (since there was no margin) and (iii) generically unacceptable (since it was not a story). So much for writing on a topic of your own choice in any form you choose! Ben survived, did mainly science subjects in secondary school where he hated English because they never told him the criteria on which assessment was based (though he is a voracious reader and loves Shakespeare), and went on to complete a degree in biochemistry and psychology at university. His middle-class parents, both working in tertiary education, had given him the coding orientation he needed to see him through. But what about other students, we wondered, who cannot see through or find a way around the hidden literacy curriculum on offer here?

Incidents of this kind confirmed for us the importance of looking closely at the language of student writing in order to build a clearer picture of what was going on. Fortunately for us we were working in Michael Halliday's linguistics department at the University of Sydney, and had the richest meaning oriented grammar of English in the world at our disposal (Halliday 1994). In addition, we were developing Halliday and Hasan's 1976 work on cohesion as a model of discourse structure (Martin 1992, Martin and Rose 2003/2007). And beyond this we had inherited useful models of social context from Halliday (1978) and Jim's teacher in Toronto, Michael Gregory (1967, Gregory and Carroll 1978). So we set to work, exploring what we found.

2.2   Types of writing in infants and primary school

As we can see from Ben's explanation, students were not all in fact writing 'stories'. And we observed that the texts that Ben's teacher might have accepted as a bona fide 'story' were not all of the same kind (as partly reflected in the different grades teachers would assign them). Here are some examples[2] of the kind of writing we found (Rothery 1989), beginning with what were overwhelmingly the two most common types of text collected.

2.2.1   Observation/comments and recounts

Text [2.2] is from a Year 3 female writer, who has been to a school swimming carnival. She relates that she went in four races and had fun that Thursday. We termed this kind of text an **observation/comment** because it comprised an observation about an experience and the student's reaction to it. In observation/comments the experience is not developed as a sequence of events; what happened is parcelled up economically as a named activity.

---

[2] In order not to repeat examples from previous publications, throughout this chapter we have often used texts collected in the 00s for purposes of illustration, not the actual texts on which our comments on the distribution of genres are based.

[2.2] Observation/comment text - language only (Year 3)

> The Swimming
> Carnival.
> I Went in The nace 4 nace
> and fun Thursday

Observation/comments tend to be realised as multimodal texts, accompanied by drawings bearing on the experience related. The images accompanying the verbal text just considered are included in [2.2'] below, including clouds, two bird's eye perspectives on the pool (divided into lanes for the races, and with the names of the writer and her peers by lane in the top one), and what appears to be a map of sorts to the right. This was the most common kind of writing we found in our survey of just over 2,300 texts, and the only kind of writing that we could be sure was undertaken by all students before leaving infants and primary school for secondary education.

[2.2'] Observation/comment - language and image

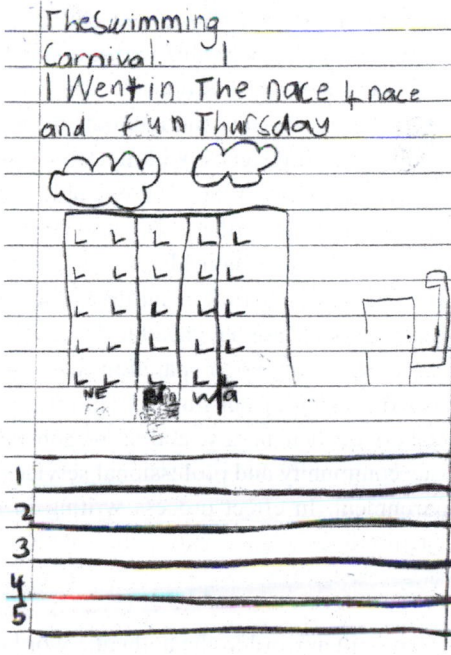

Text [2.3] is from a Year 5/6 male writer who has been to visit his father for three weeks during the summer holidays. He relates a visit to his aunt, what he got for Christmas and how he felt about seeing everyone.

[2.3] Recount (Year 5/6)

On the holiday

I went to my dads for 3 weeks an we went to ante Jhins house for crismuse. I got
Leogo and a humonic I was vere happy to se [vey?] famle BLak

We termed this kind of text a **recount**; it differs from an observation/comment
in that a temporal sequence of events is established, unpacking in this case some
of the things that happened during the holiday visit. This was the second most
common kind of writing we found, and one that most students would have
performed by the end of primary school. It might or might not be accompanied
by an illustration, depending on the length of the recount and the age of the
student. It appears that drawings were considered childish and so disappeared
over time, replaced where the student was able with extended writing, which was
more highly valued in process writing classrooms.

Taken together, observation/comments and recounts made up the great majority of the writing we collected. Colleagues working around Australia at the time
confirmed comparable results. Gray 1986, for example, found that 100% of
writing by Indigenous students in Northern Territory rural schools comprised
recounts. This shocked us when we considered the literacy demands of the
primary curriculum, ranging across themes including science, geography, history,
health and government as it does. Looking ahead to secondary school it was clear
that most students were receiving no preparation whatsoever for writing in
different subject areas. And many of our migrant students were the most fluent
English-speaking members of their family, and so responsible in some measure
for liaising with various community and professional services in a predominantly
English-speaking environment. In effect process writing in Australia had more
than confirmed Bernstein's fears about locking students into her or his 'present
tense':

As we move from the written word to the authentic word of the child, it is
quite likely that the time dimension of the transmission is changing from
the past to the present. If that is so, we must make very certain that the
new pedagogy does not lock the child into the present – in his or her
present tense. There is a danger that the new educational pull with its
emphasis on the aural might well in fact do that unless we seek to

understand systematically how to create a concept which can authenticate the child's experience and give him or her those powerful representations of thought that he or she is going to need in order to change the world outside (Bernstein 1979: 300-1).

On reflection what we found should not have surprised us. Constructivist pedagogy (and curriculum, if we can call it that) in fact proscribes teaching students how to write. Models of what is expected are not given; knowledge about language that might be used by teachers to discuss writing with students is dismissed as useless (because it supposedly cannot be used to improve writing) and harmful (since learning it takes time away from writing itself); students are encouraged to write stories across the curriculum (since 'narrative' is supposedly the 'primary act of mind' that children rely on to understand their world, a perspective taken over from Britton, e.g. 1970); and teachers do not compose texts jointly with their class for fear of intruding on students' creativity and subjectivity. In a knowledge vacuum of this kind, most students have no choice but to draw their own experience of language, which is an oral one, featuring language like that scribed in Texts [2.2] and [2.3]. The only real 'progress' we noted from K–6 for most students was that the texts got longer, as students got faster at writing their spoken language down.

2.2.2   Factual texts

Significantly, as [2.1] above shows, this was not all we found. Ben was not the only student interested in the nature of things, and so we came across writing like [2.4] below.

[2.4] Report - Goannas (Year 10 – see §4.1)

> Goannas
>
> Goannas are native animals that live in isolated place and they are reptiles
>
> Goannas are all way the same as the
>
> Goannas look as same as area where the live in. They camouflage their self with the area their colour looks like yellowish-brown and they eat insec dead animals
>
> Goannas breed about six eggs
>
> Aboriginals hunt goannas for food and the fat inside the goannas are used for medicine.

Goannas

Goannas are native animals that live in isolated place and they are reptiles.

Goannas look as same as area Where they live in. They camouflage their self with the area their colour looks like yellowish-brown and they eat insects dead animals

Goannas breed about six eggs

Aboriginals hunt goannas for food and the fat inside the goannas are used for medicine.

This Goannas report is also 'not a story': temporal sequence is not a structuring principle here, nor is the text about personal experience. Rather the text makes generalisations about a biological species – classifying goannas, describing them, commenting on reproduction and noting how they were used by Indigenous people. We termed this kind of writing a **report**, and noted that they were usually written by boys (who, like Ben, were thereby putting their implicit or explicit assessment as a 'story' writer at risk).

Like reports, [2.5] below focuses on things rather than events; but in this case it considers a single thing, not a class – here an imaginary pet.

[2.5] Description - featuring humour, focalisation (Years 3/4)

The Coolest Shark in the Underworld.
EV x

Every sea creature sees my shark
differently. The penguin think shes
The brother The great white shark
Shes a princess bin in a cuddly sort
of way.
The crab next door Thinks
Shes smart But you havent
seen The cilly crabs next door!
Even Jack Octopus Thinks
shes funny its crazy Though,
he cracks up laughing every time he sees
her mr stingray thinks shes precious
and adorable but when he takes
her on a journey she tries to bite him.
But I love my shark. I think
Shes The coolest.
im a snappy and swishy kind of way

The Coolest Shark in the World

Every sea creature sees my shark differently. The penguins think she is The brother. The great white shark

shes a princess but in a cuddly sort of way.

The crab next door Thinks shes smart But you haven't seen The cilly crabs next door!

Even the Octopus thinks shes funny. It's crazy though. he cracks up laughing every time he sees her mr stingray thinks shes precious and adorable but when he takes her on a Journey she tries to bite him.

But I love my shark. I think shes The coolest.

in a snappy and swishy kind of way.

The text describes, from different points of view, a particular shark who is variously a brother, a great white shark, a princess, smart, funny, humorous, precious, adorable, dangerous and cool (and the writer loves her great white pet). We termed this kind of writing a **description**. The move from biology (Text [2.4]) to domestic life (imagined) affords an outpouring of feeling, including those of the writer (who accordingly writes in the first person).

Notably this text includes almost no scientific information about sharks (contrasting with reports about sharks in this way; see [2.6] below). Instead, the text plays with personification (endowing animals with human consciousness) and focalisation (considering the pet shark form the imagined perspective of fellow sea creatures). These standard literary turns no doubt play a key role in attracting the assessment 'Super work' from the teacher, and demonstrate the fact that 'imagination' is not a faculty that can only be exercised in 'story' genres, and exemplify the fact that 'creativity' is a possibility with every genre (once it has been mastered of course).

In contrast with Text [2.5], which depends on personification and focalisation to impress the reader, Text [2.6] depends on research.

[2.6] Report – Shark Report (Years 3/4)

> Shark Report   9-4-08
> A shark is a type of species that lives in the sea. A shark is one of the largest sea creatures. There are 350 type of shark. A shark is shaped like a torpedo. Sandpaper is lef like a shark body. Elastic is in shark body inset of bones. A shark can grow up to 8 metres.
>
> Sharks live in Oceans. Sharks have to swim but if they dont swim they will sink or suffocate.
>
> Harmless sharks eat Plants but harmful sharks eat live meat. Sharks have up to forty two pups. Some sharks lay eggs and some have them alive. Some sharks have to defend the pups

Shark Report

A shark is a type of species that lives in the sea. A shark is one of the largest sea creatures. There are 350 type of shark A shark is shaped like a torpedo. Sandpaper is like a shark body. Elastic is in shark body inset of bones A shark can grow up to 8 meters.

Sharks live in Oceans. Sharks have to swim but if they don't swim they will sink or suffocate.

Harmless sharks eat Plants but harmful sharks eat live meat. Sharks have up to forty two pups. Some sharks lay eggs and some have them live. Some sharks have to defend the pups.

Without a time line to organise the text, students face the challenge of organising the uncommonsense information they collect. The goannas and shark reports share a common strategy in this respect, first classifying the creature in focus, then describing it, then commenting on its habits, and then reproduction. The information, in other words, is staged to achieve the texts' goals.

In our survey we noted that the complementarity of the 'literary' and 'scientific' approaches to sharks reflected in Texts [2.5] and [2.6] was gendered, with the literary texts more highly valued by primary school teachers. This places boys at a disadvantage as far as the implicit writing assessment practices of constructivist pedagogy are concerned; ironically, the few boys thus inclined were preparing themselves for the literacy demands of secondary school in a way that girls were not (Martin 1985).

Another type of 'scientific' writing we found in our survey was the **explanation**. Text [2.7] below is an explanation from biology, complementing in this respect Ben's geological interests in [2.1]. This text begins like a report, describing and locating the heart, but then moves on to explain blood circulation as a process unfolding through time.

[2.7] Explanation – The Heart (Years 5/6)

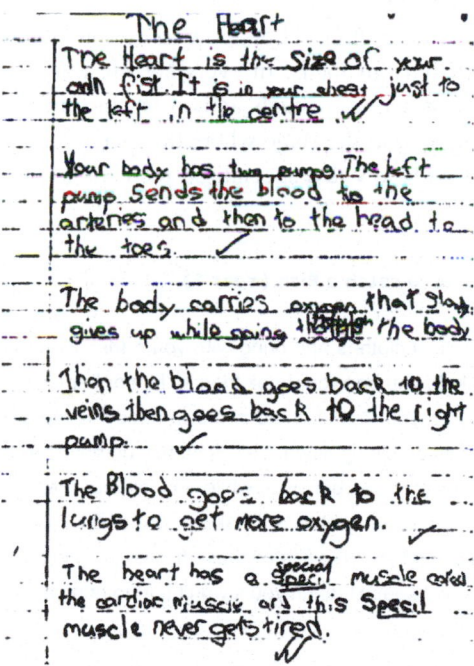

The Heart

The Heart is the size of your first. It is in your chest just to the left in the centre.

Your body has two pumps. The left pump sends the blood to the arteries and then to the head to the toes.

The body carries oxygen that slowly gives up while going through the body.

Then the Blood goes back to the lungs to get more oxygen.

The heart has a special muscle called the cardiac muscle and this special muscle never gets tired.

Students' explanation texts were very rare – in part because the genre was not modelled for students in constructivist classrooms, and in part because very little writing was done across the curriculum in thematic units focusing on physical or biological phenomena. In any case, the literary orientation of process writing was so strong that materials promoting writing as a tool for learning science at the time were recommending narrative[3] and poetry writing over other genres (Martin 1990b).

Alongside reports and explanations we occasionally came across instrumental writing about how to do things (procedure and protocol) and argumentative writing about issues (exposition and discussion). Numbers were small, since taken together explanations, procedure, protocol, exposition and discussion made up only about 2% of our sample.

Procedures provide instructions about how to do something, organised around a time line of the activity in focus. In everyday life this genre is deployed for recipes, directions, instruction manuals and so on; in school it is more likely to feature in science reports, in the stage where the methodology of the experiment is specified. Text [2.8] below is a specialised recreational procedure, explaining how to catch a fish.

[2.8] Procedure – How to catch a Fish (Year 6)

You put on your dirtiest clothes and bring with you a friend who knows how to fish. Get your friend to help you bait your hook then let him or her cast your line try and sit patiently. If you can't. your friend could come in handy to talk with. (?) play some kind of game you can do sitting down. This is so you do not have to leave your spot. When you get a nibble close your eyes while you let your friend reel it in. Get your friend to show off his or her catch and take a photo. STAND CLEAR while your friend cleans, scales and guts the fish because fish is going to smell. If you can't find a spot where the smell doesn't reach you it won't hurt to bring a peg.

Procedures are complemented by protocols, which assume you know how to do something but need some guidance on how to do it properly. They feature in civic life as rules, regulations and laws controlling behaviour – often signposted at appropriate locations. They are not organised around a time line but simply list restrictions on the activity in focus. Text [2.9] is an imaginative protocol text from early secondary school, listing.

---

[3] So instead of scientific explanations, students were writing imaginative stories such as 'Journey to the ear' (as a sound wave).

[2.9] Protocol (early secondary school)

If shoes ruled the world I think the would apply lots of laws and some of the might be

...

- People are not allowed to wear shoes.

- All of the tv shows featured shoes.

- The president would be a shoe.

- The people would be slaves to the shoes.

- Shoes were all over the world and did all of the human jobs.

Text [2.10] below is a rare example of argumentative writing, dealing with the thesis that the best pet in the world is a pet rock.

[2.10] Argument – The Perfect Pet (Year 6)

The best pet in the world is a pet that you don't have to feed, doesn't fidget and doesn't make noises in the middle of the might. The pet that fits all these categories is a pet rock. You never have to worry about it dying because it was never alive in the first place. When you take your pet rock for a walk you don't have to worry about it fighting with another rock. You don't ever have to brush it or wash its fur. Pet rocks are always good for weather predictions. It your rock is wet you know it's raining, when it starts to fly its windy and when it shakes it must be an earthquake. A pet rock will never run away, it doesn't answer back and if you don't like the colour of the rock you can paint it again. The food bill is very low for a pet rock for it will cost you nothing to feed. There are two or three things your pet rock will not do. It will not fetch a ball or stick, won't beg for food, and can't roll over for you to rub its stomach. But it also never digs up the garden and doesn't care if you change its name. Pet rocks never catch a cold or get sunburnt. They are very good for paper weights if they are heavy. Last, but not least they can be both an indoor and an outdoor pet.

A more serious implementation of the argument genre than [2.10] might deal with the issue of whether people should keep pets at all; and with guidance it might be more clearly organised into pros and cons. Reflecting no doubt (i) the relative absence of a focus on writing across the curriculum, (ii) the implicit literary bias in the largely implicit assessment processes and (iii) childish conceptions about the capabilities of infants and primary school children (Martin 1985), the relatively few examples of explanatory, instrumental and argumentative writing we found were from good writers playing with the genre, often using imaginative topics, and often for humorous effect (as reflected in [2.8] to [2.10]).

2.2.3   Narratives

In spite of the range of kinds of writing we found, including examples of the reports, descriptions, explanations, procedures, protocol and arguments (i.e. the proto-expositions and discussions reviewed above), we concluded that this kind of factual writing in effect accounted for only about 10% of the texts surveyed (Rothery 1996). The rest was story writing of some kind, mainly including observation/comments (about 40%) and recounts (about 20%); most of the rest was narrative proper, by which we mean a story in which something goes wrong. Let us explore this a little now, because in spite of their generally implicit preference for writing of this kind, we found that teachers had very little awareness of what they were reacting to when they valued a successful narrative text. Text [2.11] below can be read as a proto-narrative.

[2.11] Proto-narrative (Year 1)

The Horse

Once upon a time

there was a horse and he jumped over the fence. then he ate some apples.

The End

Text [2.11] includes various narrative features: it begins with the indexical *Once upon a time* opening featured in fairy tales, introduces the main character (a horse), arguably implicates a problem/solution sequence (i.e. the horse wanted some apples, so it jumped over the fence to get some), and closes with *The End*.

Text [2.12], from an even younger but more advanced writer, develops a canonical narrative structure more clearly.

[2.12] An early narrative (K)

> A fish was swimn inthe worta. He heerd a SPlash and a car falld in theworta car. "Help; help" said the man. The fish help the man swim to the beech.

A fish was swimn inthe worta. He heerd a SPlash and a car falld in theworta car.
"Help; help" said the man. The fish help the man swim to the beech.

Narrative features in [2.12] include setting the scene (a fish was swimming), introducing a complication (car in the water), suspending the time line to allow for some evaluation of the gravity of the situation ('Help, help' said the man) and resolving the complication with the rescue (the fish helping the man to the beach). Labov and Waletzky's 1967 proposals for basic narrative structure (Orientation, Complication, Evaluation, Resolution) are easily recognised here.

Text [2.13] below exemplifies a more developed narrative.

[2.13] A more developed narrative (Years 1/2)

> my settin on an island n middle of swamp other perion mandy Not that far from where I was standing in the swamp. I though I heard a strange gurgling noise. mandy had frosen and was looking at the swamp. I wanted to yell "run" but my throat was dry. Suddenly a yellaw slime Just on the water, then a red dot in the water. I whispered "the great scream oaslime" swamp water snake." Mandy nodded then she whisped "back away slowly" we did and hid behind some rocks. Soon the gurgling sound got faint er then it was gone. We rowed back in our boat and never came back.
>   Great   Evie   AP

> My settin on an island in middle of swamp. other person mandy not that far from where I was standing in the swamp, I thought I heard a strange gurgling noise. Mandy had frozen and was looking at the swamp. I wanted to yell "run" but my throat was dry. Suddenly a yellow slime just (appeared) on the water, then a red dot in the water. I whispered "the great screampaslime swamp water snake." Mandy nodded. Then she whispered "Back away slowly" we did. Soon the gurgling sound got farther then it was gone. We rowed back in our boat and never came back.

More developed narrative features in [2.13] include a complication developing in two phases (first the *gurgling sound* and then the appearance of the *water snake*), each with their own evaluation. The resolution similarly unfolds in steps (*moving back, the sound receding, rowing away and never coming back*). The suspenseful staging of events is further dramatised with affectually charged lexis (including one invented term) – *swamp, strange, gurgling, frozen, slime, screampaslime, whispered*. And not surprisingly, given its enactment of the conventions of the genre, the story is assessed as 'Great', despite its problems with handwriting.

Basing our analysis on texts of this kind we were able to bring to consciousness the implicit story assessment criteria of our process writing teachers, with Labov and Waletzky's staging as a basic scaffolding, and 'bonus points' given for further problematising the time line, for using non-core vocabulary to charge the text with feeling, for setting the story somewhere beyond normal everyday experience and for incorporating literary devices such as personification and shifting focalisation. But our process writing students were not being led along a pathway developing these resources. In fact only a few of our female writers were able to figure out from their own reading what their teachers were actually asking for. Most students continued to write observation/comments and recounts, based on how they had heard language used outside school and in the playground. Even where students had extraordinary experiences to draw upon, the absence of modelling and explicit discussion of how to form a narrative meant that a developmental trajectory was not embarked upon. Text [2.14], for example, has the stuff of narrative, but it is not a highly valued piece of writing with respect to the implicit assessment criteria just outlined.

[2.14] Undeveloped story (Year 5/6)

On the weekend I Play footyball Then I went to the river and I see a black snake and I see a black dog and cat my cousin Jac. my cousn Jack Jumpet out of the tree and see a black snake.

I was worry bous my cousln was near a black snake.

Accordingly many students were arriving in secondary school with the implicit idea that writing was simply spoken language written down. Text [2.15] below is a telling example from a writer in year 7 (the first year of secondary school in New South Wales).

[2.15] Anecdote (Year 7)

> When I was walking up to MS COX room I seen a suitcase. and a slimy thing hanging out and it looked like a baby octopus. AT First I was scared but when I look it wasn't that scary. Then I looked up closer I seen a face with to big eyes I jumped. It looked like a cat. I went over to open it and it was a cat playin with a baby toy. I laughed at myself and the cat looked up at me and it meowed at me. THE END.

This Text [2.15] can be interpreted as an **anecdote**, a story that reports an unusual experience in order to share an emotional reaction with listeners (Martin and Plum 1997, Rothery 1994). Here the writer has a laugh at herself for getting frightened by a pussy cat.

Needless to say, writing of this kind concerns secondary school teachers greatly, since at all levels (e.g. handwriting, spelling, punctuation, layout, non-standard grammar, spoken story-telling style) it is far from the kind of writing needed for book reports, literature essays and narrative composition in subject English, let alone writing across the curriculum in other discipline areas. We were confident infants and primary schools could do better than this, and so we set to work to turn things around.

2.3   Knowledge about language: genre

The first thing we had to do was build a model of language in social context that teachers could use to plan and deliver their writing lessons, and evaluate their students' progress. Without such a model, these pedagogic activities depended on teachers' intuitive knowledge about language, and their students' writing depended on their even more limited intuitive awareness. Our goal was to bring the linguistic nature of their students' writing to consciousness, to make the teaching of language explicit. To do so we needed to find a way to build teachers' and students' knowledge about language, or KAL.

This was especially challenging in the Australian context where progressive educators had been able to remove the last vestiges of grammar and rhetoric teaching from school and pre-service teacher training curricula (Christie 1993). As a result, the only knowledge about language that remained for most teachers was a few terms for word classes (usually called parts of speech), without any systematic criteria to recognise a noun, verb, adjective, adverb, conjunction or preposition reliably when asked to identify one. Our own linguistic framework was far richer than this, and we proceeded along the following lines, drawing on the best analyses we could muster to make explicit what was going on.

From our functional model of language we assumed that the texts students were writing were made of meanings; and since we were dealing with whole texts, we approached the analysis of their meanings from the perspective of discourse, that is, of meanings unfolding through a text. We will organise the discussion here with reference to systems of meanings in discourse that are outlined in Chapter 5 (§5.3) below, and detailed in Martin and Rose 2003/2007. Because they present two perspectives on one topic of school knowledge, we will focus on the two sharks texts introduced above: [2.5] which we called a description and [2.6] which we classified as a report. To show more clearly how meanings unfold through the texts, they are presented line-by-line, with one clause to each line (as for 2.5' below).

[2.5'] The Coolest Shark in the World

> Every sea creature sees my shark differently.
>
> The penguins think she is The brother.
>
> The great white shark [thinks] shes a princess but in a cuddly sort of way.
>
> The crab next door Thinks shes smart
>
> But you haven't seen The cilly crabs next door!
>
> Even the Octopus thinks shes funny.
>
> It's crazy though.
>
> he cracks up laughing
>
> every time he sees her
>
> mr stingray thinks shes precious and adorable
>
> but when he takes her on a Journey
>
> she tries to bite him.
>
> But I love my shark.
>
> I think shes The coolest. in a snappy and swishy kind of way.

2.3.1   Presenting knowledge

The first set of meanings we will focus on is known as **ideation**. Ideation is concerned with the nature of knowledge, including everyday, specialised and academic knowledge. Text [2.5], for example, presents the writer's everyday knowledge about sea creatures, including great white sharks, penguins, crabs, octopuses and stingrays (although her pet shark is not explicitly classified as one of her sea creatures). Just a few of many possible sea creatures are mentioned, and no biological information is provided about any of them beyond this partial inventory. The activities noted are familiar domestic ones – joking around and going on trips. Since the creatures mentioned would be familiar to most urban children from reading picture books, watching television and perhaps a trip to an aquarium, this description arguably does not depend on any research; the text is based on everyday understandings of the world, with the imaginative twist that sharks can be kept as pets, and sea creatures can think and laugh and go on excursions just like people do.

Text [2.6] on the other hand does compile scientific understandings based on research. First sharks are explicitly classified with species that live in the sea, which is then rephrased as one type of sea creature, and the number of sub-types is stated.

[2.6′] Shark Report

A shark is a type of species that lives in the sea.

A shark is one of the largest sea creatures.

There are 350 type of shark

Some aspects of shark's bodies are then described, with reference to their streamlined shape, the texture of their skin, the elastic nature of their (cartilaginous) skeleton and their size.

A shark is shaped like a torpedo.

Sandpaper is like a shark body.

Elastic is in shark body inset of bones

A shark can grow up to 8 meters.

Finally, their ocean habitat and some of their behaviours are described, including swimming, feeding and breeding.

Sharks live in Oceans.

Sharks have to swim

but if they don't swim

they will sink or suffocate.

Harmless sharks eat Plants

but harmful sharks eat live meat.

Sharks have up to forty two pups.

Some sharks lay eggs

and some have them live.

Some sharks have to defend the pups.

In this kind of text we have moved from everyday understandings of the world to scientific ones. Writing of this kind involves research, and typically depends on reading – since the biology involved by and large has to be retrieved from writing.

2.3.2   Identifying people, things and places and organising information

The complementarity between everyday and scientific knowledge in the two shark texts is also highlighted by resources for **identification**. Identification is used to introduce people, things and places into a text and to keep track of them from sentence to sentence. The writer of [2.5] introduces each thing except *sea creatures* as a specific individual who is already known to readers (*the coolest shark in the world*, *my shark*, *the penguins*, *the great white shark*, *the crab next door*, *the Octopus*, *Mr Stingray*). And five of these things are tracked through chains of reference, the longest of which refers to the pet shark (12 references).

> the coolest Shark in the world, my shark, she, she, she, she, her, she, her, she, my shark, she
>
> the crab next door, the cilly crabs next door
>
> the Octopus, he, he
>
> mr stingray, he, him

In [2.6] on the other hand each thing is generic, referring to whole classes of phenomena; and as is typical of generic reference there are only occasional short identity chains.

> sharks, they, they
>
> up to forty two pups, them, the pups

Generally indefinite reference is used to refer to these generic participants. Sharks are referred to several times in this way, alongside single mentions of bones, oceans, plants, live meat and eggs. The only definite reference is *the largest sea creatures*, which refers back to *species that live in the sea*.

> a shark, a shark, shark, a shark, a shark body, shark body, a shark, sharks, sharks, harmless sharks, harmful sharks, sharks, some sharks, some sharks
>
> bones, oceans, plants, live meat, eggs

With respect to the flow of information, the two texts organise the meanings reviewed above in complementary ways. Text [2.6] begins with a title, classifies sharks in an introduction, and then develops their description.

> Shark Report
>
> A shark is a type of species that lives in the sea.
> A shark is one of the largest sea creatures.
> There are 350 type of shark

A shark is shaped like a torpedo.

Sandpaper is like a shark body.

Elastic is in shark body inset of bones

A shark can grow up to 8 meters.

Sharks live in Oceans.

Sharks have to swim

but if they don't swim they will sink or suffocate.

Harmless sharks eat Plants

but harmful sharks eat live meat.

Sharks have up to forty two pups.

Some sharks lay eggs

and some have them live.

Some sharks have to defend the pups.

Furthermore, the starting point, or **Theme**, of each clause is overwhelmingly sharks, which serves to orient each message to the scientific topic of the text. And each clause ends with a piece of information about sharks, that is the **News** of the message (in bold below).

Themes	**News**
A shark	is a type of species that lives in the sea.
A shark	is one of the largest sea creatures.
There	are 350 type of shark
A shark	is shaped like a torpedo.
Sandpaper	is like a shark body.
Elastic	is in shark body **inset of bones**
A shark	can grow up to 8 meters.
Sharks	live in Oceans.
Sharks	have to swim
but if they don't swim	they will sink or suffocate.
Harmless sharks	eat Plants
but harmful sharks	eat live meat.
Sharks	have up to forty two pups.
Some sharks	lay **eggs**
and some	have them **live.**
Some sharks	have to defend **the pups.**

Text [2.5] also begins with a title, then introduces the different points of view of different sea creatures as an introduction, develops their perspectives and finally turns to the feelings of the author.

The Coolest Shark in the World

Every sea creature sees my shark differently.

The penguins think she is The brother.
The great white shark shes a princess but in a cuddly sort of way.
The crab next door Thinks shes smart
But you haven't seen The cilly crabs next door!
Even the Octopus thinks shes funny.
It's crazy though.
   he cracks up laughing every time he sees her
mr stingray thinks shes precious and adorable
but when he takes her on a Journey she tries to bite him.

But I love my shark.
I think shes The coolest.
in a snappy and swishy kind of way.

Clause by clause this text's development is more complicated because there are in effect two planes of 'narration'. One develops the different points of view, with sea creatures and the writer as Theme and their mental processing as News

the penguins	think
the great white shark	(thinks)
the crab next door	thinks
the Octopus	thinks
he (the Octopus)	cracks up laughing
mr stingray	thinks
I	love
I	think

The other develops what they think, with the pet shark as Theme and her evaluation as News.

she	is The brother.
she	s a princess
but	in a cuddly sort of way.
she	s smart
she	s funny.
she	s precious and adorable

> she   s The coolest.
>   in a snappy and swishy kind of way.

So as far as information flow is concerned we have two planes of experience (sea world and pet world), one projecting the other, as sea creatures evaluate the pet. As Rothery has noted (e.g. 1994; cf. Martin 1996), bringing two planes of experience together in narrative is a highly valued trope in secondary school subject English classrooms, for which the author of [2.5] appears to be well prepared.

2.3.3   Evaluating feelings, people and things

Turning to **appraisal**, which focuses our attention on feelings, the everyday world of [2.5] judges the shark's character (*coolest, cuddly, smart, cilly, funny, crazy, coolest*) and appreciates it as a pet (*precious, adorable, snappy, swishy*); and the Octopus has an outburst of feeling every time he sees her (*laughing*). In contrast Text [2.6] has just two appreciations of the danger sharks pose to humans (*harmless, harmful*). Significantly, the source of most of the evaluations in Text [2.5] is the sea creatures, an important dimension of their personification (alongside their ability to think and laugh like people do).

Finally, with respect to **conjunction**, the strongest contrast between the two texts is the recurrent use of concessive relations in Text [2.5], in bold below.

> The great white shark shes a princess
> **but** in a cuddly sort of way.
>
> The crab next door Thinks shes smart
> **But** you haven't seen The cilly crabs next door!
>
> **Even** the Octopus thinks shes funny.
> It's crazy **though**.
> he cracks up laughing
> every time he sees her
>
> mr stingray thinks shes precious and adorable
> **but** when he takes her on a Journey
> she tries to bite him.
> **But** I love my shark.
>
> I think shes The coolest.
> **(but)** in a snappy and swishy kind of way.

These concessive conjunctions (*but, even, though*) are used by the writer to qualify the evaluations of the pet shark made by different sea creatures. So not only do we have multiple points of view in Text [2.5], but each perspective is negotiated by the writer to finesse the evaluation. This kind of self-conscious fine-tuning is highly valued in the academic discourse of humanities and social sciences as one dimension of what it means to be 'critical', and is another reason for the high value placed on texts like [2.5] – especially in comparison with texts like [2.6] which authoritatively compile facts about the world.

2.3.4   Genres – configurations of meanings

There is of course more to say about these two texts. There are so many meanings involved that we cannot do justice to all of them here. Our aim is simply to illustrate how texts are made of meanings. They do not simply express meanings that exist somewhere else – texts make meanings. And when we refer to a text as a description or a report, these classifications are based on the overall configuration of meanings in that text. So the text types we establish are based on the recurrent configurations of meaning we find in our research.

Early in this phase of our work we began to refer to these recurrent configurations of meaning as **genres**. The diagram that came to be most widely used for modelling genres as recurrent configurations of meaning is presented in Figure 2.1. The co-tangential circles, one inside another, are designed to show that genres are patterns of language patterns. The double headed arrow stands for realisation – the idea that genres consist of meanings and thus that meanings construe the genre.

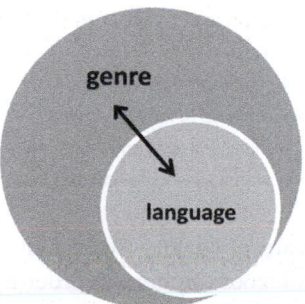

Figure 2.1: Genre realised through language – language construing genre

Having got this far, the challenge now lay in getting this information to teachers and students, in a context where, as noted above, we had no knowledge about language to work with. Clearly, starting with language was going to be problematic, since our close readings of Texts [2.5] and above assume a lot of understanding of how texts are organised. So we decided to begin not with language but with genre, and begin to re-introduce KAL from the top down. This perspective resonated with the whole text focus of process writing and whole language programs. We came to formulate our characterisation of genres for teachers as 'staged, goal-oriented, social processes' – **social** because we are inevitably trying to communicate with readers (even if they do not immediately read or respond to our work), **goal-oriented** because we always have a purpose for writing and feel frustrated if we do not accomplish it, and **staged** because it usually takes us more than one step to achieve our goals.

The report [2.6], for example, has two broad social purposes: to classify sharks and describe them; so following its Title, it includes two main stages: Classification and Description. The Description goes through three phases, which any science teacher would recognise for a report about animals: describing (i) their appearance, (ii) their habitat and (iii) their behaviour, which includes movement, feeding (or diet) and breeding (or reproduction), shown below.

Title	Shark Report
Classification	A shark is a type of species that lives in the sea.
	A shark is one of the largest sea creatures.
	There are 350 type of shark
Description	
appearance	A shark is shaped like a torpedo.
	Sandpaper is like a shark body.
	Elastic is in shark body inset of bones
	A shark can grow up to 8 meters.
habitat	Sharks live in Oceans.
behaviour	
movement	Sharks have to swim but if they don't swim they will sink or suffocate.
diet	Harmless sharks eat Plants
	but harmful sharks eat live meat.
reproduction	Sharks have up to forty two pups.
	Some sharks lay eggs and some have them live.
	Some sharks have to defend the pups.

The stages of a genre are obligatory steps that our research showed each mature instance of the genre goes through. In order to make these clear for both teachers and students, we distinguished genre stages by initial capitals, such as Classification and Description. Within each stage, any one text may go through phases that are more variable. For example, a report about animals may or may not include habitat, movement, diet or reproduction, and may include other phases depending on the writer's particular purpose. Each stage and phase of a genre has a specialised function that contributes to the social purpose of the genre as a whole. And each has characteristic language features designed to contribute to the meaning of the whole.

The staging of reports can be contrasted with staging for narrative genres, which have a very different social function. For example, the very simple narrative, Text [2.12], can be divided into the stages Orientation, Complication, Evaluation, Resolution.

Orientation	A fish was swimn inthe worta.
Complication	He heerd a SPlash and a car falld in theworta car.
Evaluation	"Help; help" said the man.
Resolution	The fish help the man swim to the beech.

We initially borrowed these terms from Labov and Waletzky's 1967 work on spoken narratives. Labov and Waletzky characterised stories without a Resolution stage as an incomplete narrative, since the problem posed was not resolved. However our research showed that stories without a Resolution were just as common, but had different social functions, such as sharing an emotional reaction to what went wrong. We termed this kind of story genre an anecdote. The critical point here is that the staging is a crucial dimension of the function of the genre, and for writing to be effective the language mobilised has to enact, stage by stage, the function of the genre.

2.3.5 Key genres for primary school

Working along these lines we developed descriptions of what we considered to be some of the key genres students should master by the end of primary school, including recount, anecdote, exemplum, observation/comment, narrative, description, report, procedure, protocol, explanation, exposition and discussion. Each of these is a technical term referring to a distinctive configuration of meaning constituting the genre. In addition, we worked out the basic staging for each genre, including technical terms for stages, as set out below in Table 2.1.

So now we had two levels of metalanguage we could provide to teachers: (i) the name of each genre, linked to its social purpose, and (ii) the stages we could expect each genre to go through. Materials supporting this metalanguage were prepared for teachers, including worksheets for students focusing on the metalanguage (e.g. Disadvantaged Schools Program 1988, Macken-Horarik et al. 1989, Christie et al. 1992, Callow 1996). Most of these are by now difficult to access, but they have since spawned a host of imitators, published by state education departments and commercial publishers, typically under the name 'text types'.[4]

---

[4] Derewianka 1991 however is still in print and is representative of the best of these materials.

Table 2.1: Genres described in the first phase of research

	genre	purpose	stages
Stories	recount	*recounting events*	Orientation
			Record of events
	narrative	*resolving a complication*	Orientation
			Complication
			Evaluation
			Resolution
	anecdote	*sharing an emotional reaction*	Orientation
			Remarkable event
			Reaction
	exemplum	*judging character or behaviour*	Orientation
			Incident
			Interpretation
Factual texts	description	*describing specific things*	Orientation
			Description
	report	*classifying and describing general things*	Classification
			Description
	explanation	*explaining sequences of events*	Phenomenon
			Explanation
	procedure	*how to do an activity*	Purpose
			Equipment
			Steps
	protocol	*what to do and not to do*	Purpose
			Rules
Arguments	exposition	*arguing for a point of view*	Thesis
			Arguments
			Reiteration
	discussion	*discussing two or more points of view*	Issue
			Sides
			Resolution

Both teachers and students in infants and primary school took readily to this kind of KAL, especially where supported by in-service programs like those run by the Disadvantaged Schools Program in eastern Sydney (see §2.4 below); by the end of the millennium, K–6/7 curricula across Australia had been strongly influenced by this genre perspective.[5] Critically, assessment practices shifted formally and informally from an implicit evaluation of all student writing as a more or less successful narrative (as for Ben's explanation above) to an explicit

---

[5] One useful point of access for reflecting on the results of these interventions is the sample of student texts, sorted by genre and assessment, available at the NSW Board of Studies website, http://arc.boardofstudies.nsw.edu.au/

analysis of specific genres in terms of how effectively they accomplished their goals.

By the early 1990s a student could leave primary school, arrive in secondary school, and when given a writing task put their hand up and ask 'What genre Miss?' Their chance of getting an informed answer was, unfortunately, very small, since our intervention had not had any significant impact on secondary school teaching. The best such students could hope for was to return to their primary school and work with former teachers there on what the writing task actually involved. And this kind of support of course was not sustainable throughout their secondary school years.

Our success in restoring KAL to the writing curriculum, beginning from the top down, encouraged us to begin introducing aspects of functional grammar in support of such programs. We were able to establish that both infants and primary school students took as readily to the grammar terms as to the genre ones (Rothery 1989, Williams 1999a, 2004, 2005a). But their teachers, their parents, the media and politicians were another story entirely. During this period governments were severely curtailing in-service resources for practising teachers, and by the mid-1990s the regional Disadvantaged Schools Program resource centres, which were so crucial to our work, had been closed down. So we were unable to provide teachers with the support they needed to learn to do close readings of language patterns realising genres. Meanwhile, circa 1995/1996, the media and politicians in New South Wales engendered a debate about whether functional grammar (which they claimed parents could not understand) should be 'imposed' on teachers and students in place of traditional grammar (good old nouns and verbs). This eruption of 'back to basics' anti-intellectualism is an instructive one for anyone interested in renovating literacy curricula; Martin 2000a, b explores some of what we learned.

In retrospect, the significant upshot of all this fervour was that genre consciousness, including terms for genres and staging, slipped comfortably into the NSW K–6 curriculum, beneath the radar as it were. But this is getting ahead of ourselves. For knowledge about genre to be effective in classrooms it was necessary to change not just how teachers looked at student texts, but how they taught students as well. So it is to issues of pedagogy as far as teaching writing is concerned that we now turn.

2.4   Teaching genre: *Language and Social Power* project

2.4.1   Getting off the literacy pendulum

As we have discussed, by the early 1980s the literacy pedagogy pendulum had swung radically from traditional, so called 'teacher-centred' positions to constructivist 'student-centred' ones as far as classroom interaction was concerned. Accordingly, most teachers would have had some experience with both styles of interaction, and so could approach genre-focused KAL from either point of view. From a traditional perspective, the desirable approach would be to present a model of a given genre, deliver a monologic lecture about it and then tell students to write. From a constructivist perspective, the approach would be to try and draw knowledge about genre out of the students with leading questions, sometimes focused on a model, sometimes not, before offering them the possibility of writing one. The traditional approach assumes that students are paying attention, can follow the monologue, and can see from one exemplar and its discussion how to successfully undertake the task. The constructivist approach assumes that students can discover all they need to know about genre themselves as two or three of their peers play the quiz show 'guess what's in my head' game with their teachers.

Our feeling was that either approach could perhaps work with the minority of students who learn to write however their teachers do or do not support them, but that both approaches were unlikely to succeed with the majority of students (and that the more implicit constructivist approach gave students from non-mainstream migrant, working-class or Indigenous backgrounds even less hope of success than the more explicit traditional one). Constructivist approaches were after all a radical reaction to traditional literacy pedagogy, and so circumscribed by its agendas; this in part explains the failure of process writing to prepare students for writing across the curriculum in primary school, disciplinary writing in secondary school and the civic literacy needed to prosper outside education in a postmodern world. By 1984 we were looking for ways to get off the pendulum, and design a pedagogy that would work for all students, regardless of their social background.

2.4.2   Guidance through interaction in the context of shared experience

As almost everyone learns to speak as they grow up at home we decided to look there to understand what it is that ensures success. Fortunately for us we had Halliday's and Painter's ground-breaking work on spoken language development to draw on (Halliday 1975, 2003, Painter 1984, 1991). And even more fortunately we were able to commission Painter to write her classic paper on the role of interaction in learning to talk and learning to write (Painter 1986). From Halliday and Painter we adopted the fundamental principle that successful language learning depends on **'guidance through interaction in the context of shared experience'**. Let us look at just a few examples of parent–child interaction from Painter 1986 to see what this means.

The first two examples show a two-year-old learning how to give reasons. In the first his dad explains why his parents cannot keep up; three months later Hal reasons in a similar context on his own:

Learning to reason

[24 months]

Hal   *[pulling Mum and Dad by the hands]*
       Want to run again.
Dad   *No, we can't run any more.*
       Daddy's too tired
       and Mummy's too tired.

[27 months]

Mum   *Why don't you get the little cars out?*
Hal   *Mummy play cars.*
       I can't play cars;
       I'm too tired.

In the next examples, Hal's Mum suggests a reason why Hal might not want some food; three months later, again in a very similar context, Hal justifies his wishes on his own.

[24 months]

Mum   *Don't you want any tea?*
       Do you want some biscuits and cheese?
Hal   *No.*
Mum   *No?*
       Not hungry.
       You're not hungry tonight, eh?

[27 months]

Mum   *Want a bit of toast?*
Hal   *No thanks.*
       I'm not hungry.

In both cases we see the parents interacting with Hal and through this interaction providing a model for him of what it is to justify behaviour; then later on, in comparable contexts, Hal takes over this kind of reasoning as his own.

What about longer texts? Where do they come from? The recount genre, which so many students have to draw on in process writing classrooms, provides a key exemplar. Here is an early example from Halliday; his son Nigel is not yet two years old (1975: 112) and is reflecting on a trip to the zoo with his mother and father where a goat had tried to eat a plastic lid he had picked up when he was petting him. A few hours later Halliday recorded the following exchange.

Learning to recount stories

Nigel	*try eat lid*
Father	*What tried to eat the lid?*
Nigel	*try eat lid*
Father	*What tried to eat the lid?*
Nigel	*goat ... man said no ... goat try eat lid ... man said no*

Note how the father's guiding interaction prepares Nigel for his more extended recount. Later that evening his mother provides further support.

Nigel	*goat try eat lid ... man said no*
Mother	*Why did the man say no?*
Nigel	*goat shouldn't eat lid ... (shaking head) goodfor it*
Mother	*The goat shouldn't eat the lid; it's not good for it.*
Nigel	*goat try eat lid ... man said no ... goat shouldn't eat lid ... (shaking head) goodfor it*

Halliday comments that this 'story is then repeated as a whole, verbatim, at frequent intervals over the next few months', with Nigel recounting on his own, without the guiding interaction of the caregivers who shared this experience with him.

In the following example from Painter (1986: 75) we see Hal at 26 months cuddling a toy giraffe and recalling a real giraffe he had seen at the zoo; his mother then prompts some further details about the experience.

[26 months]	
Hal	*[cuddling a toy giraffe]*
	I saw a big giraffe.
Mum	*Yes, what was the giraffe doing?*
Hal	*Eating /ə/ leaves.*
Mum	*What about the little giraffe?*
	Remember what he did?
Hal	*Go peepbo.*
Mum	*Yes, he was looking out of the door, wasn't he?*

Two days later when reading a picture book and coming across a picture of a giraffe Hal recounts the zoo episode on his own.

Hal	That's giraffe. I saw a big giraffe. Big giraffe eating /ə/ leaves; little giraffe go peepbo round /ə/ door.

These examples are very similar to another interaction between Halliday's son Nigel and his parents (Halliday 1975, reported in Painter 1986: 75). At 22 months Nigel tells his father about a meal he has shared with his mother, who prompts further details.

[22 months, 14 days]

Nigel	*Auntie Joan cook quack quack for you.*
Father	*Auntie Joan cooked quack quack for you, did she?*
Nigel	*Auntie Joan cook greenpea.*
Father	*And green peas.*
Nigel	*Began shout.*
Mother	*Who began to shout.*
Nigel	*Nila began to shout.*
Mother	*Did you? What did you shout?*
Nigel	*Greenpea.*

Later that same day the child reconstructs the experience on his own, shedding the interactive support his parents provided first time round (and again takes the step of repeating the story over and over in ensuing months).

Child	*Auntie Jean cook quack quack for you ... and green pea ... you began to shout GREENPEA!*

Nigel's recount about GREENPEA is in fact the very example used in Applebee and Langer's 1983 popularisation of Bruner's notion of **scaffolding** (a term introduced in Wood et al. 1976). The scaffolding metaphor captures the transitional role of caregivers' and teachers' guidance, supporting children to build their competence towards independent control. The scaffolding notion was of course derived from Vygotsky's 'zone of proximal development' (ZPD).

> It is the distance between the actual development level as determined by independent problem solving and the level of potential development as determined through problem solving under adult guidance or in collaboration with more capable peers (Vygotsky 1978: 86).

Our model of learning was informed by Halliday's and Painter's language development studies, noting correlations with Vygotskyan learning theory only later on in our work (Martin 1999a). The connections between Halliday's and Painter's functional linguistic perspective and Vygotsky's learning theory and their implications for teaching and learning are discussed by Gibbons 2002, 2006, 2009, Hammond 2001, Hasan 2005 and Wells 1999, among others. However, something that is rarely noted about Vygotsky's ZPD is that it is an assessment measure, 'determined by independent problem solving' versus 'problem solving under guidance' (1978: 86). It denotes the difference between learners' scores on these two assessment tasks, using the spatial metaphor of a 'zone'. Scaffolding likewise uses a construction metaphor, with learning as the building and the teaching as the 'scaffold'. Both metaphors reify the processes of learning as abstractions; neither accurately evoke the learning processes involved, and there are many different interpretations of what ZPD and scaffolding mean (see §6.1.5 below for examples). For us the scaffolding meta-phor does not reinforce strongly enough the fact that guidance takes place through unfolding **dialogue**, in which teachers prepare learners for tasks and follow up with elaborations.

2.4.3   Designing a curriculum genre for teaching writing

Joan Rothery was the first member of our group to try and translate the notion of 'guidance through interaction in the context of shared experience' into literacy teaching practice. She reasoned that if we could make learning to read and write more like learning to speak, then more students would be successfully appren-ticed. Working with a Year 2 and also a Year 5 class Rothery developed the following curriculum genre for teaching writing (Table 2.2). Rothery referred to her model as a 'language based approach'.

Table 2.2: Rothery's initial curriculum genre for teaching writing

1	Introducing a Genre	Modelling a genre <u>implicitly</u> through reading to and by class; e.g. read *Little Red Riding Hood*
2	Focusing on a Genre	Modelling a genre <u>explicitly</u> by naming its stages; e.g. identifying the stages of Orientation, Complication and Resolution in the tale of *Little Red Riding Hood*
3	Jointly Negotiating a Genre	Teacher and class compose the genre under focus; the teacher <u>guides</u> the composition of the text through questions and comments that provide the <u>scaffolding</u> for the stages of the genre; e.g. in a narrative the following questions may point towards a Resolution stage - how will X escape from the witch? Does she do it alone or does someone help her?
4	Researching	- Factual writing usually involves research - Selecting material for reading - Note making and summarising - Assembling information before writing
5	Drafting	A first attempt at writing the genre under focus
6	Conferencing	Teacher/pupil <u>consultation</u> - direct reference to the <u>meanings</u> of the writer's text; e.g. questions that help the writer to resolve the Complication stage of a narrative. Young writers find Complication easy but resolving their characters' problems is often hard. Conferencing is getting 'into the text', not standing aside from it.
7	Publishing	Writing a final draft that may be 'published' for the class library, thus providing another input of genre models and a great deal of enjoyable reading

The names of the last three of these stages were borrowed from process writing curriculum genres, thereby providing some continuity for process writing teachers, but with significant renovations. Conferencing, for example, was reconceived as a consultative process, with teachers in an authoritative mentoring role. And Rothery's curriculum genre as a whole is front-loaded – it introduces what students need to know up front, and constructs a text interactively with them before asking them to write on their own. So drafting and publishing have a different function in the curriculum genre as a whole, drawing as they do on knowledge about language and genre. We are taking the term 'curriculum genre' here from Christie (e.g. 2002) and using it to focus on classroom practice – interpreted as a family of spoken genres which we explored along the same lines as our exploration of written genres illustrated above in Table 2.1.

This model was presented by Jim in a plenary address to the 1986 meeting of the Australian Reading Association in Perth. On the basis of the Perth presentation, Jim and Joan were approached later that year by Mike Callaghan of the NSW Disadvantaged Schools Program, to work with him and his colleagues on teaching writing to the predominantly working-class, migrant and Indigenous students in the inner-city schools he was responsible for. As one of his principals had cautioned him, 'Don't bring us any more of that process writing ****; it doesn't work with these kids!' This led to the *Language and Social Power* project, which ran successfully with a focus on infants and primary schools in collaboration with Sydney University's Linguistics Department over the next few years. Alongside the production of materials focusing on different genres mentioned above, this project worked hard developing the pedagogy – with Joan, Mike, Mary Macken-Horarik[6] and others playing key roles.

One of their first steps was to recontextualise Rothery's sequence of stages as a teaching/learning cycle (TLC) which could be entered at different points and re-cycle specific stages depending on the needs of students (Disadvantaged Schools Program 1989, Macken-Horarik et al. 1989). Over time the teaching/learning cycle was reconceptualised in various forms, which developed and foregrounded different aspects on the pedagogy. In the initial phase the major stages were referred to as Modelling, Joint Negotiation of Text and Independent Construction of Text (Figure 2.2).

---

[6] Mary Macken-Horarik in fact undertook her pedagogy and curriculum research as part of a joint LERN (Literacy and Education Research Network) and NSW Department of Education initiative, before joining the DSP. LERN was formed by Bill Cope, Mary Kalantzis, Gunther Kress and Jim Martin in 1987 with a focus on post-progressive developments in language and social science education (Cope and Kalantzis 1993). One offshoot is the regular international LERN Conferences organised by Cope and Kalantzis.

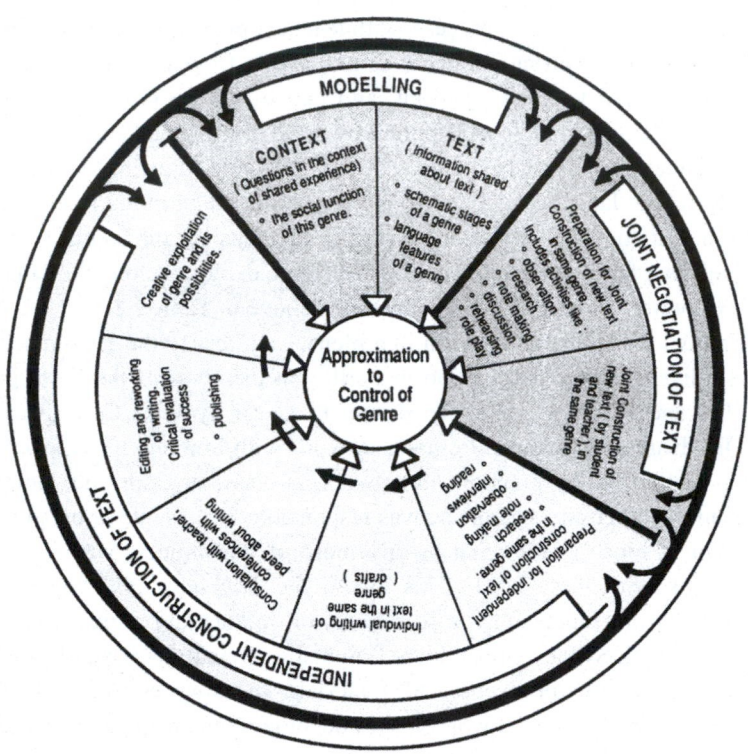

Figure 2.2: Early *Language and Social Power* project teaching/learning cycle

As Figure 2.2 indicates, Modelling involved setting the genre in its cultural context and discussing its stages and language features. Joint Negotiation of Text involved first building up the field for a new text on a different but related topic in the same genre and then jointly constructing a text, with the students making suggestions and the teacher adapting them for writing on the board, butcher paper or OHP in front of the class. Independent Construction of Text involved a sequence of sub-stages: building up another field, writing the text, submitting it for consultation with the teacher, editing and 'publishing', and as a final step making time for creative exploitation of the genre once it had been mastered (placed last since we concurred with Bakhtin's notion that creativity depends on mastery of the genre; Bakhtin 1986).[7]

Over time, teachers' experience was that at least one cycle benefited all students, although some students needed more cycles of modelling and joint construction than others before writing on their own, and writers who would

---

[7] As we discovered by around 1990, Bakhtin's conception of what he called 'speech genres' (first published in English in 1986 but developed decades earlier) was remarkably close to our own, anticipating it by more than a generation.

have succeeded in either traditional or progressive paradigms could often make do with just a Modelling stage. Successive cycles could be organised for smaller groups of students in a class as more students were able to write independently in the genre. Our educational linguists also found that successful implementation of the cycle generally depended on consultants working alongside teachers in their classrooms through demonstrations and face-to-face feedback as a follow-up to in-service presentations. 'Guidance through interaction in the context of shared experience' in other words was just as important for teachers learning this mixed-mode curriculum genre (involving speaking and scribing) as for their students learning a written one (involving the transformation of speaking into writing).

Based on feedback from teachers this early TLC was revised as Figure 2.3 below (Murray and Zammit 1992).

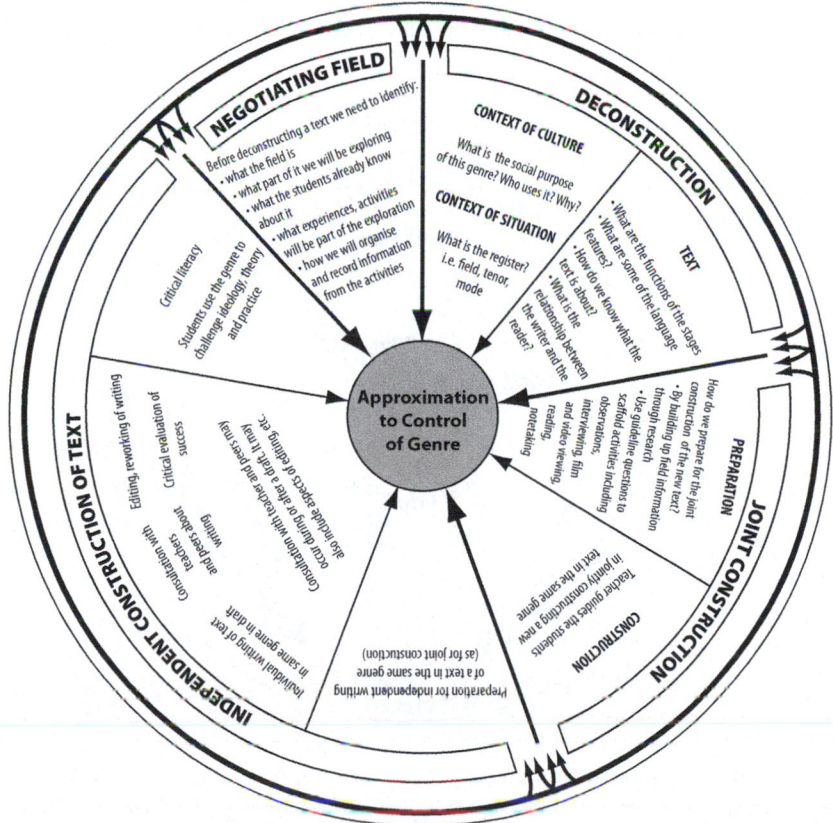

Figure 2.3: Later *Language and Social Power* project teaching/learning cycle

The main stages now consist of Deconstruction (formerly Modelling), Joint Construction and Independent Construction of Text; in addition a fourth stage, Negotiating Field, has been added, to emphasise the importance of shared experience of the subject matter when teaching genre. Foregrounding field in this way made it easier for teachers to see how to build genre writing into thematic units of work across the curriculum ('writing to learn' as the notion of embedded literacy teaching was phrased at the time). Negotiating field can draw on a number of different research activities, after which the information gathered can be usefully organised by teacher and students in point form as a resource for writing in one or another stage.

The introduction of the term 'Deconstruction', and 'critical literacy' under Independent Construction, reflects the influence of educators drawing on cultural studies and critical theory (cf. New London Group 1996). In other words, the main anxiety about genre-based literacy programs had shifted from the effect of genre writing on creativity to its effect on students' ability to critique the texts they were reading and the social realities they naturalised.

The TLC was refined in the next stage of the research, the *Write it Right* project outlined in Chapter 3 below, as the elegantly presented three-stage model in Figure 2.4.

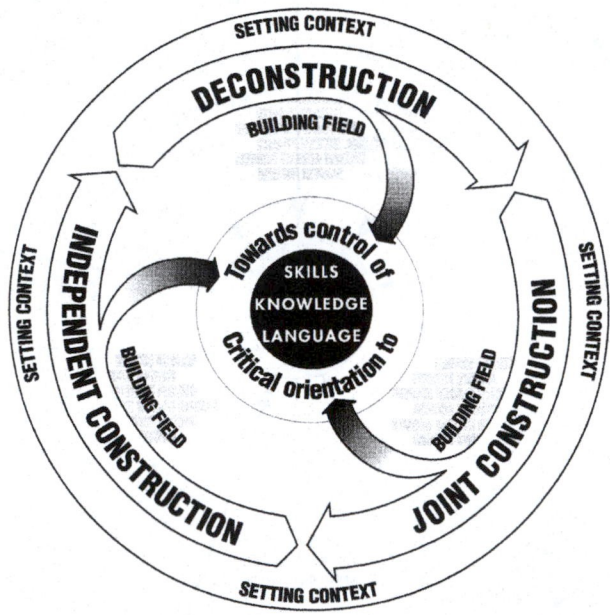

Figure 2.4: *Write it Right* teaching/learning cycle (Rothery 1994)

As we can see from the diagram, setting context and building field are now more appropriately positioned as key concerns of each stage of the cycle. At the centre of the model, the goal has been refined as *Towards control of* and *critical orientation to genre* and *text*, reflecting the relation between genre and language modelled in Figure 2.1 above – namely, the idea that genres consist of meanings and thus that meanings construe the genre.

The introduction of a 'critical orientation' alongside 'control' reflected our response to the concerns of the critical theorists that teaching the genres of power (as they were referred to in DSP materials and Cope and Kalantzis 1993) in some sense denigrated other genres (for example, the spoken genres of working-class, migrant and Indigenous communities) and ran the risk of subsuming non-mainstream students into mainstream (e.g. patriarchal, bourgeois, homophobic) cultural norms.[8] Our response was twofold. On the one hand we decided as an issue of social justice that it was important to make the genres required for success in education and life beyond school as widely available as possible. On the other we concluded that a critical perspective on genre depended on both mastery of the genres being critiqued and mastery of the genres being used to critique.

2.5 Negotiating meaning: teacher–student interactions

In this section we will look at teachers and students in different kinds of negotiation, depending on the work they were doing in one or another phase of the TLC as a whole. In reviewing these episodes we need to keep in mind that both globally and locally genre writing pedagogy is designed to hand over control to students by first establishing common ground and then making meaning with them – before asking them to write on their own.

The examples of interaction we will show are taken from a Year 6 class of mainly migrant students (Vietnamese and Middle Eastern background). They are working on exposition, have been through one cycle of Deconstruction, Joint Construction and Independent Construction and have already written independently on the issue of whether voting should be compulsory (which it is in Australia). The teacher is embarking on a second cycle to improve their control of the genre, so they already have a lot of shared KAL to draw on.[9]

In particular, the teacher is working on the challenge of previewing arguments in the Thesis stage (the introduction to an exposition) without actually giving the arguments, and then making sure everything mentioned in the preview is picked up in the Argument stage (the body of an exposition) – without being repetitive

---

[8] Anxieties of critical theorists at the time are discussed in Fairclough 1992, Freedman and Medway 1994a, b, Green and Lee 1994, Lee 1996, Luke 1996. Some of their concerns are addressed in Cranny-Francis and Martin 1993, 1994, 1995, Macken-Horarik 1997, 1998, Martin 1991, 1999a, b, Martin and McCormack 2000, Veel 1995. Martin 2000c and Martin and Rose 2003/2007 discuss the connections between our functional linguistic approach to text analysis and critical discourse analysis (CDA).

[9] Our thanks to Julie McCowage and her students at Lakemba Public School for their enthusiastic participation in the development of the TLC pedagogy and the teaching/learning cycle from which these texts arise.

(see Figure 2.5). So in effect we are in a second Deconstruction phase, looking critically at models of the genre produced by the class at the end of the first cycle. Recycling in this way allows all students to benefit from the feedback on individual expositions.

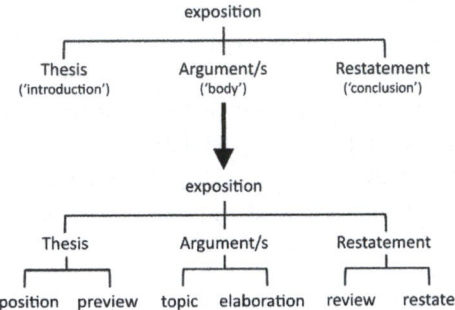

Figure 2.5: A pathway of genre development for exposition

We will look first at how the principle of handover is managed locally in the Deconstruction and Joint Construction stages, and then look at handover globally from the perspective of the TLC as a whole.

2.5.1   Deconstruction stage

From a local perspective, the teacher begins monologically, considering a successfully organised exposition:

Negotiating Deconstruction

Teacher   *OK. So she's very clearly given her three Arguments. Can everyone see that? And the very interesting thing is that she lets you know in the Introduction what those three Arguments are going to be. She hasn't told you what they're going to be; she's just mentioned them.*

She then continues, in the same turn, with a warning about including too much detail in the Thesis.

Teacher   *Can you see the difference? Because people started in that introduction going on to the Argument. You don't mention (sic) it there; you only mention it. You don't go into the ... giving the reasons for the Argument. Can you see the difference?*

In a subsequent turn she makes the point that previewed arguments must be expanded later:

Teacher   *The other thing is if you mention an Argument in your introduction, or your Thesis, you have to make sure it's in your ... Arguments.*

Further on, she invites the students to give this information back to her, using the teacher device of saying the words up to the desired response, with a rising tone.[10]

Teacher	*So whatever you mention in your introduction, you have to make sure you mention in your ...?*
Students	*... Arguments.*
Teacher	*... in your Arguments.*

As we can see, the notion of guidance through interaction in the context of shared experience shapes the micro-structure of the pedagogy. The teacher first makes her point about the introduction on her own; then she reconstructs her message in an exchange of turns (Martin and Rose 2003/2007) with the students supplying the missing information in a turn of their own. By the end of the stage, the students construct the relevant points on their own in full responses to relatively open trigger questions.

Teacher	*O.K. So there's a few things to think about. What are some of the things I mentioned you are going to try to think about when we do this one today? Filippa?*
Filippa	*Not to, um, put an Argument into the Thesis.*
Teacher	*Good. Right.*
Teacher	*Something else, to think about. Yes.*
Linh	*The Argument that you're doing has to be like the topic or Thesis that you choose.*
Teacher	*Right. So you make sure you mentioned all your Arguments in your Thesis. Good.*

Globally, we find the same pattern, on a longer wavelength as it were. The teacher works through several student texts, reinforcing her point that the first paragraph has to introduce the arguments but not actually present them. At this stage the teacher is doing most of the talking, building up deeper shared understandings about the genre development she is addressing.

> *So, you can see very clearly she has just stated the reasons. [pointing at model text] Now, some people, the other day when they did it, when they were giving the reasons, they gave the whole explanation and they gave all their exposition in the introduction. You don't give ... explain in detail. You just mention the reason ...*
>
> *Let's have a look at another one ...*
>
> *So once again, that person is very clearly ... told you what the paragraphs are going to be about. The other thing is if you mention an argument in your introduction, or your thesis, you have to make sure it's in your ... arguments. What some people did the other day was they all had these wonderful ideas in their introduction or thesis and I was all ready to read about them and I got to*

---

[10] Technically speaking the teacher introduces a break in the rhythm (a silent foot) before the Tonic syllable (Halliday and Greaves 2008): //^you don't/go into the/^.../giving the/reasons for the/Argument//

the end and they hadn't talked about all these things that they told me they were going to tell me...

She's actually explained her argument, hasn't she? Her argument is, um, people may not vote, um, and that's all she needed to say, that people may not vote, and then she's gone on to say that no one would get elected, then the candidate would get their friends to vote for them and therefore it wouldn't be fair and some areas would be represented and others wouldn't be if people don't vote. She's actually expanded on her ... arguments. Remember, you don't have to expand on them in the ... intro...duction. You just have to ... mention them.

Once the teacher has worked through enough examples to make her point she shifts to a much more dialogic form of interaction to consolidate the new knowledge about genre.

Teacher	*O.K. So there's a few things to think about. What are some of the things I mentioned you are going to try to think about when we do this one today? Filippa?*
Filippa	*Not to, um, put an argument into the thesis.*
Teacher	*Good. Right. Something else.*
Richard	*Don't repeat yourself.*
Teacher	*Don't repeat. Excellent. Something else. Who can think of something? Yes.*
Nicole	*Don't put any other ideas in the paragraph you are talking about.*
Teacher	*Good girl. Keep all the paragraph unified. Don't start introducing new ideas into the same one. Something else, to think about. Yes.*
Linh	*The argument that you're doing has to be like the topic or thesis that you choose.*
Teacher	*Right. So you make sure you mentioned all your arguments in your thesis. Good.*
Richard	*Give another word which refers to 'secondly' and 'thirdly'.*
Teacher	*Yes, where you can find some other words.*
Lynette	*In a paragraph.*
Teacher	*Right ... Yes, Filippa.*
Filippa	*Um, it, um, if you write smaller paragraphs you could expand them,*
Teacher	*Yes. You have to try to think of ways to expand them. And what we are going to do this morning is try and bring some of our ideas together to get used to doing a little ...*
Iain	*Make sure you space to start a paragraph.*
Teacher	*Good boy. Make sure you space, so who knows there is a paragraph there?*
Loukia	*The person that's reading it.*
Teacher	*Good girl. Anything else that you can think of? Who can think of another point that was mentioned this morning? Any other issues?*
Filippa	*Remember indentation.*
Teacher	*Right. That's fine. We have mentioned that. Anything different? O.K. Thank-you.*

Here we see the familiar Initiation Response Feedback (IRF[11]) triadic interaction noted by Sinclair and Coulthard 1975 for classroom interaction. Critically the

---

[11] Referred to by Mehan 1979 as Initiation Reply Evaluation (IRE); Gibbons (2002, 2006, 2009) develops this perspective in relation to scaffolding and her work on what she calls 'bridging discourses'.

teacher is not using this pattern of interaction to build up knowledge about genre; rather, she is using it to confirm the understandings she has already invested in the students. From a generic perspective this is a dialogic example of the protocol genre, in which the teacher and her students are consolidating guidelines about how to write an exposition. The protocol thus culminates the Deconstruction stage of the TLC, before starting the Joint Construction.

2.5.2   Joint Construction stage

Satisfied that the students are ready to move on, the teacher moves to the Joint Construction stage of the TLC, where the first task is to build up a new field. The argument this time is about reasons for going to school. The teacher initiates this activity as follows:

Negotiating Joint Construction

Teacher   *Now. What we're going to do is - I haven't talked about this very much - the reasons to go to school. I want you to get together in a group, say of about four people (you can organise yourselves) and jot down, just jot down the ideas. You don't have to write it in ... sentences or paragraphs or anything else. We're just jotting down ideas - reasons why you think it's important that children do go to school or reasons why you think that children shouldn't go to school. O.K. Make sure they're sensible; make sure they're logical ... O.K. ... and organised. Does anyone want to ask any questions first before they go away and have a go? Alright. Can you get this computer paper out, Richard, please?*
Get yourselves into a group. Have one person jotting the notes as everyone gives their ideas.

She then encourages the groups to start organising their ideas:

Teacher   *What I want you to do is now read through your list of ideas, go right through them, check that you've got all the main points that you wanted to get down, and then, some people will have already started doing this, linking any similar ideas together. So join them up, any ideas that you think would go together, work well together ...*
Alright, once you've done that, once you've linked it all up and you're quite happy with it, come and sit on the mat. You've got two minutes then to link the things together.

In the next phase the teacher works with the class to jointly organise the ideas, as exemplified below. The basic task here is to familiarise students with the ideas collected from different groups and sort them into packages of information which will later constitute the arguments of the exposition. The results of this phase (which could be formulated as word maps, tables, lists etc.) have to be kept visible for the whole class (via white board, black board, butcher paper, OHP or smart board) during Joint Construction. The interaction here is similar to that in the forthcoming Joint Construction phase, with students making suggestions based on their discussions in small groups and the teacher guiding them to organise their ideas.

Teacher	*Right. O.K. Now, let's try and get these into an order so we can organise how many paragraphs or how many new ideas we are going to introduce. Can someone sort of help me work that out?*
	O.K. Who can see the main thing that keeps coming … the whole way through? Lisa?
Lisa	*Learn about a wide range of subjects.*
Teacher	*Right. This seems to be one of the most important things, doesn't it? So we can put say a '1' next to it. Where else does it come up again?*
Lisa	*Put that with the '1' [pointing at the notes]*
Teacher	*Right. So we can put '1' against that - that could all be part of the same … paragraph, then, couldn't it? Somewhere else - the same sort of thing where we can link it together? Can you find any other links? Filippa?*
Filippa	*Use your education to get a good job.*
Teacher	*Right. Now, would that be a new idea? Or is it the same, do you think? It all follows on; everything leads to help you to the next thing but you've got to try and organise it so you've got one complete. Remember that glue - trying to get that paragraph to stick together? We want to have a complete paragraph and then another complete paragraph. Do you think that one would work as a follow-up? After you've got your knowledge and you've applied all these skills, what are you going to be able to do there?*
Safira	*Support your family.*
Teacher	*Support your family by what?*
Safira	*A job.*
Teacher	*A job. So that would really be another paragraph, wouldn't it? That would be that paragraph, together, talking about that. Yes, Linh?*
Linh	*Good ideas on how to behave and how to live.*
Teacher	*Um. Learn about a wide range of subjects and good ideas on how to behave. Yes, um, the only thing is, though, what's going to happen to this paragraph? It's going to be absolutely … Ss. … long, huge.*
Teacher	*Huge. So maybe we can almost have sub-paragraphs of the same thing. If we stick say all the education and learning in that paragraph, these are more socialising skills, aren't they? - getting friends, learning how to behave, following rules - they could all form one paragraph, couldn't they? So if we put good ideas, all friends, that could be all of 3.*

By this point the teacher and class have negotiated a Thesis stage for their exposition, which previews reasons for going to school:

> *I strongly believe children should go to school for the following reasons: education is free, it can fulfill your time, parents can work and they won't have to worry about you while you are at school. You can learn about a wide range of subjects, which will give you a tremendous amount of*

knowledge and ultimately help you in choosing your career. Finally, it is a place where you learn to socialise and develop in a warm and friendly atmosphere.

Now they are working on their first and second arguments. The text the teacher scribes on the board is in quotes below. Her guiding role involves taking the spoken suggestions of the students and reworking them as necessary into appropriate written expression. This kind of interaction gives all students the experience of writing collaboratively with an expert before writing on their own and makes learning to write much more like learning to talk than in alternative traditional and progressive pedagogy encounters. Decades of working with teachers has convinced us that successful Joint Construction is the most powerful classroom practice currently available as far as learning written genres is concerned.

Teacher	*Right. So 'Firstly, you learn about a wide range of subjects, for example, maths, science, computers, social studies, spelling, art, craft, reading, language, library, scripture, learning a new language … learning a new language.'*
Teacher	*O.K. Keep going. What else …? Yes. Siraj?*
Siraj	*We learn about other things - people's cultures and religions.*
Teacher	*Right. We've got here Firstly, you learn about a wide range of subjects. Maybe we can put after subjects … um, [?] of subjects, cultures and people - could we put that in there? So we could put that in. So Firstly, you learn about a wide range of subjects, cultures and people. For example, and then we could go on to our for example. So that gets some of the other things in. Filippa?*
Filippa	*We also learn about sport.*
Teacher	*Yes. Well, I'll put sport in there, because sport wasn't mentioned. I'll put it in there, sport. O.K. So we can put it in there. Anything else, there? Um, well, sport and health. O.K. What else have we got up there on the board with 1? So once we've done all these things, what have we gained?*
Students	*Knowledge. [teacher scribes; some children read along]*
Teacher	*O.K. So, um, ultimately, this allows us to achieve a greater understanding of the world and increase our knowledge. O.K. So, next paragraph. Let's have a look. Who can start? Look at the number 2s now. What's another good argument? Um, Safi? Um, um, Rana?*
Rana	*It gives you an education to help you get a job and to work.*
Teacher	*Alright. Now, secondly we really need to link that a little bit with the first paragraph. So what could we say? Secondly, by achieving this, what did we just achieve? Yes.*
Teacher and Students	*This knowledge.*
Teacher	*We will be then what?*
Teacher and Students	*Be in a better position to … to get a job. And to pursue our … careers.*
Filippa	*And support a family.*
Teacher	*Secondly, after achieving this knowledge, it will then put all individuals who*

> *attend the school, in a position [some students reading along] O.K. So can you*
> *read that for me, Nicole? Nicole*

Teacher   *Good. And what else? Can we develop that a little bit more? Is there anything*
there that you can add to that from the board? Daad?

Daad   *And you can support your family or yourself from your job.*

Teacher   *Right. Um, so this will enable the individual to then support themselves or their*
… [unison] families.

> *You noticed here I've used the word individual rather than say myself. I could*
> *say myself if I was writing it for myself, but considering I'm not, I'm writing for*
> *everyone, that's why I'm using the word individual. If you were writing it, if you*
> *were trying to convince your audience, you could take two ways. If you used the*
> *word individual, it means everyone that ever goes to school, which is a stronger*
> *statement than if it's just your own statement referring to … you. So, you have to*
> *think about that when you're writing, think about who's reading it and which is*
> *going to make the stronger statement. Words like that will either make it*
> *stronger and make more, make the piece of writing more powerful, which is*
> *what you wanted to do, isn't it? You want to make the reader really believe what*
> *you're saying. So, sometimes you have to choose your words; it's not always a*
> *good idea to write from your own personal thing. Me, me, me or I, or we or us or*
> *you. Sometimes you might make it broader and make it the whole, all children*
> *in general, all schools in general. So that's something you have to think about*
> *when you're writing as well.*

The interactions we are looking at here make explicit reference to knowledge about genre, which has been introduced in the previous cycle. The genre is exposition, and its stages are referred to more and less technically (as introduction or Thesis, and as Arguments, explanation or reasons). In addition, as the final turn by the teacher above indicates, there is discussion of specific word choices in relation to the purpose of the genre. In particular, the teacher is discussing the choice of first or third person in relation to specific or generic reference, but without using any terms from either traditional or functional grammar.

Towards the end of this TLC, in discussion with the teacher, an ESL teacher who was observing the lesson does explicitly refer to this issue using the term third person, but this is subsequently followed up non-technically with the class by their teacher:

ESL   *Why did I change from 'you' to 'individuals', from 'our' to 'their'. 'Their own self-*
teacher   *discipline', and from 'friendships we make' to 'they make'?*

Loukia   *Because we're not talking about one person; we're talking about a lot of people.*

Teacher   *Excellent. Good girl.*

> *Because, up here in our first two paragraphs, remember we talked about it*
> *generally, we didn't talk about it being 'you or ourselves'. So when we got down*
> *to the third paragraph we started talking about individuals in referring to us,*
> *saying 'you and we and they', so we had to go back to generally speaking instead*

	of 'you' …
ESL teacher	*Everyone*
Teacher	*Back to everyone, the word 'individuals' and the word 'their' and 'they' which makes it … what?*
Ss	*general.*
Teacher	*Everyone. Not specific. Alright. Thanks.*

This shift reflects the absence of any shared linguistically informed knowledge about grammar, an issue we will address more fully in Chapter 5, taking this episode as a point of departure.

2.5.3   Writing outcomes

The final version of the text jointly constructed in this lesson is presented below, and provides another model of the genre for the class – in addition to the 25-30 expositions written at the end of the first cycle, the exposition jointly constructed in that cycle, and the model used in the Deconstruction stage there.

[2.16] Exposition (Year 6)

I strongly believe children should go to school for the following reasons: education is free, it can fulfill your time, parents can work and they won't have to worry about you while you are at school. You can learn about a wide range of subjects, which will give you a tremendous amount of knowledge and ultimately help you in choosing your career. Finally, it is a place where you learn to socialise and develop in a warm and friendly atmosphere.

Firstly, you learn about a wider range of subjects, cultures and people. For example, in maths, science, computers, social studies, spelling, art, craft, reading, language, library, sport, health, scripture, learning a new language and many more subjects. So ultimately, this allows us to achieve a greater understanding of the world and increase our knowledge.

Secondly, after achieving this knowledge, it will then give all the individuals who attend school a better chance to pursue their own career or job prospects. This will enable the individual to support themselves or their families.

Finally, at school, people learn how to behave, socialise with other children, share with each other, play, have fun, learn to be responsible, have their own self-discipline, obey the school rules and form friendships which they may keep for life.

I hope I've convinced you that children should attend school for the reasons I have mentioned, and hopefully every individual will have the wonderful opportunity to attend school.

And there will soon be another 25-30 models produced at the end of cycle two. Here's one of them, considering the civic issue of whether to build an amphitheatre in a park just down the road from the school.

[2.17] Exposition (Year 6)

> *Exposition for: Should an amphitheatre be built in Wiley Park? [Filippa]*
>
> *I strongly believe that the amphitheatre in Wiley Park should be built for these following reasons, such as: it attracts more people to the area, shops and public transport will earn a larger profit, people will become more interested in Wiley park, and it is suitable for all ages.*
>
> *My first reason is that it will bring more people to our area because there are not many main attractions in our community and it can be something to remember our bi-centenary by in years to come.*
>
> *Another point to mention is shops will earn more money, for example, the new restaurant which will be built with in the amphitheatre. And not to forget Public transport which will create more money for the government and will be more easier for the disabled to travel by if they wish to do so.*
>
> *And last but not least it is not only for the grown ups but it is also suitable for children for example, there will be entertainment such as concerts, plays and shows. In my opinion from a child's point of view I think it's going to be fun and it's about time the council did something like this.*
>
> *I hope I have convinced you that we should have a amphitheatre at Wiley Park.*

Later in the year that these texts emerged, Joan and Jim were unofficially banned from working with teachers in NSW schools during a state election campaign. The then Labor government was promoting a traditional 'back to basics' (including grammar) approach to literacy teaching, at the same time as its Department of Education was releasing a Writing K–12 syllabus which was radically progressive in orientation (e.g. process writing, whole language, poetry and narrative across the curriculum, grammar at point of need, if at all) – all this at the same time as we were having considerable success with our genre-based post-progressive pedagogy in several schools. In response to this political intervention, the class of Year 6 students we have just been considering, who Jim was working with at Lakemba Public School, took it on themselves to protest by writing expositions to the Minister of Education on why genre writing was a good thing (allowing for one anti-genre exposition, on the grounds that genre writing had been scheduled during that student's favourite part of the curriculum). They were very proud to control a genre that mattered as far as public issues affecting them were concerned.[12] It made them feel grown-up and ready to make the move to secondary school.

Throughout our work many critics have raised concerns about genre teaching locking students into writing constrained by models and thus preventing them

---

[12] One can never be sure about the impact letter writing campaigns of this kind might have; but as part of this controversy LERN was able to lobby the Minister of Education to establish a joint LERN/NSW Department of Education project through which Mary Macken-Horarik produced a pioneering set of genre-based literacy materials (Macken-Horarik et al. 1989).

from expressing themselves in meaningful ways.[13] In this chapter we have done what we can to allay these fears by showing that all forms of language development, whether spoken or written, depend on modelling and repetition; this is how we learn language. But this does not mean we cannot adapt what we have learned in ways that are meaningful to us once we have taken control. By way of drawing this chapter to a close, Texts [2.18] to [2.20] below show further examples of students taking control, taken from Jon Callow's work (Callow 1999, Ng et al. 1999) with a class of Year 6 at Dulwich Hill Public School (another school in our Metropolitan East Disadvantaged Schools Program). The students' local swimming pool had recently been closed due to recurring structural damage caused by its location next to a goods train line. The students Jon was working with launched a campaign for a replacement pool, which included a brochure distributed to local residents and letters to the mayor [2.20].

[2.18] Students' brochure

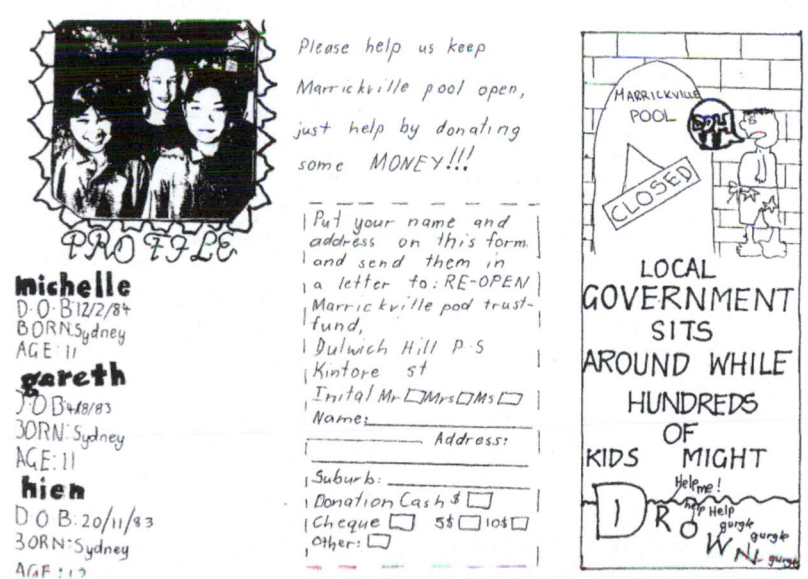

One of their letters to Mayor Cotter is also shown below as [2.21].

---

[13] Significantly, to our knowledge, these 'concerns' have never been pressed beyond the scare-mongering phase and backed up with research demonstrating the doomsday scenarios supposedly inflicted on students by genre-based literacy programs; Reid 1987 and Freedman and Medway 1994a, b include some engaging repartee.

[2.19] Student form letter to Mayor Cotter

Dulwich Hill Public School

Kintore Street, Dulwich Hill 2203   Phone: 559 2699 Facsimile 559 5676

Dear Mr _Cotter_____,

I Michelle Vuong, a student from Dulwich Hill Public School (D.H.P.S.) am very concerned about this issue of the Marrickvile Pool being closed down.

In our class, we surveyed the children and found out that:
-75% of kids can't swim
-80% of kids used Marrickville Pool
-Most children who can swim, learnt to swim at Marrickville Pool
-If swimming lessons were free or cheaper, 100% of children would learn to swim
-100% of children demand Marrickville Pool to be re-opened
-Marrickville Pool was the most used facility.
We were all very surprised about these results.

In our school, fewer and fewer children are attending and participating in our school swimming carnivals. Not because their parents won't let them, but because they don't know how to swim and parents fear for their safety.Just Imagine if somebody you knew, had drowned in the local beach or pool. Who is to blame?The pool maybe?or the people who didn't bother to help re-open the Local Pool? Thousands of kids can't swim (including me), and almost the same number are drowning all over the World. If kids don't know how to swim they will live their lives in fear of water. I am just one of very concerned children. Parents can't afford to travel miles just to get to a pool. What about poor families? What we need are cheap "Learn To Swim" programmes and publicity to encourage worried parents that swimming lessons are safe, nessesary and enjoyable for their child. We need Marrickville pool re-opened NOW!!!!!

Thank you for taking the time to read my letter and I hope you take this issue seriously as I and my fellow class mates do. Please consider these arguments and please help us in our battle to re-open our local pool so that more children are incouraged to learn to swim.

From a very concerned child,
Yours Sincerely,

Michelle.V

Michelle Vuong.

Luka also wrote an exposition [2.20] which he has recontextualised as a formal protest letter appropriate to its mode of delivery (including school letterhead, salutation, self-introduction, subject, message, valediction, name and signature); the exposition functions as subject and message in letter. From this we can see how students can adapt genres in meaningful ways to their own purposes, including as many arguments as necessary (four not three in this text) and adjusting to the mode of transmission (e.g. business letter, essay, letter to the editor, editorial, political speech).

[2.22] Luka's letter to Mayor Cotter

Dulwich Hill Public School

Kintore Street, Dulwich Hill 2203   Phone: 559 1699 Facsimile 559 3676

Dear Mr Cotter ,

Allow me to introduce myself, I am Luka Marsi & I am from the Aqua Party and a student from Dullwich Hill Public School, & my class have been discussing and investigating the matter & cost, closing down of Marrickville Pool. We are very anxious to see it renovated & reopened.

Here are some of the reasons why you should make the opening an important issue.

Firstly, after a long hot summer, Marrickville residents appear no closer to reclaiming their local Swimming Pool. Marrickville Pool was the most used facility in Marrickville

Secondly only 25% of students surveyed in our school can swim. More people could drown & would blame local polititions.

Thirdly we also need a local pool to us down when it's hot. (A pool is a solution for this hot hot HOT weather!) Families have a local, fun, and healthy place to go swimming together

Finally a local pool would be useful for poorer people, – because some BIG families aren't able to afford public transport to travel so far.

So according to the survey responses, we need a local pool for more swimming lessons (I agree on this) Thank you for readi -g my letter, & taking your time. I hope you will help us by renovating the pool, be very careful with all those expenses!

From a caring and concerned child
Yours sincerely ~~Luka Marsi~~ Luka Marsi

In response to the pool campaign the school's principal received complaints from local politicians about the inappropriateness of students involving themselves in local affairs along these lines – complaints that were strongly rebuffed by the school. The students did not get their pool,[14] but they did make an impact, because their control of genre afforded them the opportunity to get involved.

---

[14] Council funding constraints meant that it was not until two decades later that work was completed on the redevelopment of another pool site to help meet the needs of local residents.

2.6   Teaching AND learning

In the twelve months or so before this book was drafted, Jim attended an international e-learning conference in Hong Kong and the annual meeting of TESOL (Teachers of English to Speakers of other Languages) in Boston. In the presentations he attended the verb *teach* was never mentioned. Teaching was taboo. Such was the dominance of progressive ideologies of learning, now generally re-presenting themselves as social constructivist (as outlined in Chapter 1), that teaching had to be conceived as facilitating learning. The idea of an e-teaching conference would be, apparently, unthinkable. Teachers had indeed learnt to bite their tongues, at least when it came to talking about their work.

We often wonder what parents would make of this, if they were fully aware of what was going on. Parents like the mother below, advising her six-year-old child on how to accept a birthday invitation by phone (from Painter 1986: 80):

Child	*I don't know what to say.*
Mother	*Well, first you say 'This is David.' and then you say that you will be able to go to John's party.*
	[Child dials the number and starts talking into the dialling tone]
	No, wait for some one to pick up their phone and say hello to you.
Voice	*Hello.*
Child	*This is David. I'm going to come to John's party.*
	[after child hangs up]
Mother	*There, good. Next time, after you've said your name, give them a chance to speak before you go on.*

Parents like the father and mother below helping their four-year-old son formulate an abstraction (from Painter 1999: 121):

Father	*This car can't go as fast as ours.*
Child	*I thought - I thought all cars could - all cars could go the same - all cars could go the same (pause) fast ...*
Mother	*The same speed.*
Child	*Yes, same speed.*

Parents like those scaffolding the spoken recount texts reviewed above. How would their children have learned to speak if everyone around them was busy biting their tongues? The point here of course is that as Halliday and Lemke have argued, we are all born with a predisposition to both teach and learn:

[J]ust as children are predisposed to learn, so parents, and 'others', are predisposed to teach ... Lemke (1984) has shown that a theory of learning must take account of the human predisposition to teach – as well as of the teaching function, in a broader sense, that is a feature of the environment as a whole (Halliday 2003: 238).

Traditional education emphasises, probably too strongly, the teaching disposition; by the same token, constructivist education has emphasised, certainly too strongly, the learning one. Genre-based literacy pedagogy was designed to get teachers off this pedagogy pendulum and develop strategies which both teach and learn.

In addition, as Painter (e.g. 1996, 1999) has shown, we also share a disposition to talk about language as we teach and learn it. And we naturally take advantage of the words language uses to talk about itself (e.g. *word*, *call*, *mean* in the examples below).

Painter 1996: 54 (Stephen 2:6)

[Stephen enters childcare centre and addresses a staff member]

Stephen	*I've got a paper*
Carer	*Oh let's have a look. What's on the paper? (opening folded sheet) Do you know?*
Stephen	*Um, **that's words (pointing) that's words**.*

Painter 1996: 57 (Stephen 2:10)

(fingering missing toggle on his raincoat)

| Stephen | *I need a coat - a coat - **what's it called**?* |

Painter 1996: 59 (Stephen 3:7)

Mother	*You're naughty boys to throw them up there.*
Stephen	*Hal did it, by accident.*
Mother	*Well, Hal's naughty then.*
Stephen	***Not by accident; that's not naughty, that's mean (pause) you say sorry.***

Painter 1996: 59 (Stephen 3:10)

(Stephen approaches mother holding up a complicated duplo structure)

| Stephen | ***Balance means you hold it on your fingers and it doesn't go on the floor.*** |

Here are some further examples of language about language from Jim's children when they were between four and six years of age:

meaning/wording	*You're tricking/joking ...*
meaning/wording	*What does drown mean?*
wording	*I know what running comes from run!*
wording/scribing	*That says Daddy; that's my 'H' (looking at pavement) ...*
scribing/sounding	*Handbag has got 'b'*

scribing/sounding   *If Phoebe didn't have a silent 'o', it would be fubby*
sounding   *Not carrot* [15] *Daddy, [p] [p] [p] [p] parrot ...*

As Halliday comments (for further details see Painter 1999, Chapter 5 'The construal of semiosis as process'):

> The earliest linguistic terms an English-speaking child learns to use are not terms like *noun* and *verb*, or even *word* and *sentence*; in fact they are not nouns at all – they are verbs, typically *say* and *mean* [1:9], and shortly afterwards *tell* ... He also has a clear concept of naming ... at 20 months, *what that*, and at 24 months, *what's that called?* ... By the time he is two years old, the child has a considerable awareness of the nature and functions of language. When he starts to talk, he is not only using language; he is also beginning to talk about it. He is constructing a folk linguistics, in which (i) saying, and (ii) naming-meaning, denote different aspects of the same symbolic act (Halliday 1977: 32-33).

Genre-based literacy pedagogy takes advantage of the disposition to teach and learn and the disposition to talk about language while doing so by designing a mentoring role for teachers into the TLC and by providing relevant under-standings about language to share with students drawing on functional linguistic theory. We will return to the issue of why everyday pre-school ways of talking about language are not enough in institutionalised learning contexts in Chapter 5.

Having established the foundations of social literacy in infants and primary school, we next turned our attention to secondary school writing. This meant we had to focus our attention on embedding genre writing in subject areas and carefully consider the nature of disciplinary knowledge from a linguistic per-spective. These tasks fell to the *Write it Right* project, the next phase of our action research.

---

[15] At one stage Jim's son called parrots carrots, a usage Jim has persisted with teasingly over the years – prompting the resistance here.

3 *Write it Right/the Right to Write*[1]

This chapter focuses on the genres that students are expected to read and write in the secondary school, described in the Sydney School project's second phase, the *Write it Right* project. The knowledge realised in these genres is described in terms of three broad semantic tropes: classification, cause-and-effect and evaluation. These semantic themes are exemplified in a range of genres in science and history. The critical resource for building uncommonsense knowledge is then explored - grammatical metaphor. The chapter concludes by presenting the range of written genres from perspectives of categories (typology) and tendencies (topology).

3.1 Embedded literacy:[2] the *Write it Right* project

Around the same time the *Language and Social Power* project was taking off in Sydney, we began to explore the nature of literacy in specific subject domains. Inspired by the work by Halliday on scientific discourse (Halliday 2004), Jim directed a project focusing on the language of physical geography and history, working with Suzanne Eggins and Peter Wignell (Eggins et al. 1993, Martin et al. 1988, Wignell et al. 1989, Wignell 1994).[3] It also became clear from our work

---

[1] *Write it Right/the Right to Write* was our preferred compromise as a name for the secondary school/workplace project; our funding bodies, an employers' group and a government agency, would not however accept 'the Right to Write' phrasing. As educators and linguists, we were understandably just as uneasy about the connotations of 'Write it Right', but bound by the funding it attracted to enable the research.

[2] Embedded literacy is a widely used term for embedding literacy teaching in curriculum learning. Another widely used term with a similar connotation is 'integrating literacy'.

[3] The geography and history research was funded by the Australian Research Council.

in disadvantaged schools that we needed to extend our work on genre to more effectively address writing across the curriculum in primary school and writing in different subject areas in secondary school. In 1990 Sue Doran, then Executive Officer of the Metropolitan East Disadvantaged Schools Program (DSP), secured funding from the Australian Education and Training Foundation (1990–1994) for a large-scale action research project focusing on the relation between secondary school and workplace discourse (reviewed in Veel 2006). This work developed through the early 1990s concentrating on three workplaces (science industry, Rose et al. 1992; media, Iedema et al. 1994; and administration, Iedema 1995) and on several subject areas (including English, Rothery 1994; geography, Humphrey 1996; history, Coffin 1996; mathematics, Veel 1999). We will have to set aside the workplace research here; key references to this elision include Christie and Martin 1997, Martin and Veel 1998, Iedema 1997a, b, 2003, Rose 1997, 1998 and White 1997, 1998, 2000.

In 1996 the neo-conservative Howard Government ended the federally funded Disadvantaged Schools Program (two decades after its founding as part of Whitlam's socialist education reforms). Although the NSW Department of School Education (as it was known at the time) maintained a Disadvantaged Schools Centre at Erskineville for a number of years, it shifted its focus statewide, becoming known as the State Equity Centre. The innovative research, materials production and distribution practices initiated in the former Metropolitan East DSP were scaled back. A consequence was that research reports on mathematics and creative arts could not be completed, and that the extensive materials prepared for teachers and students across subject areas could not be effectively in-serviced or distributed. Ongoing debates about literacy teaching and controversy over the teaching of grammar led to misgivings among some politicians and NSW Education Department bureaucrats, with the consequence that the institutional impact of the *Write it Right* project on Australian secondary schools was severely diminished. The work has survived, however, in the collective memory and ongoing inventions of the educational linguists noted above and those inspired by them. For example, *Lexis Education* (http://www.lexised .com) has developed extensive language and literacy in-service programs drawing heavily on and extending *Write it Right* research. It also underpins the *Reading to Learn* methodology described in Chapter 4 below.

3.2   Genre and field

As we saw in Chapter 2, shared experience is a crucial dimension of genre-based pedagogy, since genres are always about something; if this knowledge is not shared it is very difficult for students to concentrate on the structure of the new language they are being scaffolded to learn. And as we noted there, this shared knowledge may involve everyday domestic experience or specialised understandings that we learn in school. We have to be careful here, since in multi-cultural societies, we cannot take one common experience of domestic and community life for granted. But keeping this caveat firmly in mind, it is generally the case that the knowledge about sea creatures assumed in Text [2.5] depends more on commonsense experience than the knowledge in Text [2.6], which has to be accessed elsewhere:

> [2.5] Every sea creature sees my shark differently. The penguins think she is The brother. The great white shark shes a princess but in a cuddly sort of way. The crab next door Thinks shes smart But you haven't seen The cilly crabs next door! …

> [2.6] A shark is a type of species that lives in the sea. A shark is one of the largest sea creatures. There are 350 type of shark A shark is shaped like a torpedo. Sandpaper is like a shark body. Elastic is in shark body inset of bones A shark can grow up to 8 meters …

Similarly, the knowledge about sequences of activity in Text [2.3] would be relatively easy to share (a little work on Christian religious festivals in some cultural contexts notwithstanding) compared with the school work needed to build up shared expertise for Text [2.7].

> [2.3] I went to my dads for 3 weeks an we went to ante Jhins house for crismuse. I got Leogo and a humonic…

> [2.7] … The left pump sends the blood to the arteries and then to the head to the toes. The body carries oxygen that slowly gives up while going through the body. Then the Blood goes back to the lungs to get more oxygen …

Critically, different genres (description, report, recount, explanation etc.) are tuned to different kinds of experience. And in secondary school this means that each subject area will have its own relatively distinctive suite of genres, as outlined in the work by Coffin, Humphrey, Rothery and Veel mentioned above. We will return to this issue and its implications for organising secondary school curricula in §3.8 below. But before pursing this we have to establish the different kinds of meaning that all knowledge, whether commonsense or schooled, is actually made of.

3.3 Understanding things: classification and composition

3.3.1 Learning to classify at home

As Halliday and Painter have shown, in their second year of life children are no longer restricted to naming individuals with what are essentially 'proper names' but are already developing the ability to use words to refer to classes of things – to generalise across phenomenal instances with common nouns (Halliday 1993/2003: 334-5). And this means working out how to classify things, a process described by Painter 1999 in some detail. Here is an example of Stephen's parents helping him sort out whales and fish in his third year of life.

[3.1] age 2:7

(looking at a picture book)

Mother	What's that?
Stephen	It's a bub- um (pause) a fish.
Father	Yes, good boy, it's a whale.
Stephen	I thought it's a whale; it's - it **is** a fish.
Mother	Yes, a big, big, big fish.

A little over a year later, they are continuing to explore the classification of animals together:

[3.2] age 3:8

(Stephen is examining animal jigsaw puzzle pieces)

Stephen	There isn't a fox; and there isn't - is a platypus an animal?
Mother	Yes.
Stephen	And is a seal an animal?
Mother	Yes (shepherding Stephen to bathroom).
Stephen	And is er- er- er- er-
Mother	You do your teeth while you're thinking. (Painter 1996: 57)

Where appropriate, classification may focus on what members of classes are made of or their parts, i.e. their composition:

[3.3] age 2:7

Mother	And do you remember what that is? (= picture in book)
Stephen	Mm.
Mother	What is it?
Stephen	It's a house.
Mother	It's a house, special house and what's it made of?
Stephen	Oh (pause) snow.
Mother	Yes, that's right, it's made of ice.
Stephen	Made of ice.
Mother	And it's called an igloo.
Stephen	Igloo. (Painter 1999: 85)

[3.4] age 3:8

Stephen	Snakes and worms, they don't have legs.
Mother	They don't have what, darling?
Stephen	Legs. Snakes and worms don't have legs.
Mother	Ah no.
Stephen	But lizards do.

And classifications are ongoingly adjusted, often with explicit reference to criteria. Of special interest here is the intervention of Stephen's four and a half year older brother Hal, who complicates the process by bringing the specialised knowledge he has learned at school into the discussion.

[3.5] age 3:8

(Mother asks Stephen if he knows the word dog, which is in the book they are looking at)

Stephen	No.
Mother	It's an animal.
Stephen	Rabbit?
Mother	No, it's 'dog'.
Stephen	Dog's not an animal!
Mother	Yes it is.
...	
Stephen	It's, it's just a dog.
Mother	Yes, but dogs are animals.
Stephen	No, they aren't.
Mother	Well, what's an animal then?
Stephen	Um (?a) giraffes an animal.
Mother	Oh, I see, you think animals is only for zoo animals.
Stephen	Yeh.
Mother	Dogs are animals too, they're tame animals. And cats, cats are animals too. Did you know
Hal	(chipping in) And people, we're animals.
Stephen	We're **not**. (Painter 1996: 63)

Stephen resists the schooled knowledge in this exchange; and a year later he laughs his mother off when she suggests that people are *creatures*:

[3.6] age 4:4

(Mother and Stephen are discussing whether whales kill people)

Mother	There may be one kind of whale that can, but most whales are nice creatures.
Stephen	They're not creatures Mum, they're whales.
Mother	Yes; creature is anything that's alive.
Stephen	Are **we** creatures?

Mother	Yeh.
Stephen	No, we're not! (laughing) (Painter 1966: 65)

But in another year Stephen will be in school, coming to terms with the fact that there are both commonsense and uncommonsense ways of classifying experience, even if the school promotes its classifications as true and pre-school knowledge as false (e.g. the idea that some of the 'stars' we see in the sky with the naked eye are **really** planets and many of them are **actually** galaxies).

3.3.2   Classification in school

The work we see Stephen, his elder brother and parents doing in these examples is related to the organising work we saw the teacher doing with her class in Chapter 2, as they sorted out the ideas for their exposition. One phase of that negotiation was resolved by distinguishing *discipline that people enforce upon you* and *self-discipline*.

[3.7] Building field for joint construction

Nicole	*Discipline.*
Teacher	***Discipline****. O.K.*
...	
Filippa	*Good ideas on how to behave.*
Teacher	*Right. Share with each other and in discipline. That can be what - **self-discipline**, so you can learn to look after yourself and control yourself and it can be discipline that other people enforce upon you - you have to learn to accept **rules**. So, it can be **two sorts**, can't it? Your **self-discipline** - that means you go home and do your homework at night, and you don't need someone to say, 'Hurry up; it's 4:30; it's time to do your homework.' You can just go in, do it yourself and look after yourself. And it can also mean discipline that's coming from ... other ... people - **obeying the rules**. If we have school rules, what do you have to do?*
Students	*Obey them.*
Teacher	*And you have to learn to follow them. When you leave school and go out and get a job, what will you have to do then?*
Students	*Obey the work rules.*
Teacher	*Obey the work rules. So you've got to learn to accept. If people ask you to do something usually there is a ... a reason. Sometimes it mightn't be good and you might discuss that, but you have to learn to accept. If someone says that is what's going to happen, sometimes you just have to go a ... along with it. You can, maybe discuss your way out if it, but sometimes you do have to do what they say. So I'll put self there, and I'll put rules there. Alright. So that means the two sorts of discipline. Right.*

The teacher's elaborations here sub-classify two types of discipline, giving the simple taxonomy in Figure 3.1.

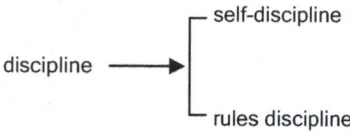

Figure 3.1: Subclassification of discipline

The difference here in school is that the classification process now establishes abstractions – concepts about non-sensory experience which the teacher defines for the class: *Your self-discipline – that **means** you go home and do your homework at night, and you don't need someone to say, 'Hurry up; it's 4:30; it's time to do your homework.' You can just go in, do it yourself and look after yourself.* The abstractions then enable the class to consolidate information in their final argument:

> *Finally, at school, people learn how to behave, socialise with other children, share with each other, play, have fun, learn to be responsible, **have their own self-discipline, obey the school rules** and form friendships which they may keep for life.*

The same kind of classification and abstraction process sets up the abstraction *wide range of subjects* in [3.8].

[3.8] Classifying school subjects

> Teacher   *... Now, let's try and get these into an order ... Who can see the main thing that keeps coming through the whole way through? Lisa?*
>
> Lisa   *Learn about a wide range of subjects.*

This abstraction plays a key role in modelling for the students how to flag their arguments in their introduction without spelling them out:

> *You can learn about **a wide range of subjects**, which will give you a tremendous amount of knowledge and ultimately help you in choosing your career.*

And it also enables them to set up a topic sentence for their first argument, which both links back to their introduction and is then spelled out in their argument:

> ***Firstly, you learn about a wider range of subjects, cultures and people.** For example, in maths, science, computers, social studies, spelling, art, craft, reading, language, library, sport, health, scripture, learning a new language and many more subjects. So ultimately, this allows us to achieve a greater understanding of the world and increase our knowledge.*

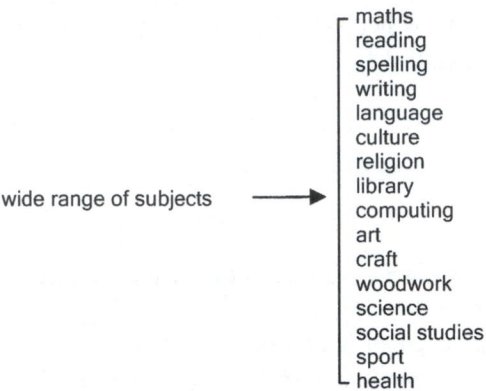

wide range of subjects ⟶ maths
reading
spelling
writing
language
culture
religion
library
computing
art
craft
woodwork
science
social studies
sport
health

Figure 3.2: Generalising a set of subjects

From these examples we see the important ways in which students experience continuity and discontinuity as they move from home to school. They are still classifying their world. But now the classifications are based on specialised criteria, and often involve abstractions. And the taxonomies they build are used not just to talk about the ongoing experience of the child's immediate sensory environment but are used to develop various realms of knowledge that are specific to each discipline, and to organise the writing where this specialised knowledge is stored.

3.3.3   Classification in science

Building up specialised classifications of uncommonsense experience becomes even more important as students move into science and related subjects in secondary school. We will consider an example from the general field of electricity here, beginning with a relatively accessible report [3.9] by Jim Lesurf for his website 'The Scots Guide to Electronics',[4] which he originally designed to help students at St Andrews University learn some basic electronics. This is one kind of material a secondary school student might well uncover surfing on the web. For many students it is the kind of material they have to depend on to supplement handouts distributed in class (which often provide just a glimpse of the understandings involved) – all the more so if these students do not have access to a textbook or have a strong preference for online over print materials even when they do (Jones 2007, 2008).

In terms of genre, Text [3.9] is a report, as it makes generalisations about entities. Specifically, it is a classifying report, since its function is to classify different substances that conduct electricity (as opposed to descriptive reports which would focus on just one phenomenon; e.g. the goannas and sharks reports

---

[4] http://www.st-andrews.ac.uk/~www_pa/Scots_Guide/intro/electron.htm

in Chapter 2). It begins by setting out the Classification system, and then works through the Description stage – with a phase devoted to each major type of conducting substance, and two sub-types.

[3.9] Classifying conductors

Classification	The materials used in electronics can be divided into three basic types.
	Conductors
	Insulators
	Semiconductors
Description	[...]
type 1	**Conductors**
	Most of the conductors used in electronics are metals like copper, aluminium and steel. Conductors are materials that obey Ohm's law and have very low resistance. They can therefore carry electric currents from place to place without dissipating a lot of power. As a result, metals are useful as connecting wires to carry electrical signals from place to place. They help ensure that most of the signal's power reaches its destination instead of warming up the wires in between! ...
type 2	**Insulators**
	Glass, most polymers (plastics), rubber and wood are all examples of insulators. These are materials which will refuse to carry an electric current. They are useful for jobs like coating electric wires to prevent them from 'shorting together' or giving you a shock. Silk and cotton are also good insulators (when they're dry!!) and some of the mains wiring in very old houses once used them - but by modern standards this was pretty dangerous since you could get a shock when wet or a spark would set them alight when dry! ...
type 3	**Semiconductors**
	All the transistors, diodes, integrated circuits, etc. used in modern electronics are built using a range of semiconductors. The basic property of a semiconductor is given away by its name - it 'conducts a little bit'. A semiconductor will carry electric current, but not as easily as a normal conductor.
type 3a	Some materials are intrinsic semiconductors. The semiconducting properties occur in these materials naturally. However, most of the semiconducting
type 3b	materials used in electronics are extrinsic. This means that left to themselves they are excellent insulators. These materials are turned into semiconductors by doping them with small amounts of foreign atoms ...

[http://www.st-andrews.ac.uk/~www_pa/Scots_Guide/info/comp/conduct/conduct.htm]

The uncommonsense criterion used to establish this classification is the ability of substances to conduct electricity (high, low or in between). Semiconductors are further classified as intrinsic or extrinsic with respect to another criterion (whether they have been 'doped'[5] or not to adjust their atomic structure). The taxonomy constructed here is outlined in Figure 3.3.

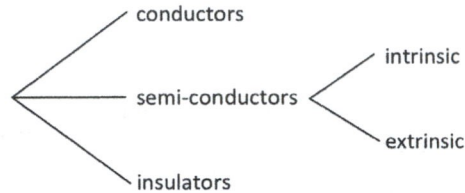

Figure 3.3: Classification of conducting substances

Outside of biology, diagrams of this kind are seldom used in secondary school to represent classification systems. Students have to construe the system (i.e. learn through language), by reading not viewing. Sometimes headings highlight the system as in Text [3.9] above; sometimes key terms are highlighted (using bold, italics, underlining, colour or as 'clickable' links, explicitly flagged as such or not, in web-based texts); sometimes there is an explicit Classification stage; sometimes there is a separate paragraph for each sub-typing phase, with or without a topic sentence foregrounding the phase. Any one or combination of these highlighting strategies may be used – or none at all, in which case many students may have trouble seeing that a classification process is underway at all. Text [3.10] illustrates a canonical Classification stage.

[3.10] Classification naming three types

> Classification   All materials can be **classified into three groups** according to how readily they permit an electric current to flow. These are: **conductors, insulators and semiconductors** (Glendinning 1980).

Text [3.11] has this stage but it only introduces conductors and insulators; semi-conductors are introduced later on in the report:

[3.11] Classification naming only two types

> Classification   All the practical effects of electricity are produced by the movement of electrons. In electrical work generally, materials can be **grouped as either conductors or insulators**.
> Description   [...]
> type3   In addition to this there are materials in which the degree can be varied. These are called **semi-conductors**... (Jenneson 1980: 23)

---

[5] Lesurf further subclassifies extrinsic semi-conductors as n-type or p-type depending on how they are doped – with donor atoms or acceptor ones (see §3.7 below).

And Text [3.12] similarly notes that there are two groups, but without immediately specifying them by name; once again the third term in the system, semiconductors, arises later in the text:

[3.12] Classification naming no types

Classification	As far as the ability to carry electricity is concerned, we can **place most substances into one of two groups**.
Description	
type 1	The first group contains materials with many electrons that are free to move. These materials are called **conductors** because they readily carry or conduct electric currents. Conductors are mostly metals but also include graphite.
type 2	The second group contains materials with very few electrons that are free to move. These materials are called **nonconductors** and are very poor conductors of electricity. Nonconductors can be used to prevent charge from going where it is not wanted. Hence they are also called **insulators**. Some common insulators are glass, rubber, plastic and air.
type 3	There are a few materials, such as germanium and silicon, called semiconductors. Their ability to conduct electricity is intermediate between conductors and insulators. **Semiconductors** have played an important role in modern electronics (Heffernan and Learmonth 1983: 212).

However they are textured (i.e. woven into text), specialised classifications of this kind are one key dimension of knowledge building in secondary school and are critical to guiding students to read and write report genres. The criteria by which conducting substances are classified in Texts [3.9]–[3.12] (i.e. their atomic structure) draw our attention to the other key dimension of building specialised knowledge about things – their composition. To explore this we have to go deeper into the structure of conducting substances, since it is the nature of their atomic composition that is crucial. Lesurf's website takes us deeper down this path, but here we will look at another type of report that describes the parts of an atom [3.13].

[3.13] Compositional report

Classification	The atom is a basic unit of matter that consists of a dense, central nucleus surrounded by a cloud of negatively charged electrons.
Description	
part 1	The atomic nucleus contains a mix of positively charged protons and electrically neutral neutrons (except in the case of hydrogen-1, which is the only stable nuclide with no neutrons).
part 2	The electrons of an atom are bound to the nucleus by the electromagnetic force.
part 3	Likewise, a group of atoms can remain bound to each other, forming a molecule (http://en.wikipedia.org/wiki/Atom).

This text is a compositional report rather than a classifying one, as it generalises the parts of atoms, which are also parts of molecules. Unlike classifying reports, compositional ones are often supported by a diagram such as that in Figure 3.4. As with Figure 3.3 above, the labelled image enables the reader/viewer to grasp at a glance the overall structure of the knowledge which unfolds more prosaically, in more detail, in print.

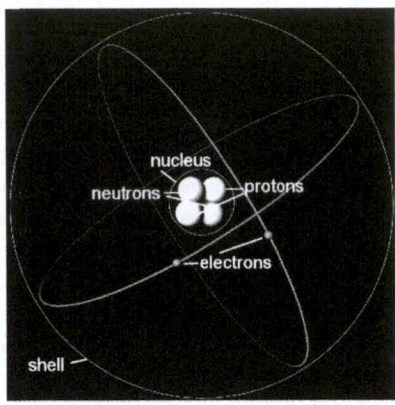

Figure 3.4: Compositional structure of a helium atom 4

(http://www.radartutorial.eu/21.semiconductors/hl04.en.html)

In science and related subjects the world is extensively re-classified and re-composed; and the classifying and compositional reports doing a lot of this work introduce large numbers of technical terms. The definitions of these terms (including of course the criteria defining them) and their relations to one another (as classes and parts) constitute the new knowledge about things which students have to understand. These new concepts are not directly available to the senses, and so we do not have words for them in our everyday vocabulary. We cannot see, touch, hear, feel or taste them. Rather, we learn them, as part of institutionalised teaching/learning (i.e. school). The critical point we are making here is that all of this uncommonsense knowledge is made of meaning, and has to be learned through the specialised language and images through which it is construed.

3.3.4   Classification in social sciences

Some subject areas are of course more technical than others. If we move to the humanities end of the curriculum, we still find descriptive, classifying and compositional reports. In history, for example, significant people and places are classified as in [3.14].

[3.14] Classifying people

A devout Roman Catholic, Diem was fervently anti-communist, nationalist and socially conservative. Historian Luu Doan Huynh notes, however, that 'Diem represented narrow and
extremist nationalism coupled with autocracy and nepotism'. As a wealthy Catholic, Diem was
viewed by many ordinary Vietnamese as part of the elite who had helped the French rule Vietnam;
Diem had been interior minister in the colonial government. The majority of Vietnamese people
were Buddhist, and were alarmed by actions such as his dedication of the country to the Virgin
Mary (http://en.wikipedia.org/wiki/Vietnam War).

Most specialised classification in history is in fact borrowed from other fields
– for example, the classification of 'Rainbow Herbicides' and the diseases linked
to the notorious Agent Orange in Text [3.15].

[3.15] Classifying things

The defoliants, which were distributed in drums marked with color-coded bands, included the
'Rainbow Herbicides' – Agent Pink, Agent Green, Agent Purple, Agent Blue, Agent White, and,
most famously, Agent Orange, which included dioxin as a by-product of its manufacture. About 12
million gallons (45,000,000 L) of Agent Orange were sprayed over Southeast Asia during the
American involvement. A prime area of Ranch Hand operations was in the Mekong Delta, where
the U.S. Navy patrol boats were vulnerable to attack from the undergrowth at the water's edge.
...

The U.S. Veterans Administration has listed prostate cancer, respiratory cancers, multiple
myeloma, type II diabetes, B-cell lymphomas, soft tissue sarcoma, chloracne, porphyria cutanea
tarda, peripheral neuropathy, and spina bifida in children of veterans exposed to Agent Orange.
Although there has been much discussion over whether the use of these defoliants constituted a
violation of the laws of war, the defoliants were not considered weapons, since exposure to them
did not lead to immediate death or incapacitation (http://en.wikipedia.org/wiki/Vietnam War).

When it comes to classifying historical events, however, historians do establish classifications of their own. These may or may not involve technical terms
(i.e. proper names for phases of history such as *WWII, the Gulf War, the Long
March, Mabo, the Sharpeville Massacre, the Renaissance* etc.). In Text [3.16]
below, initial upper case letters designate the *Indochina Wars* as a proper name;
but the first, second and third wars are not technicalised in this way.

[3.16] Classifying historical events

There were three Indochina Wars: the first was to remove the French; the second, the North
Vietnamese campaign to unify the country; and the third, the clashes between Vietnam, Cambodia
and China. All three wars saw massive loss of life and social and economic dislocation within the
region. The period marked the end of western imperialism and forced the USA to acknowledge

that there were limits, even as a superpower, to its capacity to determine the fate of other nations (Dennett and Dixon 2003: 474).

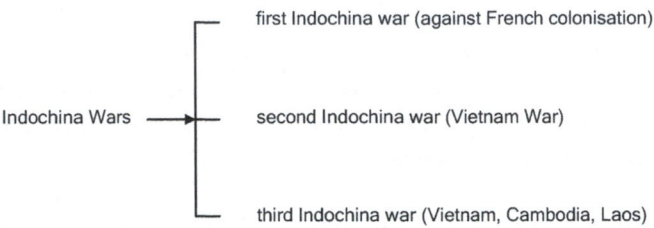

Figure 3.5: Classification of the Indochina Wars

Even where historians agree on the classification, the lack of technicalisation means that various terms can be used for the same phase of history, as exemplified in [3.17], [3.18] and [3.19] below. One advantage of this is that it allows the same events to be named from different points of view, more and less explicitly loaded with the values of those using the terms (e.g. *Dirty War* and *Anti-French Resistance War* in lieu of the *First Indochina War*; cf. *la Guerra de las Malvinas/the Falklands War*).

[3.17] First Indochina War

The First Indochina War (also known as the French Indochina War, Anti-French War, Franco-Vietnamese War, Franco-Vietminh War, Indochina War, Dirty War in France, and Anti-French Resistance War in contemporary Vietnam) was fought in French Indochina from December 19, 1946, until August 1, 1954 …

(http://en.wikipedia.org/wiki/First_Indochina_War)

[3.18] Vietnam War

Various names have been applied to what is known as the Vietnam War. These have shifted over time, although Vietnam War is the most commonly used title in English. It has been variously called the Second Indochina War, the Vietnam Conflict, the Vietnam War, and, in Vietnamese, Chiến tranh Việt Nam (The Vietnam War) or Kháng chiến chống Mỹ (Resistance War against America)

(http://en.wikipedia.org/wiki/Etymology_of_the_Vietnam_War)

[3.19] Sino–Vietnamese War

The Sino-Vietnamese War … also known as the Third Indochina War, known in the PRC as […] Counterattack against Vietnam in Self-Defense) and in Vietnam as […] War against Chinese expansionism, was a brief but bloody border war fought in 1979 between the People's Republic of China (PRC) and the Socialist Republic of Vietnam.

(http://en.wikipedia.org/wiki/Sino-Vietnamese_War)

Compositional reports in history introduce students to the structure of physical phenomena (e.g. temples, cities, battle lines) and human agencies (e.g. armies, governments, education systems). Once again, almost all specialised decomposition is borrowed, typically from the fields the historian is addressing. Text [3.20] outlines the organisation of the underground tunnel complexes used by the Vietnamese as bases during the Resistance War against America, beginning with Cu Chi, but immediately developing generalisations. Each sentence describes one or more parts of the complex, in bold below.

[3.20] Compositional report in history

Classification	The base area at Cu Chi was a vast network, with nearly 200 miles of **tunnels**. Any facility used by the guerrillas - a **conference room** or **training area** - had almost immediate underground access.
Description of parts	Hidden **trapdoors** led below, past **guarded chambers**, to long **passages**. At regular intervals, **branches** led back to the surface and other secret **entrances**. Some **openings** were even concealed beneath the waters of streams or canals.
	At the deeper levels, there were chambers carved out for **arms factories** and a **well** for the base's water supply.
	There were **store rooms** for weapons and rice, and there was sometimes a **hospital** or **forward aid station**.
	Long **communication tunnels** connected the base with other distant complexes.
	Base **kitchens** were always near the surface, with long, carved-out **chimneys** designed to diffuse cooking smoke and release it some distance away.
	Near the kitchens were the guerrilla's **sleeping chambers**, where they could survive for weeks at a time if need be.
	Everywhere on the top level, there were **tunnels** leading upwards to hundreds of hidden **firing posts** for defence of the base.
	(http://www.pbs.org/battlefieldvietnam/guerrilla/index.html)

As in science, labelled images often support, or even function in place of, compositional reports of this kind (Figure 3.6 below). The knowledge developed here is specialised, but not technical. It names sensory phenomena, which students can observe in photos or cross-sectional diagrams (or on site if a class visit is possible). So, unlike science, students to not have to learn a battery of terms defined in terms of criteria based on sense-augmenting technology, mathematics and decades or even centuries of record keeping.

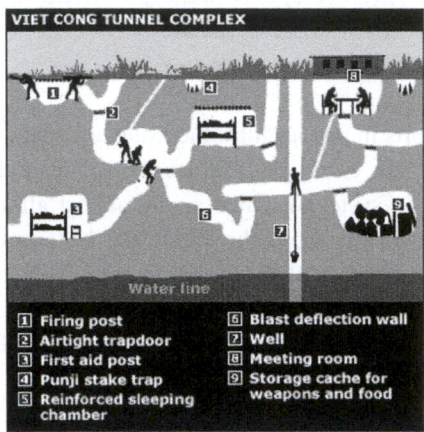

Figure 3.6: Typical Viet Cong tunnel complex

(http://news.bbc.co.uk/2/hi/asia-pacific/720577.stm)

3.4   Understanding processes: activity sequencing

3.4.1   Time, cause and effect

In Chapter 2 we gave some examples of Hal at two years of age learning to reason in dialogue with his parents. Exploring cause/effect relations is a central feature of language development in the home documented in Painter 1999, who includes a telling example illustrating Stephen's indignation when his mother fails to offer an acceptable explanation.

[3.22] age 3:6

Stephen	Why (?) clouds and it does rain?
Mother	Why does it rain?
Stephen	Why - why - there are clouds and it does start to rain and we don't like it.
Mother	(confused) Why does it rain when we don't want it to?
Stephen	Mm.
Mother	I don't know.
Stephen	**You have to tell me something!** (Painter 1999: 213)

By the time he arrives at school Stephen has been apprenticed into reasoning on his own – about the relative speed of vehicles for example.

[3.23] age 4:5

Stephen	Mum, can bikes go faster than cars? Can bikes go faster than cars?
Mother	You're always asking me that.
Stephen	I can't remember.
Mother:	They go about the same.
Stephen	What about vans? (ponders) Vans go faster than cars **so** vans should go faster than motorbikes. (Painter 1999: 304)

As we can see, Stephen has now learnt to reason that 'a happens so b should happen'. Cause-and-effect relations of this kind are an important resource for explaining uncommonsense phenomena in school. In primary school science there is a tendency for explanations to foreground sequence in time over cause/effect, since these are apparently seen as more transparent for young learners. Text [2.8] introduced in Chapter 2 featured an activity sequence of this kind.

[2.8] Heart explanation

The left pump sends the blood to the arteries
and **then** to the head to the toes.
The body carries oxygen that slowly gives up **while** going through the body.
Then the Blood goes back to the lungs
to get more oxygen.

Here most relationships between events are marked explicitly by temporal conjunctions (*then*, *while*), alongside one purposive relation (signalled by *to*). In spite of the foregrounding of sequence in time,[6] the explanation is really about why the heart pumps blood through the body (in order to give it oxygen) and why it goes back to the heart via the lungs (in order to get more oxygen). Although this text answers the question of why the heart pumps blood, most of the cause/effect relations are left implicit, so the reader must infer cause/effect from the temporal sequence. In order to do so the reader needs to know the function of the explanation genre – to explain causes and effects – and to recognise texts like this as explanations (and not simply a recount of events).

In the following explanation [3.24], lightning is explained in temporally unfolding terms. This explanation goes through four distinct phases that were not marked by paragraphing in the original version, but we have labelled below.

---

[6] Science discourse does include some sequentially organised texts which do not imply causality; for example, procedural recounts, in which the steps undertaken during an experiment are recorded (Martin and Rose 2008).

[3.24] Explanation of lightning

explanation sequence	Warm air rises in hot clouds and encounters cold air, charging the particles in the cloud making them both positive and negative and this is called static electricity. When enough positive and negative charges occur, they build up too much energy and explode in a flash of light that we call lightning. This flash of light helps balance out the number of negative and positive charges in the atmosphere.
2 types of lightning	Sometimes the flash of light is movement within the cloud and sometimes it is movement between the atmosphere and the ground. The movement between the atmosphere and the ground is the reason that tall objects on earth like trees are struck by lightning.
thunder and lightning	Light travels faster than sound, and because of this, we see the flash of lighting before we hear the clap of thunder. There is thus a direct relationship between thunder and lightning; they are not separate phenomena.
duration	Thunder and lightning lasts only as long as is necessary to get all the electrical charges in the atmosphere back in balance.

In the initial explanation sequence, most of the temporal links are left implicit; we have to understand from expectations about the genre that one event is following another. The implicit temporal relations have been added here in parentheses.

Warm air rises in hot clouds
and (**then**) encounters cold air,
(**then**) charging the particles in the cloud
(**then**) making them both positive and negative...
When enough positive and negative charges occur,
(**then**) they build up too much energy
and (**then**) explode in a flash of light...
(**then**) This flash of light helps balance out the number of negative and positive charges in the atmosphere.

But there is more to understand than just the implicit temporal sequence. In scientific texts of this kind, the sequences are really **implication sequences**, because the relations between events are actually contingent ones: i.e. **if** this happens, **then** this ensues (*if warm air rises in hot clouds then it will encounter cold air*). In this kind of sequence each event is both a condition for the next (*if*) and an effect of the preceding event (*then*), diagrammed in Figure 3.7.

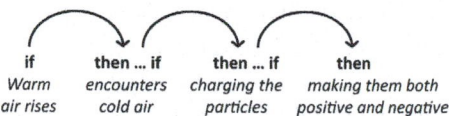

Figure 3.7: Implication sequence

The second phase distinguishes two types of lightning, and explains how phenomena get hit by lightning on the ground. In this case the cause/effect relationship is realised inside a single clause rather than between two clauses. In order to realise cause and effect this way one event and the causal relation are expressed as nouns (*the movement* …, *the reason* ...) and the other event modifies *the reason*.

Cause		Effect
The movement between the atmosphere and the ground	is	**the reason** [[that tall objects on earth like trees are struck by lightning]]

A more spoken version would express this sequence as two clauses linked by a conjunction, so: the electric energy moves between the atmosphere and the ground and **so** tall objects are struck by lightning.

The last phase explains why we hear thunder after lightning:

Light travels faster than sound,
and **because of this**, we see the flash of lighting
before we hear the clap of thunder.

In this case the cause/effect is again realised inside a clause; but this time cause is realised through a prepositional phrase (*because of this*), and 'this' picks up the reason from the preceding clause (i.e. that *light travels faster than sound*).

Cause	Effect
and **because of this**	we see the flash of lighting before we hear the clap of thunder

This phase then concludes with 'thus', making explicit that, although we experience lighting and thunder as separate events, there is a direct relationship between them – they are two aspects of the same phenomenon:

There is **thus** a direct relationship between thunder and lightning;
they are not separate phenomena.

Note that the causal conjunction ***thus*** refers here to the scientific reasoning involved, rather than to cause-and-effect relationships obtaining among the phenomena themselves. This kind of logical relation is discussed further in Chapter 5 (§5.2.2).

The final phase of the text explains that thunder and lightning continue until a balance of electrical forces in the atmosphere is achieved (via a purposive relation signalled by *to*):

> Thunder and lightning lasts only as long as is necessary
> **to** get all the electrical charges in the atmosphere back in balance.

Technical terms commonly arise in the course of explanations; two explanation sequences in [3.24] are named with the technical terms *static electricity* and *lightning*.

> Warm air rises in hot clouds
> and encounters cold air,
> charging the particles in the cloud
> making them both positive and negative and **this is called static electricity**.

> When enough positive and negative charges occur,
> they build up too much energy
> and explode in a flash of light **that we call lightning**.

Set up in this way, lightning is no longer just an everyday term for the play of light we observe during storms in the sky; it is now, in addition, a technical scientific term that distils the explanation we have been tracking here. So the same word now belongs to two fields (to both common- and uncommonsense worlds), with distinct meanings in everyday life and in science.

Some topics in science lend themselves to explanations organised around sequence in time (e.g. coal formation, glacial movement, evolution). Other topics lend themselves to a less sequentially organised, more 'theoretical' explanation (e.g. sound, heat, seasons) (Unsworth 1997a, b, c, 1999a, b, 2001a, Veel 1992, 1997). In order not to place too high a burden on readers (like us) who have struggled with physics in the past and/or forgotten it long ago, we will stick with relatively sequentially organised explanations here.

Some phenomena have alternative explanations. For example, the precise way in which lightning forms is unresolved, and a number of alternative explanations have been proposed. The Wiki website reviews a number of these, beginning with the electrostatic induction hypothesis [3.25] below, which follows a similar explanation sequence as [3.24] above.

[3.25] Alternative explanation for lightning

Phenomenon	According to the electrostatic induction hypothesis charges are driven apart by as-yet uncertain processes.
Explanation sequence	Charge separation appears to require strong updrafts which carry water droplets upward,
	supercooling them to between -10 and -20 °C.
	These collide with ice crystals to form a soft ice-water mixture called graupel.
	The collisions result in a slight positive charge being transferred to ice crystals,
	and a slight negative charge to the graupel.
	Updrafts drive the less heavy ice crystals upwards,
	causing the cloud top to accumulate increasing positive charge.
	Gravity causes the heavier negatively charged graupel to fall toward the middle and lower portions of the cloud,
	building up an increasing negative charge.
	Charge separation and accumulation continue
	until the electrical potential becomes sufficient to initiate a lightning discharge,
	which occurs when the distribution of positive and negative charges forms a sufficiently strong electric field (http://en.wikipedia.org/wiki/Lightning).

In addition to this 'electrostatic induction hypothesis', the website also includes the 'polarisation mechanism hypothesis' and 'Gurevich's runaway breakdown theory'. Texts which explore alternative explanations without advocating one over another can be referred to as **explorations**. Advocating one position over another on the other hand gives rise to argument genres, including **exposition**, **discussion** and **challenge**, which we will touch on in §3.5 below.

There is of course a great deal more to say about taxonomies and implication sequences in science (cf. Martin 2007a, b). In particular, we do not have space to explore the importance of mathematical symbolism and visual images in multi-modal genres (Martin and Rose 2008, O'Halloran 2005, Unsworth 2001b, 2008, Veel 1998). Nor do we have space to consider macrogenres – the combinations of reports, explanations, procedures and related genres that make up textbooks, websites, research articles and longer school assignments that accumulate knowledge of complementary kinds (Hood 2010, Martin 2002a, Martin and Rose 2008, Swales 1990, 2004). Our concern here is simply with establishing the fundamentals of knowledge structure in uncommonsense fields. These fundamentals include the use of language and supporting images to construe (i) a reclassification of familiar concepts and classification of new ones, (ii) a recomposition of familiar concepts and composition of new ones and (iii) alternative explanations of familiar processes and novel explanations of new ones. Because it is made of language, this knowledge is packaged as the genres that science has evolved to consolidate its uncommonsense perspective on the universe and is stored as writing.

3.4.2   Time and cause in history

Turning to the humanities discourse of history we have to come to terms with a different kind of uncommonsense knowledge, equally or even more abstract but much less technical than that of science (Coffin 2006, Martin 1993a, b, 2002b, 2003, Veel and Coffin 1996). Since history is concerned with recording and interpreting the past, we will begin with a focus on activity unfolding through time – with texts construing a sequence of events. These are used to focus on events in which the details of what happened are historically significant.

The examples we use here are all drawn from the field of the long period of conflict in Vietnam. The first Text [3.26] is a recount of the My Lai massacre in 1968. It is an excerpt from a letter by Ron Ridenhour, which led to exposure of the cover-up by Defence Department officials.[7] The recount begins with an Orientation that establishes the sources of the story. The Record of events then goes through two phases, which we have labelled here. The first phase has less detail; the second phase goes into more, gruesome, detail. The time sequence is construed by temporal conjunctions, in bold below.

[3.26] Recount of event

Orientation (sources)	It was June before I spoke to anyone who had something of significance to add to what I had already been told of the 'Pinkville' incident. It was the end of June, 1968 when I ran into Sergeant Larry La Croix at the USO in Chu Lai. La Croix had been in 2nd Lt. Kally's[8] platoon on the day Task Force Barker swept through 'Pinkville'. What he told me verified the stories of the others, but he also had something new to add. He had been a witness to Kally's gunning down at least three separate groups of villagers. 'It was terrible. They were slaughtering villagers like so many sheep.'
Record summary of events	Kally's men were dragging people out of bunkers and hootches and putting them together in a group. The people in the group were men, women and children of all ages. **As soon as** he felt that the group was big enough, Kally ordered a M-60 (machine gun) set up and the people killed. La Croix said that he bore witness to

---

[7] An early player in the cover-up was Major Colin Powell, who concluded in a 1968 report responding to charges of American atrocities that 'relations between American soldiers and Vietnamese civilians are excellent'; ever a team player, Powell would later consummate his role as a right-wing spin master in his notorious address to the UN in support of the Iraq War (http://www.consortiumnews.com/archive/colin3.html).

[8] The reference is to Second Lieutenant William Calley, the only American soldier convicted in relation to the massacre; sentenced to life imprisonment and hard labour he ultimately served three and a half years of house arrest in an American military prison.

detailed
recount

this procedure at least three times. The three groups were of different sizes, one of about twenty people, one of about thirty people and one of about 40 people. **When** the first group was put together Kally ordered Pfc. Torres to man the machine-gun and open fire on the villagers that had been grouped together. This Torres did, but **before** everyone in the group was down he ceased fire and refused to fire again. **After** ordering Torres to recommence firing several times, Lieutenant Kally took over the M-60 and finished shooting the remaining villagers in that first group himself. Sergeant La Croix told me that Kally didn't bother to order anyone to take the machine-gun **when** the other two groups of villagers were formed. He simply manned it himself and shot down all villagers in both groups (http://www.law.umkc.edu/faculty/projects/ftrials/mylai/ridenhour_ltr.html).

Except for exceptional episodes of this order, historians cannot afford to chronicle history as a sequence of events in such detail. Their job is rather to generalise across events and the people involved. To manage this they partition the past into phases of activity undertaken recurrently by groups of people, in addition to the great men who are singled out as history makers, such as General Giap and Ho Chi Minh in Text [3.27] below. Each new phase of activity is signalled by a time phrase, in bold here.

[3.27] Historical recount

In August 1945 the French colony of Indo-China (Vietnam, Laos and Cambodia, now called Kampuchea) was occupied by British and Nationalist Chinese troops after the surrender of the Japanese who had seized it **in 1941**. **In October 1945** the French returned determined to re-establish their control, especially in Vietnam. French forces easily re-occupied the southern portion of Vietnam, but were faced in the north with a new communist regime which had been established in their absence by the communist leader Ho Chi Minh. **During the war** Ho had led the resistance to the Japanese occupation of Vietnam, and after the war led a communist-dominated organisation which represented Vietnamese nationalist aspirations. Ho's organisation was known as the Viet-Minh. The French were determined to retake northern Vietnam and **in 1946** began military operations against the Viet-Minh, thus triggering the first Indo-China War.

In late 1946 the French forced the Viet-Minh, led by General Vo Nguyen Giap, out of Hanoi and into the hills of northern Vietnam. **By 1948** it appears that the Viet-Minh were beaten. However, the victory of the communists in China gave the Viet-Minh secure bases on the Vietnam-China border, as well as a source of military supplies. **In January 1951** the strengthened Viet-Minh attempted an all-out assault on Hanoi but were easily defeated by the superior French fire power. Nevertheless, the French could not defeat the Viet-Minh in guerilla warfare, despite the fact that France had 100000 troops in Vietnam and was backed b the United States, which **by 1953** was paying 78% of the cost of the war.

In early 1953 Giap began to move his forces across Vietnam to invade Laos and support the communist guerilla army there, the Pathet Lao. The French attempted to block this move by setting up a major base at Dien Bien Phu. They positioned 15000 of their best combat troops at Dien Bien Phu and hoped to force the Viet-Minh into open combat. The French expected Dien

Bien Phu to be a slaughtering ground for the Viet-Minh. Instead the reverse happened. The Viet-Minh besieged the French garrison at Dien Bien Phu and for two months pounded the base with artillery, which the French had assumed could not be brought through the jungle. Using human wave attacks the Viet-Minh overwhelmed Dien Nien Phu **on 7 May, 1954**. With the fall of Dien Bien Phu, French power in Vietnam collapsed.

In July 1954, at a Geneva peace conference it was agreed Vietnam would be divided along the 17th parallel. North of this line was to be a communist state of North Vietnam led by Ho Chi Minh, while south of the 17th parallel a non-communist government supported by the Americans was established. Elections were to be held **in March 1956** with the intention of reuniting the country. Both Laos and Cambodia (now Kampuchea) were granted independence, as well as neutral status (Condon 1987: 492).

These phases unfold through time, as did [3.26] above, but they make use of **setting in time** rather than **sequence in time** to do so. In terms of genre, we can contrast **historical recounts** like [3.27] that recount phases in time with detailed recounts of events like [3.26]. By organising unfolding events in phases in this way historians in effect turn activity sequences into part-whole structures – the past is decomposed into stages. Important pieces of this division can then be named, as we saw earlier in Text [3.16] above, which named each of the Indo-china Wars. So as far as recording the past is concerned, historians recast time as a kind of 'thing', and break it up into significant segments. This shift from **sequence in time** to **setting in time** is a fundamental dimension of building uncommonsense knowledge in humanities and social science subjects that deal with the past, such as art history, literary studies, social work, media studies, economics and historical linguistics.

Like scientists, however, historians are also expected to explain – to move beyond packaging up what happened to interpreting why things turned out as they did. This gives rise to **historical accounts** which not only progress through phases, but which also establish cause/effect relations between events, both within and between phases. A historical account of this kind is exemplified in [3.28] below, with settings in time underlined and causal relations in bold (implicit causal relations are made explicit in parentheses).

[3.28] Historical account

France began its conquest of Indochina in the late 1850s, and completed the pacification by 1893. The Treaty of Huế, concluded in 1884, **formed the basis** for French colonial rule in Vietnam for the next seven decades. **In spite of** military resistance, most notably by the Can Vuong of Phan Dinh Phung, by 1888, the area of the current-day nations of Cambodia and Vietnam was made into the colony of French Indochina (Laos was added later). Various Vietnamese opposition movements to the French rule existed during this period, such as the Viet Nam Quoc Dan Dang who staged the failed Yen Bai mutiny in 1930, but none were ultimately as successful as the Viet Minh common front, controlled by the Communist Party of Vietnam, founded in 1941 and funded by United States and Chinese Nationalist Party in its fight against Japanese occupation.

During World War II, the French were defeated by the Germans in 1940. For French Indochina, **this meant** that the colonial authorities became Vichy French, allies of the German-Italian Axis powers. In turn **this meant** that the French collaborated with the Japanese forces after their invasion of French Indochina during 1940. The French continued to run affairs in the colony, **but** ultimate power resided in the hands of the Japanese.

On May 1941, the Việt Minh was founded as a league for the independence from France. The Việt Minh also opposed Japanese occupation in 1945 **for the same reason**. The United States and Chinese national party supported them to weaken Japanese influence over Vietnam. **However**, they did not have **enough** power **to** fight actual battles at first. Ho Chi Minh was suspected of being a communist and jailed for a year by the Chinese national party.

Double occupation by France and Japan continued until the German forces were expelled from France and the French Indochina colonial authorities started holding secret talks with the Free French. (**because**) Fearing that they could no longer trust the French authorities the Japanese army interned them all on March 9, 1945 and assumed direct control themselves through their puppet state of the Empire of Vietnam under Bảo Đại.

During 1944-1945, a deep famine struck northern Vietnam **due to** a combination of poor weather and French/Japanese exploitation. According to Ho chi Minh's speech in August, 1 million people died of starvation (out of a population of 10 million in the affected area). (**by**) Exploiting the administrative gap that the internment of the French had created, the Viet Minh in March 1945 urged the population to ransack rice warehouses and refuse to pay their taxes. Between 75 and 100 warehouses were **consequently** raided. This rebellion against the **effects** of the famine and the authorities that were partially **responsible for** it bolstered the Viet Minh's popularity and (so) they recruited many members during this period (http://en.wikipedia.org/wiki/Vietnam_War).

Such historical accounts are comparable to the scientific explanations discussed above; they do not simply chronicle – they explain why. In such texts, a variety of causal relations are expressed in a variety of ways, including conjunctions (e.g. *because, but, however, by, to*) nouns (*the **reason**, the **effects**, the **basis***), verbs (*this **meant**, **forms** the basis*), adverbs and adjectives (*consequently, responsible for*) and prepositions (***in spite of*** *resistance*, ***for*** *the same reasons*, ***due to*** *a combination*). Alongside the causal meanings of *because, so, to, due to, consequently, reasons, effects*, we also find meanings realised by conjunctions like *in spite of, but* and *however* that are 'counter-causal' – instead of *a* happening, *b* happens. These relations are known as **concessive** (Martin 1992, Martin and Rose 2003/2007).

3.4.3   Factors and consequences

Explaining why may involve more than a simple cause/effect relationship with one event following on as the result of another. There can be complex causes and complex effects. In this case the chronological unfolding of a text has to give way to make room for the presentation of multiple cause/effect relations. In Text

[3.29] below, two factors affecting America's involvement in Vietnam are reviewed. The factors and their outcome are labelled here.

[3.29] Factorial explanation

Phenomenon: outcome	America's response to developments in Vietnam was dramatically influenced by two events:
Explanation	
factor1	- in 1949, China fell to the communists. This intensified the fears of a global communist expansion, and led to criticism of the Democrat President Truman from members of the rival Republican Party in the US. Republicans blamed Truman for 'losing China'
factor2	- in 1950, President Truman saw the outbreak of the Korean War as a deliberate challenge to world peace and his policy of containment. The containment policy had been put in place in march 1947 as the Truman Doctrine, with the intention of halting the global spread of communism by supporting anti-communist regimes ... (Dennett and Dixon 2003: 435).

We refer to this type of text as a **factorial explanation**. Conversely in [3.30], two of the effects of the Vietnam War are presented in a **consequential explanation**, including a cause and its multiple consequences, labelled here as cons 1, cons 2, etc.

[3.30] Consequential explanation

Phenomenon: cause	The Vietnam war, which is the main topic of this chapter, also had a major impact on the twentieth century national history of the USA and was one of the defining events of the Cold War.
Explanation	
cons 1	Professor David Kennedy of Stanford University has argued that the cost and trauma of the Vietnam War produced a 'crisis of confidence' in the USA. Until the Vietnam War, Americans had generally felt confident in their ability to mould events through the exercise of their ingenuity, energy and vast economic resources. Vietnam proved to be a problem that they couldn't manage.
cons 2a	The Vietnam conflict gave rise to social division and distrust of government in the US. It ended the political career of President Lyndon Johnson and his dreams of major social reform.
cons 2b	It also produced, in the case of Richard Nixon's presidency, a siege mentality that contributed directly to the infamous Watergate Scandal (1973-74) and the resignation, in disgrace, of Nixon.
cons 2c	Because of the Vietnam War, as part of the wider conflict in Indochina, a generation of Americans identified with anti-conscription and anti-war protest movements.

cons 2d   Many of the social and political effects evident in the US were also present
             in Australia (Dennett and Dixon 2003: 426).

Relations of causes to effects in [3.29] and [3.30] are diagrammed in Figure 3.8.

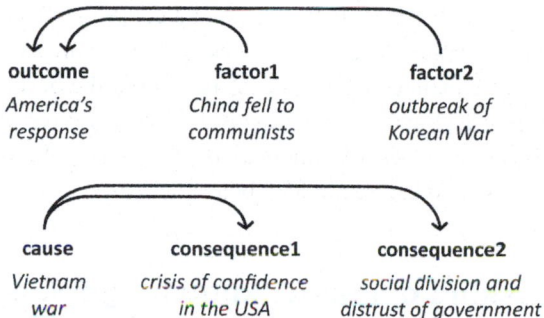

outcome   **factor1**   **factor2**
America's   *China fell to*   *outbreak of*
response   *communists*   *Korean War*

cause   **consequence1**   **consequence2**
Vietnam   *crisis of confidence*   *social division and*
war   *in the USA*   *distrust of government*

Figure 3.8: Factorial and consequential explanations

While the factors in [3.29] are presented in point form, the consequences in [3.30] are introduced as one of the defining moments of the Cold War, and then each introduced with a topic sentence and then elaborated. The rhythm by which the information flows is illustrated through indentation below.

[3.30'] Information flow in a consequential explanation

The Vietnam war, which is the main topic of this chapter, also had a major impact on the twentieth century national history of the USA and was one of the defining events of the Cold War.

> Professor David Kennedy of Stanford University has argued that the cost and trauma of the Vietnam War produced a 'crisis of confidence' in the USA.

>> Until the Vietnam War, Americans had generally felt confident in their ability to mould events through the exercise of their ingenuity, energy and vast economic resources. Vietnam proved to be a problem that they couldn't manage.

The Vietnam conflict gave rise to social division and distrust of government in the US.

>> It ended the political career of President Lyndon Johnson and his dreams of major social reform. It also produced, in the case of Richard Nixon's presidency, a siege mentality that contributed directly to the infamous Watergate Scandal (1973-74) and the resignation, in disgrace, of Nixon. Because of the Vietnam War, as part of the wider conflict in Indochina, a generation of Americans identified with anti-conscription and anti-war protest movements. Many of the social and political effects evident in the US were also present in Australia.

Because they deal with complex cause and effect relations, factorial and consequential explanations have to be organised rhetorically rather than chronologically, something which sets them apart from recount genres. The nature of the knowledge, in other words, makes different demands on the way the writing (and its reading) unfolds. We will take up the question of how causality is managed grammatically in explanations in §3.6 below.

As with science, history has evolved a range of genres for consolidating different kinds of knowledge – recounts for detailed sequences of events, historical recounts for phases of time, accounts for foregrounding causal connections between events and phases, and factorial and consequential explanations for phenomena with multiple causes and effects. Much more explicitly than in science genres, whose main concern is consensus about the best available understandings of the physical and biological world, history genres deal with values around which consensus takes a lot more effort to sustain. We turn to history's axiological perspective on the past in §3.5 below.

3.5 Expressing opinions: knowledge and values

So far in this chapter we have focused on the nature of the uncommonsense things and activities students encounter in secondary school. In doing so we have so far limited our focus to the uncommonsense 'facts of the matter', setting aside the values students also have to learn. We will turn briefly to these axiological understandings here, beginning with history, where the need to take up a position on people and their activities is relatively clear (Coffin 1997, 2000, 2003, 2006).

3.5.1 Evaluating history

In contemporary secondary school history, a lot of emphasis is put on interpreting primary sources. And sources often include judgements that students will have to read and adjudicate. Ridenhour's letter, for example, from which we excerpted the recount in [3.26] above, does faithfully document what happened at My Lai, based on his interviews with soldiers who were there and experienced it first hand. But it also asserts the veracity of his account, and includes Ridenhour's judgements on the events, which he explicitly characterises as dark, bloody, barbaric and black as part of appealing to the government officials and congressmen to whom he wrote for justice (only one of whom, Morris Udall, acted on the information). More of Ridenhour's letter is presented as [3.26'] below, with key judgements in bold.

[3.26'] Evaluations of events

> It was late in April, 1968 that I first heard of 'Pinkville' and what allegedly happened there. I received that first report with some skepticism, but in the following months I was to hear similar stories from such a wide variety of people that it became impossible for me to disbelieve that something **rather dark and bloody** did indeed occur sometime in March, 1968 in a village called 'Pinkville' in the Republic of Viet Nam.

...

After hearing this account I couldn't quite accept it. Somehow I just couldn't believe that not only had so many young American men participated in such an act of **barbarism**, but that their officers had ordered it.

...

This account of Sergeant La Croix's confirmed the rumors that Gruver, Terry and Doherty had previously told me about Lieutenant Kally. It also convinced me that there was a very substantial amount of **truth** to the stories that all of these men had told. If I needed more convincing, I was about to receive it.

...

Exactly what did, in fact, occur in the village of 'Pinkville' in March, 1968 I do not know for certain, but I am convinced that it was something **very black** indeed. I remain irrevocably persuaded that if you and I do truly believe in the principles, of **justice** and the **equality** of every man, however **humble**, before the law, that form the very backbone that this country is founded on, then we must press forward a widespread and public investigation of this matter with all our combined efforts. I think that it was Winston Churchill who once said **'A country without a conscience is a country without a soul, and a country without a soul is a country that cannot survive.'** I feel that I must take some **positive** action on this matter. I hope that you will launch an investigation immediately and keep me informed of your progress. If you cannot, then I don't know what other course of action to take.

The historical recounts which do the bulk of the chronicling work in secondary sources also include evaluation, although this tends to come at the beginning or end of phases of activity (Coffin 1997, 2003). For example, the historical recount [3.27] above presents itself as an objective record of what went on until it reaches a turning point in the American involvement in Vietnam. The chronicle continues as follows.

[3.27 continued]

When no elections were held in Vietnam in 1956, communist guerilla activity recommenced. Between 1957 and 1959 the communists increasingly attacked the American-backed government of South Vietnam headed by Ngo Dinh Diem. In 1960 a national liberation front was established by the communists in South Vietnam and 20,000 guerillas, known as the Vietcong, began a major assault on the Diem government. The United States sent 1300 military advisers to South Vietnam in 1961 to help Diem's regime resist the Vietcong. However, the **corrupt** South Vietnamese regime was **unable to effectively** resist the communists even after Diem was replaced (he was shot by one of his own generals) in November 1963 (Condon 1987: 492-3).

This phase explicitly judges Diem's regime as 'corrupt' and appreciates the significance of its resistance to the communists as 'ineffective'. Explanations regularly include explicit evaluation of this kind, as in Texts [3.29] and [3.30] above. Some of the explicitly evaluative comments from these texts are high-lighted in bold here.

America's response to developments in Vietnam was **dramatically** influenced by two events:

in 1949, China fell to the communists. This **intensified the fears** of a global communist expansion

in 1950, President Truman saw the outbreak of the Korean War as a **deliberate** challenge to world peace and his policy of containment.

The Vietnam War, which is the main topic of this chapter, also had a **major** impact on the twentieth century national history of the USA and was one of the **defining** events of the Cold War

Professor David Kennedy of Stanford University has argued that the cost and trauma of the Vietnam War produced a **'crisis of confidence'** in the USA.

In spite of the relatively opinionated nature of such evaluations, in historical recounts, accounts and explanations they are presented as uncontested. Students are thus positioned to accept the judgements of the historian in question. At the same time students are sometimes cautioned to be very careful about passing judgements of their own, as in the exhortation from a secondary school history textbook [3.31] below.

[3.31] Hortatory exposition

We should be very careful about passing judgements on some incident or person in history. Firstly, the events under study probably took place in a setting and at a time much different from our own. What seems totally unreasonable behaviour to us in our time and place might not have been generally regarded as such in another time and place. Secondly, we should make sure that we have access to as much information as possible about the events and the people involved before passing judgment. Finally it is necessary for us to establish criteria by which we can make the judgment (Hoepper et al. 1996: 121).

This text displays the canonical structure of an **exposition** of the hortatory type, starting with the exhortation to 'be very careful', followed by three supporting arguments signalled by *firstly*, *secondly*, *finally*. Note, however, that the writer does not proscribe all judgement, but rather *prescribes* the conditions for making judgements.

Unlike historical recounts, accounts and explanations, expositions do present opinions as contested, and marshal arguments in support. Text [3.31] in effect warns students to treat their own opinions as contestable. The fact that they read historians making uncontested judgements all the time is no doubt what makes this warning contestable, and so something that needs to be argued for. Text [3.32] below, primary source material from an address by American president Lyndon Johnson, deals with the highly contested issue of American involvement in Vietnam. It is also a hortatory exposition, designed to rally support for the war effort. The exposition stages of Thesis and Arguments are labelled here, with each supporting argument as a phase.

[3.32] Exposition as a presidential address

Thesis	Over this war, and all Asia, is the deepening shadow of Communist China. The rulers in Hanoi are urged on by Peking. This is a regime which has destroyed freedom in Tibet, attacked India, and been condemned by the United Nations for aggression in Korea. It is a nation which is helping the forces of violence in almost every continent. The contest in Vietnam is part of a wider pattern of aggressive purpose. Why are these realities our concern? Why are we in South Vietnam?
Arguments	
argument 1	We are there because we have a promise to keep. Since 1954 every American President has offered support to the people of South Vietnam. We have helped to build, and we have helped to defend. Thus, over many years, we have made a national pledge to help South Vietnam defend its independence. And I intend to keep our promise. To dishonour that pledge, to abandon this small and brave nation to its enemy, and to the terror that must follow, would be an unforgivable wrong.
argument 2	We are also there to strengthen world order. Around the globe, from Berlin to Thailand, are people whose well-being rests, in part, on the belief that they can count on us if they are attacked. To leave Vietnam to its fate would shake the confidence of all these people in the value of American commitment, the value of America's word. The result would be increased unrest and instability, and even wider war.
argument 3	We are also there because there are great stakes in the balance. Let no one think for a moment that retreat from Vietnam would bring an end to conflict. The battle would be renewed in one country and then another. The central lesson of our time is that the appetite of aggression is never satisfied. To withdraw from one battlefield means only to prepare for the next. We must stay in Southeast Asia, as we did in Europe, in the words of the Bible: 'Hitherto shalt thou come, but no further.' ...

(http://www.pbs.org/wgbh/amex/vietnam/psources/ps_policy.html)

3.5.2   Supporting evaluations

History students, since their perspective is retrospective (not prospective like Johnson's in [3.32]), are expected to argue not about what should happen but what did happen – about contestable evaluations of past events. In Text [3.33] below a Year 12 student presents arguments in favour of the proposition that the defeat of America and South Vietnam was inevitable. We have included the exposition's Thesis and Restatement below, and excerpted the topic sentence from several of its key arguments (indented). Explicit evaluations are highlighted in bold.

[3.33] Student's exposition

It was **inevitable** that the USA and the Republic of Vietnam would be defeated in the Second Indochina war of 1965-1973 because of the **effective** strategies used by the North, with the use of Guerrilla warfare and the Ho Chin Minh trail. The south was defeated because their tactics like using conventional ground warfare and air warfare and their Pacification Campaigns were **totally inappropriate** for the war in Vietnam.

> …
>
> The US tactics were **wrong**
>
> …
>
> The goal of the NVA and VC was to unify North and South as one nation by defeating the US and their allies. This cause became an **all consuming** one.
>
> …
>
> The US and SV were **very disadvantaged**.
>
> …
>
> But the main reason, and **most effective** part of the VC's strategy was that they had a **cause**.
>
> …
>
> The US and RoV Social policies were also a **failure**, and a **major part** to the **inevitability of their loss**.
>
> …

It was **inevitable** that the US and RoV were to be defeated in the Second Indochina war. What attributed to this defeat were **not only the strengths** of the North's strategy of guerrilla warfare and the **vital success** of the Ho Chi Minh Trail in supplying the troops. The strategy of the US and the South was **hopeless in all senses** for this type of war. Their use of conventional techniques and Pacification programs in the end pushed the people to believe they are in fact the enemy. The fact that the North has an **emotional cause appealing** to the whole of the people and the **all-round inappropriate** strategy of the south and US it was **inevitable from the start** that the South would be defeated.

As we can see, several arguments are presented in support of the inevitability of defeat, and support is also given for the evaluations in each of these. For example, in the first supporting argument, the student does not just claim that US tactics were *wrong*. This evaluation is backed up with two phases of detail about US operations, first on the ground and then in the air. Both phases unfold as relatively objective accounts of what went on, avoiding contestable evaluations.

[3.33'] Supporting argument

The US tactics were wrong. Fighting a conventional war against a guerrilla war, the US should have learnt from the previous Indochina War between the French and the Vietnamese.

> 'History repeats itself. It comes in cycles. Lessons and reflections exist everywhere, but no one seems to learn' - Arnold J Toynbee 'Contested Spaces'
>
> The US and RoV armies were efficiently equipped to meet conventional invasion, with tanks only used for 'Coup D'état' also defensive role, armoured personnel carriers (APC's) could only be used in dry weather and heavy artillery used as defence. The US

went about the war using the "Search and Destroy" method this meant they located a VC unit, attacked and returned to base. This was self-defeating as VC would hear the fleet of planes from miles away and have time to run, hide or prepare an ambush. Soldiers plodded through rice fields and dense jungle, weakened by the heat and rain, attacked by insects and leeches, misery/boring, threat of VC, booby traps waiting to be stepped on or triggered. The US was victorious in set battles, like Khe Sanh in 1967-1968. The battle was a major attack by the NVA, a total of 10,000 NVA killed and 500 US killed. But these battles did not deter the North, but the US was furious with the amount of deaths.

     As a form of Conventional warfare, the US used helicopters, jets and bombers to rain death on NV, beginning in May 1965 and continued for three years. 800 tons of bombs, rockets and missiles on the North's military establishments, bridges, roads, rail lines, fuel storehouses. A total of 7,000,000 tons was dropped. Napalm, jellied petroleum that sticks to skin and burns through to the bone, was used in the Rolling Thunder raids and throughout the South against suspected enemies or supply lines. The Americans controlled the air space, but the North also possessed highly effective air defences. S.A.M and M.i.G fighter planes effectively caused considerable damage to US planes. On many occasions, large bodies of NVA troops were caught before they got into action.

This objective support also includes an appeal to authority – to a famous historian this time, not the Bible of Johnson's oration. The challenge of being critical yet objective is solved by composing a text which backs up contestable evaluations with historical 'facts', thereby satisfying the expository admonitions in [3.31] above – i.e. to contextualise thoroughly and sensitively, and provide criteria for judgements.

3.5.3   Contesting history and science

Our major concern to this point in this section has been to show that subjects like history are not just about knowledge of uncommonsense things and activities. They are also about the specialised evaluations students learn to make about this knowledge. As part of this, students have to also learn to argue in favour of their judgements of character and behaviour and appreciations of the significance of events. In general, the evaluations students learn reflect the stance of the curriculum, textbooks and their teachers, who keep an eye on the kinds of attitude that school examinations reward.[9] For modern history in Australian secondary schools, this currently involves a left of centre stance, which a former neo-con government tried to stigmatise as 'black arm-band' history because of its tendency to side with people who suffered under colonialism. In other parts of the world, alternative sensibilities are propagated, and comparably surveilled by church and state.

---

[9] Martin et al. 2010 discuss this issue with reference to the role of '-isms' in history discourse and Maton's notion of axiological cosmology; the description of Diem in Text 3.14 above referenced several of these: communism, nationalism, conservativism, autocracy, colonialism, Catholicism, Buddhism.

In science, opinions may matter, especially where an ecological perspective is taken up (Veel 1998, Martin 2002a). But generally in science it is the facts that count. Contesting hypotheses arise, as we saw in relation to the formation of lightning in Text [3.25] above. But in secondary school science, students are not expected to argue for one or another of these; they are not after all in a research environment where they can contribute to a resolution. This is because science resolves differences through experimentation that brings relevant evidence to bear, not through arguments; and students are apprenticed into this reasoned perspective on evolving knowledge about the physical and biological world. This is currently a matter of serious concern for the training of science teachers in education faculties in Australia and elsewhere, where a critical/constructivist ideology has become hegemonic. Ignorance about the social processes in which knowledge is negotiated by practising scientists has spawned a widespread view of science as a one-sided view of the world that students should learn to contest. Recent graduates report to us that they have not been trained in techniques for building up students' knowledge of the discipline, but instead to critique scientific knowledge from a constructivist stance.

3.6   Building knowledge: grammatical metaphor

So far in this chapter we have outlined the kinds of meaning that constitute knowledge in science and history. The main meanings we considered were **things** in §3.3, **activity sequences** in §3.4 and **opinions** in §3.5. Within activity sequences we looked at both temporal and causal connections between events, and made a distinction between sequencing events in time (e.g. *and then*) and setting them in time (e.g. *in early October 1967*).

3.6.1   Meanings and wordings

We now need to look a little more closely at how these meanings are constructed at the level of grammar, clause by clause. This discussion of grammar is recapitulated in more detail in Chapter 5 (§5.2). We will preview it here in order to further explore written ways of knowing in the school. We will start with examples from Ridenhour's recount of the My Lai massacre, introduced in Text [3.26] above. In another part of his letter, Ridenhour reports the beginning of fellow soldier Butch Gruver's recount of the massacre as follows:

> The other two companies that made up the task force cordoned off the village so that 'Charlie' Company could move through to destroy the structures and kill the inhabitants.

In this sentence, Gruver introduces six 'entities' (people or things) that belong to two groups – the American task force and their Vietnamese target.

the task force, the other two companies, 'Charlie' Company;

the village, the structures, the inhabitants

As the attack unfolds, these entities participate in four events – two companies cordon off the village to keep villagers from escaping while 'Charlie' Company moves in.

The other two companies …[10] **cordoned off** the village

'Charlie' Company **could move** through

('Charlie' Company) to **destroy** the structures

('Charlie' Company) **kill** the inhabitants.

In terms of grammar, each of these entitiles is realised as a **nominal group** (a group of words around a noun) – *the other two companies*, *Charlie Company*, *the village*, *the structures*, *the inhabitants*. Each event is realised by a **verbal group** (one or more verbs) – *cordoned off*, *could move*, *destroy*, *kill*. The events are connected to one another by purpose and addition, creating a sequence of activity. Each connection is realised by a **conjunction** – *so that*, *to*, *and* – relating the events in the activity sequence to one another.

conjunction	nominal group	verbal group	nominal group
	= entity	= event	= entity
	The other two companies	cordoned off	the village
so that	'Charlie' Company	could move through	
to		destroy	the structures
and		kill	the inhabitants.

Ridenhour's initial reaction to Gruver's recount was a natural one for a fellow soldier – he couldn't quite believe it:

When 'Butch' told me this I didn't quite believe that what he was telling me was **true.**

His opinion here is realised grammatically as an adjective – *true* – describing his evaluation of what Gruver was saying.

The meanings of the recount match their grammatical wordings, as outlined in Table 3.1 below.

---

[10] The embedded clause *that made up the task force* is elided here since its function is not to advance the activity sequence but to clarify the composition of the task force.

Table 3.1: Meaning matching wording (congruent realisations)

meaning	wording	examples
entity (people/things)	nominal group	*The other two companies*
event	verbal group	*cordoned off*
figure (event + entities)[11]	clause	*The other two companies cordoned off the village*
activity sequence	clause complex	*so that 'Charlie' Company could move through to destroy the structures and kill the inhabitants.*
opinion (attitude)	adjective	*true*

These congruent relations between meanings and wordings are mapped onto the model of language strata we introduced in Chapter 1, as Figure 3.9.

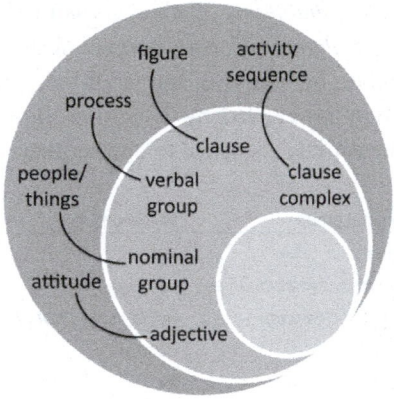

Figure 3.9: Meaning matching wording (congruent realisations)

Significantly, these relations are the kind that Nigel, Hal and Stephen depended on when first learning language in their homes. Here, as for them, people and things are realised by nominal groups, and actions and relationships are realised by verbal groups; similarly relations between events are signalled by conjunctions between clauses, and opinions are realised as adjectives that characterise things, events and activities. The relationship between meaning and wording is thus a direct one; our young language learners, along with the caregivers interacting with them, mean what they say and say what they mean. This relationship between meaning (technically **discourse semantics**) and wording (technically **lexicogrammar**) is referred to in functional linguistics as a **congruent** one.

---

[11] To simplify the presentation we will set aside the circumstances in figures at this point in the discussion (i.e. extent and location in time and place, manner, accompaniment and so on).

3.6.2   Meanings mismatching wordings

Ridenhour, however, is a mature speaker, crafting the most important letter of his life. And for various reasons his meanings do not always match his wordings. Taking attitude, for example, at one point he wants to qualify how strongly he was coming to believe in what he was hearing about My Lai. So instead of saying it was *true*,[12] he writes that he was convinced that there was *a very substantial amount of truth* to it. By expressing his opinion as a noun in a nominal group instead of an adjective, he opens up the possibility of quantifying it, and thus fine-tuning his degree of conviction at this penultimate point in his investigation.

> It also convinced me that there was **a very substantial amount of truth** to the stories that all of these men had told.

This contrasts with his initial reaction, in which he qualifies the degree to which he believed Butch's story, not how true it was.

> When 'Butch' told me this I didn't quite believe that what he was telling me was **true**, but he assured me that it was and went on to describe what had happened.

In fact, a close reading of Ridenhour's letter (along with a spoken recount of events which he gave at Tulane University in December 1994[13]) reveals that when Ridenhour departs from the congruent meaning/wording relations in Table 3.1 he is usually expressing attitude. The activity sequence Gruver recounts, for example, is referred to nominally as *an act of barbarism*:

> (Gruver recount)
>
> ...
>
> After hearing this account I couldn't quite accept it. Somehow I just couldn't believe that not only had so many young American men participated in such an act of **barbarism**, but that their officers had ordered it.

And he also evaluates event sequences nominally as *slaughter* and *murder*:

> (Gruver recount)
>
> ...
>
> It was so bad, Gruver said, that one of the men in his squad shot himself in the foot in order to be medivaced out of the area so that he would not have to participate in the **slaughter**.
>
> I'm not talking about something that's ambiguous, I'm talking about **murder**. I'm talking about

---

[12] It is of course possible to grade adjectives like true as *fairly true, quite true, very true, completely true* and son on; but Ridenhour wants to be more careful than this, and nominal groups give him more scope to adjust his charge.

[13] http://www.law.umkc.edu/faculty/projects/ftrials/mylai/Myl_hero.html#RON

somebody walking right up, pointing a gun and, without provocation, pulling the trigger.

Some specific events making up part of the sequence are also charged with feeling (e.g. *a **burst** of 16 (M-16 rifle) rifle fire* below):

> Then the captain's RTO (radio operator) put a **burst** of 16 (M-16 rifle) fire into him. It was so bad, Gruver said, that one of the men in his squad <u>shot</u> himself in the foot in order to be medivaced out of the area so that he would not have to participate in the slaughter.

Where events are not being attitudinally charged, Ridenhour is more likely to express them verbally (e.g. *transferred* and *trying to ambush* below), although some events are realised as nouns (especially where commonly expressed as such in military parlance; e.g. *orders for a transfer* and *to protect the infantry soldiers from ambush* below):

> In late April, 1968 I was awaiting orders for **a transfer from HHC, IIth Brigade to Company 'E,' 51st Inf, (LRP)**, when I happened to run into Pfc 'Butch' Gruver, whom I had known in Hawaii. Gruver told me he had been assigned to 'C' Company 1st of the 20th until April 1st when he <u>transferred</u> to the unit that I was headed for.
>
> Gruver told me he had been assigned to 'C' Company 1st of the 20th until April 1st when he went out to fly around in this village and to protect the infantry soldiers from **an ambush**. They got on line, literally they made a line long enough for all the men in two infantry companies to stretch out in one long line and then they started walking through the village. Our job was to fly over the village and to fly behind the village to see if anybody was either <u>trying to ambush</u> them or to flee.

Ridenhour's texts are autobiographical recounts and so the generally congruent relation between meaning and wording is appropriate, especially taking into account that one of his recounts was spoken (his Tulane University address). The complementary congruent and 'incongruent' wordings we are exploring here are outlined in Table 3.2.

Table 3.2: Meaning matching and mismatching wording

meaning	congruent wording	'incongruent' wording
attitude	[adjective] *true*	[noun] *truth*
figure	[clause] *he transferred to the unit*	[nominal group] *a transfer from HHC, 11th Brigade to...*
activity sequence	[clause complex] *somebody walking right up, pointing a gun and, without provocation, pulling the trigger*	[noun] *murder*

These **incongruent** relations between meanings and wordings are mapped onto the model of language strata as Figure 3.10.

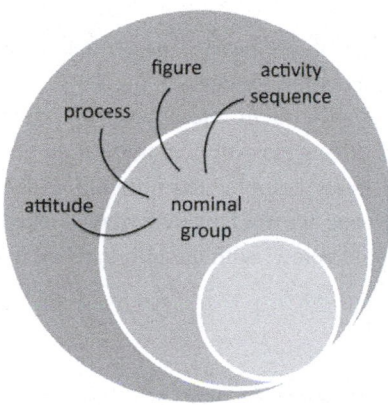

Figure 3.10: Meaning mismatching wording (incongruent realisations)

Once we move from more personal spoken recounts like Ridenhour's to historical recounts like [3.27] above, incongruent wording becomes far more common, although it is seldom attitudinally charged. This is because incongruence is useful for generalising across events and helping to package them up in phases of time (shown in bold here).

[3.27'] Historical recount

> Using **human wave attacks** the Viet-Minh overwhelmed Dien Nien Phu on 7 May, 1954. With **the fall of Dien Bien Phu**, French power in Vietnam collapsed.
>
> In August 1945 the French colony of Indo-China (Vietnam, Laos and Cambodia, now called Kampuchea) was occupied by British and Nationalist Chinese troops after **the surrender of the Japanese** who had seized it in 1941. In October 1945 the French returned determined to re-establish **their control**, especially in Vietnam. French forces easily re-occupied the southern portion of Vietnam, but were faced in the north with a new communist regime which had been established in their **absence** by the communist leader Ho Chi Minh. During the war Ho had led **the resistance** to the Japanese occupation of Vietnam, and after the war led a communist-dominated organisation which represented **Vietnamese nationalist aspirations**. Ho's organisation was known as the Viet-Minh. The French were determined to retake northern Vietnam and in 1946 began military operations against the Viet-Minh, thus triggering the first Indo-China War.

The nominal expressions *human wave* ***attacks***, *the* ***fall*** *of Dien Bien Phu, the* ***surrender*** *of the Japanese, their* ***absence***, *the* ***resistance*** *to the Japanese* ***occupation*** and *Vietnamese nationalist* ***aspirations*** all function in this way in [3.27']. A tremendous amount of military activity was going on, concisely encapsulated in these wordings.

3.6.3   Cause in the clause

Comparable encapsulation of events is also critical in historical accounts and explanations. In these genres the pressure is on not just to package up events as phases of time, but to organise them into appropriate causes and effects as well. Formulating causes and effects may involve more than one incongruent wording, which can result in relatively complicated nominal expressions (compared with the simpler nominal groups we find in everyday spoken language). Examples from text [3.29] are in bold below, with the nominalised events underlined.

[3.29'] Historical account

> America's response to <u>developments</u> in Vietnam was dramatically influenced by two events:
> - in 1949, China fell to the communists. This intensified **the <u>fears</u> of a global communist <u>expansion</u>**, and led **to <u>criticism</u> of the Democrat President Truman from members of the rival Republican Party in the US**. Republicans blamed Truman for 'losing China'
> - in 1950, President Truman saw **the <u>outbreak</u> of the Korean War** as a deliberate **<u>challenge</u> to world peace and his policy of <u>containment</u>**. The <u>containment</u> policy had been put in place in March 1947 as the Truman Doctrine, with **the <u>intention</u> of halting the global <u>spread</u> of communism by supporting anti-communist regimes**. At the same time that Truman committed US forces to Korea, he ordered a **major military <u>assistance</u> package** for the French in Indochina. American aid was administered by the Military Assistance and Advisory Group Indochina (MAAGI). Aid to the French and the forces of SOV in the form of weapons and equipment amounted to between $2.6 and $3 billion (Dennett and Dixon 2003: 435).

More spoken variations on some of these would include *they **feared** that the communists would **expand** around the world, the Korean War **broke out**, America tried to **contain** communism*. More significantly, because causes and effects are now realised inside clauses as nominal groups, the causal relations connecting them have to be specified inside clauses as well. In our discussion of science explanations [3.24] and historical accounts [3.28] above we noted the variety of ways in which cause was expressed (using conjunctions, verbs, prepositions, nouns, adverbs and adjectives). When cause is expressed inside the clause, the main incongruent wordings involve nominal groups, prepositional phrases and especially verbal groups. Text [3.30] above, a consequential explanation, has examples of each of these.

[3.30'] Consequential explanation

> The Vietnam war, which is the main topic of this chapter, also had **a major impact** on the twentieth century national history of the USA and was one of the defining events of the Cold War.
> Professor David Kennedy of Stanford University has argued that the cost and trauma of the Vietnam War **produced** a 'crisis of confidence' in the USA. Until the Vietnam War, Americans had

generally felt confident in their ability to mould events **through** the exercise of their ingenuity, energy and vast economic resources. Vietnam proved to be a problem that they couldn't manage.

The Vietnam conflict **gave rise to** social division and distrust of government in the US. It ended the political career of President Lyndon Johnson and his dreams of major social reform. It also **produced**, in the case of Richard Nixon's presidency, a siege mentality that **contributed** directly to the infamous Watergate Scandal (1973-74) and the resignation, in disgrace, of Nixon. **Because of** the Vietnam War, as part of the wider conflict in Indochina, a generation of Americans identified with anti-conscription and anti-war protest movements. Many of the social and political effects evident in the US were also present in Australia.

The pattern of figures realised by nominal groups, with their causal relation realised by verbal groups is diagrammed in Figure 3.11.

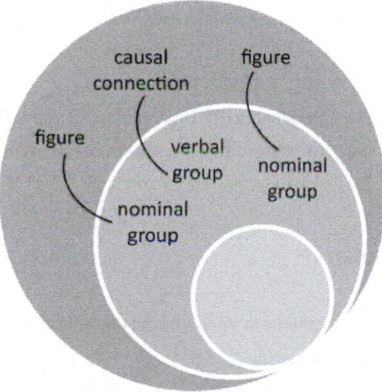

Figure 3.11: Cause realised as a verbal group

Table 3.3: Cause in the clause in consequential explanation [3.30′]

cause	causal connection	effect
the cost and trauma of the Vietnam War	**produced** (verbal)	a 'crisis of confidence' in the USA
the Vietnam conflict	**gave rise to** (verbal)	social division and distrust of government in the US
It (the Vietnam conflict)	**produced** (verbal)	a siege mentality
that (a siege mentality)	**contributed** (verbal)	to the infamous Watergate Scandal (1973-74) and the resignation, in disgrace, of Nixon
Vietnam war	**because of** (prepositional)	a generation of Americans identified with anti-conscription and anti-war protest movements

the exercise of their ingenuity, energy and vast economic resources.	**through** (prepositional)	their ability to mould events
the Vietnam war	**a major impact** (nominal)	on the twentieth century national history of the USA

By realising causal connections inside the clause, historians are able to fine tune the effect of one event upon another. In [3.30], for example, a contrast is set up between events which *had a major impact* on others with those that simply *contributed*; and the verbal groups *produced* and *gave rise to* fill in the middle ground as far as causal impact is concerned.

... contributed to ... gave rise to ... through ... produced ... because of ... a major impact ...

————————————————————————————————————▶

force of causality

Another advantage of realising cause/effect relations between historical events inside the clause is that it makes room between clauses to organise texts which are not chronologically organised. This is managed through bullet points in the factorial explanation [3.29] above.

[3.29'] Factorial explanation

> America's response to **developments** in Vietnam was dramatically influenced by two events:
> - in 1949, China fell to the communists ...
> - in 1950, President Truman saw the **outbreak** of the Korean War as a deliberate **challenge** to world peace and his policy of **containment** ...

Contributing factors could be further scaffolded with conjunctions in a more fully developed essay (e.g. *first of all*, *in addition*). The canonical exposition [3.31] above explicitly scaffolds its argument structure with conjunctions flagging the sequence of their presentation.

[3.31'] Exposition

> We should be very careful about passing judgements on some incident or person in history.
> **Firstly**, the events under study probably took place in a setting and at a time much different from our own ...
> **Secondly**, we should make sure that we have access to as much information as possible about the events and the people involved before passing judgment.
> **Finally** it is necessary for us to establish criteria by which we can make the judgement.

Firstly, secondly, finally are not, to be sure, specifying the sequence in which the research activities prescribed should be put into practice – since they are all relevant, all the time. Rather their function is to organise the arguments. This text-organising function is known as internal conjunction.

3.6.4   Building technicality in science

Cause in the clause is also an important resource in scientific explanations for packaging information as cause and effect. In science, however, it is not used to anywhere near the same extent to fine tune causality – since scientific reasoning depends on simple cause/effect relations, not contextually sensitive interpretations of just how one thing affects another. The lightning explanation [3.25] above consistently reasons inside the clause to outline one hypothesis about how lightning is formed, and depends on multiple nominal realisations of events to do so. These nominalisations are in bold below and causal connections underlined.

[3.25'] Lightning explanation

According to the **electrostatic induction** hypothesis **charges** are <u>driven apart</u> by **as-yet uncertain processes**. **Charge separation** <u>appears to require</u> **strong updrafts** which carry water droplets upward, supercooling them to between -10 and -20 °C. These collide with ice crystals to form a soft ice-water mixture called graupel. **The collisions** <u>result</u> in **a slight positive charge** being transferred to ice crystals, and **a slight negative charge** to the graupel. Updrafts <u>drive</u> the less heavy ice crystals upwards, <u>causing</u> the cloud top to accumulate **increasing positive charge**. Gravity <u>causes</u> the heavier negatively charged graupel to fall toward the middle and lower portions of the cloud, <u>building up</u> an increasing negative charge. **Charge separation and accumulation** continue until **the electrical potential** becomes sufficient to <u>initiate</u> **a lightning discharge**, which occurs when **the distribution of positive and negative charges** forms a sufficiently strong electric field.

Table 3.4: Cause in the clause in science explanation [3.25]

cause	causal connection	effect
as-yet uncertain processes	are driven	charges
strong updrafts which carry water droplets upward, supercooling them to between -10 and -20 °C.	appears to require	charge separation
the collisions	result in	a slight positive charge being transferred to ice crystals, and a slight negative charge to the graupel
gravity	causes	the heavier negatively charged graupel to fall toward the middle and lower portions of the cloud

[the heavier negatively charged graupel to fall toward the middle and lower portions of the cloud]	**building up**	an increasing negative charge.
Charge separation and accumulation continue until the electrical potential	**becomes sufficient to initiate**	a lightning discharge
the distribution of positive and negative charges forms a ... strong electric field	**sufficiently** [14]	which (a lightning discharge) occurs

Most of the incongruent wordings in [3.25] involve technical terms such as *electrostatic induction* and *positive charge*, precisely because definitions regularly depend on such wording to distil the right package of meaning as an uncommonsense thing. To explore this let us return to Lesurf's classification of conducting substances, introduced in Text [3.9] and Figure 3.3 above. Lesurf subclassifies extrinsic semi-conductors as follows:

> There are two main types of semiconductor materials:
> • intrinsic - *where the semiconducting properties of the material occur naturally i.e. they are intrinsic to the material's nature.*
> • extrinsic - *the semiconducting properties of the material are manufactured, by us, to make the material behave in the manner which we require.*

And he then notes the two most common ways of manufacturing the semi-conducting properties of extrinsic semi-conductors.

> Several different semiconducting materials exist, but the most common semiconductor material is Silicon and the two most common methods of modifying the electronic properties are:
> • *Doping - the addition of 'foreign' atoms to the material.*
> • *Junction effects - the things that happen when we join differing materials together.*

Notice here that the definition of doping is the incongruent nominal group *the addition of foreign atoms to the material*, and that the technical term for the second method is itself the incongruent nominal group ***junction effects***. Lesurf then redefines doping with another incongruent nominal group (*the process by which* …), and subsequently 'unpacks' the defining process (establishing two further technical terms, *bulk* and *dopant* as he goes):

> Doping is **the process by which** engineers change an insulating material into a semiconductor. The basic process inserts a small 'population' of a foreign element into the crystal lattice of the

---

[14] Cf. an alternate wording which makes the causality more transparent: *when the distribution of positive and negative charges forms an electric field strong enough to cause a lightning discharge.*

insulator. For example, we might insert some boron atoms into a lump of - otherwise very pure - silicon. It is conventional to call the main material the *bulk* and the small number of foreign atoms the *dopant.*

The result of this kind of doping is then outlined by way of defining n-type extrinsic semi-conductors; the anaphoric phrase *in this way* gathers up the meanings being distilled as 'n-type' semi-conductors:

> The **effect** of doping is to provide the bulk material with a population of free electrons which have been 'borrowed' from - or *donated* by - the dopant. Semiconductors manufactured in this way are called n-type because the free charge carriers we have created are negative (electrons) and there are no corresponding holes in the valence band.

Note the cause-in-the-clause noun *effect* used here. An alternative process, which adds a dopant which freely accepts electrons rather than donating them, establishes the 'p-type' extrinsic insulators. The resulting uncommonsense classification of conducting substances is outlined in Figure 3.12.

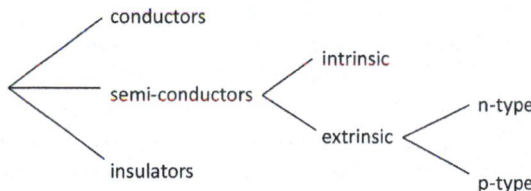

Figure 3.12: Further classification of conducting substances

As we can see, building an uncommonsense classification of this kind, and thereby establishing its technical terms, takes a lot of explaining. And we have only touched on Lesurf's reader-friendly account here. The point we are emphasising through this scientific domain is that if it were not for incongruent wordings, then technical terms, their definitions, the criteria by which they are defined, resulting classifications and decompositions and attendant theoretical relations could not have been established (Halliday and Martin 1993, Martin and Veel 1998, Halliday 2004). Similarly, without incongruent wordings, phases of Vietnam war history, the -isms involved, the ways that events affect one another, the ways outcomes are valued, and arguments about how to interpret the past could not have been formulated (Coffin 2006, Martin and Wodak 2003, Schleppegrell 2004). Scientific and historical understandings, like all uncommonsense ones, are built up through incongruent language; and learning to read and write language of this kind is thus the most important task faced by students in secondary school.

3.7   Mapping the genres of schooling

The *Write it Right* project mapped the major genres that students need to control for success in the secondary school. Figure 3.13 sets out the most common ones as a taxonomy organised by their social purposes, and by contrasts in their features. The function of this map is to provide teachers with an overview of the tasks they need to prepare their students for.

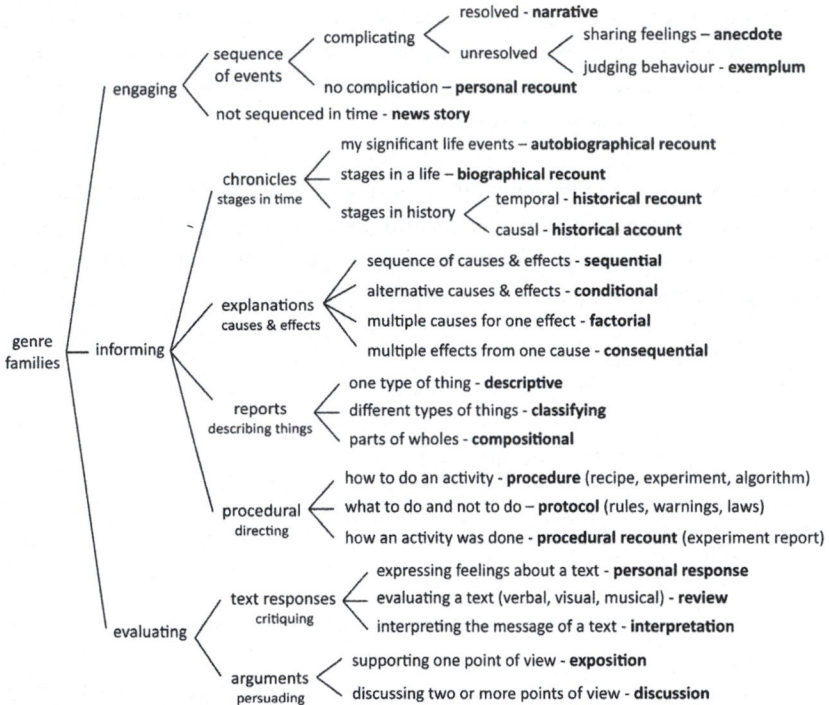

Figure 3.13: Map of genres in school

Figure 3.13 can be used to introduce teachers to systematic principles for selecting and analysing texts in their curriculum programs, starting with the social purposes of genres, their stages and phases. The names for each genre constitute the first level of metalanguage they can use to teach reading and writing. The taxonomy is summarised for teachers as follows, in terms that connect with their own knowledge of their curricula. In other words, teachers are already familiar with these genres, but without explicitly naming them. Naming and organising them in this taxonomy brings that intuitive knowledge of genres to consciousness – a first and necessary step in being able to teach them explicitly.

The first choice in the genre map is between texts whose central purpose is to engage, inform or evaluate. Any text has multiple purposes; it is its primary purpose that shapes its staging, and the family of genres it belongs to. A common purpose of stories is to engage readers, so a focus of teaching stories is on the language that authors use to engage readers. A common purpose of factual texts is to inform readers, so a teaching focus is on the information they present. The common purpose of evaluating texts is to evaluate either texts, in the case of text responses, or issues and points of view, in the case of arguments. So a teaching focus with these genres is on the evaluative language that writers use to evaluate and persuade.

Engaging: stories

There are five main types of stories: a recount simply recounts a series of events, but in a narrative the central characters resolve a complication; anecdotes share feelings about a complicating event that is not resolved, while an exemplum judges people's character or behaviour. Unlike the other story types, news stories (in western broadsheet newspapers, especially English ones) are not sequenced in time, but first engage the reader with a newsworthy event and then report different angles on it.

Informing: chronicles, explanations, reports, procedures

The set of genres that we have grouped as 'chronicles' includes autobiographical recounts, in which the writer recounts the major events in his or her life; biographical recounts tell the stages in a person's life; historical recounts and accounts cover the stages in a period of history; stages are connected temporally in recounts but causally in accounts. Explanations are concerned with causes and effects: sequential explanations explain a sequence of events; conditional explanations present alternative causes producing different effects (if ... then); factorial explanations explain multiple causes for one effect; consequential explanations explain multiple effects of one cause. Procedural texts include procedures for doing experiments and observations, using technology, or making things, as well as algorithms or operations in maths; protocols tell what not to do, such as rules and warnings; procedural recounts outline the steps that have been done in a procedure, such as experiment reports and observation reports. Reports classify and describe things: a descriptive report classifies and describes one kind of thing; a classifying report classifies different types of things; a compositional report describes parts of wholes.

Evaluating: arguments and text responses

Text responses evaluate texts (verbal, visual, musical): personal responses express feelings about a text, often with a retelling of the story; reviews describe the text and make a judgement about it; interpretations interpret the message that a text symbolises. Argument genres evaluate issues and points of view: expositions argue for a point of view, but discussions debate two or more points of view about an issue.

The second level of metalanguage is the names for stages that each genre goes through to achieve its social purpose. These are set out in Table 3.5.

Table 3.5: Genres and stages

	genre	purpose	stages
Stories	recount	recounting events	Orientation Record of events
	narrative	resolving a complication in a story	Orientation Complication Resolution
	exemplum	judging character or behaviour in a story	Orientation Incident Interpretation
	anecdote	sharing an emotional reaction in a story	Orientation Remarkable event Reaction
Histories	autobiographical recount	recounting life events	Orientation Record of stages
	biographical recount	recounting life stages	Orientation Record of stages
	historical recount	recounting historical events	Background Record of stages
	historical account	explaining historical events	Background Account of stages
Explanations	sequential explanation	explaining a sequence	Phenomenon Explanation
	conditional explanation	alternative causes and effects	Phenomenon Explanation
	factorial explanation	explaining multiple causes	Phenomenon: outcome Explanation: factors
	consequential explanation	explaining multiple effects	Phenomenon: cause Explanation: consq.
Procedures	procedure	how to do experiments and observations	Purpose Equipment Steps
	procedural recount	recounting experiments and observations	Purpose Method Results
Reports	descriptive report	classifying and describing a phenomenon	Classification Description
	classifying report	classifying and describing types of phenomena	Classification Description: types
	compositional report	describing parts of wholes	Classification Description: parts
Arguments	exposition	arguing for a point of view	Thesis Arguments Reiteration
	discussion	discussing two or more points of view	Issue Sides Resolution
Text Responses	review	evaluating a literary, visual or musical text	Context Description of text Judgement
	interpretation	interpreting the message of a text	Evaluation Synopsis of text Reaffirmation
	critical response	challenging the message of a text	Evaluation Deconstruction Challenge

As we explore these genres in this book (and in Martin and Rose 2008), we usually go a step further than their stages, to name and discuss the phases they go through within each stage. Where stages are obligatory steps that each instance of the genre typically goes through, phases are often more variable (as we noted in Chapter 3). For example, stories of all types are created from phases such as settings, problems, characters' reactions to problems, solutions and descriptions. How these are arranged depends very much on the ingenuity of the author, discussed in Chapter 4 below. On the other hand, phases in some factual genres are more predictable, such as the **type** phases that distinguish classifying reports [3.9-12] above, and the **part** phases that distinguish compositional reports [3.13].

A third perspective to round off the discussion of genres and knowledge in the school curriculum is the topology of genres and their purposes in Figure 3.14 below.

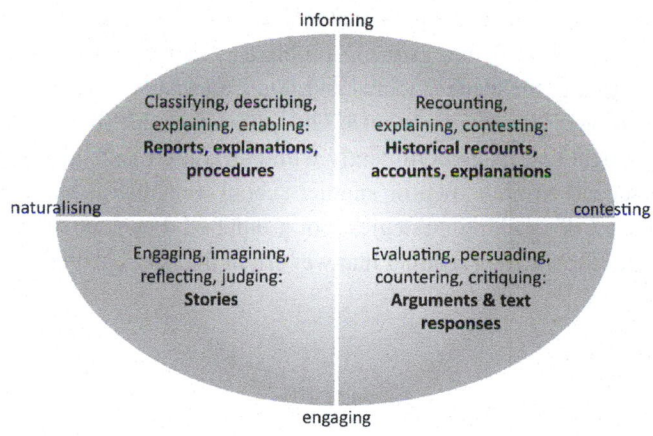

Figure 3.14: Genres and types of knowledge in the school curriculum

In contrast to the typological organisation of Figure 3.13 (categorising as either/or), this topology organises genres in terms of their tendencies along two axes – the extent to which their primary purpose is to provide information about a field or to engage readers' feelings and judgements – and to present things and events as natural, or to contest viewpoints about them. The social purposes of the genres in the top left, top right and bottom right quadrants have been discussed in this chapter; stories and text responses will be explored further in Chapter 4.

However, these categorisations are only tendencies. For example, the texts in the top left tend to present scientific or technological information as fact, more natural than contestable, so that contested scientific hypotheses often stand out as newsworthy. On the other hand, we expect the historical texts in the top right to take a position in relation to other views, more or less explicitly. If history is presented merely as fact it may be regarded as either dull or one-sided. Arguments and text critiques are by definition contesting other voices, but in deft hands their conclusions can flow so naturally that they appear uncontestable. And stories can weave their writers' judgements into the events so seamlessly that the reader scarcely realises they are moralising at all.

Any particular text can be positioned along these two axes, towards their centres or their margins. One of the principles for analysing texts, that we have endeavoured to emphasise and model here, is that teachers need to look at each text with open eyes, using the guidelines we present here, combined with their knowledge of the curriculum subject and a healthy dose of commonsense.

We said earlier that any genre has multiple purposes – so, for example, stories and arguments can certainly inform readers, as well as engage them, and science and history need to engage their readers, as well as inform them. Of course, science and history texts will not engage students who are not sufficiently literate to read them. An unfortunate path that publishers and education departments have taken in reaction to this growing problem is to try and make curriculum texts more engaging for these students and less informative – so they look more like magazines and less like textbooks. Our position is directly opposite: every student has a right to engage confidently with curriculum texts at the same level as the top students in their own or another school. For this to happen, teachers need a better set of teaching strategies, not a dumbed down set of texts. It is to these strategies for teaching reading that we turn in the next chapter.

4 *Reading to Learn*

This chapter outlines the third generation of genre pedagogy, known as *Reading to Learn*. The chapter begins with its starting point in Indigenous education in Australia, and then outlines two key components: the design of classroom interactions and the model of reading. It next outlines strategies for reading three sets of genres: stories, factual texts and arguments. Each section includes strategies for preparing for reading, for reading in detail, and for using what has been learnt from reading to write new texts. The focus is on integrating reading and writing with learning the curriculum in the primary and secondary school.

4.1 From learning to write to *Reading to Learn*

The *Reading to Learn* program outlined in this chapter extends genre pedagogy's principle of embedded literacy, to integrate the teaching of reading and writing across the curriculum at all levels of school and beyond. To this end it is grounded in the research in language and writing pedagogy described in Chapters 2 and 3, and also incorporates strategies for teaching reading, in an integrated approach that has been designed and refined through extensive classroom application and teacher professional learning programs (Rose 2005, 2007, 2008a, 2011a, b, Rose and Acevedo 2006, Koop and Rose 2008).

Although it is now implemented in mainstream education programs across Australia and internationally, *Reading to Learn* was initially designed to meet the needs of Indigenous school students from remote communities in central Australia, with whom David had worked for many years. His mentors in this work were the Pitjantjatjara elders, Nganyintja and Charlie Ilyatjari, who ran cultural and education programs for young people at risk in the Pitjantjatjara communities. Nganyinytja (to whom this book is dedicated) had been the first Indigenous teaching assistant in the region in the 1950s. By the 1980s, she and other community leaders and parents were deeply concerned that their children were finishing primary school with little or no literacy in English, and no possibility of completing secondary or further education (Tjungutu Uwankaraku 1985, Jabangardi Poulson 1988, Lester 1993, Martin 1990a, Rose 1992).

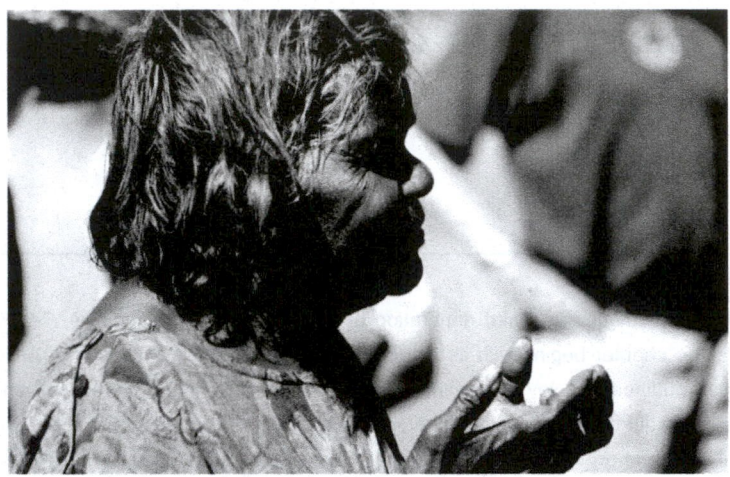

Figure 4.1: Nganyinytja speaking on education in 1993

To address this need, David initiated the project *Scaffolding Reading and Writing for Indigenous Children in School*, in collaboration with Brian Gray and Wendy Cowey of the Schools and Community Centre, Canberra University (Rose, Gray and Cowey 1999). In the early 1980s, Gray had developed successful strategies for teaching Indigenous children to read, using texts their teachers had written together with them (Gray 1986, 1987, 1990). At the Schools and Community Centre, Gray, Cowey and colleagues had developed a program for teaching children who were failing to read in upper primary years (Axford, Harder and Wise 2009). The scaffolding reading program emphasised building understanding of a text before starting to read it, and carefully planning teacher–learner interactions to provide maximum support.

In the first phase of this project, David worked with teachers of Pitjantjatjara secondary school students to synthesise the genre writing pedagogy and *Write it Right* research with these reading strategies, producing encouraging results. At the start of the project's first year, almost all these secondary students, even up to Year 10, were reading at junior primary levels despite continual intensive one-on-one support in classes and homework from tutors and ESL specialists. By the end of the project's first year, all students were reading at age-appropriate levels (McRae et al. 2000, Gray, Rose and Cowey 1998). One such student was Craig, whose report on Goannas we met in Chapter 2, reproduced here as [4.1].

[4.1] Craig's initial writing sample

> Goannas
>
> Goannas are native animals that live in isolated place and they are reptiles
>
> ~~Goannas are all way the same as the~~
>
> Goannas look as same as area where the live ~~they~~ in. They camouflage their self with the area their colour looks like yellowish-brown and they eat insec dead animals
>
> Goannas breed about six eggs
>
> Aboriginals hunt goannas for food and the fat inside the goannas are used for medicine.

Craig was a Year 10 student with Pitjantjatjara as his first language and the dialect known as Aboriginal English as his second. He had attended the primary school in his community until Year 7, exposed to the usual mix of whole language, process writing, phonics and sight word drills known as a 'balanced approach' in Australian primary schools. He had then attended an urban secondary school with intensive ESL support and tutoring for three years. This text was written following lessons on the topic (reptiles) and joint construction of the report genre. Its standard was typical, not only for Craig but for all the Indigenous students in his secondary school program, and for many others all over Australia. His teacher, Wayne Wearne-Jarvis, then used the techniques of Detailed Reading and Rewriting (described below in this chapter) in a lesson sequence beginning with a primary school text about goannas, then with a secondary school text on the same topic, then set a research task for the students to write their own report on an animal of their choosing. Craig independently researched and wrote the report on Komodo dragons shown in Text [4.2], two months after the goannas Text [4.1].

Text [4.2] is a first draft, in which Craig still has issues with English grammar but few problems with understanding and explaining the field he has researched. This report went on for another page after this one, providing more detail about a topic which he clearly found fascinating. After a few more months of teaching, Craig was consistently researching and writing well-organised texts in standard English, such the first draft of a report on butterflies in Text [4.3].

[4.2] Craig's writing after 2 months

The largest of all lizards would be the Komodo Dragon which has a strong body also long tail. The Komodo Dragon has scales all over it's body and can grow to ten feet long. The Komodo Dragon has very visible hearhole and you can see their nostrils on the end their snout. The Komodo Dragon has the same tongue like the goanna in Australia the tongue is forked like a snake. The Komodo Dragon has teeth, less than an inch long which is covered by spongy gum

The Komodo Dragon is a Einsiten of it own world or reptiles. The Komodo Dragon knows that he has caught food before in area were these animals. The Komodo Dragon ambushe it's prey the dragon knows that there is a goat or a deer coming towards him the way the dragon knows because it's has a tongue sticking out of it mouths When the animal gets close to the dragon the dragon does not show no sign of excitement.

The dragon has six-sens which is a combation on smell and taste. When the Komodo dragon sticks its tongue out the chemical on the goat or the deer is collected by the tongue then the chemical from the animal is drops down to the pad then the information is sent to the brain. The komodo dragon then tries to kill the prey. If the dragon bites the deer then the deer dies in a different way which poison by the dragon bite. If the dragon gets it prey it bites it's throat and shakes crazy and then it swallows it's prey, the dragon swallows it prey to help thick gobs of spit

The largest of all lizards would be the Komodo Dragon which has a strong body also long tail. The Komodo Dragon has scales all over its body and can grow to ten feet long. The Komodo Dragon has very visible hearhole and you can see their nostrils on the end of their snout. The Komodo Dragon has the same tongue like the goanna in Australia the tongue is forked like a snake. The Komodo Dragon has teeth, less than an inch long which is covered by spongy gum.

The Komodo Dragon is a Einstein of its own world of reptiles. The Komodo Dragon knows that he has caught food before in an area where there (are) animals. The Komodo Dragon ambush its prey the dragon knows that there is a goat or deer coming towards him the way the dragon knows because it has a tongue sticking out of it. When the animal gets close the dragon does not show no sign of excitement.

The dragon has six-sense which is a combination of smell and taste. When the Komodo dragon sticks its tongue out the chemical on the goat or the deer is collected by the tongue then the chemical from the animal drops down to the pad then information (is) sent to the brain. The Komodo Dragon then catches the prey and tries to kill the prey. If the dragon bites the prey then it dies in a different way which (is) poisoned by the dragon bite. If the dragon gets its prey it bites its throat and shakes crazy and then it swallows its prey. The dragon swallows its prey it helps thick gobs of spit …

[4.3] Craig's writing after 6 months

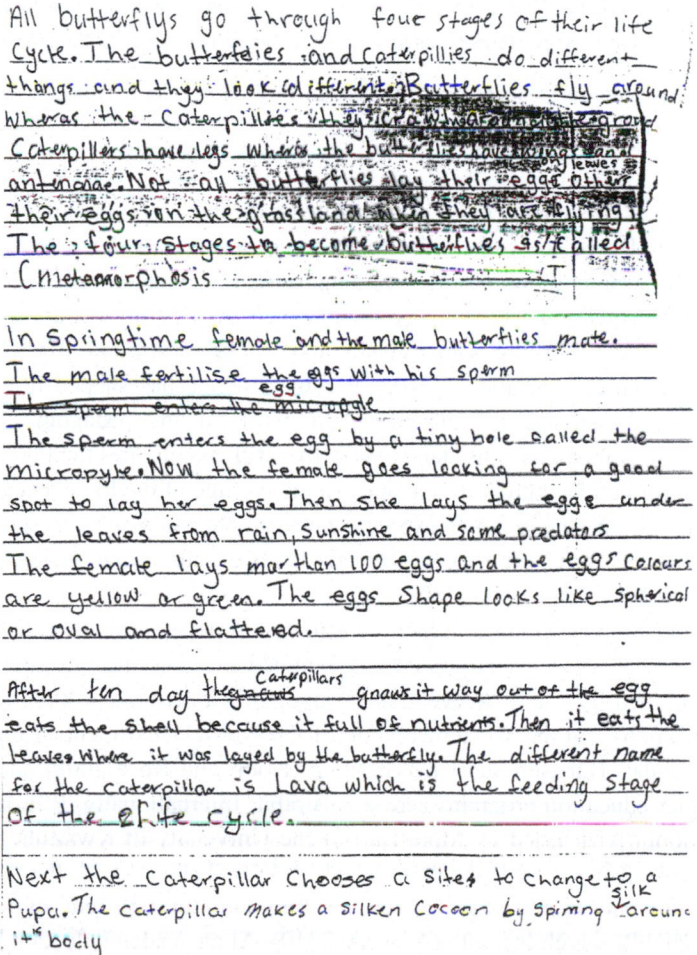

All butterflies go through four stages of their life cycle. The butterflies and caterpillars do different things and they look different. Butterflies fly around wheras the caterpillars crawl around on the ground. Caterpillars have legs wheras the butterflies have wings and antennae. Not all butterflies lay their eggs on leaves. Others lay their eggs on the grassland when they are flying. The four stages to become butterflies is called metamorphosis.

In springtime female and male butterflies mate. The male fertilise the eggs with his sperm. The sperm enters the egg by a tiny hole called a microphyle. Now the female goes looking for a spot to lay her eggs. Then she lays the eggs under the leaves (away) from rain, sunshine and some predators. The female lays more than 100 eggs and the eggs colours are yellow or green. The eggs shape looks like spherical or oval and flattened.

After ten days the caterpillar gnaws it way out of the egg and eats the shell because it is full of nutrients. Then it eats the leaves where it was layed by the butterfly. The different name for the caterpillars is lava which is the feeding stage of the life cycle.

Next the caterpillar chooses a site to change to a pupa. The caterpillar makes a silken cocoon by spinning silk around its body...

The success of students like Craig attracted national attention and led to many requests for David to work with school programs across the country. In the decade since, many thousands of Australian school students have benefited from the teacher professional learning program which became known as *Reading to Learn* (or R2L). Working with teachers and teacher educators at all levels of school and further education, across all subject areas, has shaped the methodology to be broad and flexible enough to work in any pedagogic situation. Independent evaluations consistently show that R2L accelerates the literacy of all students, from all backgrounds and ages, at an average of double expected learning rates, and up to four times expected rates for the students who started with the weakest skills. The most consistent results are with whole classes (Culican 2006, Rose 2011c, Rose et al. 2008).

Key education programs that have contributed to developing the R2L program and professional learning program have included the Catholic Education Office Melbourne, led by Claire Acevedo and Sarah Culican (Culican 2006, Rose and Acevedo 2006) and the Western Region of the NSW Department of Education, led by Lyndall Harrison and Cheryll Koop (Koop and Rose 2008), along with many other education programs across Australia. Internationally, R2L has taken root in South Africa, led by Mike Hart of the University of KwaZulu Natal, in Afghanistan, Kenya and Uganda, initiated by Fran Tolhurst with the Aga Khan Foundation, and in Scandinavia, led by Ann-Christin Lovstëdt of Sweden's Multilingual Research Institute (Acevedo 2010). At an academic level it has been implemented with international, Indigenous and mainstream students at universities around Australia (Rose, Chivizhe, McKnight and Smith 2004, Rose et al. 2008), and in South Africa, China, Indonesia and Latin America. It has also been the subject of PhD research in South Africa, Australia and China (Chen 2010, Childs 2008, Culican 2007, Liu 2010).

4.2   A functional perspective on reading

The chapter is organised as follows. To begin with, the task of learning reading is addressed from two perspectives: the problem of teaching reading in the classroom, and the nature of the reading task itself. This sets the context for describing the *Reading to Learn* methodology, which involves a set of strategies for reading and writing that can be applied in various teaching contexts. The strategies vary across the genres outlined in Chapters 2 and 3; strategies are described for working with stories (§4.3), factual texts (§4.4) and arguments (§4.5). Each of these sections begins with strategies for working with texts at primary or junior secondary level, and then extended with strategies for more challenging texts. More intensive strategies for teaching foundation literacy skills are outlined in §4.6, and strategies for teaching beginning literacy in the first years of school are described in §4.7.

4.2.1   Designing classroom interactions

One of the issues that became apparent early in the *Scaffolding Reading and Writing* project, and later in all manner of school contexts, was that the problems with reading experienced by Indigenous students are also experienced by a significant proportion of students from all backgrounds. Not only are these students unable to read at the levels they need in order to engage in the school curriculum, but they are also less likely to engage actively in classroom learning. As mentioned in Chapter 1, the teachers we work with report that only a minority of their students consistently respond to their classroom questions with answers that the teacher can affirm; most respond rarely and less successfully, while others barely participate. From classroom studies, Nuthall (2005: 919) reports that:

> teachers are very largely cut off from information about what individual students are learning. Because of the numbers of students that teachers have to manage simultaneously, and because of the individuality of student learning, teachers must rely on routines and rituals that we believe are good for students … Typically, a few students contribute the majority of the ideas, a few more students contribute one or two ideas, and most students are silent.

Moreover, the proportions in each group vary with the socioeconomic context of the school. Teachers in lower socioeconomic areas report the fewest number of students who consistently respond, often just one, two or three out of a class of 20 or 30. In Indigenous community classrooms, where no students are able or willing to respond to teacher questions, the result is the communication break-down described by Malcolm (1991) and the widespread turn to undemanding busywork reported by Folds (1987).

This presents a double challenge for reading pedagogy in the school. On one hand we need to provide teachers with a set of strategies that can rapidly develop students' reading and writing skills; on the other they need to deliver these strategies to whole classes of students with a wide range of abilities and engagement in learning. Furthermore, the students most in need of the strategies' benefits are often the least engaged and responsive in the classroom. One response to this problem has been to divide the class into 'ability groups' in which students read and discuss different levels of texts. The outcome of this practice, as we discussed in §1.3.3, is to widen the gap between high- and low-achieving students. Instead, teachers need tools to redesign their classroom discourse to engage and support their weakest students, while continuing to extend their most successful students. So on top of delivering an effective reading and writing pedagogy, we needed a better understanding of how learning actually occurred through teacher–learner interactions.

With respect to reading, a fertile place to start is in parent-child reading in the home. In reading with their young children, parents work with a repertoire of strategies to draw their attention, model behaviours, affirm them and elaborate their understandings, in order to engage them in the act of reading as a meaningful activity (Rose 2010a). How this engagement with books develops is illustrated in the following interaction between a mother and her 18-month-old child (from McGee 1998: 163), around *The Three Little Pigs* [4.4]. The extract includes three cycles of interaction, over four pages of the book. Although the primary purpose of the reading activity is shared pleasure rather than teaching, parent-child reading is nevertheless a learning activity, in which the child's task is to identify elements in the story. In each cycle in [4.4] below the mother focuses the child's attention, the child identifies an element, and the mother elaborates. These elements of the learning exchange are included in the nuclear model we developed in Chapter 1, as Figure 4.2.

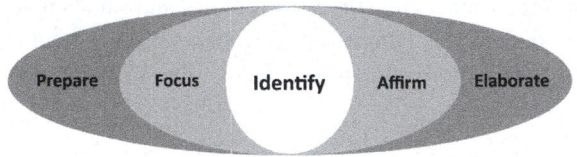

Figure 4.2: Phases in parent-child reading exchange [4.4]

[4.4] Parent-child reading at age 1:6

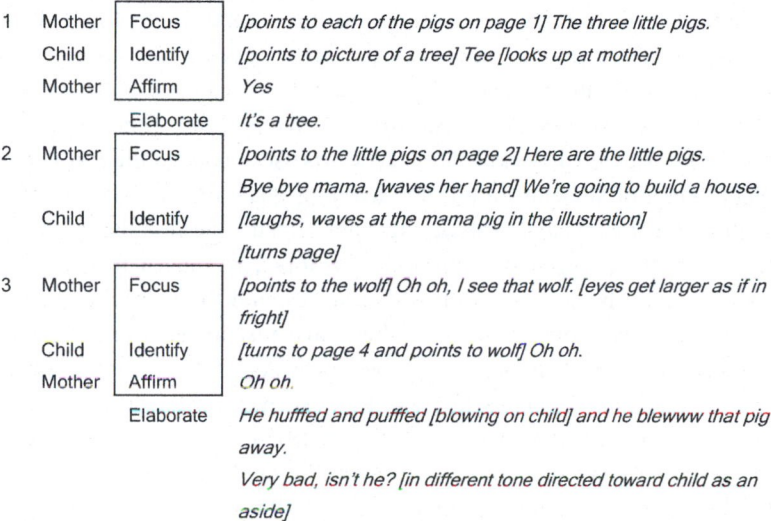

1	Mother	Focus	*[points to each of the pigs on page 1] The three little pigs.*
	Child	Identify	*[points to picture of a tree] Tee [looks up at mother]*
	Mother	Affirm	*Yes*
		Elaborate	*It's a tree.*
2	Mother	Focus	*[points to the little pigs on page 2] Here are the little pigs.*
			Bye bye mama. [waves her hand] We're going to build a house.
	Child	Identify	*[laughs, waves at the mama pig in the illustration]*
			[turns page]
3	Mother	Focus	*[points to the wolf] Oh oh, I see that wolf. [eyes get larger as if in fright]*
	Child	Identify	*[turns to page 4 and points to wolf] Oh oh.*
	Mother	Affirm	*Oh oh.*
		Elaborate	*He hufffed and pufffed [blowing on child] and he blewww that pig away.*
			Very bad, isn't he? [in different tone directed toward child as an aside]

In the first Focus, the mother points and names the story's main characters. The child does not simply imitate her mother, but responds with her own innovation by pointing and naming a tree in the picture. After affirming her, the mother elaborates by modelling correct pronunciation in a full sentence. In the second cycle, the Focus progresses from identifying characters to engaging the child's empathy with them, *Bye bye mama* [waves her hand], and expectancy of events to come, *We're going to build a house*. These are not the words in the text, but what is happening in the picture, explained in terms the child understands, so she responds by laughing and waving at the picture. In the third cycle, the Focus extends to emotional reactions, with the apprehensive *Oh oh, I see that wolf*, interpreting the pig's facial expression with her own, modelling empathy with the character. The child responds by identifying the next picture of the wolf and repeating *Oh oh*, and the mother elaborates by reading the words on the page and blowing on the child, imitating the wolf in the image. Recognising the wolf's behaviour in both words and image then provides a context for judging his character: *Very bad, isn't he?*

In this brief excerpt, the child's attention has been drawn to features that identify main characters, engage readers in their activities, expect sequences of events, enact emotional reactions, and judge their behaviour. The mother carefully and deliberately interprets the meanings in the book for the child. She adjusts, translates and reduces the meanings expressed by words and images in the book, down to the level of spoken language she knows the child will understand. The continual affirmations serve to engage the child in the activity of story reading, but they also give intense positive value to the meanings that the mother presents and the child repeats. Each exchange of value-laden meanings then expands the child's capacity for understanding a further elaboration, which the mother usually takes advantage of.

Patterns of learning interactions in the home exemplified in [4.4] are recontextualised in the school as the 'IRF' cycles of classroom discourse, discussed in Chapter 2 above (Alexander 2000, Christie 2002, Gibbons 2002, Lemke 1990, Mercer 2000, Nassaji and Wells 2000, Sinclair and Coulthard 1975). Perhaps the key skill that teachers possess is the ability to interact with a whole class of students around the learning goals of a lesson. Teachers initiate each interaction cycle by asking the class a focus question that is relevant to the task they are engaged in – discussing a topic, reading a text, or constructing another text. The students' task is then to respond to the teacher's question, and the answer may come from what they have just learnt, from the text they are reading, or from their previous experience. As in the parent–child exchanges above, students' responses are always evaluated by the teacher, and are then usually elaborated (the 'feedback' slot in IRF terms). The elaboration contains the teaching goal; the students' response is the stepping stone that allows the teacher to bridge from what students already know to new knowledge that is the goal of the lesson. As can be seen, our nuclear analysis of learning tasks is equally applicable to classroom exchanges, as it is to parent–child exchanges.

Although such classroom exchanges are the very marrow of teaching practice, teachers learn these skills primarily through experience, both as students themselves and as practising teachers, rather than being explicitly taught them in their teacher training. One dimension of the *Reading to Learn* program is to bring teacher's intuitive knowledge of this classroom discourse to consciousness, and to use it to explicitly design teaching practice. The aim is that all students in a class can be equally supported (as we outlined in Chapter 1, §1.3.3) to read and write challenging texts at the level they should be for their grade and subject area.

4.2.2   The reading task

Exchange [4.4] illustrates how with very young children, parents explain what is happening in the pictures before they start reading the story. A glance at most children's picture books shows why this is necessary, as their fields are often fantastic and well outside of young children's experience. These books are explicitly designed to depend on parents' guidance for children to understand them. The parent–child discussion of picture books happens at three levels:

1. pointing and naming what is happening in the pictures,
2. relating what is happening to preceding or following events, e.g. *We're going to build a house* or *Oh oh, I see that wolf!*,
3. relating what is happening to experience or values beyond the text, e.g. *Very bad isn't he?*

By the time children are three or four years old, there may be less of this preparation before starting reading, but there are still the same three levels of discussion. At this age, parents often ask children to name picture elements themselves, to remember or predict what did or will happen, and to relate it to their experience; but parents also still provide a lot of information in interaction with the child. In the following example [4.5] from Williams' major study of parent-child reading (1995: 359), the mother simply names the book and starts reading as the child looks on, but as she turns the pages she asks the child to remember repeated events, and to infer what is happening from the pictures.

[4.5] Parent-child reading at age 4

Mother	**Focus**	*This is called 'A lion in the meadow.'*
	[reads]	*The little boy said, 'Mother, there's a lion in the meadow.' The mother said, 'Nonsense little boy.' [turns page] The boy said, 'Mother, there's a big yellow lion in the meadow.'*
Mother	**Focus**	*And the mother said ...? Remember?*
	[reads]	*'Nonsense little boy.' [turns page] And the boy said, 'Mother, there is a big, yellow, whiskery roaring lion in the meadow.'*
Mother	**Focus**	*Looks like there is, doesn't it? [referring to the picture]*
	[reads]	*The mother said, 'There you go, making up stories again. There's nothing in the meadow except grass and trees. Go and see for yourself.' But the boy said, 'I'm scared because there's a lion there.'*

The mother's questions focus on the patterns that are repeated with variations in each episode – what the boy and his mother said – and the evidence in the pictures. Next she asks the child to interpret the events from his experience. In this case, the child's task is to propose a response from his experience, rather than identify an element in the text, so this move is labelled Propose. Again the Focus-Propose-Affirm nucleus of each exchange is outlined (and diagrammed in Figure 4.3).

Mother	Focus	*Do you think there was really truly a lion?*
Child	Propose	*Yes.*
Mother	Focus	*Why do you think so?*
Child	Propose	*'Cause he's not dreaming.*
Mother	Affirm	*Yeah he's not dreaming. Yeah, I think you're right.*
	Focus	*How do you know he's not dreaming?*
Child	Propose	*Because he went out to the garden and saw the lion.*
Mother	Affirm	*So it's not a dream.*

Figure 4.3: Nuclear phases in parent-child reading [4.5]

Here again are the three levels: identifying elements in the story, inferring connections from page to page, and interpreting events from experience. We will use terms that are widely recognised by teachers to refer to these three reading levels, as **literal**, **inferential** and **interpretive**.

- Literal meanings are accessible within the words of a sentence or the image on a page.
- Inferential meanings are recoverable from other parts of the text – preceding or following sentences, pages, sections or images.
- Interpretive meanings require application of the reader's experience or values to interpret what is going on.

The fourth level of reading is often referred to as 'decoding', that is recognising words from their patterns of letters. We put 'decoding' in quotes because in fact all levels of language encode meanings, and reading involves decoding meanings at all levels. But as 'decoding' is widely used to refer to recognising words from their letter patterns, we will use it in that sense here. These four levels of reading correlate with the levels of language in social context that we outlined in Chapter 1. Decoding relates to the graphological level of letter patterns in words, literal to the grammatical level of patterns within sentences, inferential to the discourse level of patterns across texts, and interpretive to the contextual level of experience and social relations beyond the text, illustrated in Figure 4.4.

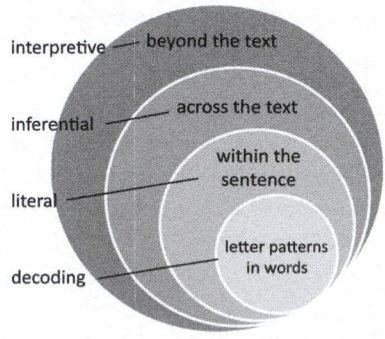

Figure 4.4: Levels of reading behaviours and language in context

For children in literate middle-class families, as illustrated in [4.4] and [4.5], learning to read begins with their parents guiding them to identify, infer and interpret meanings, long before they learn to decode letter patterns. The process begins with parents talking through the pictures with children, guiding them to identify elements in the pictures and discussing the field of the story. As the discussion follows the sequence of the book, from page to page, the child becomes familiar with the sequence of phases or episodes in which the story unfolds. Each episode is typically presented on one or two pages, and episodes typically follow a repeated pattern – a characteristic of children's picture books that the mother focuses on above in 'A lion in the meadow'. In other words, repeated episodes is a typical configuration of the picture book genre. So at the interpretive level, the child is guided to recognise the patterns in which the field of the story unfolds through this genre.

At the inferential level, the parent also guides the child to infer discourse connections across the text, even before reading the words, such as *We're going to build a house* or *Oh, oh, I see that wolf.* This guidance through the field, the genre, and patterns of discourse prepares young children to comprehend the words of the story as they are read. The parent will reinforce and elaborate these interpretive and inferential levels of understanding as the words are read and re-read. Eventually the child will be able to say the words along with the parent, and understand what they mean, at each level. By the time the child is three or four years old, their language repertoire will have grown to the point where the caregiver can often simply read the words, and discuss their inferential and interpretive meanings afterwards, as in exchange [4.5] above.[1] Williams' research on semantic variation in parents' reading styles (1995, 1999b, 2001) suggests that children from middle-class families are more likely to have experienced guidance with respect to interpretive meanings (discussed further in §4.7.2 below). Before starting school, such children may well have read and re-read hundreds of books with their parents, discussing their meanings at each level. Adams 1990 reports that children in middle-class families spend up to 1000 hours in parent-child reading before they start school. Although they may not have yet learnt to decode letter patterns, they are reading at every other level, and are already literate in most senses of the word. When these children start school, virtually all their teachers need do is show them correspondences between sounds and letters, together with more shared reading, and they rapidly learn to read independently.

---

[1] Freebody and Luke (1990) present a parallel perspective on reading they call the 'four roles of the reader'. These roles can be correlated with the genres we described in Chapters 2 and 3 as follows. As stories engage readers, the role as 'text participant' is foregrounded; as factual texts inform, the role as 'text user' predominates; evaluating texts foreground the role as 'text analyst' – text responses analyse particular texts, arguments analyse them in general. In *Reading to Learn*, we use text analysis as the pathway for teachers and students to become adept decoders, participants and users of texts.

From the discussion above we can draw the following key principles:

1. Reading involves four levels of meaning: **decoding** words from their letter patterns, **identifying** meanings within sentences, **inferring** connections across a text, and **interpreting** relations to the social context of a text.
2. Children learn to read through explicit guidance by caregivers and/or teachers (not by discovering it for themselves in a 'print rich environment').[2]
3. Guidance takes highly predictable forms as cycles of interaction, in which the parent **focuses** attention on a feature of the text, the child **identifies** the feature, and the parent **affirms** their response. In addition the parent may **prepare** the child by saying what to look for, and may **elaborate** with further information after affirming the child's response.
4. Elaborations may be interactive, in which the parent asks a **focus** question, the child **proposes** a response from their experience, and the parent **affirms**, and may further **elaborate**.
5. Classroom interactions follow similar patterns. Teachers ask focus questions and build on students' responses to elaborate their teaching goals; but teachers often prepare only if they get no response or the wrong response from students, and this preparation may be tuned into the needs of just a few 'responsive' students.
6. Reading development occurs over time. It begins with a high level of support in which parents tell the child what is happening in the story before reading the words, and later, as the child's language experience develops, they may provide less preparation before reading.
7. In the early stages, parents provide most of the literal, inferential and interpretive meanings in a text, and in later stages children may be guided to identify, infer and interpret meanings themselves as the text is read.
8. Children are not expected to start decoding themselves until they are thoroughly familiar with written ways of meaning; and learning to decode letter patterns becomes easy once they are familiar with the meanings of words.

We have applied these principles to designing a pedagogy for explicitly teaching reading and writing at all levels of education. The *Reading to Learn*

---

[2] The constructivist approach to reading, whole language, claims that children learn to read for themselves in a 'print rich environment' (Graves 1983, Cambourne 2003). Hattie's 2009 meta-analysis found that 'whole language programs have negligible effects on learning to read – be it on word recognition or comprehension' ($d = 0$).

pedagogy constitutes a set of tools that teachers can apply at any points in their curriculum programs, whenever learning tasks involve reading or writing. Simply put, there are nine sets of strategies in the program, which provide three levels of support for reading and writing.

Level 1	Preparing for Reading	Joint Construction	Individual Construction
Level 2	Detailed Reading	Joint Rewriting	Individual Rewriting
Level 3	Sentence Making	Spelling	Sentence Writing

These nine sets of strategies are presented as a set of options for integrating reading and writing with the curriculum in Figure 4.5.

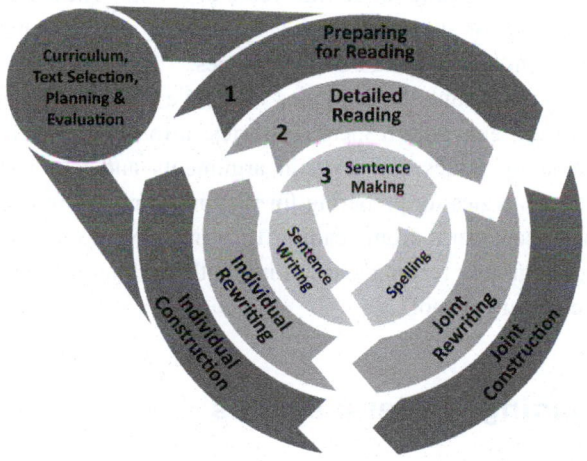

Figure 4.5: Three levels of strategies in Reading to Learn

Cycle 1 corresponds to the genre writing teaching/learning cycle described in Chapter 2 above. But as the starting point is with teaching reading, the first set of strategies here is called **Preparing for Reading**. This includes strategies for supporting students to read texts in the curriculum, along with deconstructing model texts for writing (termed Deconstruction in the genre writing TLC in Figure 2.4 above). This level of strategies links directly with curriculum goals at each stage of schooling, including the knowledge that is learnt through reading, and the evaluation of learning through writing. The language focus at this level is particularly on the structures of whole texts.

The strategies in cycle 2 provide a higher level of support for students to read the language of curriculum texts with detailed comprehension, and to use the language they have learnt from reading in their writing. The language focus at this level is on patterns of meaning within and between sentences. Short passages are selected from curriculum texts for Detailed Reading, followed by Rewriting of the passage using the same language patterns. As well as detailed comprehension and writing skills, these strategies are used to develop detailed knowledge about language at the levels of grammar and discourse.

Cycle 3 consists of intensive strategies that are used to teach foundation skills in reading and writing in the context of curriculum texts (described in §4.6 below). One or more sentences are selected from Detailed Reading passages for Sentence Making activities, in which students cut up and manipulate words and word groups. Words are then selected from these sentences to practise Spelling, including letter patterns, letter–sound correspondences, and letter formation. The knowledge of meanings, wordings and spelling gained from these activities is then practised in Sentence Writing. These strategies are used regularly in the primary school, for additional support in secondary school, and for teaching beginning reading and writing in the first years of school. They are also effective in providing support for students learning English as an additional language in TESOL contexts, and for learning other languages.

In this chapter we outline the strategies that have been developed for reading three kinds of texts: engaging readers in stories, informing readers with factual texts, and evaluating issues and texts in arguments and text responses. Each section includes strategies for preparing for reading, for reading in detail, and for using what has been learnt from reading to write new texts. The focus is on techniques for integrating reading and writing with learning the curriculum in the primary and secondary school.

4.3   Engaging readers: stories

4.3.1   Preparing for reading stories

Preparing for Reading is the first phase in the R2L program (Figure 4.6). It begins at the interpretive level of comprehension, with the background knowledge or field that learners need to know about to access a text. This discussion of the field need not include everything that happens in the text, because these details will emerge as it is read. Rather a brief outline of key elements is sufficient, so as not to overload learners with details before starting to read. In any case, the text is likely to be part of a topic that is being studied in a class, which will give students the field knowledge they need to access the text. This knowledge may only need briefly revising before reading.

The second step in preparing for reading is then to preview the sequence in which the field unfolds through the genre. This is the key phase in parent-child reading described above, in which the learner is guided to recognise what is going on in each episode or phase of the text, by talking through the pictures before reading the words. The same principle can be applied to texts at any level or any subject, by summarising the sequence in which the text unfolds.

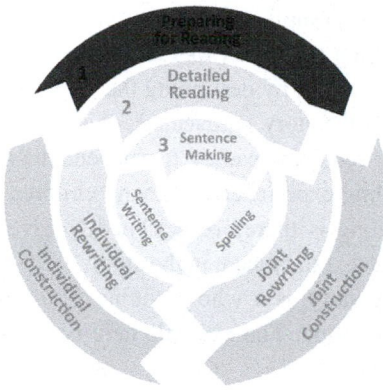

Figure 4.6: Preparing for Reading in the R2L program

We can start to illustrate this technique with the novel *Fantastic Mr Fox* by Roald Dahl (2007: 13), which is aimed at eight to ten-year-old readers. This is a useful text as a starting point here, as its field is relatively simple, but it is written with a host of rich language resources. The novel as a whole is a serial narrative, with a series of Complications that are finally resolved in the last chapters (a common pattern in children's and adult fiction, Rothery and Stenglin 1997). Before reading it with the class, the teacher could preview it as follows.

> *This book is about Fantastic Mr Fox and his fight with three farmers who want to shoot him. The reason they want to shoot him is that Mr Fox steals their chickens, ducks and geese to feed his family. Mr Fox and his wife and children live in a hole in the ground, on top of a hill under a huge tree. Every night he goes out to steal chickens, ducks and geese from the farmers. Their names are Farmer Boggis, Farmer Bunce and Farmer Bean, and they are horrible men. Here are the characters in the book [opening to first page illustrations]. You can see Mr Fox is dancing in his coat and his scarf. Here's Mrs Fox, and here are their children, the Small Foxes. How many are there? - Four. Right. Here's Mr Fox's friend Badger. And here's fat Farmer Boggis, and skinny Farmer Bean, and mean Farmer Bunce.*

> *The farmers decide to shoot Mr Fox, so one night they wait around his hole with shotguns, until he comes out. They almost get him, but he jumps back in his hole. Then they try to dig him out with shovels, but the Fox family dig a tunnel away from them, so the farmers can't catch them. Then they try to dig them out with big tractors. They dig away half of the hill, but they still can't catch them, so they decide to wait beside the Foxes' hole until they starve. The Foxes have nothing to eat for days, but then Mr Fox gets an idea that might save them. So let's start reading the story and find out what happens. It starts by describing the three farmers.*

The only background knowledge that needs preparing for this text is the basic premise of the story, along with the main characters. The teacher then summarises the sequence of Complications and temporary Resolutions, up to the point where it starts getting resolved (*Mr Fox gets an idea*). However, the novel actually starts quite differently, by describing the farmers, so that the reader must wait until the premise of the story is revealed. This type of device is common in children's literature. It requires readers to suspend their expectations, and so assumes a level of reading experience that many children do not have. The brief preparation before reading is therefore designed to give all students sufficient understanding of the context to engage in the story.

After introducing the story as a whole, the next step is then to prepare each chapter before it is read aloud. The example here is for Chapter 3, in which the first Complication occurs.

> *This chapter is called The Shooting [pointing at heading]. We're going to find out what happens when Farmers Boggis, Bunce and Bean are waiting outside Mr Fox's hole that night. It starts with Mrs Fox asking Mr Fox to bring back a fat duck for dinner. She tells him to be careful, but they don't know that the farmers are waiting for him. He creeps out of his hole very carefully, checking for any signs of danger, and he's just about to climb right out when he see's something shining and realises it's a gun. So let's find out what happens.*

This preparation first relates the chapter to the preceding events (the farmers waiting outside the hole), and then summarises the key events that follow. As in the preparation for the book, the twist at the end is not revealed, until it is read aloud to the class. The preparation thus both supports and motivates students to attend to the text as it is read.

This chapter is a complete narrative within itself, with the Orientation^ Complication^ Resolution structure discussed in our Chapter 2 above. The Orientation is very long, as the Foxes decide on ducks for dinner, Mrs Fox warns Mr Fox to be careful, and he slowly creeps out of his hole. In contrast, the Complication is very short – just one paragraph – with a twist in the last sentences of the chapter. Here are the last two pages of the chapter, with the Orientation, Complication and Resolution labelled. In addition, the story phases within each of these stages are also labelled.

[4.6] Extract from *Fantastic Mr Fox*

Orientation

...

setting	Mr Fox crept up the dark tunnel to the mouth of his hole. He poked his long handsome face out into the night air and sniffed once. He moved an inch or two forward and stopped. He sniffed again. He was always especially careful when coming out from his hole. He inched forward a little more. The front half of his body was now in the open.
problem	His black nose twitched from side to side, sniffing and sniffing for the scent of danger. He found none, and he was just about to go trotting forward into the

	wood when he heard or thought he heard a tiny noise, a soft rustling sound, as
	though someone had moved a foot ever so gently through a patch of dry leaves.
reaction	Mr Fox flattened his body against the ground and lay very still, his ears pricked.
	He waited a long time, but he heard nothing more.
solution	'It must have been a field-mouse,' he told himself, 'or some other small animal.'
re-setting	He crept a little further out of the hole ... then further still. He was almost right out
	in the open now. He took a last careful look around. The wood was murky and
	very still. Somewhere in the sky the moon was shining.

Complication

problem1	Just then, his sharp night-eyes caught a glint of something bright behind a tree
	not far away. It was a small silver speck of moonlight shining on a polished
problem2	surface. Mr Fox lay still, watching it. What on earth was it? Now it was moving. It
	was coming up and up ... Great heavens! It was the barrel of a gun! Quick as a
problem3	whip, Mr Fox jumped back into his hole and at that same instant the entire wood
	seemed to explode around him. Bang-bang! Bang-bang! Bang-bang!

Resolution

re-setting	The smoke from the three guns floated upward in the night air. Boggis and Bunce
	and Bean came out from behind their trees and walked towards the hole. 'Did we
	get him?' said Bean.
solution	One of them shone a flashlight on the hole, and there on the ground, in the circle
	of light, half in and half out of the hole, lay the poor tattered bloodstained remains
	of ... a fox's tail. Bean picked it up. 'We got the tail but we missed the fox,' he
	said, tossing the thing away.

Phases such as these, among others, can be found across all types of stories, from children's to adult fiction (Martin and Rose 2008, Rose 2006a). Settings present characters, events, places, times; problems create tension; reactions express characters' feelings, which can intensify tension; solutions release tension. Within the Orientation here, the author builds and releases tension by having Mr Fox react to a small noise, then decide it is nothing. This episode foreshadows the Complication to come. The Complication then builds rapidly with a series of worsening problems that Mr Fox reacts to, until the wood explodes with the sounds of shotguns. It is not until the last sentence that the tension is finally released.

The analysis of phases in a text can inform the preparation before reading, particularly if the text is difficult or challenging for students. The text we are considering here is relatively accessible; but this extract could be prepared in more detail as follows.

Remember Mrs Fox told Mr Fox to be careful, but they don't know that the farmers are waiting for him. This part starts with Mr Fox creeping very slowly out of his hole, sniffing the air for signs of danger. Then he heard a little sound that made him lie flat, but nothing happened so he decided it must have just been a mouse. As he crept further out, he could see a little bit because the moon was shining, then he saw something shining behind a tree. What do you think it was? - The farmers. That's right, it was one of their guns shining in the moonlight. Just as Mr Fox jumped back in the hole they all shot their guns. There was lots of smoke, so they didn't know if they got him until they shone a torch. So let's see if they did get him.

This type of preparation summarises the sequence of phases identified in the analysis above, in terms that all students can understand, including its key events, and using many of the words from the passage. It also starts by relating the passage to the preceding events. Such a preview gives students a map of how the text will unfold, including a series of signposts so that they will recognise key elements as they occur. No student will struggle to comprehend what is happening at each step, so all will be able to follow the words closely as they are read. If the text is read aloud, weaker readers need not struggle to decode unfamiliar words as it is read to them. If students are likely to find the text comparatively easy to follow, the preview can be brief, as in the chapter preparation above. If the text is more challenging, the preview can be more detailed, summarising its phases.

Following the text with general comprehension, as it is read aloud, then forms a basis for interpreting its details. After reading this chapter, the class could have a discussion about some of its key elements, led by the teacher. For example, the teacher could ask:

- if the ending was expected (and name it as a 'twist'),
- if the shooting came as a surprise, and review the way that the author built tension through a series of problems,
- why the entire wood seemed to explode,
- how Mr Fox could see the gun, reviewing elements such as *the moonlight shining on a polished surface.*

Such cycles of preparing, reading and then elaborating are not too far from the kinds of teaching activities that experienced teachers normally use in literary studies. Teachers typically provide background knowledge so that students can access a challenging text, and discuss interpretations after reading. One key difference here is in the kind of preparation, which carefully previews the phases through which the plot unfolds, enabling all students to follow the text with understanding. To plan such a preview, the teacher must first select an ideal passage, such as this one from *Fantastic Mr Fox*, then analyse it closely to identify its phases. These analyses can be enhanced by knowing the kinds of phases expected in stories, such as the settings, problems, reactions and solutions above (described in Martin and Rose 2008, Rose 2006a, 2011a). Most importantly they involve looking closely at what the author is doing at each step as the text unfolds, and interpreting why. Such close text analysis is often a revelation for teachers, not only to recognise the complexity of choices that the author has made, but the potential difficulty for their students to read and comprehend the text at inferred and interpretive levels.

This in turn can inform teachers' selection of texts to read with their students. Texts that are easy to read may enable weaker readers to access them with minimal support, but will not show sufficient literary technique for a worthwhile discussion after reading. The point of preparing for reading is to enable all students to access challenging texts. The strategy of preparing for reading enables the whole class to work with texts that challenge the top readers, with the teacher's guidance. Repeated preparation, joint reading and elaborating discussion eventually enables weaker readers to independently read the texts the class is working with, and ultimately other texts at the same level.

The same principle of preparing, reading and elaborating may also be used with longer literary texts, such as novel chapters, short stories and drama. As shown above for *Mr Fox*, the teacher can preview the longer text in less detail, distilling key elements from the plot, which act as signposts that students will recognise as the text is read. The combination of preparing and reading the text as a whole, and then close reading of a passage, can provide the support and insights for students to read the remainder of the text closely, and identify its significant elements. The whole text should be read first, at least up to the selected passage, to give students a framework for comprehending the passage. Novels should be read up to and including the chapter containing the selected passage.

Preparing for reading can also be used for academic discourse in tertiary education, with lecturers preparing subsequent course readings at the end of each lecture, by summarising how the field unfolds through each text. Taking a few minutes at the end of each lecture to prepare students for their readings can go a long way to overcoming students' inability or unwillingness to read them. This practice both enables and motivates students to study course readings with at least general comprehension, and this in turn provides the foundation for them to comprehend the next lecture. Preparing in this way involves lecturers looking closely at the texts they expect students to read, and this can inform both their text selection and how they structure their lectures (Rose 2008b, Rose, Lui-Chivizhe, McKnight and Smith 2004, Rose et al. 2008).

After preparing, reading and discussing a text, there are two options for the next step. If the text could serve as a model for writing a new text, the lesson could go straight to a Joint Construction that follows the same stages and phases as the model (discussed in §4.3.4 below). However, to enable all students to read the text with a full depth of understanding, and to use its author's language resources in their own writing, one or more short passages can be selected for Detailed Reading, whose place in the program is shown in Figure 4.7.

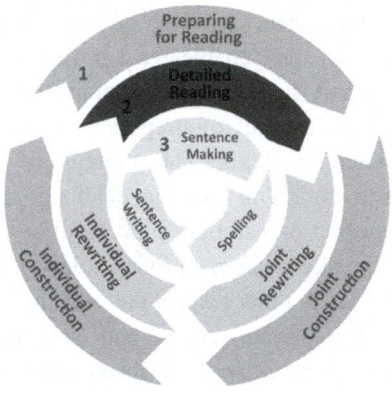

Figure 4.7: Detailed Reading in the R2L program

4.3.2   Detailed Reading of stories – language resources for engaging readers

In Detailed Reading, the teacher guides students to identify wordings within each sentence of a short passage from the reading text, and then elaborates their meanings in more depth and detail. This intensive activity takes some time, so short passages are typically selected that can be worked through in 20 or 30 minutes. Passages are selected with the most elaborate language resources – the very ones for which students need more guidance to read with understanding, and which they can use in turn in their writing. For example, one section of the passage above that offers rich opportunities for Detailed Reading is the Complication, with its mounting problems and reactions by Mr Fox. To give it a context we could also include the setting that precedes the Complication.

> He crept a little further out of the hole ... then further still. He was almost right out in the open now. He took a last careful look around. The wood was murky and very still. Somewhere in the sky the moon was shining.
>
> Just then, his sharp night-eyes caught a glint of something bright behind a tree not far away. It was a small silver speck of moonlight shining on a polished surface. Mr Fox lay still, watching it. What on earth was it?
>
> Now it was moving. It was coming up and up ... Great heavens! It was the barrel of a gun!
>
> Quick as a whip, Mr Fox jumped back into his hole and at that same instant the entire wood seemed to explode around him. Bang-bang! Bang-bang! Bang-bang!

This passage is ideal for Detailed Reading, because it:

- uses rich language resources for building tension in stories, through a series of mounting problems and character's reaction,
- includes a series of descriptive devices that expand the images of the scene (analysed in Chapter 5, §5.1.5 below),

- is engaging for the students and lends itself to writing their own passage using the same language resources (§4.3.3 below),
- could easily be worked through in about 15 minutes of class time.

Students use highlighters or pens to mark groups of words in each sentence as they are read and discussed. The Detailed Reading technique here begins by reviewing the context and phases of the selected passage.

Detailed Reading transcript for *Fantastic Mr Fox* [4.6]

Prepare passage	*Remember this is the Complication, where poor old Mr Fox gets shot. Mr Fox had almost climbed right out of his hole, and was looking around. It was dark but the moon was shining. So that's the setting. Then there's a little problem that makes Mr Fox worry. He saw something shining behind a tree, and he wondered what it was. Then the problem gets worse because the shiny thing started moving up and up, and he realised it was a gun. He jumped back in his hole as fast as he could, at the same time as the farmers all shot their guns at him.*

The teacher then reads the passage aloud. The next step is then to prepare the first sentence of the passage, giving students the inferred meaning of the sentence in terms they will all understand, and then reading the sentence aloud as students read along.

Prepare sentence	*The first sentence tells us how carefully Mr Fox came out of his hole. Look at the sentence as I read it. 'He crept a little further out of the hole … then further still.'*

This sentence preparation enables all students to understand the sentence as it is read, hearing the words as they see them. It is a crucial step for three reasons:

1. It correlates the written words with their spoken expression, as a sequence of meanings that students can understand. Because its meaning has been prepared, students need not struggle to understand the sentence. Because it is read to them, they need not struggle to decode unfamiliar words. This reduces their semiotic load, enabling them to process the complexity of meanings, wordings and soundings as easily as possible.
2. It provides a meaningful context for identifying and understanding each wording within the sentence, as they are highlighted and discussed.
3. As the students have heard the words articulated, they will be able to see and say the words aloud when the teacher asks them to identify and highlight them.

The next step is to give students a meaning cue for the first wording, along with a position cue. This is termed a Prepare move in Detailed Reading, as follows.

Prepare   *At the start of the sentence it tells us how he moved.*

All students can now see the specific word referred to by this general cue *how he moved*. However, the teacher then asks a particular student to say the words, typically with a Focus question, that repeats the meaning cue:

Focus   [student name] *Can you see the word that says how he moved?*

As the preparation – first of the whole sentence, then of the wording – enables every student to read the words confidently, this question can be addressed to any student, including the weaker readers in the class. Note that the meaning cue is repeated to be completely unambiguous, and the position cue that precedes the question makes it as easy as possible. The aim is to reduce the semiotic load and emotional stress on students, so that they can focus on identifying the wording from the meaning cue. Consequently every student can be equally engaged in the discussion and, most importantly, be affirmed by the teacher. The students' task is simply to identify the wording in the text.

Student	**Identify**	*Crept.*
Teacher	**Affirm**	*Exactly right.*

The stronger the affirmation, the better it can make students feel about their success, which sharpens their attention and engagement. So affirmations can be more than just *yes* or *OK*, without becoming cloying. Phrases like *exactly right*, *excellent, fantastic* can simply roll off the teacher's tongue. This simple technique thus actively engages all students in the discussion. At the same time it enables every student to read the words with comprehension, although they may be well beyond their independent reading competence.

The teacher then directs the class to exactly which words to highlight, in order to ensure that all students can identify and mark the same words.

Direct   *Let's highlight 'crept'.*

Their success in reading the wording then forms a sound basis for deepening their understanding, in an elaboration phase.

Elaborate   *Creeping means going very slowly, and keeping as low as you can, so no-one will see you. Mr Fox is creeping because he's a bit scared so he's being very careful.*

Here the teacher first defines the word, and then explains it in the context of the events. The next wordings are then identified using a similar sequence of moves.

Again the nucleus of each exchange consists of Focus-Identify-Affirm (outlined), but now each exchange is deliberately prepared, students are directed to highlight, and an elaboration follows.

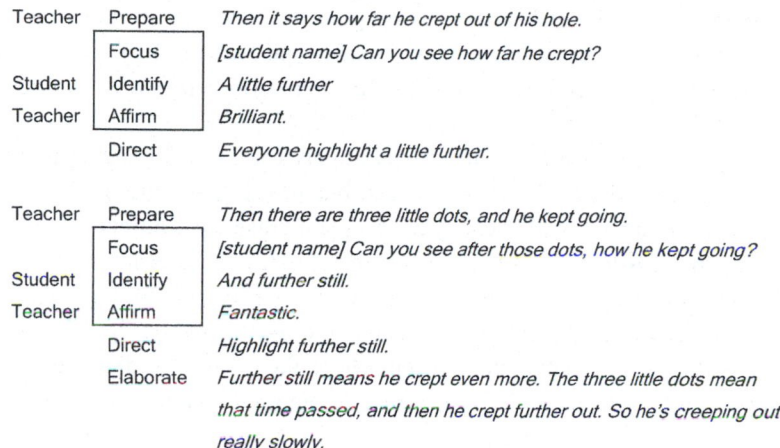

Teacher	Prepare	*Then it says how far he crept out of his hole.*
	Focus	*[student name] Can you see how far he crept?*
Student	Identify	*A little further*
Teacher	Affirm	*Brilliant.*
	Direct	*Everyone highlight a little further.*

Teacher	Prepare	*Then there are three little dots, and he kept going.*
	Focus	*[student name] Can you see after those dots, how he kept going?*
Student	Identify	*And further still.*
Teacher	Affirm	*Fantastic.*
	Direct	*Highlight further still.*
	Elaborate	*Further still means he crept even more. The three little dots mean that time passed, and then he crept further out. So he's creeping out really slowly.*

Here the teacher focuses on the three elements that express how slowly Mr Fox crept out of his hole – *a little further*, then three dots, then *further still*. A little further is prepared with a 'wh' cue *how far*, as it is relatively easy to understand. Where wordings are easy to read and understand, they can be prepared with literal meaning cues such as *who, what, when, where, how far*. After giving this cue, the teacher hands control to the students to do the task themselves. With 'wh' cues the task is to identify specific wordings from these general meanings. This mental labour is what makes the learning transferable to reading other texts. Such general meanings focus students' attention on the semantic functions of word groups that make up sentences, including people (who), things (what), processes (what doing), places (where), times (when) and qualities (how, what like). Students rapidly learn to recognise these chunks of meaning in other sentences and texts, and often come to predict the teacher's questions in Detailed Reading.

In contrast, *further still* is a little further from young children's everyday language, so it is prepared with a synonym they will understand, *kept going*, along with a precise position cue, *after those dots*. Whenever students are unlikely to understand the wording, it is essential to tell them what it means so they can identify and comprehend it. With synonyms or paraphrases, the task is to identify an unfamiliar wording from the familiar meaning cue. This develops students' capacity for building up their knowledge of words and structures as they read.

To this end, the elaborations above extend students' lexical knowledge, by defining words and structures in terms of the particular context in this sentence. Here *further still* and the three dots are defined, and their overall meaning in the context is explained. Continual definitions in context such as these guide students to use contextual clues as they read, and to infer the meanings of wordings. This is a more effective technique for expanding students' vocabulary and grammar knowledge than attempting to memorise words or grammar structures out of context, or relying on dictionaries for definitions. Furthermore, students are guided through the elaborations to imagine the scene, i.e. to interpret the word- ings in the sentence in terms of the images and feelings they evoke: *Mr Fox is creeping because he's a bit scared so he's being very careful ... So he's creeping out really slowly.*

In sum, where wordings are comparatively easy to read and understand, they can be prepared with literal 'wh' cues; but where they may not be understood, they are prepared with synonyms or paraphrases. Elaborations subsequently guide students to infer connections across the text, and to interpret the context. These principles apply at all ages, from young children up. Any text worthy of Detailed Reading will involve inferential and interpretive levels of meanings that are scaffolded in elaborations, even where the literal wordings are apparently transparent. We can see the same principles applied with the following sentences.

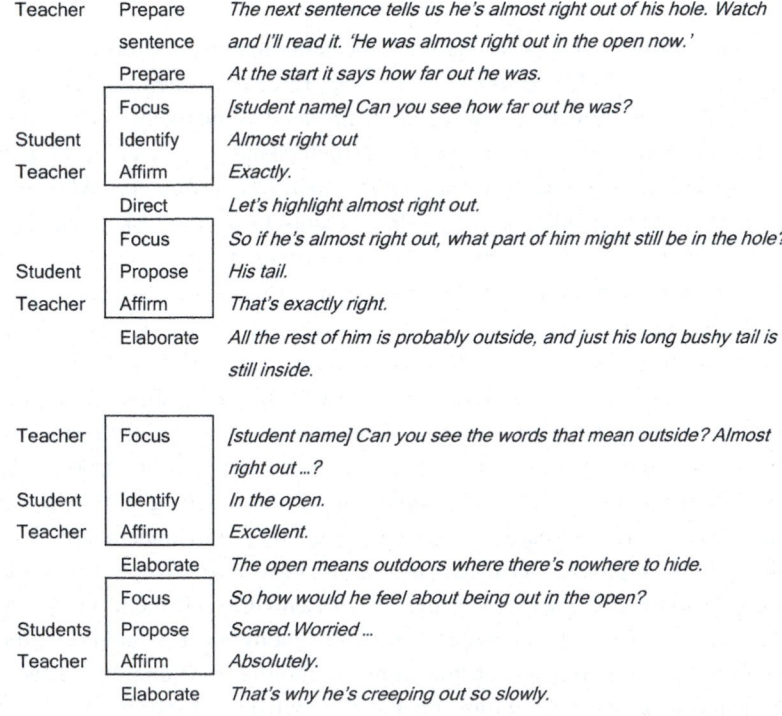

Teacher	Prepare sentence	*The next sentence tells us he's almost right out of his hole. Watch and I'll read it. 'He was almost right out in the open now.'*
	Prepare	*At the start it says how far out he was.*
	Focus	*[student name] Can you see how far out he was?*
Student	Identify	*Almost right out*
Teacher	Affirm	*Exactly.*
	Direct	*Let's highlight almost right out.*
	Focus	*So if he's almost right out, what part of him might still be in the hole?*
Student	Propose	*His tail.*
Teacher	Affirm	*That's exactly right.*
	Elaborate	*All the rest of him is probably outside, and just his long bushy tail is still inside.*

Teacher	Focus	*[student name] Can you see the words that mean outside? Almost right out ...?*
Student	Identify	*In the open.*
Teacher	Affirm	*Excellent.*
	Elaborate	*The open means outdoors where there's nowhere to hide.*
	Focus	*So how would he feel about being out in the open?*
Students	Propose	*Scared. Worried ...*
Teacher	Affirm	*Absolutely.*
	Elaborate	*That's why he's creeping out so slowly.*

In this exchange, the teacher engages the students interactively in elaborations, by asking them to imagine what part of Mr Fox might still be in the hole, and then how he would feel out in the open. In this kind of exchange the teacher's Focus question guides students to propose a response from their knowledge or experience, in contrast to identifying wordings in the text. The Focus question is phrased in such a way that students' responses can always be affirmed. Note also that the teacher gives a precise position cue in the second cycle, by reading up to the required words with a rising tone *Almost right out ...?* This common teacher question technique is deployed in Detailed Reading to ensure that students can see exactly which words to identify.

The next sentence is prepared with its inferred meaning, that is, why he looked around.

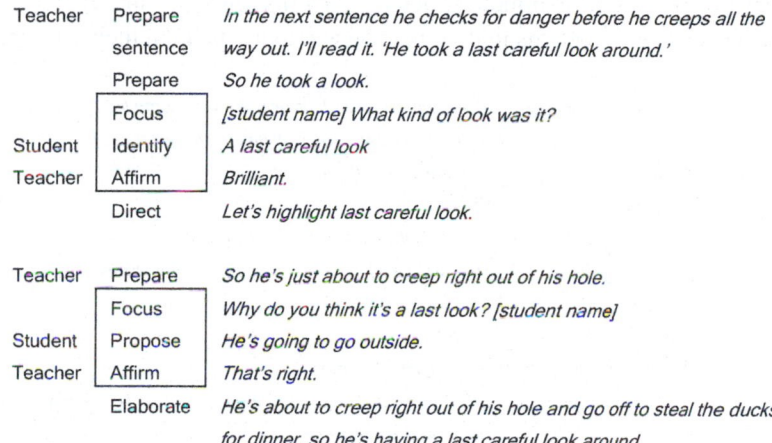

Teacher	Prepare sentence	*In the next sentence he checks for danger before he creeps all the way out. I'll read it. 'He took a last careful look around.'*
	Prepare	*So he took a look.*
	Focus	*[student name] What kind of look was it?*
Student	Identify	*A last careful look*
Teacher	Affirm	*Brilliant.*
	Direct	*Let's highlight last careful look.*

Teacher	Prepare	*So he's just about to creep right out of his hole.*
	Focus	*Why do you think it's a last look? [student name]*
Student	Propose	*He's going to go outside.*
Teacher	Affirm	*That's right.*
	Elaborate	*He's about to creep right out of his hole and go off to steal the ducks for dinner, so he's having a last careful look around.*

Here *a last look* could be ambiguous, as he is about to get shot, so the teacher first prepares with the inferred meaning (that he is about to creep out of his hole), and then asks a student who is likely to infer the right response. The next sentences describe what he sees, but this logical connection to the preceding sentence is implicit, so the teacher makes it explicit.

Teacher	Prepare sentence	*The next two sentences describe what he sees. Look while I read them. 'The wood was murky and very still. Somewhere in the sky the moon was shining.'*
	Prepare	*The first sentence describes two qualities of the wood.*
	Focus	*[student name] What's the first quality?*
Student	Identify	*Murky*
Teacher	Affirm	*Fantastic.*
	Direct	*Highlight murky.*
	Elaborate	*Murky means that it was dark so you could see a little bit but not much.*
	Focus	*[student name] What's the next quality?*
Student	Identify	*Very still.*
Teacher	Affirm	*Great.*

| Direct | *Highlight very still.* |
| Elaborate | *So it's a dark night and nothing is moving.* |

Here the teacher draws students' attention to a pattern of two similar items, by asking students to name one at a time. Repeated patterns are common in both literary and factual texts, at the levels of words, word groups, clauses and sentences – in pairs, triplets, quadruplets. They generally imply some similarity between the elements, which can be brought out in elaborations (see §5.2.5). Here the teacher explicitly names them as qualities of the wood. Guiding students' attention to common structural patterns such as this enables them to recognise similar patterns in their reading and to use them in their writing.

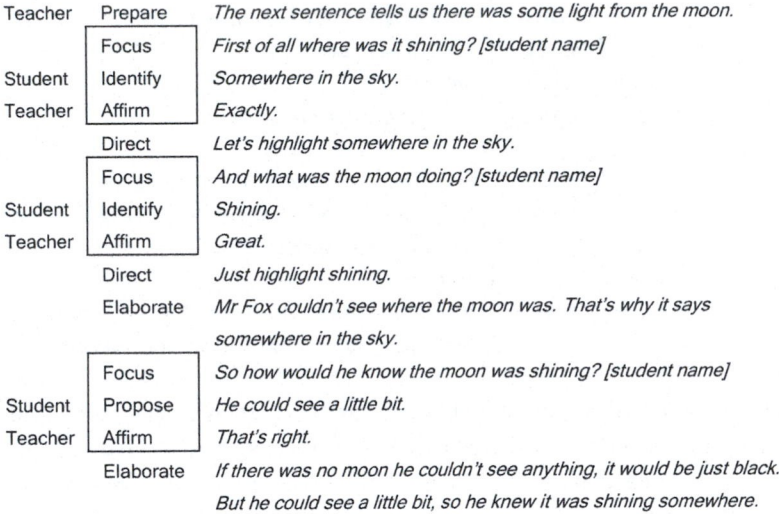

Teacher	Prepare	*The next sentence tells us there was some light from the moon.*
	Focus	*First of all where was it shining? [student name]*
Student	Identify	*Somewhere in the sky.*
Teacher	Affirm	*Exactly.*
	Direct	*Let's highlight somewhere in the sky.*
	Focus	*And what was the moon doing? [student name]*
Student	Identify	*Shining.*
Teacher	Affirm	*Great.*
	Direct	*Just highlight shining.*
	Elaborate	*Mr Fox couldn't see where the moon was. That's why it says somewhere in the sky.*
	Focus	*So how would he know the moon was shining? [student name]*
Student	Propose	*He could see a little bit.*
Teacher	Affirm	*That's right.*
	Elaborate	*If there was no moon he couldn't see anything, it would be just black. But he could see a little bit, so he knew it was shining somewhere.*

In this elaboration, the teacher guides the class to interpret the implicit meaning of *somewhere in the sky*. The phrase itself is easy to read so it is just prepared with *where*, but its significance would be invisible to many readers. Notice that the student responds with words the teacher used in discussing the previous sentence, *could see a little bit*. This information is important for the next sentence, in which he sees something shining, but at first cannot tell what it is.

Although this has been a long discussion about Detailed Reading of just one paragraph, the actual time taken for the interaction cycle in the classroom is just a few minutes. There is no need to labour any of the learning points, as the same types of language features will be encountered again and again, in this and other Detailed Reading sessions.

After completing each sentence, it can be read aloud by the class, and the whole passage can be read again when the Detailed Reading is complete. The teacher can then label the phases on a projected version of the passage that the whole class can see, as students label the phases in their own copies. This reinforces the structures of the text, and provides more detail. The passage is highlighted and labelled by way of illustration as follows.

setting	He crept a little further out of the hole … then further still. He was almost right out in the open now. He took a last careful look around. The wood was murky and very still. Somewhere in the sky the moon was shining.
problem1	Just then, his sharp night-eyes caught a glint of something bright behind a tree not far away. It was a small silver speck of moonlight shining on a polished surface.
reaction	Mr Fox lay still, watching it. What on earth was it?
problem2	Now it was moving. It was coming up and up …
reaction	Great heavens! It was the barrel of a gun!
reaction	Quick as a whip, Mr Fox jumped back into his hole
problem3	and at that same instant the entire wood seemed to explode around him. Bang-bang! Bang-bang! Bang-bang!

Note that grammatical words such as pronouns and articles are often not highlighted, in order to leave gaps between wordings as students highlight them. After 20 minutes or so of such Detailed Reading, every student in a class will be able to read the passage with detailed understanding. Teachers invariably find that their weakest students can now read a passage that is far beyond their normal independent reading scores, although they will not necessarily be able to read other texts at the same level, as this will require repeated practice with the kind of guidance illustrated above. In addition, students will come to recognise the language choices that the author has made in writing the Detailed Reading passage. Accordingly, the next activity is to rewrite the passage, using the same language resources. This both reinforces students' control of the reading text and prepares them for writing their own texts. The place of Joint and Individual Rewriting is shown in Figure 4.8.

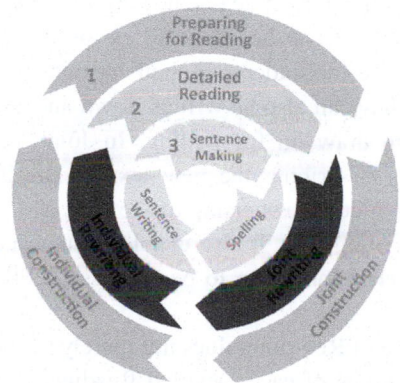

Figure 4.8: Joint and Individual Rewriting in the R2L program

4.3.3   Joint and Individual Rewriting – appropriating language resources

The aim of Rewriting is to guide students to appropriate the language resources of accomplished authors into their own writing. Experienced authors do this themselves, more or less intuitively. Rewriting makes this process conscious, by focusing on the language features that have been discussed in Detailed Reading. Rewriting with stories involves following the same language patterns as the sentences analysed in Detailed Reading, but with a new field – i.e. new characters, events, settings. This strategy supports students to practise the complex task of writing a new text by using the language patterns of a familiar text. The process begins with Joint Rewriting, in which the teacher guides students to apply a new field to the sentence patterns. The teacher's role in Joint Rewriting is critical, as an authoritative guide for language choices. But because the class has already thoroughly discussed the author's language choices in Detailed Reading, it is easy for all to see how the process works, and to actively participate.

The field is chosen by the class, after brainstorming a range of ideas, each of which may be written on the board. As many ideas as possible are listed on the board, for later Individual Rewrites, and one is chosen for the Joint Rewrite. The original passage is projected so that all can see, and the teacher guides the class to choose new details for each segment of the text. The teacher prepares students for selecting ideas, by pointing out what the author has done at each step in the model text, and asking what choices could be made for the class text. Students' responses may then be evaluated and elaborated, by rephrasing or extending, to fit the requirements of the developing Rewrite. The teacher, in other words, gives the class whatever language resources are needed for the text, incorporating the students' ideas into a coherent product. Joint writing does not mean trying to get ideas out of students that they do not have; rather the purpose is for the teacher to provide the language resources they need to learn, drawing on their own repertoires as much as possible.

As ideas are generated for each segment, they may be written on the board, and arranged in groups that can be added to as the text unfolds. These 'word banks' become a resource for students in their Individual Rewriting, along with ideas for new fields. They can also be written down and expanded later, as more permanent resources to draw on for writing. In Joint Rewriting, students are encouraged to take turns scribing the new text on the board, rather than the teacher. This gives all students ownership of the text, and prepares them directly for the Individual Rewriting task. It also enables issues such as grammar, spelling, punctuation and letter formation to be addressed collectively as the text is written.

Crucially the practice of Rewriting does not merely support students to use the particular language features of each Detailed Reading passage. Rather repeated practice following Detailed Reading teaches them *how to* recognise interesting and useful language features in their reading, and to borrow them into their writing. A key resource for this learning process is metalanguage that is applied to language features as texts are rewritten. Metalanguage can be introduced in Joint Rewriting, or terms which have been introduced previously can be applied and reinforced here.

To illustrate how Rewriting works, here is the Complication again, with significant boundaries marked with a slash, where they are not already marked with punctuation.

> Just then, his sharp night-eyes/ caught a glint/ of something bright/ behind a tree not far away.
>
> It was/ a small silver speck of moonlight/ shining on a polished surface.
>
> Mr Fox lay still, watching it.
>
> What on earth was it?
>
> Now it was moving.
>
> It was coming up and up …
>
> Great heavens! It was the barrel of a gun!
>
> Quick as a whip, Mr Fox jumped back into his hole/
>
> and at that same instant/ the entire wood/ seemed to explode around him.
>
> Bang-bang! Bang-bang! Bang-bang!

To do a Rewrite of *Fantastic Mr Fox*, the starting point is to select a character that is a likeable rogue, who could be in danger from an enemy. Popular choices for this type of character have included animals such as a cat, lizard or snake, or cartoon characters like Sylvester the Cat, the Roadrunner or Bart Simpson. One idea chosen to Rewrite the Detailed Reading passage above was to substitute Peter Rabbit for Mr Fox, as follows.

Rewrite using sentence patterns from Text [4.6]

> *All of a sudden, his long twitching ears/ caught the sound/ of something moving/ behind the garden close by.*
>
> *It was a squeaking and rumbling sound/ rolling along the gravel path.*
>
> *Peter Rabbit froze stiff, listening.*
>
> *What could it be?*
>
> *It kept rolling along,*
>
> *Getting closer and closer …*
>
> *Dear Lord! It was Mr MacGregor's wheelbarrow!*
>
> *Like a shot, Peter leaped towards the garden gate*
>
> *but almost at once/ Mr MacGregor's rake/ came crashing down towards him.*
>
> *Whoosh-Bang! Swish-Smash! Swipe-Crunch!*

The teacher-student exchange in Joint Rewriting is illustrated as follows. Again the nucleus of each exchange is outlined. Metalanguage terms shared by the class are in bold.

Joint Rewriting of Text [4.6]

Teacher	Direct	*OK, let's read the **first problem** together.*
Students	[read	*Just then, his sharp night-eyes caught a glint of something bright*
	aloud]	*behind a tree not far away. It was a small silver speck of moonlight*
		shining on a polished surface.
Teacher	Focus	*What's the **problem** here?*
Student	Identify	*He saw something shining.*
Teacher	Affirm	*Right.*
Teacher	Prepare	*So what's going to be our **first problem**?*
	Focus	*Will Peter Rabbit see or hear something?*
Students	Propose	*Mr MacGregor. A bird. Fox.*
Teacher	Affirm	*[scribing ideas] Great.*
	Elaborate	*Remember it has to be something very dangerous, and Peter*
		doesn't know what it is yet.
Teacher	Prepare	*Let's say Mr MacGregor is coming.*
	Focus	*What could Peter hear before he sees him?*
Students	Propose	*Talking. Shouting. Footsteps. Wheelbarrow.*
Teacher	Affirm	*[scribing] Good ideas.*
	Elaborate	*Let's go with Mr MacGregor's wheelbarrow, that Peter hears.*

The discussion opens with the term **problem**, which was introduced in the earlier reading, and written as a label on the projected text. Students recognise the type of story phase it refers to and can use it to start planning the new text. Note that the teacher provides less precise guidance for students' responses than in Detailed Reading, but still makes final decisions about what to write, and provides ideas where necessary. The aim of Detailed Reading was to support all students to read the passage fluently with literal, inferential and interpretive comprehension, and high personal engagement, and this required precise preparations and affirmations for each student. Once this has been achieved, support can be reduced so that students can exercise their inferential and interpretive comprehension more freely.

This reduction in support is necessary in Joint Rewriting, for students to propose ideas from their own repertoires, as a step towards Individual Rewriting. Support is still maintained by pointing to the wordings in the Detailed Reading passage, and naming the type of language feature to propose, but Focus questions are more open. For example, *What's the problem here?* asks students to identify the nub of the problem from within two sentences, without a position cue. But this task was prepared for by earlier discussion in Detailed Reading, and in turn prepares students to propose a similar problem for the new text. Similarly, the teacher's elaboration, *Remember it has to be something very dangerous, and Peter doesn't know what it is yet*, explicitly refers back to the Detailed Reading discussion. This prepares them to propose similar ideas, from which the teacher settles on the sound of Mr MacGregor's wheelbarrow. Once these key elements of the field have been built up, rewriting starts with a precise preparation, including a position cue, the type of language feature (conjunction) and its definition *very quickly*.

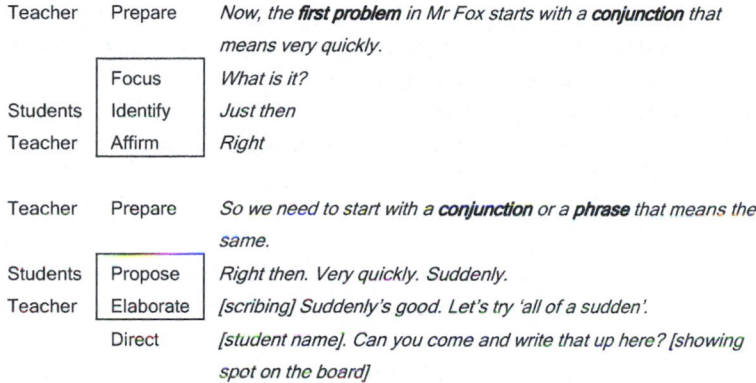

The definition *very quickly*, plus the terms **conjunction** or **phrase** prepares students to propose appropriate ideas, which the teacher affirms but rephrases with *All of a sudden*. Note that the student starts scribing on the board only after the whole wording has been decided on.

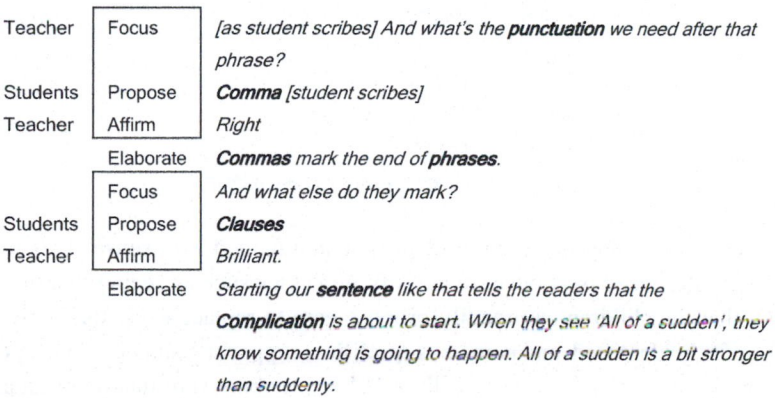

Here the teacher reinforces the function of **commas** to mark **phrases**, engages the children to reinforce the function of **commas** to mark **clauses**, and then elaborates with the function of sentence starters like 'Just then' or 'All of a sudden', to signal the **Complication**.

While this signalling function is explained, it is quite abstract, so it is not given a name at this point. Later, however, after the class has encountered many such instances, the term **Theme** could be introduced, and the idea of a **marked**

Theme (see §5.3.1 below). This is a general principle for introducing meta-language: students need to understand a wording before it can be named as a type of language feature, which is why metalanguage is introduced in elaborations. And they generally have to experience the language feature and its name several times, before they can fully grasp and remember it. (The same applies to teachers and linguistics students.)

Teacher	Focus	*Now [pointing at next word group], what did Mr Fox **sense** with?*
Students	Identify	*Sharp night-eyes*
Teacher	Affirm	*Right.*
	Focus	*So what is Peter Rabbit going to **sense** with?*
Students	Propose	*Ears.*
Teacher	Affirm	*Exactly.*

Teacher	Prepare	*So Mr Fox's eyes were sharp night eyes.*
	Focus	*What **qualities** can we give to Peter Rabbit's ears?*
Students	Propose	*Long. Pink. Furry. White. Listening.*
Teacher	Affirm	*Good [scribing], they are all **qualities** of rabbits' ears.*
	Elaborate	*Let's say they are long so they can hear well*

Teacher	Prepare	*And rabbits' ears also twitch from side to side when they are listening.*
	Focus	*Have you ever seen that? [demonstrating with hands] Have you seen a dog's or cat's ears twitch?*
Students	Propose	*[laughter] Yes.*

Teacher	Focus	*So how are we going to say that?*
Students	Propose	*His long twitching ears.*
Teacher	Affirm	*Great.*
	Direct	*[student name], can you write that next?*

The next wording is precisely identified, and named with **sense**. This has clearly been introduced previously to classify processes such as seeing, hearing, feeling, so that the children can readily propose ears to replace eyes. Its details are then precisely identified, and named as **qualities**, supporting students to propose ideas, which the teacher rephrases with *twitching*, making sure that all students understand its meaning. This is sufficient support for students to construct the word group as a whole.

Metalanguage is clearly a valuable resource in this activity to direct attention and support students to propose appropriate ideas for the new text. The projected text allows the teacher to manually point at the wordings under focus. Meta-language enables us to point verbally at the type of language feature we are interested in. Metalanguage used here includes semantic terms: **Complication, problem, senses, qualities,** and class terms: **conjunction, phrase, clause,**

sentence, along with punctuation: **comma**. The range of metalanguage that can be used in class discussion is surveyed in Chapter 5 below.

The teacher paces the Rewriting process as fast as necessary to complete the task. Instead of struggling to get ideas from the class for every little component of the text, the teacher provides much of it, while guiding the class to propose key elements that s/he knows they will be able to, and repeating items s/he has just said. This requires judgements about the kinds of language resources that students have, and what needs to be supplied by the teacher. A crucial strategy for making such judgements is for teachers to practise the Rewrite before attempting it with the class. The class Rewrite will be different from the teacher's practice run, but s/he will have a good idea about where to steer it, and potential pitfalls as it is written.

Rewriting is as beneficial for successful students as it is for struggling writers, for first language speakers as it is for speakers of other languages, and for senior secondary and tertiary students as it is for beginning readers and writers. Like Detailed Reading, it enables students to write texts that may be well beyond their independent competence, by supporting them to recognise and use the language resources of accomplished authors. This closely supported analysis and application enhances the skills of all students.

Initially, more successful students may find Individual Rewriting as constraining as others find it liberating. These students may be used to intuitively appropriating the language resources of the authors they read, using them creatively, and being rewarded by their teachers. Some initially refuse to follow the constraints of close rewriting, but they soon find that their products are less polished than those who have followed the patterns, including students who are usually poor writers. Top writers in a class come to realise that these exercises are invaluable to help them improve.

One of the advantages of Individual Rewriting is that more successful students are able to work independently, applying their wider repertoire to the task, which allows the teacher to spend more time with other students, offering ideas and guiding their practice. As a result, students who can usually write no more than a sentence or two can quickly gain the confidence to write pages of coherent text, following repeated practice with Rewriting and Joint Construction.

4.3.4   Joint and Individual Construction – constructing whole texts

Rewriting is not an end in itself. Its function is to build up language resources that students will then be able to use in their own writing. As we described in Chapter 2, the Joint Construction activity is designed to support students to write successful whole texts in various genres. Rewriting contributes to this by giving students control over the language resources that will be used in Joint Construction and eventually in their independent writing. In order to build sufficient language resources, teachers generally like to do Detailed Reading and

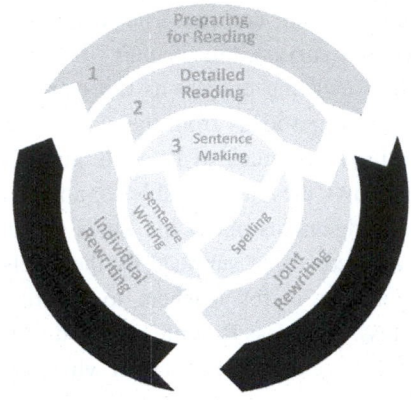

Figure 4.9: Joint and Individual Construction in the R2L program

Rewriting on two or three short passages, before each Joint Construction. One criterion for selecting Detailed Reading passages is thus to provide language resources that will contribute to writing whole texts.

The Joint Construction process in *Reading to Learn* extends the strategies developed in earlier phases of genre pedagogy discussed in Chapter 2. A key development here is the analysis of phases within each stage of the genre. The analysis of texts such as the passage from *Fantastic Mr Fox* [4.6] provides more fine-grained models for constructing new stories, using the same sequence of phases. Thus Joint Construction follows not only the stages of the genre, but also exactly the same phases as the particular text used as a model. In the case of stories, this supports students to practise using the sophisticated rhetorical tropes of accomplished authors. Examples from [4.6] are the use of a minor problem, reaction and solution within the Orientation, creating tension that foreshadows the Complication. Within the Complication is the technique of building tension through a series of worsening problems and intensifying reactions, culminating in a crisis. And within the Resolution, a re-setting maintains the tension until the final twist at the end.

To support students to follow such elaborate techniques, the model text is projected on the board or wall, and prepared, read and discussed as described for Preparing for Reading in §4.3.1 above. The teacher then guides the class to identify each phase in the text, and writes a label for it beside the relevant paragraph, as in Text [4.6] above. The students also need their own photocopies of the text. As the class text is labelled, they label their own copies. This serves to reinforce both the structure of the model, and the metalanguage used to discuss it.

Next a new field for the text is brainstormed by the class, including new characters, events and settings. As many ideas as possible are listed on the board for students to choose from when they write their own. As the text is written, the teacher keeps referring to the phases of the original text projected on the wall, and, as students and teacher generate ideas for wording each event, they can be listed on the board. The teacher guides the class to propose appropriate wordings and organise them coherently. That is, the teacher is authority in this activity, providing students with the language resources to construct a successful text based on the model.

The following example of a Joint Construction [4.7] follows the same phases as Dahl's narrative. In this case it is again Peter Rabbit as the protagonist instead of Mr Fox.

[4.7] Joint Construction using phases from Text [4.6]

Orientation

setting	*Peter Rabbit was feeling very hungry. He poked his pink button nose through a hole in the garden gate. He pushed himself through the hole, until he was almost inside the garden.*
problem	*His long ears turned from side to side, listening for any sound of Mr MacGregor, the gardener. He was just about to go hopping towards the carrot patch when he heard the sound of crunching gravel.*
reaction	*Peter froze. He peered about looking for the source of the noise.*
solution	*A robin flew up from the path. 'Oh, that's all it was,' he told himself.*
setting	*He hopped off happily towards the vegetables. The scent of fresh carrots and radishes was overwhelming.*

Complication

problem1	*All of a sudden he heard the crunching sound again. What on earth could it be?*
problem2	*Then through the carrot tops he saw a wheelbarrow coming around the garden shed. Oh dear, it's Mr MacGregor!*
problem3	*Like lightning Peter hopped back towards the gate, just as a rake swooped down towards his poor head.*

Resolution

solution	*'Aha, got you this time,' hooted Mr MacGregor. There lying sprawled on the ground, skewered by the rake, was the torn remains of … Peter's pretty blue jumper.*
	'Fiddlesticks,' muttered the gardener, 'he's slipped away again.'

This Joint Construction is less detailed than the original, and does not incorporate the sentence-by-sentence Rewriting we showed earlier. The primary aim in this particular case was simply to practise structuring a whole text, and in order to complete this task there may not be enough time to expand it with the detail explored in Rewriting. In addition, rather than students taking turns to scribe on the board, it is typically the teacher that scribes the Joint Construction, as the class decides what to say and how to say it, as we described in Chapter 2.

Following this Joint Construction, each phase is labelled as above, and students can copy the joint text with its labels into their workbooks. Students can then attempt their own narrative, again following exactly the same pattern of phases. They now have two models – Dahl's original and the jointly constructed one, together with the ideas listed on the board. This activity is termed **Individual Construction** (in contrast to Independent Construction in Chapter 3). At this point, students are not yet at the point of independently writing a completely new narrative on their own; rather, they are practising using the same narrative devices as the teacher guided them to use in the Joint Construction. This is a further innovation on the original genre writing TLC described in Chapter 2, one designed to provide a higher level of support for all students to create accomplished texts, including the most and least successful students in the class.

4.3.5   More challenging texts – metaphor and messages

Although its language resources are rich and varied, *Fantastic Mr Fox* is written for eight to ten-year-old children. Beyond the middle primary level, texts become more complex and their language features more elaborate; in particular, metaphor becomes a pervasive feature. Furthermore, their social function extends beyond simply entertaining readers, to encoding messages about character and the nature of social life (Christie and Macken-Horarik 2007, 2011, Rothery 1994, Rothery and Stenglin 1997, 2000). At these levels, the reading and writing strategies have to focus as much on interpreting these messages as on the complexity of language.

To illustrate, the novel *Follow the Rabbit Proof Fence* (Pilkington 1996) encodes messages about tenacity and the sanctity of family and children, in contrast to the heartlessness and brutality of the policy of Indigenous child removal in Australia. Pilkington's novel addresses curriculum goals well beyond simply reading and writing stories, in social studies as well as literature studies. It could be studied as part of a curriculum unit explicitly designed to address issues in Australian history, Indigenous perspectives, human rights and other values. Reading the book can tell the teacher just what needs to be covered in the curriculum unit, in order to contextualise the story for students.

In class, the book as whole and each chapter in turn can be prepared before reading, as outlined above for *Mr Fox*, with background knowledge and a preview of the events to come. But with *Rabbit Proof Fence*, each preparation may involve more background and more detail in the preview, so that students can follow with understanding as it is read. And after reading each chapter, there would of course be many opportunities for interpretation in class discussion.

In order to give all students access to both the story and its interpretations, one or more passages can be selected for closer reading, including Detailed Reading. The following passage [4.8] is ideal, as it includes the pivotal events in the novel when the girls are removed from their family, forms a coherent story in itself, and encodes key messages of empathy with the family's grief, in contrast with antipathy to the heartlessness of their children's removal. The story in this case is not a narrative, as it is not resolved. Instead it concludes with the family's reactions to the events, the type of story known as an anecdote. The stages of an anecdote are Orientation, Remarkable Event and Reaction. Within these stages, each phase is also labelled.

[4.8] Extract from *Follow the Rabbit Proof Fence*

Orientation

...

setting   Molly and Gracie finished their breakfast and decided to take all their dirty clothes and wash them in the soak further down the river. They returned to the camp looking clean and refreshed and joined the rest of the family in the shade for lunch of tinned corned beef damper and tea.

Remarkable Event

problem   The family had just finished eating when all the camp dogs began barking, making a terrible din. 'Shut up,' yelled their owners, throwing stones at them. The dogs whined and skulked away.

description   Then all eyes turned to the cause of the commotion. A tall, rugged white man stood on the bank above them. He could easily have been mistaken for a pastoralist or a grazier with his tanned complexion except that he was wearing khaki clothing.

reaction   Fear and anxiety swept over them when they realised that the fateful day they had been dreading had come at last. They always knew that it would only be a matter of time before the government would track them down.

problem   When Constable Riggs, Protector of Aborigines, finally spoke his voice was full of authority and purpose. They knew without a doubt that he was the one who took children in broad daylight - not like the evil spirits who came into their camps at night. 'I've come to take Molly, Gracie and Daisy, the three half-caste girls, with me to Moore Rive Native Settlement,' he informed the family.

reaction   The old man nodded to show that he understood what Riggs was saying. The rest of the family just hung their heads, refusing to face the man who was taking their daughters away from them. Silent tears welled in their eyes and trickled down their cheeks.

problem   'Come on, you girls,' he ordered. 'Don't worry about taking anything. We'll pick up what you need later.' When the two girls stood up, he noticed that the third girl was missing. 'Where's the other one, Daisy?' he asked anxiously. 'She's with her mummy and daddy at Murra Munda Station,' the old man informed him. 'She's not at Murra Munda or Jimbalbar goldfields. I called into those places before I came here,' said the constable. 'Hurry up then, I want to get started. We've got a long way to go yet. You girls can ride this horse back to the depot,' he said, handing the reins over to Molly. Riggs was annoyed that he had to go miles out of his way to find these girls.

Reaction

reaction   Molly and Gracie sat silently on the horse, tears streaming down their cheeks as Constable Riggs turned the big bay stallion and led the way back to the depot. A high pitched wail broke out. The cries of agonised mothers and the women, and the deep sobs of grandfathers, uncles and cousins filled the air. Molly and Gracie looked back just once before they disappeared through the river gums. Behind them, those remaining in the camp found sharp objects and gashed themselves and inflicted deep wounds to their heads and bodies as an expression of their sorrow.

reaction   The two frightened and miserable girls began to cry, silently at first, then uncontrollably; their grief made worse by the lamentations of their loved ones and the visions of them sitting on the ground in their camp letting their tears mix with the red blood that flowed from the cuts on their heads.

comment   This reaction to their children's abduction showed that the family were now in mourning. They were grieving for their abducted children and their relief would come only when the tears ceased to fall, and that will be a long time yet.

Before reading this passage, it could be prepared as follows. We can assume that the novel has been read up to this point, so that the students know who Molly and Gracie are, why the family are camping in the riverbed, and about the government policy that Constable Riggs is carrying out.

This is a key passage in the novel, in which Molly and Gracie are taken from their family by the policeman, Constable Riggs. It begins peacefully. Remember the family went camping for the weekend, and collected lots of bush food. The girls slept in the dry riverbed and their mothers made breakfast for them. In this part, the girls go to wash their clothes in a pool in the riverbed, called a soak, and then have lunch with their family. Suddenly all the dogs start barking, and a white man appears on the bank of the river above them. The family recognise that he is a policeman by his khaki uniform, and realise that he has come to take their girls away, and that fills them with fear. Riggs announces why he has come, and the family hang their heads, knowing there is nothing they can do about it. There is a small problem for Riggs, because Daisy is not with them, so he will have to go out of his way, which annoys him. But that is nothing compared to the terrible grief that Molly, Gracie and the family feel, as Riggs leads them away, knowing that they may never see each other again.

This preparation summarises the sequence of phases in the analysis [4.8]. After reading, the passage could be interpreted in more depth. For example, we could discuss the significance of Molly and Gracie washing their clothes between breakfast and lunch – perhaps indicating that they were not dirty or neglected, one of the stereotypical prejudices often cited for removing Indigenous children from their families. We might ask about the significance of Riggs' *authority and purpose*, and why the family just hang their heads. Crucially, the contrast between the family's grief and Riggs' annoyance at having to go out of his way encodes the central message of the novel, steering the reader towards empathy with the humanity of Indigenous families and children, and antipathy towards the government policy that separated them. In this context, unfamiliar grieving actions like gashing heads seem more understandable than the inhumane act of taking children from their families.

Within the text, we could discuss the author's strategy of beginning with a peaceful setting, shattered by the dogs barking, which foreshadows the problem to come. The tension is then held by pausing the action to describe what the family see, and we enter their emotional world as they realise who it is and are overcome with fear. The external events that follow are controlled by Riggs, as he informs, orders and demands information, but the internal world of feelings is the domain of the girls and their family, as they react to each of the problems that Riggs presents to them. As the problems worsen, so the reactions intensify, culminating with their agonised cries and gashing of heads. The final comment returns the story to the present, as the author steps in to explain their behaviour, and subtly shifts from a story in the past to the future for Indigenous people as a whole, as *their relief would come only when the tears ceased to fall, and that will be a long time yet.*

It is a great piece of writing, full of subtlety and grace. Experienced readers may absorb these subtleties while devouring the novel, without consciously noticing them all. Less experienced readers could miss many, and not recognise the message they convey. Others may simply struggle to comprehend what is going on. The discussion after reading brings all this subtlety to consciousness, making the author's techniques explicit for all to see. The preparation before reading enables all students to engage with the text as it is read, and thus to participate meaningfully in the elaboration that follows.

4.3.6   Detailed Reading – unpacking metaphor

An experienced practitioner of Detailed Reading could work through this entire passage with a class of secondary students in around 30 minutes. Alternatively, we could just do Detailed Reading on the paragraphs that include the most elaborate language and implicitly encode messages for the reader to interpret. For example, the following two paragraphs use rich language resources for constructing description and reaction phases in stories, and include a series of metaphors and idioms that need to be unpacked for students to understand, at the same time showing them how to recognise and infer the meaning of metaphors and idioms in general.

> Then all eyes turned to the cause of the commotion. A tall, rugged white man stood on the bank above them. He could easily have been mistaken for a pastoralist or a grazier with his tanned complexion except that he was wearing khaki clothing.
>
> Fear and anxiety swept over them when they realised that the fateful day they had been dreading had come at last. They always knew that it would only be a matter of time before the government would track them down.

The first sentence here includes three instances of inferential meaning. It begins with a lexical metaphor *all eyes turned*; literally just their eyes turned, but the inferred meaning is that 'everyone turned around to look at the same time' (see §5.1.6 below). It ends with a grammatical metaphor (§5.1.7) *the cause of the commotion*, in which the dogs barking is referred to as *the commotion* and what made them bark as *the cause*. The sentence is prepared with its inferred meaning, and then the first lexical metaphor with its inferred meaning, as follows.

Detailed Reading for Text [4.8]

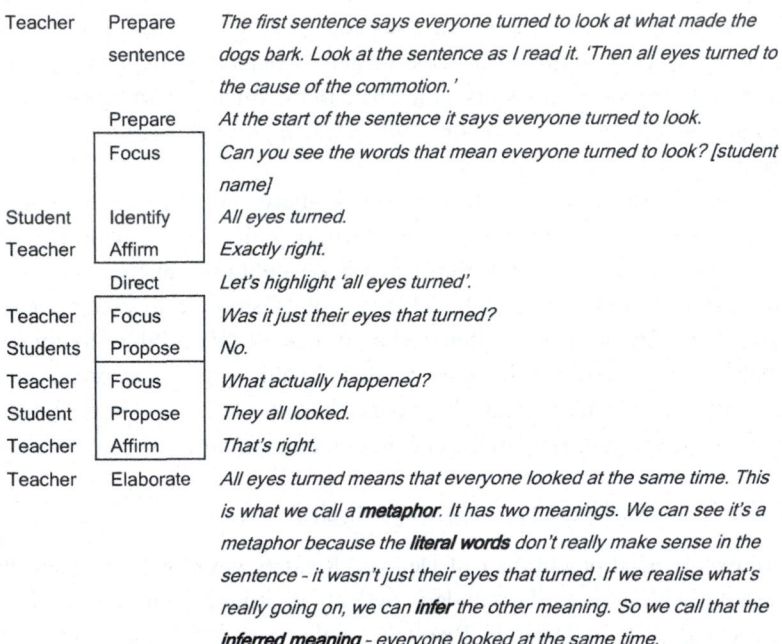

Teacher	Prepare sentence	*The first sentence says everyone turned to look at what made the dogs bark. Look at the sentence as I read it. 'Then all eyes turned to the cause of the commotion.'*
	Prepare	*At the start of the sentence it says everyone turned to look.*
	Focus	*Can you see the words that mean everyone turned to look? [student name]*
Student	Identify	*All eyes turned.*
Teacher	Affirm	*Exactly right.*
	Direct	*Let's highlight 'all eyes turned'.*
Teacher	Focus	*Was it just their eyes that turned?*
Students	Propose	*No.*
Teacher	Focus	*What actually happened?*
Student	Propose	*They all looked.*
Teacher	Affirm	*That's right.*
Teacher	Elaborate	*All eyes turned means that everyone looked at the same time. This is what we call a **metaphor**. It has two meanings. We can see it's a metaphor because the **literal words** don't really make sense in the sentence - it wasn't just their eyes that turned. If we realise what's really going on, we can **infer** the other meaning. So we call that the **inferred meaning** - everyone looked at the same time.*

One technique for elaborating lexical metaphors such as *all eyes turned* is to draw students' attention to the fact that the literal wording does not exactly make sense in the context of the sentence and that the inferred meaning is quite different. The next step here is to define the inferred meaning more precisely, and to name it as a metaphor, introducing metalanguage for this type of language feature. The concept of a metaphor could now be consolidated by asking students to think of related metaphors that they know.

Teacher	Prepare	*There are lots of metaphors about eyes, like 'keep your eyes on the ball'. It doesn't really mean take your eye out and stick it on the ball, does it?*
	Focus	*What does it really mean?*
Students	Propose	*Keep watching the ball.*
Teacher	Affirm	*Right, keep watching closely.*
	Focus	*What other metaphors do you know like that?*
Students	Propose	*Keep your eyes peeled. An eye for an eye. Easy on the eye. Out of the corner of your eye.*
Teacher	Affirm	*Brilliant.*

> Elaborate   *These are all metaphors that stand for a different meaning. Others are the apple of my eye, a sight for sore eyes, an eye-sore.*

Metalanguage is built up and reinforced through elaboration moves in Detailed Reading. After introducing the term 'metaphor' above, the next time a metaphor is encountered, the teacher may ask the class, *What do we call a wording with two meanings?* Some students will be able to respond correctly (often the more experienced readers), which the teacher can affirm and then refine the definition, perhaps again asking students to apply their experience. Over time all students will come to recognise metaphors automatically, and understand and use the term appropriately. This approach to building metalanguage works effectively because students are repeatedly encountering instances in meaningful contexts, with the teacher's guidance. This is precisely how language learning happens in the home, as we outlined in Chapter 2. It is more effective than attempting to teach language systems out of context, as sets of rules, and more effective than not explicitly teaching metalanguage at all.

The following grammatical metaphor, *the cause of the commotion*, could be prepared with the concrete events it refers to: *what made the dogs bark*.

Teacher	Prepare	*Next it tells us what made the dogs bark.*
	Focus	*[student name], can you see the words that mean what made the dogs bark?*
Student	Identify	*The cause of the commotion.*
Teacher	Affirm	*Brilliant.*
	Direct	*Let's highlight 'cause of the commotion'.*
	Elaborate	*A commotion is a lot of noise and activity.*
	Focus	*What was the commotion here?*
Students	Propose	*The dogs barking.*
Teacher	Affirm	*Exactly.*
	Focus	*And what do you think was the cause of the commotion?*
Student	Propose	*The white man. Riggs. The policeman.*
Teacher	Affirm	*That's right.*
	Elaborate	*That's why the dogs started barking, before the family saw him.*

After defining *commotion*, students are guided to infer what the commotion was, and what its cause was – in other words to give back the inferential meaning that the teacher gave them in the preparation. This provides a context for preparing the next sentence, by making the relation between the two sentences explicit.

An important point to make here is that not everything in each sentence needs to be defined, explained or named. Close scrutiny of any text worth reading will reveal a plethora of options for discussion. It can be as hard to choose which items not to elaborate as it is to identify what does need elaborating. If Detailed Reading is a regular teaching practice, then these choices become part of long-term planning of teaching programs.

Detailed Reading of this kind achieves the dual outcome of enabling the weakest students in a class to fluently read passages of dense literary text, at the same time as exploring its meanings to a level that would challenge the top students in any class. The technique can be applied to any literary text – novels, poetry, drama – at any stage of schooling. In such a curriculum unit, the teaching goal may not be story writing, in which case story Rewriting and Joint Construction may not be appropriate further steps in the teaching sequence. Rather, a major goal in literary studies in the secondary school is to interpret texts, so the key texts that students need to write are in fact text responses. We will return to this type of curriculum focus when we discuss arguments and text responses below, and look at how we can guide students to respond to texts such as *Follow the Rabbit Proof Fence*.

4.4   Informing readers: factual texts

Social purposes for reading and writing factual texts are generally quite different from those for the literary texts we have been exploring so far. By factual texts we mean the chronicles, explanations, reports and procedures that form the core curricula of school subjects such as history, geography, science, technology and maths. In the factual domain, the goal of reading is most generally to acquire knowledge about the topic presented in the text, and the function of writing is commonly to demonstrate what students have learnt about a topic.

We saw in Chapter 3 how types of knowledge are structured differently, from the synoptic evaluations of history to the technical hierarchies of scientific knowledge. In Chapter 1 we suggested that the structuring of knowledge also varies across the years of schooling. In the primary school, the curriculum tends to be organised around 'themes' that are considered of special relevance for children. Teachers are expected to select topics from different subject areas that are related to the term's theme.

One rationale for this approach to curriculum is that more children will be engaged in personally relevant themes than in a sequence of topics in academic subjects. Two consequences of this perspective are (i) that the overall structuring of each subject area may remain invisible to students and teachers, and (ii) the fragmented approach may not lend itself to systematically building up knowledge in any one subject area. It is nevertheless possible within this kind of framework to give students an understanding of how knowledge is organised in each subject – by showing them how to read and write knowledgably in the topics selected.

When they arrive in the secondary school, students are confronted with a curriculum that is in fact differentiated into subject areas, and each subject is organised by the knowledge structure of the discipline. If they have learned how to read and write the kinds of texts that build knowledge in each subject area, they will be well prepared to succeed in this type of curriculum. But as all secondary teachers know, a minority of students are in fact well prepared when they arrive in their classrooms, some are moderately prepared, and others have little preparation at all. By and large secondary teachers feel too constrained by the sheer volume of curriculum they are expected to cover to spend adequate time providing their less-successful students with what they need to successfully engage with their subjects.

The strategies outlined here are designed to enable primary teachers to make the structuring of various school subjects explicit for their students, and for secondary teachers to efficiently integrate the teaching of reading and writing with learning the curriculum of each subject. The starting point is with Preparing for Reading; in the case of secondary school disciplines, this often involves a strong focus on building field knowledge before coming to the text.

4.4.1   Preparing for Reading factual texts

We can illustrate how reading and writing can be explicitly integrated with curriculum teaching, and how subject knowledge can be explicitly integrated with reading and writing, with reference to a science topic from the junior secondary school. The topic we will focus on is the structure and function of cells, which is part of a curriculum unit on cells in living things. This unit would be studied over about half a term in the first year or two of Australian secondary schools, and follows another unit on classification of living things. Figure 4.10 is from a text book covering these curriculum units (Haire et al. 2004), setting out topics in the chapter on cells.

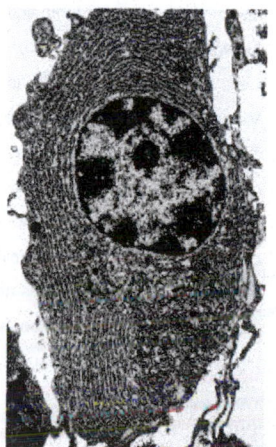

CHAPTER 5 *Cells 92*

Thinking about — Cells 93

5.1   A whole new world   94
5.2   It's a small world   96
5.3   In focus   98
5.4   Zooming in on life   100
5.5   In the five kingdoms   102
5.6   The spice of life   104
5.7   Focus on plants   106
5.8   Science issues — Viruses — Living or not?   108

Putting it all together 110

Extension — Interrupted travelling 112

Reflection 113

Figure 4.10: Topics in a science curriculum unit.
This material is reproduced with permission of John Wiley & Sons Australia.

Figure 4.11 is a double page spread from one of these topics, concerning the structures, functions and types of cells across the kingdoms of life. In this spread there are six short texts, each with a heading, as well as associated diagrams, tables, and activities designed to test students' comprehension of the texts. Such texts are known as **macrogenres**, as they consist of a series of smaller genres (see Martin and Rose 2008 for a detailed discussion of genre complexes of this kind). Three of the texts are re-presented as Text [4.9] for ease of reading.

[4.9] Three reports in Figure 4.11

5.5 In the five kingdoms

No matter how different an organism looks on the outside, its cells have the same basic structure.

Cells of the five kingdoms

Although the basic cell structure is the same, variations in the design are used to classify organisms into five main groups or kingdoms. The five different kingdoms are Animalia (animals), Fungi (e.g. mushrooms), Plantae (plants), Prokaryotae (also called Monera) (e.g. bacteria and bluegreen bacteria) and Protista (a mixture of organisms that don't fit into the other groups) (e.g. algae and protozoans).

The brain of the cell

A largish round structure called the nucleus is the control centre of the cell. It contains chromosomes that contain information to keep the cell alive and working properly. Organisms that consist of cells without a membrane around the nucleus are called prokaryotes. Those with cells that have a membrane around the nucleus are called eukaryotes. Prokaryotes such as bacteria were the first type of organisms to appear on Earth. Eukaryotes appeared about a billion years later. Plants, animals, fungi and protistans are examples of organisms containing eukaryotic cells.

All wrapped up

Cells are wrapped in a cell membrane, which controls what goes into and comes out of the cell. Material made of small particles moves in and out of cells through pores in the cell membrane. Sometimes this movement requires energy. This movement is necessary to supply substances needed by the cell and to remove wastes.

Cytoplasm is the part of the cell inside the cell membrane but outside the nucleus. In the cytoplasm hundreds of chemical reactions take place, transferring energy, storing food and making new substances. This activity within the cell is called its metabolism.

Some cells have another boundary around the cell membrane, called the cell wall. This gives protection, support and shape to a cell.

Preparing for Reading begins with the field (background) knowledge that students would need to access Text [4.9], including:

- Organisms, cells, structure and function
- Chemical reactions, energy, substances, wastes

In the five kingdoms

No matter how different an organism looks on the outside, its cells have the same basic structure.

Cells of the five kingdoms

Although the basic cell structure is the same, variations in the design are used to classify organisms into five main groups or kingdoms. The five different kingdoms are
Animalia (animals),
Fungi (e.g. mushrooms),
Plantae (plants),
Prokaryotae (also called Monera) (e.g. bacteria and blue-green bacteria) and
Protista (a mixture of organisms that don't fit into the other groups) (e.g. algae and protozoans).

The brain of the cell

A largish round structure called the **nucleus** is the control centre of the cell. It contains chromosomes that contain information to keep the cell alive and working properly. Organisms that consist of cells without a membrane around the nucleus are called **prokaryotes**. Those with cells that have a membrane around the nucleus are called **eukaryotes**. Prokaryotes such as bacteria were the first type of organisms to appear on Earth. Eukaryotes appeared about a billion years later. Plants, animals, fungi and protistans are examples of organisms containing eukaryotic cells.

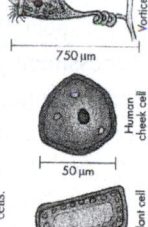

Bacterium — 3 µm · Plant cell — 100 µm · Human cheek cell — 50 µm · Vorticella — 750 µm

Some differences in the basic cell design in the five kingdoms

Characteristic	Kingdom				
	Animalia (animals: e.g. lizards, fish, spiders, earthworms, sponges)	Fungi (e.g. yeasts, moulds, mushrooms, toadstools)	Plantae (plants: e.g. ferns, mosses, conifers, flowering plants)	Prokaryotes/Monera (bacteria and blue-green bacteria)	Protista ('leftovers': e.g. algae, protozoans)
number of cells	multicellular	usually multicellular but some unicellular	most multicellular	single-celled	single-celled or multicellular
nucleus	nucleus with membrane	nucleus with membrane; some fungi have several nuclei per cell	nucleus with membrane	no membrane-bound nucleus	nucleus with membrane
cell wall	absent	present	present	present	present in some
large vacuole	absent	absent	present	absent	present in some
chloroplasts	absent	absent	present	present in some	present in some

The original two kingdom system has been highlighted. As scientists gained more knowledge they introduced more kingdoms.

All *wrapped* up

Cells are wrapped in a **cell membrane**, which controls what goes into and comes out of the cell. Material made of small particles moves in and out of cells through pores in the cell membrane. Sometimes this movement requires energy. This movement is necessary to supply substances needed by the cell and to remove wastes.

Cytoplasm is the part of the cell inside the cell membrane but outside the nucleus. In the cytoplasm hundreds of chemical reactions take place, transferring energy, storing food and making new substances. This activity within the cell is called its **metabolism**.

Some cells have another boundary around the cell membrane, called the **cell wall**. This gives protection, support and shape to a cell.

Micro *factories* and *departments*

Structures called **organelles** are found in the cytoplasm of eukaryotes. They include mitochondria, chloroplasts, vacuoles and starch grains. The **mitochondrion** (plural: mitochondria) is the 'powerhouse' of the cell, because it supplies energy. **Chloroplasts** contain the green pigment **chlorophyll** which is used in **photosynthesis** (making food using sunlight). A **vacuole** is a large cavity in the cytoplasm which is filled with a watery fluid. Vacuoles store water and dissolved substances. In plants, this fluid is called **cell sap**. Vacuoles are partly responsible for the firmness of plants. Prokaryotes do not have organelles.

One cell or more?

Some organisms are made up of a single cell and are described as being **unicellular**. In this case the cell has to do all of the required jobs itself. Unicellular organisms reproduce by cell division, that is one cell divides into two cells. **Multicellular** organisms are made up of many cells with different types of cells doing different jobs. Most plant and animal species, including humans, are multicellular organisms. Reproduction, growth and repair in multicellular organisms involve cell division.

A *Paramecium* is a unicellular animal. — 300 µm
A *Euglena* — 100 µm

How big is small?

The size of cells may also vary between organisms, and within a multicellular organism. Most cells are too small to be seen without a microscope. Special, very small units of measurement are used to describe their size. The most commonly used unit is a **micrometre** (µm) where 1 µm equals 1 millionth of a metre. Most cells are in the range of 1 µm (bacteria) to 100 µm (plant cells).

Activities

Remember
1. What do all living things have in common?
2. Why is the nucleus important to the cell?
3. State the names of the five kingdoms and use the table to determine which kingdoms contain organisms that are eukaryotes.
4. What is the purpose of the cell membrane?
5. Why does cell division take place in:
   (a) a unicellular organism
   (b) a multicellular organism?
6. State the differences between a mitochondrion, a chloroplast and a vacuole.

Think
What are the advantages, if any, of the five kingdom system?

Using data
Use the table on page 102 to answer the following questions.
1. In which kingdom(s) do the cells of an organism:
   (a) not have a cell wall, large vacuole or chloroplasts?
   (b) have a cell wall, large vacuole and chloroplasts?
   (c) have a cell wall, but no large vacuole or chloroplasts?
   (d) have a cell wall and nucleus without a membrane around it?

Use the cell diagrams on pages 102 and 103 to answer questions 2–4.
2. Construct a table with the following headings: 'Name of organism' or 'type of cell', and 'Cell size (µm)'.
3. Show the sizes of the cells on a graph, with the horizontal axis representing the type of cell and the vertical axis representing the size of cell. Sketch each cell as accurately as you can, in the correct position on the graph. Which are the smallest and biggest?
4. Determine the average size for the cells shown on pages 102 and 103.

Create
Make a labelled model of a cell from one of the kingdoms. Use materials available at home, such as egg cartons, cottonwool and plastic drink bottles.

PLANTAE · ANIMALIA · FUNGI · PROKARYOTAE/MONERA · PROTISTA

Figure 4.11: Double page on one topic. This material is reproduced with permission of John Wiley & Sons Australia.

Planning a lesson unit involves selecting texts for students to read, as well as presenting the topic in the classroom. Carefully reading selected texts reveals the knowledge that must be presented and sequenced for students to access the texts. Lesson planning thus becomes a two-way process: selecting texts to fit the lesson, and shaping the lesson to fit the texts. Textbooks like this one are generally organised to build up knowledge in steps. In theme-based programs in the primary school, and where textbooks are not used in the secondary school (such as in 'lower ability' classes), the job of sequencing knowledge falls to teachers, who may or may not be well positioned to take up this challenge.

Assuming these topics have been studied previously, they may be briefly revised in class discussion, before starting on the text. The next step is to sum-marise the text in terms that all students can understand and engage with. Plan-ning for this involves identifying the key information in each paragraph. In addition, there may be diagrams and tables that re-present or exemplify infor-mation in the verbal texts or provide additional information that has no verbal support. This may be a particular challenge with current textbooks and websites, which are designed to appeal to young readers with fragmented magazine style layouts. The relation between texts and images in these macrogenres can be difficult to recover, making them harder to read than more traditional textbooks that systematically use images in support of verbal texts. Complicating this is the naïve assumption that images are more transparently understood than writing, and can thus be used instead of writing, especially for weaker students.[3]

A further consideration is the assessment tasks that may culminate each section in a textbook (both traditional and magazine style), and are designed to test literal, inferential and interpretive comprehension, such as these from Figure 4.11.

Remember

1. What do all living things have in common? (literal)

2. Why is the nucleus important to the cell? (inferential)

3. State the names of the five kingdoms (literal) and use the table to determine which kingdoms contain organisms that are eukaryotes. (inferential)

4. What is the purpose of the cell membrane? (inferential)

Taking these questions into account, the text could be orally prepared as follows. (Figure 4.6 is reproduced here to remind us where we are in the R2L program.)

---

[3] The actual nature of the complementarity of words and images in building disciplined knowledge is usefully explored in Jones 2007, Martin and Rose 2008, Unsworth 2001a, 2008.

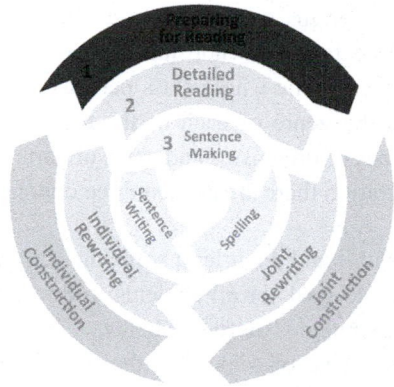

Figure 4.6': Preparing for Reading in the R2L program

Ideally the whole text would be projected for the class so that the teacher can pinpoint elements, and each student would have their own copy to highlight and retain.

> *These pages describe the structures and functions of cells in the five kingdoms of life. You can see there are six short texts about different aspects of cells' structure, each with a heading. There are diagrams that relate to these texts, and a table at the bottom that summarises the information. At the end are Activities for you to do after reading it.*
>
> *It starts by saying what all organisms have in common, their cells have the same basic structure. The first short text is a report about the five kingdoms of life, with a diagram beside it showing examples in each kingdom. Let's say the names of each kingdom - Animalia, Fungi, Plantae, Prokaryotae, Protista (repeating). What organisms can you see in each kingdom?*
>
> *Can you see what the next text is called? - The brain of the cell. Right. It's a report about the structure of cells and focuses on the nucleus which controls the cell. That's why they call it the brain of the cell, and why it is important. Simple cells like bacteria have no membrane or boundary around the nucleus. They are called prokaryotic. Cells in all other organisms do have a membrane around the nucleus. They are called eukaryotic. Let's all say prokaryotic and eukaryotic (repeating).*
>
> *The next text on the next page is a report about the membrane that covers the cell. Can you see what it's called? - All wrapped up. Right. It describes the purpose of the membrane, then it describes the substance within the membrane called the cytoplasm. Let's say cytoplasm (repeating). Then it describes the chemical reactions in the cytoplasm called metabolism. Say metabolism (repeating).*

The purpose of asking students to voice the headings of each text as it is prepared is so that they can identify the parts of the text as it is read, and will recognise the headings. Likewise, they are guided to say technical terms aloud to make these unfamiliar words more familiar as they read. And they are also supported to read the diagrams and tables, and relate them back to the texts. Interpersonally, the preparation is not just a teacher monologue about an unfamiliar topic, but engages the whole class personally and actively. Note also that the teacher names the genre of each of the texts; in this case they are all reports that describe types of organisms and cells, or parts of cells.

Following this preparation there are at least three options for reading the text:

1. Students may read it and do at least some the activities independently. This is the ultimate goal for all students, following practice with the more supportive strategies discussed below.
2. The whole text can be read aloud, either by the teacher or with the students taking turns. More support can be given by preparing and reading one short text at a time, repeating the preparations given earlier.
3. The text can be read paragraph-by-paragraph, with a preparation for each paragraph and discussion of key points after reading it. As each paragraph is elaborated, students can be guided to highlight key information in it. These activities are known as **paragraph-by-paragraph reading** and **text marking**. They can be used with any longer texts to guide students to identify key information. This information can then be used for note making, discussed in §4.4.4 below.

Here is an example of paragraph-by-paragraph reading and text marking, for the first paragraph of the textbook page [4.9].

Exchange in paragraph-by-paragraph reading and text marking

| Teacher | **Prepare paragraph** | *OK. This first little report classifies the five kingdoms of life. Follow the words as I read it. 'Although the basic cell structure is the same, variations in the design are used to classify organisms into five main groups or kingdoms. The five different kingdoms are Animalia (animals), Fungi (e.g. mushrooms), Plantae (plants), Prokaryotae (also called Monera) (e.g. bacteria and bluegreen bacteria) and Protista (a mixture of organisms that don't fit into the other groups) (e.g. algae and protozoans).'* |
| | **Elaborate** | *So there are differences in the cells of each kingdom that scientists use to classify them.* |

Here the teacher briefly restates the earlier preparation, reads the paragraph aloud, and elaborates its key message. The elaboration is then continued interactively, as follows.

Teacher	Direct	*Let's say their names again.*
	Focus	*What's the first one?*
Students	Identify	*Animalia*
Teacher	Affirm	*Right*
	Elaborate	*That's the Latin name for animals.*
Teacher	Focus	*Next*
Students	Identify	*Fungi*
Teacher	Affirm	*Yes*
	Focus	*What's an example of Fungi?*
Students	Identify	*Mushrooms. Toadstools.*
Teacher	Affirm	*Exactly*
	Focus	*Next, what's the Latin name for plants?*
Students	Identify	*Plantae*
Teacher	Affirm	*Right*
	Focus	*Let's say the next one together. Prokaryotae.*
Students	Identify	*Prokaryotae*
Teacher	Affirm	*Very good*
	Elaborate	*They are also called Monera*
	Focus	*What are the examples of Prokaryotae?*
Students	Identify	*Bacteria and bluegreen bacteria*
Teacher	Affirm	*Yep*
	Focus	*And last?*
Students	Identify	*Protista*
Teacher	Focus	*Can you see the two examples of Protista?*
	Identify	*Algae and protozoans*
Teacher	Affirm	*Exactly.*
Teacher	Elaborate	*Algae are plant-like organisms including seaweeds. Protozoans are single cell organisms that move about like animals.*
	Focus	*Have a look at Protista in the diagram. Can you see the tiny hairs on those big cells?*
Students	Attend	*[look at diagram]*
	Elaborate	*They wave about so the cell can move through water.*

Students are asked to identify each kingdom, and the examples in brackets, through a series of Focus questions without preparations, as the earlier discussion before and during reading prepared them for this. However, the teacher increases support as the task gets harder, such as pronouncing *Prokaryotae*, and explaining the category *Protista*, which is the furthest from commonsense. Again this last elaboration is done interactively by guiding students' attention to the diagram and explaining it. Text marking then proceeds by guiding students, with meaning and position cues, to identify key wordings, as follows.

Teacher	Prepare	*Now, let's highlight some key information here. We'll start with the topic sentence.*
	Focus	*First of all what's the same about all these organisms?*
Students	Identify	*Basic cell structure*
Teacher	Affirm	*Brilliant*
	Direct	*Let's highlight basic cell structure at the beginning of the text.*
	Focus	*Next, can you see the word that means they vary?*
Students	Identify	*Variations.*
Teacher	Affirm	*Exactly right.*
	Elaborate	*That's the differences between them.*
	Focus	*Then can you see what the variations in design are used for?*
Students	Identify	*Classify organisms*
Teacher	Affirm	*Right*
	Elaborate	*Scientists classify organisms into different kingdoms by differences in their cells.*
	Direct	*Now let's just highlight the names of the kingdoms.*
	Focus	*What are they?*
		...

Again little preparation is needed for this sentence, as it was prepared by the preceding discussion, but the teacher further elaborates by explaining the technical terms *variations* and *classify*. In both the reading and text marking, Focus questions are directed here to the class as a whole. The preceding discussion should support most students to respond successfully. However, individual students can also be asked to respond, to ensure that all students are equally engaged.

A critical point here, which applies across the whole methodology, is that comprehension is continually reinforced and extended, by returning to the text through the series of strategies. Preparation before reading the whole text supports overall comprehension. This general level of comprehension then provides a platform for preparation and reading the paragraph, which in turn gives a platform for extending comprehension in the elaboration, which is then reinforced and further extended in text marking.

Rather than expecting students to grasp a topic through oral teacher explanations, along with oral exploratory question and answer routines, student understanding is built up through a series of reading tasks that are prepared and elaborated. Each successive task is more detailed and difficult, but is grounded by students' success with preceding tasks. The first task is to follow the oral preparation, repeat technical words as the teacher says them, and identify the headings and visual images with the teacher's guidance. The second task is to follow the words of the paragraph as it is read aloud. The third is to identify and say wordings in the paragraph, with the teacher's guidance. And the fourth is to mark key information. At each of these four task levels, understanding is extended through elaborations.

4.4.2   Detailed Reading of factual texts – technical and abstract language

Following preparation and reading of the whole text (with or without text marking), a short passage can be selected for Detailed Reading and Rewriting. The aims of Detailed Reading and Rewriting with factual texts are to support students to read and write technical and abstract language, and to comprehend the field in depth and detail. While Detailed Reading and Rewriting are only done on short passages of text, the skills they give students transfer to reading and writing other texts over time.

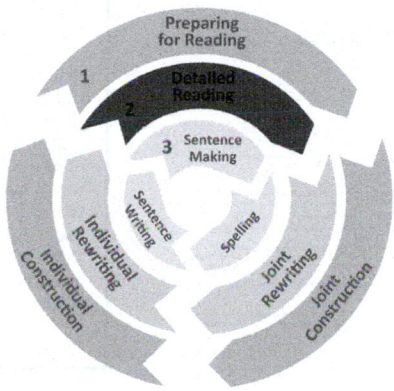

Figure 4.7′: Detailed Reading in the R2L program

Figure 4.12 is a short passage selected for Detailed Reading and Rewriting from Text [4.9]. Purposes for Selecting such a short passage for Detailed Reading could include the need to focus on:

- key elements for understanding the topic in depth;
- dense technical or abstract language that needs unpacking;
- good models for structuring one or more parts of the genre that students will be writing for assessment.

Before Detailed Reading this passage could be prepared as follows.

> *This is a report about the parts of cells. Because it describes what cells are composed of, we call it a compositional report. Each paragraph describes one structure in the cell and what it does, in other words its function. The first paragraph describes the skin that cells are wrapped in - called a membrane - and the function of the membrane - controlling what comes in and goes out of the cell. The second paragraph describes what's inside the membrane - a jelly-like substance called the cytoplasm (everyone say cytoplasm). Then it describes what happens in the cytoplasm - lots of chemical reactions - called metabolism (everyone say metabolism). The last paragraph describes a layer that some cells have outside the membrane, called a cell wall.*

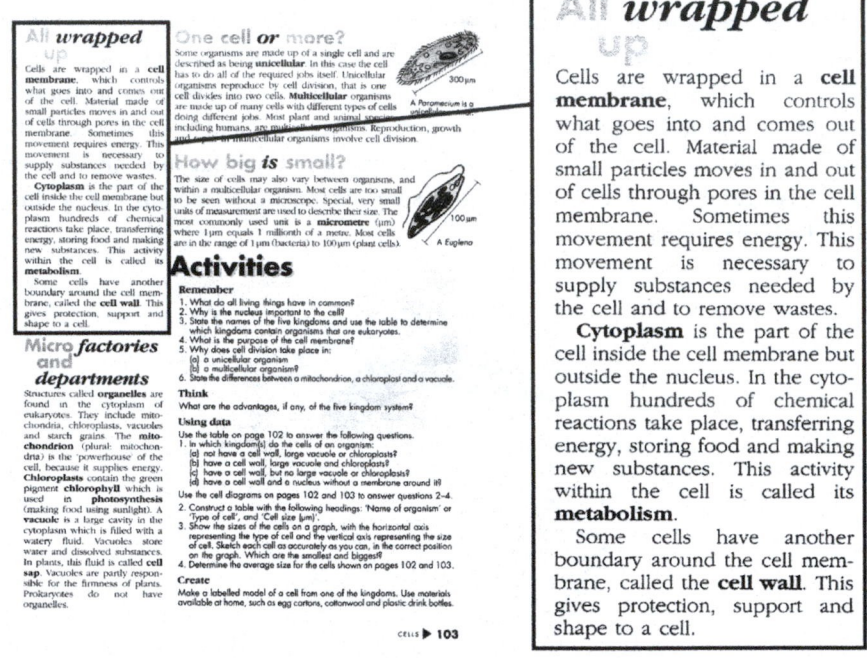

Figure 4.12: Passage Selected for Detailed Reading

This preparation provides more detail than preparing the whole text, and it focuses on the structuring of the text in three phases – membrane, cytoplasm, cell wall – each describing a structure and its functions. The text would then be read to the class. The Detailed Reading exchange is illustrated here with the second paragraph, which perhaps contains the most technicality in this text.

Detailed Reading of Text [4.9]

Teacher	Focus	*Can you see what the next phase is about?*
Students	Identify	*Cytoplasm*
Teacher	Affirm	*Right*
	Direct	*Let's highlight cytoplasm.*
	Elaborate	*The cytoplasm is like the body of the cell.*

The teacher starts by asking the class to identify what the phase is about, an easy task as it is the first word in bold, and they have already practised saying it. The next wordings in the sentence are easy to read, so students can identify them without precise preparation, as follows.

Teacher	Prepare sentence	*The first sentence describes where the cytoplasm is. 'Cytoplasm is the part of the cell inside the cell membrane but outside the nucleus.'*
Student	Focus	*[student name] What's it inside of?*
	Identify	*the cell membrane*
Teacher	Affirm	*Exactly.*
	Direct	*Let's do inside the cell membrane.*
Student	Focus	*[student name] What's it outside of?*
	Identify	*the nucleus*
Teacher	Affirm	*Right.*
	Direct	*Do outside the nucleus.*
	Focus	*Have a look at the diagram of a Paramecium at the top right of the page. Can you see the dark nucleus and the membrane around the cell?*
Students	Attend	*[look at diagram]*
	Elaborate	*The cytoplasm is the grey part inside the membrane but outside the nucleus.*

While *inside* and *outside* are easy enough to read, they provide an opportunity to relate the text to the diagrams on the page (reproduced here as Figure 4.13), ensuring that all students can visualise the biological structure the image is illustrating.

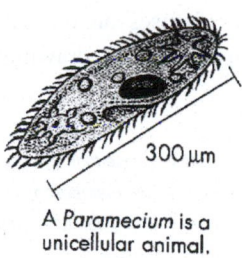

300 μm

A *Paramecium* is a unicellular animal.

Figure 4.13: Diagram of Paramecium referred to in Detailed Reading

Teacher	Prepare sentence	*The next sentence tells us what happens in the cytoplasm. I'll read the sentence. 'In the cytoplasm hundreds of chemical reactions take place, transferring energy, storing food and making new substances.'*
Student	Focus	*[student name] Can you see what takes place in the cytoplasm?*
	Identify	*hundreds of chemical reactions*
Teacher	Affirm	*Exactly right.*
	Direct	*Let's just highlight chemical reactions.*

Teacher	Prepare	*Then it says three things those chemical reactions do, three functions.*
	Focus	*[student name] What's the first one?*
Student	Identify	*transferring energy*
Teacher	Affirm	*That's right.*
	Direct	*Just highlight energy.*
	Elaborate	*Transferring energy means taking energy from a chemical reaction to do other work.*
	Focus	*For example, what work does the cell membrane need energy for?*
Student	Propose	*Move particles in and out*
Teacher	Affirm	*Exactly.*
	Focus	*[student name] What's the next function of chemical reactions?*
Student	Identify	*Storing food*
Teacher	Affirm	*Right.*
	Direct	*Highlight that.*
	Elaborate	*One way cells store food is by converting nutrients into glucose.*
	Focus	*[student name] What's the next function?*
Student	Identify	*Making new substances*
Teacher	Affirm	*Exactly.*
	Direct	*Highlight new substances.*
	Elaborate	*Our cells make hundreds of different chemicals.*

We can assume the class knows about chemical reactions, which is not elaborated. Instead the teacher focuses on their three functions, repeating the term *function*, and elaborating each one, drawing on students' prior learning where possible.

Teacher	Prepare sentence	*The last sentence tells us what it's called. 'This activity within the cell is called its metabolism.'*
	Focus	*First of all, what's the word at the beginning that means what happens? [student name]*
Student	Identify	*This activity*
Teacher	Affirm	*Right.*
	Direct	*Highlight activity.*
	Elaborate	*Activity means what's going on.*
	Focus	*And what's it called? [student name]*
Student	Identify	*Metabolism*
Teacher	Affirm	*Brilliant*
	Direct	*Let's all say metabolism again.*
Students	Identify	*Metabolism*
	Elaborate	*Metabolism is all the activity, everything that goes on inside your body, in every cell.*

As well as defining *metabolism*, the teacher uses this opportunity to reinforce the meaning of *activity* here, as it is commonly used in science to refer to a series of processes. Detailed Reading thus provides continual opportunities for introducing and reinforcing general concepts in a field (such as biology here), as well as the specific information in the text.

4.4.3   Joint and Individual Rewriting – (re)presenting information

After Detailed Reading of a factual text, the information that has been highlighted can be used for Joint and Individual Rewriting.

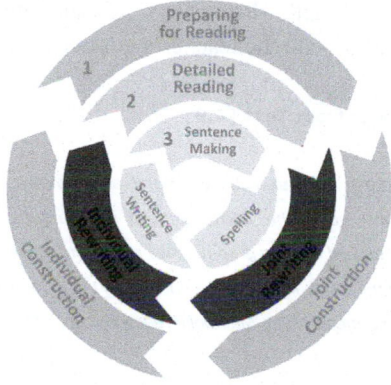

Figure 4.8′: Joint and Individual Rewriting in the R2L program

The first step in Rewriting is to write the highlighted information as notes. A very fruitful strategy for doing so is for students to take turns scribing the notes on the class board, as other students tell them what to write from their own highlighted texts. This is a cooperative activity in which the dictating student must clearly articulate the words, and spell them out if necessary, as the scribing student writes the words. The students are largely in control of the task at this point, since they understand the words they have highlighted, and can focus on saying and writing them. But this negotiation also provides many opportunities for the teacher to further discuss meanings as the words are written up, and to enhance students' skills in spelling and handwriting. Guiding students to spell in syllables using this activity can rapidly enhance the spelling skills of all students (see Spelling in §4.6 below).

A simple technique for note making from the highlighted text is to mark the information taken from each sentence in the original text with a dot point, with a dash between each word group; this helps keep the chunks of meaning clear and groups them into the information units they were highlighted from. Notes from different paragraphs can be separated with a line. The notes can then be labelled to make the structure of the text explicit, as follows:

membrane	*structure*	cell membrane - what goes into and comes out of the cell
	functions	small particles - in and out - pores
		movement requires energy
		supply substances needed by the cell - remove wastes.
cytoplasm	*structure*	cytoplasm - inside the cell membrane - outside the nucleus
	functions	chemical reactions - energy - food - new substances
		activity - metabolism
cell wall	*structure*	some cells - another boundary - cell wall
	functions	protection - support - shape

The function of Joint Rewriting of factual texts is then to explore the options for re-expressing these notes with different wordings, and to practise writing coherent technical language with the teacher's guidance. Here is an example:

[4.10] Rewrite using notes from Text [4.9]

> *All cells are covered in a thin skin called a membrane. Small particles move in and out of the cell through pores in the membrane. These particles include substances that the cell uses and wastes that must be removed. Energy is sometimes needed to move these particles in and out.*
>
> *Inside the cell membrane, but outside the nucleus, is the cytoplasm. Chemical reactions in the cytoplasm are known as metabolism. Metabolic reactions store food, create new substances and transfer energy.*
>
> *Some cells have a cell wall around the membrane, which protects the cell, supports it and gives it shape. For example, plant cells have cell walls.*

The teacher guides the class to order the sequence of elements, using a variety of grammatical structures, while maintaining the overall structure of phases, and the structure-function pattern within each phase. Metalanguage can again be drawn on as a key resource to facilitate this guidance, as illustrated by the following exchange. Its metalanguage terms are in bold.

Joint Rewriting exchange for Text [4.10]

Teacher	Focus	OK, what's the **first structure** we need to write about? [pointing at notes]
Students	Identify	Cell membrane
Teacher	Affirm	Right.
	Prepare	So in our **first sentence**, let's **define** what a membrane is.
	Focus	What did we say it was?
Students	Propose	A skin
Teacher	Affirm	Right, a thin skin.

Here the teacher is guiding the class to begin with a definition of the structure, before describing its functions (whereas the original included both structure and function in the first sentence).

Teacher	Prepare	*So let's start the **sentence** with what our readers already know, the object we're talking about.*
Students	Propose	*Cells*
Teacher	Affirm	*Yep.*
	Focus	*How many cells have a membrane? Just some cells?*
Students	Propose	*All cells*
Teacher	Affirm	*Great.*
	Direct	*[student name] Can you come and write that up here?*
Student		*[student scribes 'All cells']*
Teacher	Affirm	*Beautiful*
	Elaborate	*So that's the starting point of our **sentence**. We call that the **Theme** of the sentence, what it starts with.*

The teacher now starts guiding the class to organise the sentence, and introduces the term Theme, that can be repeated and redefined later. Note that the student starts scribing only when the wording has been decided on.

Teacher	Focus	*Now, what do all cells have?*
Students	Propose	*A membrane*
Teacher	Affirm	*Right*
	Focus	*And what did we say a membrane is?*
Students	Propose	*A thin skin*
Teacher	Affirm	*Exactly*

Here the teacher elicits a definition that was given during the Detailed Reading. Part of planning for Detailed Reading is to include elements that will go into a Rewrite.

Teacher	Prepare	*So let's put that next, and then the name 'membrane' at the end as the **new information**.*
	Focus	*So what's our **sentence** going to be? We have three bits of information – All cells, thin skin and membrane.*
Students	Propose	*All cells have a thin skin*
Teacher	Affirm	*Great.*
	Elaborate	*Let's say they're covered with a thin skin.*
	Focus	*Called?*
Students	Propose	*A membrane.*
Teacher	Affirm	*Brilliant*
	Direct	*[student name] Can you write that? All cells are covered in a thin skin called a membrane.*
Students		*[student scribes]*

Finally the teacher guides the class to order the three elements that have been elicited, providing additional words where needed to construct the whole scientific sentence.

When the Rewrite is complete, on the board and in students' copies, it can again be labelled with its phases, as in the notes, thus reinforcing both the structure and the terms used to discuss it. Students then use the notes for their own Individual Rewrites. The aim is to vary sentence patterns as much as possible from both the original passage and the Joint Rewrite, while maintaining the field, the overall structure, and scientific language. Some students have the language resources to do so independently, allowing the teacher to work with other students and provide them with more options.

Rewriting passages in the text can then form a foundation for practising short answers to questions, such those in the Activities section in Figure 4.11 above, applying the skills developed to assessment tasks in the subject area. Alternatively, rewriting can ground the writing of longer texts, as we discussed for stories above, using Joint Construction.

4.4.4 Joint and Individual Construction – writing from notes

A central goal for working with factual texts is to develop skills that students can use for independent research projects. These skills include (i) reading technical and abstract texts with understanding, (ii) identifying key information in the texts, (iii) making notes from this information, and (iv) using these notes to write new texts. These are essential skills for research tasks in primary and secondary school, and ultimately for mitigating the escalating pandemic of plagiarism in tertiary institutions, as students undertake research by downloading texts from the web and cutting and pasting them into submissions.[4] Joint Construction of whole texts is an essential step in developing these skills.

We have discussed writing from notes in the Rewriting activity with a short passage, but students also need to learn to apply these skills to longer stretches of text. To this end, the information that has been highlighted in paragraph-by-paragraph reading and text marking can be written on the board as notes, as described above for Joint Rewriting. During and after writing of the notes, they can be discussed and labelled with the phases that the text is going through.

---

[4] Most of these students have never been taught skills in note making and rewriting from notes, and in any case may find the material they are cutting and pasting too challenging to read. Without the kind of embedded literacy support we are describing here, threats and penalties for plagiarism have little effect, other than encouraging students to try to cut and paste more skillfully to avoid detection.

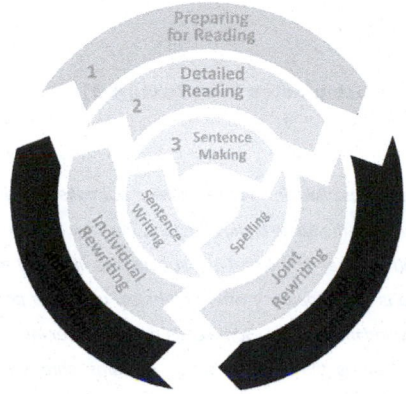

Figure 4.9′: Joint and Individual Construction in the R2L program

Text [4.9], from which the notes below were made, is a macrogenre, consisting of three short reports. The notes condense this macrogenre into a single text, namely a compositional report with two functions: to describe the basic structures of cells, and to classify them by their differences. The notes can be labelled with its stages and phases as follows.

Classification	• *basic cell structure - same - variations - classify organisms*
	• *kingdoms - animalia - fungi - plantae - prokaryotae - protista*
Description	• *nucleus - control centre*
nucleus	• *contains chromosomes*
	• *cells without a membrane around the nucleus - prokaryotes*
	• *membrane around the nucleus - eukaryotes*
	• *prokaryotes - bacteria*
	• *plants, animals, fungi and protistans - eukaryotic cells*
membrane	• *cell membrane*
and cytoplasm	• *supply substances - remove wastes*
	• *cytoplasm - inside the cell membrane - outside the nucleus*
	• *chemical reactions - transferring energy, storing food - making new substances - metabolism*
	• *another boundary - cell wall*
	• *protection, support - shape*

Once the notes are on the board, the teacher can guide the class to construct a new text using this information. This works differently form the process of Joint Construction with stories, described earlier. There, the same pattern of story phases was repeated with a new field – new characters, events, settings. With a factual text, the general organisation is followed, but the same field is used, based on the notes. The principle here is the same throughout genre-based pedagogy – using a familiar field and/or genre to practise the complex skills involved in writing a new text. Text [4.11] is an example of a Joint Construction, written from the notes above.

[4.11] Joint Construction using notes from Text [4.9]

Cells in organisms

All organisms are classified in five kingdoms: animalia, fungi, plantae, prokaryotae and protista. Their cells all have the same basic structure, but they are classified by their differences.

Cells are covered in a membrane that lets substances like food and water in, and wastes out. Inside the membrane is the cytoplasm, where chemical reactions produce energy, food and new substances. This is called metabolism. Some cells have another layer called a cell wall.

Within the cytoplasm is the nucleus, which contains chromosomes that control the cell's functions. Prokaryotes like bacteria have no membrane around their nucleus. Cells in the other kingdoms are all eukaryotes, which have a membrane around the nucleus.

In the course of rewriting, many different options for re-expressing the notes can be discussed, building up resources for students to apply in their own writing. One type of option is to re-order sequences of information, at the levels of word groups, clauses, sentences and paragraphs. For example, the first paragraph here is re-ordered to begin with classification of organisms (which flows from the preceding topic on classification), followed by the structure of cells (which is discussed in following paragraphs).

Students can write the new text in their books as it is constructed. The stages and phases of the text can then be labelled on the board and in students' copies, reinforcing the metalanguage. A next step can then be for students to write their own version from the same notes, in Individual Construction. The aim is for students to rework it from the Joint Construction, while still maintaining the organisation and information. Again, maintaining the familiar field and genre supports students to practise the complex tasks of writing their own texts. More successful writers will be able to create excellent texts independently and quickly, giving the teacher time to support other students with alternative ideas.

In any curriculum unit, there could be two or more sessions of Detailed Reading and Rewriting of factual texts before each Joint Construction, to build up students' language resources towards independent research and writing. The independent writing task that these activities prepare for is to write a text in the same genre, but with a new field that has been independently researched. For this culminative task students identify key information from source texts, using text-marking and note-making techniques on their own, and then use this information to write their own text. As students' skills develop, text marking, note making and joint constructions may be started in the class with the teacher's guidance, and completed individually (or in groups). In the secondary school, in particular, as texts get longer and with limited class time, Individual Constructions may be done at home.

4.4.5 Abstract texts – controlling grammatical metaphor

The factual Text [4.9] we discussed above describes a technical field, the biology of cells. The focus of teaching is on the language that realises this field, including technical terms and the grammar of classifying, describing and explaining. Because the text is aimed at junior secondary students, the grammar is comparatively accessible. For example, there is relatively little grammatical metaphor; where there is, it is directly linked in the text to congruent activities and things. For example, *material made of small particles moves in and out of cells –> this movement is necessary.*

By contrast, texts in social sciences and humanities tend to be loaded with grammatical metaphor, as they construct and evaluate abstract concepts about social life. From the upper primary years, students need to learn how to read grammatical metaphor and eventually to use it to construct their own texts. Preparing for Reading, Detailed Reading and Rewriting can all be used to support students to control grammatical metaphor. For example, the following passage [4.12] is an explanation of events in recent South African history, from a middle secondary textbook (Nuttal et al. 1998). Abstract things in this text are highlighted in bold. Most of these abstractions stand for activities that have been nominalised; that is, activities that are expressed as nouns instead of clauses involving processes, people and concrete things (discussed in §3.6 above and §5.2.7 below). Linking these abstract things with each other are verbs that express causal relationships between activities. These verbs are underlined.

[4.12] Historical explanation showing abstraction

> **Revolutionary days**: The 1984 to 1986 **uprising**
>
> In the mid-1980s **South African politics** erupted in a **rebellion** in black townships throughout the country. The government's **policies of repression** had bred **anger and fear**. Its **policies of reform** had given rise to **expectations** amongst black people of **changes** which the government had been unable to meet. The **various forces of resistance**, which we outlined in the previous section, now combined to create a **major challenge** for the government.

In this text three factors are given for *a rebellion*: *policies of repression, policies of reform* and *forces of resistance* combining. However, there are no explicit conjunctions linking the rebellion to these causes; the text simply assumes that students can recognise these connections from their experience of factorial explanation genres. To make sure all students can read and comprehend such texts, these causal links need to be made explicit, and abstractions and their causal relations need to be unpacked in terms that all students can understand.

The starting point for this unpacking is Preparing for Reading. As this is a short but relatively dense text, it can be prepared by paraphrasing each sentence in more commonsense terms. This means 'de-nominalising' many of the abstractions – by turning them back into activities that involve people and concrete things, and making logical relations between activities explicit with conjunctions. The preparation begins with a synopsis of the text's purpose, relating it to the sequencing of historical events. Abstractions that have been unpacked to activities are in bold; logical relations that have been made explicit are underlined.

> The particular time we're going to look at is this one here, the mid-1980s, so it's 1984, 1985, 1986. Now this is when the next student uprising started in townships like Sobantu. This little part of the textbook is about why the violence started in the townships at that time.
>
> But it starts off telling us that **people were rebelling** in the black townships, and <u>there were three reasons for this</u>. <u>Because</u> the government, <u>on one side</u> they had a policy to **keep the people down, to repress the people with the police and the army**. And of course <u>this made the people</u> **very angry and frightened**.
>
> So they had this policy <u>on one side</u> of **keeping people down**, <u>but on the other side</u>, they **promised to make things better for the people**. <u>But then</u> they <u>didn't give the people enough money to actually make things better</u>. So **people expected things to get better** and they didn't.
>
> <u>The third reason</u> was that **all the parties fighting apartheid** <u>joined together to make it</u> **very difficult** for the government.

This construal of the events is more like the everyday grammar that students are used to, in which people undertake activities in place and time. It follows the same sequence as the text, and uses many of the same lexical items, but in a form that all students will understand. They are now in a position to follow the wording of the text as it is read aloud.

The next step is to unpack each abstraction again in Detailed Reading, illustrated as follows. This starts with the heading *Revolutionary days,* which the teacher unpacks, and *uprising*, which the students are guided to unpack.

Detailed Reading of Text [4.12]

Teacher	Prepare	*We'll start off with the heading. The heading's called Revolutionary days.*
	Elaborate	*So of course it's the days when the revolution started. That's why they call it Revolutionary days.*
	Prepare	*And then it tells us when the uprising started.*
	Focus	*Now have a look at your text, and can anybody tell us when it started? Revolutionary days the …? What's the first year there?*
Students	Identify	*1984*
Teacher	Affirm	*1984!*
	Focus	*1984 to when?*
Students	Identify	*to 1986*
Teacher	Affirm	*To 1986, OK!*
	Direct	*Highlight that first for me, OK?*

	Prepare	*And then the next words tell us … it's a word for a rebellion.*
	Focus	*Can you see what it is? 1984 to 1986 …?*
Students	Identify	*Uprising.*
Teacher	Affirm	*Uprising, that's exactly right!*
	Direct	*Do the whole lot, OK, 1984 to 1986 uprising.*
	Focus	*You know why it's called an uprising? Because what did the people do?*
Students	Propose	*Rise up.*
Teacher	Affirm	*The people rose up, yes.*
	Focus	*And who were they rising up against?*
Students	Propose	*The government.*
Teacher	Affirm	*The government, that's right*

The abstraction *uprising* is prepared with a synonym familiar to the students – *rebellion*. The elaboration then guides them to re-express the noun *uprising* as a process *rising up*, and to put the people back into the process, thereby re-expressing the abstraction as commonsense. Next, the first sentence is prepared by paraphrasing the metaphor *politics erupted* with the more familiar *trouble blew up* and unpacking *rebellion* as *people were rebelling*.

Teacher	Prepare sentence	*Now the first sentence tells us that the trouble blew up in the townships, and that the people were rebelling against the government. Look at the sentence as I read it. 'In the mid-1980s South African politics erupted in a rebellion in black townships throughout the country.'*
	Prepare	*Now that sentence starts by telling us when they were rebelling.*
	Focus	*Who can see the words that tell us when?*
Students	Identify	*In the 1980s.*
Teacher	Affirm	*Is she right? OK!*
	Direct	*Let's all do mid-1980s.*
	Prepare	*Then it tells us that South African politics blew up.*
	Focus	*Can you see the word that tells us South African politics blew up? South African politics …?*
Students	Identify	*Erupted.*
Teacher	Affirm	*Erupted! Is he right?*
Students		*Yes*
	Direct	*Let's do that one.*
	Prepare	*The reason they use the word erupted is because that's what volcanoes do.*
	Focus	*Have you heard that before? A volcano erupts?*
Students	Propose	*Yes.*
Teacher	Focus	*So what were the townships like? They were like …?*
Students	Propose	*Volcanoes.*
	Affirm	*Exactly right.*
Teacher	Elaborate	*They were like a volcano, and there was all this pressure inside, waiting to blow up and erupt, with all this anger the people were feeling about the government's repression.*

The multilayered lexical metaphor *politics erupted* is unpacked interactively, by first guiding students to recognise that the townships are being compared to a volcano, and then explaining that the people's emotions are compared with the pressure inside it. No attempt is made at this point to explain the abstraction *politics*. This is not a grammatical metaphor standing for an activity, like *uprising*; rather it is a technical term in the context of social sciences, and its meaning has been previously defined in the unit of study.

The next sentence is prepared by making its logical relation to the first sentence explicit, and unpacking the abstractions.

Teacher	Prepare sentence	*Now the next sentence tells us the reasons that you had this rebellion - because the government had a policy of keeping people, of repressing people, and this made the people angry and frightened. Now everybody look at the sentence as I read it, OK. 'The government's policies of repression had bred anger and fear.'*
	Prepare	*Now this sentence starts by telling us which policy it was. It was a policy that repressed people.*
	Focus	*Can anybody tell me what that policy was? The government's policies of ...?*
Students	Identify	*Repression.*
Teacher	Affirm	*Repression! Is that right?*
Students		*Yes.*
Teacher	Direct	*OK, do the whole lot, government's policies of repression.*
	Elaborate	*Repression means you're keeping people down, you're repressing them.*

	Prepare	*The government's policies made the people angry and frightened.*
	Focus	*And who can tell me the words that mean angry and frightened. They had bred ...?*
Students	Identify	*Anger and fear.*
Teacher	Affirm	*OK! Anger and fear.*
	Direct	*Let's all do that ... Have we all got that? OK, beautiful.*
	Elaborate	*OK, we're on to the next sentence. So that was one policy they had, to keep people down, to repress them.*

The very abstract *policies of repression* is prepared with both its grammatical function *which policy it was*, and its discourse meaning *a policy that repressed people*, as well as a precise position cue *government's policies of...?*. The elaboration then restates the commonsense definition, as an activity involving people. The causal metaphor *had bred anger and fear* is unpacked as commonsense *made them angry and frightened*. The last elaboration then provides a context for the contrasting factor *policies of reform*.

This particular lesson was conducted with a class of about 50 South African secondary students with English as an additional language, and weak English literacy – including some who were still attempting to read letter-by-letter. Within about 20 minutes of Detailed Reading they could all read the passage fluently along with the teacher, and answer a range of comprehension questions about it.

The next step in developing control of abstraction is to make notes from the Detailed Reading and do a Rewrite from the notes. The notes consist of the abstract wordings from the text. The teacher guides the class to rewrite these in the more commonsense terms that were used to prepare and elaborate abstractions in the Detailed Reading. The notes that students made on the board were as follows, with labels added as they were written and discussed.

heading	• *1984 to 1986 uprising*
outcome	• *mid-1980s - rebellion - black townships*
factor1	• *government's policies of repression - anger and fear*
factor2	• *policies of reform - expectations - changes - government - unable to meet*
factor3	•*various forces of resistance - major challenge for the government*

The genre here is factorial explanation, the stages of which include the Outcome, and two or more factors as Explanation. One Joint Rewrite produced by the students was as follows.

[4.13] Rewrite using notes from Text [4.12]

> ### *The Rebellion of 1984-1986*
>
> *There was an uprising in the mid-1980s in South African townships. Because the government repressed the people, they were frustrated and frightened. Because the government promised changes, the people expected things to get better, but the government couldn't provide their needs. So all the parties resisting apartheid came together and started serious trouble for the government.*

Complex rewriting of this could be facilitated by the use of some basic metalanguage, with the class explicitly discussing clauses, conjunctions, nouns and verbs at least (but this knowledge about language was not available in the lesson discussed above). In order to explicitly discuss grammatical metaphor, students would need to understand that congruent nominal groups express the meaning 'thing' and that congruent verbal groups express the meaning 'process' – as a basis for recognising that grammatical metaphors re-express processes and qualities as nominal groups (see §5.2.7 below).

4.4.6   Writing abstract discourse – (re)packaging information

Metalanguage becomes even more useful when it comes to teaching students how to write abstract discourse, once they can read and unpack it. But learning how to read abstract discourse with understanding, and to rewrite it in more commonsense terms, are necessary first steps. These skills can be built up through continual guided practice, ideally in the upper primary years, and then into junior secondary, using the techniques outlined above. By the time they reach middle secondary at least, students need to be developing skills in writing abstract discourse in social sciences and humanities subjects. For this they need to understand the functions of grammatical metaphor – for example, to condense information and package it in chunks, as starting points or **Themes** of clauses, and end points or **News**, shown in [4.12′]

[4.12′] Historical explanation showing Themes and News

Themes	News
In the mid-1980s South African politics	erupted in a rebellion in black townships throughout the country.
The government's policies of repression	had bred anger and fear.
Its policies of reform	had given rise to expectations amongst black people of changes
which the government	had been unable to meet.
The various forces of resistance	now combined to create a major challenge for the government.

Here the passage is divided into one clause per line. The Theme of each clause is an abstract thing which stands for activities. Causal verbs (*erupted, had bred, had given rise to, to create*) link these to other abstract things which are News (or the actions themselves are News – *unable to meet, now combined*) (see §5.2.7). The basic strategy for teaching this kind of writing is to use a text like [4.12] as a model for Rewriting, using the same sentence structures but with different content, as we described for stories above. Detailed Reading of the passage can focus on the information structure of the text as a whole and of its sentences – and the critical role of grammatical metaphor in packaging activities as Themes and News. These patterns can be discussed in elaborations, after students understand the meanings of each abstraction.

Before or after this Detailed Reading, information about a new topic could be built up by reading, text marking and note making. In Joint Rewriting this information can be organised into the same information structures as the model. For example, later events in the same history unit could be written as a factorial explanation with the same structures, as in [4.14] here.

[4.14] Rewrite using sentence patterns from text [4.12]

By the late 1980s, the apartheid system	*was under siege on many fronts.*
International economic sanctions	*were crippling the economy.*
The internal movement for change	*had gathered strength and legitimacy*
which the government	*was no longer able to counter.*
Political, military and economic factors	*were overwhelming the government and forcing it to negotiate a transfer of power.*

As with the literary devices in stories, this type of exercise needs to be practised repeatedly, in Joint and Individual Rewriting, for students to develop confident control over abstract written discourse.

4.5 Evaluating issues and texts: arguments and text responses

The focus for reading and writing arguments and text responses is on the one hand the issues or texts being studied in a curriculum unit, and on the other hand the rhetorical resources for evaluating issues, points of view and texts, and for organising a coherent persuasive argument. Key systems of language resources here are **appraisal** for evaluating (§5.3.5) and **conjunction** for organising the text (§5.3.2). The ways in which these resources are used by authors are highly variable and, in the most accomplished hands, elaborate and subtle. These techniques can only be learnt by attending closely to what such authors do. Preparing for reading and Joint Construction in the manner we have described, following the stages and phases of a model, are useful for practising conjunction. Detailed Reading and Rewriting are ideal for practising appraisal.

4.5.1 Preparing for reading arguments

A curriculum unit with an argument as its goal for writing may involve a series of readings around a particular issue to be debated, including factual texts that provide background information relevant to the issue, and texts that debate it, as well as texts that do both. These texts can be used to build the field for subsequent writing, as well as providing models for persuasive writing.

In order to build the field, the strategies of text marking and note making that we outlined for factual texts are equally applicable to all kinds of reading. As a text is read, the teacher can guide students to identify key elements and mark them in the text with pencils or highlighters. These elements can then be written as notes, along with notes made from oral discussions. The goal is for students to ultimately do this themselves – marking reading texts and making their own notes, across all subject areas.

A simple example of a model for Joint Construction at upper primary level is the following discussion [4.15], which debates the issue of the media using sports people to promote alcohol and tobacco. It is presented here with stages and phases labelled. After stating the issue, the two sides are previewed. Each side, for and against, is presented in a topic sentence, and supporting reasons are given. Finally, the sides are reviewed, and then resolved in favour of side 2.

[4.15] Model discussion

Issue	Whenever we turn on the TV or radio, we are dazzled by sports heroes
preview	celebrating their victory by drinking alcohol or smoking tobacco. At first, we may think it is entertaining and harmless, but if we examine the issue more closely, questions arise in our minds about the effect these advertisements have on people.
Sides	**side 1 - for**
topic	There are several reasons why sporting heroes should promote alcohol and
reasons	tobacco products. Firstly, there would be more income for the tobacco, brewing and advertising communities to spend on sporting facilities, bodies and teams. This would lead to greater sponsorship and promotion of sport. Secondly, people themselves have to make the decision whether they want to smoke or drink. Advertisements cannot force you.
	side 2 - against
topic	On the other hand, there are many reasons why sporting heroes should not
reasons	promote tobacco and alcohol products. One important reason is that it may be a cause of under-age drinking and smoking, as it encourages sports fans to feel good about these behaviours. Secondly, it appears that sporting people promoting these products are not showing respect for their own bodies. Finally, smoking and drinking are hazardous to health, and young people should be discouraged from taking them up.
Resolution	Even though there seem to be reasonable arguments for sporting heroes
review	promoting such products, the advertising of these products may be bad for the health and well-being of young Australians. Therefore it has more disadvantages than advantages.

This model could be used both for Joint Construction and for Detailed Reading and Rewriting of short extracts. For the purposes of Joint Construction, the text would be read and discussed by the teacher and class, and then labelled as above, on both the projected class copy, and students' individual copies.

4.5.2   Detailed Reading of arguments – rhetorical resources for persuasion

The focus of Detailed Reading and Rewriting of arguments is to practise reading and writing the complex patterns of appraisal that authors use to persuade their readers. For this purpose, one or more paragraphs can be selected from texts used for reading in the curriculum unit, or from the writing model. An example of the latter, which contains some useful appraisal patterns, is the first paragraph.

> Whenever we turn on the TV or radio, we are dazzled by sports heroes celebrating their victory by drinking alcohol or smoking tobacco. At first, we may think it is entertaining and harmless, but if we examine the issue more closely, questions arise in our minds about the effect these advertisements have on people.

Attitudes expressed here include *dazzled, celebrating, entertaining* and *harmless*. The writer attempts to include the reader by sourcing experiences and attitudes to *we*. The for-side is sourced as *we may think*, but the against-side is introduced with the more academic sounding *if we examine the issue more closely*. The for-side is thus presented personally and positively; but the against-side is objectified as *questions arise in our minds*. Students can be guided to recognise these patterns in Detailed Reading, illustrated as follows. This could be done before or after using this text for Joint Construction.

Detailed Reading of Text [4.15]

Teacher	Prepare sentence	*The first sentence states the **issue** - that sports heroes promote smoking and drinking in the media. 'Whenever we turn on the TV or radio, we are dazzled by sports heroes celebrating their victory by drinking alcohol or smoking tobacco.'*
	Focus	*OK, so how often do we see this when we turn on the TV? [student name]*
Student	Identify	*Whenever*
Teacher	Affirm	*Right.*
	Direct	*Let's highlight whenever*
	Focus	*And what are the two **media** we turn on. [student name]*
Student	Identify	*TV or radio*
Teacher	Affirm	*Exactly*
	Direct	*Highlight TV or radio*
	Focus	*Then what's the **feeling** we get? [student name]*
Student	Identify	*Dazzled*
Teacher	Affirm	*Yep*
	Direct	*Highlight dazzled*
	Elaborate	*Dazzled means feeling amazed, but it also means getting blinded by bright lights.*
	Prepare	*Then it says how sports heroes **appreciate** their victory.*
	Focus	*[Student name]?*
Student	Identify	*Celebrating*
Teacher	Affirm	*Absolutely*
	Direct	*Let's highlight that.*
	Elaborate	*So they're enjoying themselves.*
	Prepare	*Then it tells us **two ways** they celebrate their victory.*
	Focus	*[student name] What's the first way?*
Student	Identify	*Drinking alcohol.*
Teacher	Affirm	*That's right.*
	Direct	*Highlight drinking alcohol.*
	Focus	*[student name] What's the second way?*
Student	Identify	*Smoking tobacco.*
Teacher	Affirm	*Absolutely.*
	Direct	*Highlight smoking tobacco.*
	Focus	*So what's the purpose of showing these images in the media?*
Students	Propose	*Advertising. Promoting.*
Teacher	Affirm	*Exactly right. That's the **issue** here.*

Here the teacher has focused on elements that will need consideration in the following Rewrite: the conjunction *whenever*, which has the effect of amplifying the issue; the classification of TV and radio as media; the classification of *dazzled* as a feeling and the elaboration of its double meaning; the classification of *celebrating* as enjoyment; the grouping of smoking and drinking as two ways to celebrate; and finally the provision of guidance for students to interpret the issue.

4.5.3   Joint and Individual Rewriting – appropriating rhetoric

Focusing attention and discussing these elements in Detailed Reading pays off in Joint Rewriting. The goal is for students to follow the same patterns in Individual Rewrites, which will deal with different issues. The starting point is therefore to brainstorm a variety of issues students could write about. One will be chosen for the Joint Rewrite and students can choose others for their own Individual Rewrite. In the following example, the issue selected is fast food advertising. First the key elements of the issue need building up, before writing begins, as follows.

Joint Rewriting of Text [4.15]

Teacher	Focus	OK, if our **issue** is media advertising fast food to young people, where do they see these ads?
Students	Propose	TV. Billboards. Movies. Magazines. Internet.
Teacher	Affirm	Right.
	Focus	So all these things are kinds of what?
Students	Propose	Media.
Teacher	Affirm	Exactly.
	Prepare	Now we turn on the TV, but not billboards, magazines or the internet.
	Focus	We need a **verb** that means we get into the media. [student name]
Student	Propose	Access the media.
Teacher	Affirm	Perfect.

Here the teacher focuses the class's attention on media advertising. They Propose ideas from everyday experience, which the teacher guides them to classify as media. One student is then picked to supply the required verb *access*. Now the teacher starts pointing out elements of the first sentence that will be rewritten.

Teacher	Prepare	Now the writer here starts off with 'we' [pointing at text] - we turn on, we are dazzled, we may think. She does this to include the reader in the discussion. We can be a bit more subtle than this. Let's wait until we present **our side** to say 'we'.
	Focus	Who is it that is accessing the media? That is targeted by these ads?
Students	Propose	People. Children. Young people.
Teacher	Affirm	Great. Let's go with young people.

	Focus	*And how often do they see these ads? [pointing at text]*
Students	Propose	*Whenever. All the time. Every time.*
Teacher	Affirm	*Excellent. We'll start with every time.*
	Direct	*[student name] Can you come out and write that?*
		[student scribes 'Every time young people access the media']
Teacher	Affirm	*Fantastic.*
	Prepare	*Now that's the first part of our sentence.*
	Focus	*What do we call that part of the sentence?*
Students	Propose	***A clause***.
Teacher	Affirm	*Exactly right.*
	Focus	*And what do we need at the end of the clause?*
Students	Propose	*A comma [student scribes]*
Teacher	Affirm	*Perfect. Thanks [student name].*

The sourcing of attitudes to *we* was not discussed in Detailed Reading, so as not to overload students with an explanation of sourcing. This is an important general point – as we return to the text through a series of activities, not everything needs to be discussed at once. Some elements are best left to joint writing activities. Nevertheless, there are always elements that can be introduced briefly in earlier activities – elements that we may not expect students to grasp immediately, but can then be repeated later with more understanding.

Teacher	Focus	*Now it won't be 'we' that are dazzled, will it?*
Students	Propose	*They.*
Teacher	Affirm	*Exactly*
	Focus	*And what happens to them when they see these ads? We need another **verb** that expresses their feeling.*
Students	Propose	*Bamboozled. Amazed. Mesmersised. Bombarded. Overwhelmed…*
Teacher	Affirm	*Excellent. [scribing notes]*
	Elaborate	*Most of these are very strong. At the beginning we need to tone it down so we don't sound too biased against fast food ads. We need a verb that's more neutral. Let's start with exposed.*

At this point, the teacher can organise these alternative attitudinal resources on a chart as stronger or weaker, positive or negative – evaluating them and adding other options. One effective activity to build these resources is to draw a graph, with a positive/negative axis and a stronger/weaker axis, and to position each verb on the chart, according to its relative value in each of these directions; the chart can be elaborated as examples are generated in writing activities, or encountered in reading. This can enable students to see at a glance the appropriate verbs to propose for each context.

	Focus	*And what are they exposed to. What do they see?*
Students	Propose	*Ads. Images.*
Teacher	Affirm	*Exactly. Images.*
	Direct	*[student name] Can you come out and write that?*
		[student scribes 'they are exposed to images']
Teacher	Focus	*Images of what? Not sports heroes. Who do they see in ads for fast food?*
Students	Propose	*Happy people. Thin people. Healthy people. Families.*
Teacher	Affirm	*Great.*
	Elaborate	*Let's say happy healthy families.*
		[student scribes 'of happy healthy families']
Teacher	Affirm	*Beautiful*
	Focus	*Now sports heroes celebrate their victory. What are our families doing?*
Students	Propose	*Enjoying*
Teacher	Affirm	*Yep.*
	Focus	*And what are they enjoying?*
Students	Propose	*Food. Fun. Happy meals. Being together. Time together …*
Teacher	Affirm	*Perfect.*
	Elaborate	*Let's say they're enjoying quality time.*
		[student scribes 'enjoying quality time']
Teacher	Affirm	*Yep.*
	Focus	*And what are two things they are doing, instead of smoking and drinking?*
Students	Propose	*Eating and drinking. Eating fast food.*
Teacher	Affirm	*Right, eating fast food is one.*
	Focus	*What are they drinking?*
Students	Propose	*Soft drinks.*
Teacher	Affirm	*Great.*
	Focus	*What's another name for soft drinks that doesn't sound as nice?*
Students	Propose	*Sugar drinks. Lolly water. Fizzy drinks.*
Teacher	Affirm	*Let's say fizzy drinks. It doesn't sound that good but it isn't obviously biased.*
	Focus	*And what's the **conjunction** we need? [pointing at text]*
Students	Propose	*By.*
Teacher	Affirm	*Right.*
	Elaborate	*By means how they are enjoying quality time, by eating and drinking. That's the **means** by which they are doing it.*
		[student scribes 'by eating fast food and drinking fizzy drinks.']
Teacher	Affirm	*Perfect.*

Through each cycle, the teacher focuses on the elements of the model, and guides students to draw on their experience to build up the new field, rephrasing and extending their proposals where necessary. This process is repeated through the preview phase, to construct a Joint Rewrite as follows.

[4.16] Rewrite using appraisal patterns from Text [4.15]

> *Every time young people access the media, they are exposed to images of happy healthy families enjoying quality time by eating fast food and drinking fizzy drinks. On one hand, many people believe fast food is nutritious and delicious. However, if we study the research carefully, the evidence suggests that promotion of fast food may have a detrimental effect on the health of young people.*

This Rewrite closely follows the patterns of appraisal and conjunction in the model. With Individual Rewrites, students write to their own choice of issue, following the same sentence patterns, with different choices for appraisal. Their options for doing so can be supported by building up word banks on a chart, as outlined above, or as lists. Another key resource is the choice of conjunctions for scaffolding the argument. Here the teacher has guided the class to propose *on the other hand*, which was also used to introduce side 2 in the model text. Ideally, the class could have a list of conjunctions to choose from, organised by their functions in connecting events or organising the text (see Table 5.9 below). Such a list can be enlarged as a poster, or copied and pasted in students' work books.

4.5.4   Joint and Individual Construction – organising arguments

An example of a Joint Construction that follows the stages and phases of the model discussion begins as follows. The issue the class has discussed is media promotion of fast food. Before starting the Joint Construction, the issue may be reviewed, and arguments made for and against. These may be summarised on the board as notes. Following the model text, two reasons for and three reasons against have been decided on. In the exchange below, metalanguage is highlighted in bold.

Exchange during Joint Construction based on Text [4.15]

Teacher	Focus	*[pointing at first sentence of model text] OK, what's the first thing we need to tell our readers?*
Student	Propose	*The **issue***
Teacher	Affirm	*Exactly.*
	Focus	*So what's the **issue** we're writing about?*
Students	Propose	*Fast food. Media advertising. Promoting junk food.*
Teacher	Affirm	*Right.*
	Focus	*And who's it promoted to?*
Students	Propose	*People. Consumers. Children. Young people.*
Teacher	Affirm	*Great. [scribing notes on board]*
	Elaborate	*Let's say it's promoted to young people, which includes children.*

The teacher's purpose in scribing students' proposals on the board is to give the class options when they come to write their Individual Constructions. The teacher then makes the final choice and explains why.

Teacher	Prepare	*So we have three **elements** for our **issue statement** - fast food, media and young people.*
	Focus	*What's our **sentence** going to be? Let's start with fast food. [student name]?*
Student	Propose	*Fast food is promoted to young people in the media.*
Teacher	Affirm	*Fantastic.*
	Prepare	*Let's make it more of an **issue**. We need to make the **statement** stronger.*
	Focus	*How much is it promoted?*
Students	Propose	*Lots. All the time. Heavily.*
Teacher	Affirm	*Excellent.*
	Elaborate	*Let's say fast food is heavily promoted by the media to young people. [scribes on board]* *So this is now controversial. It's an issue that needs to be discussed.*

Here one student is chosen to construct a sentence with the three elements, but this needs amplifying to make it an issue worth debating – so the teacher guides the class to Propose amplifying appraisals.

Teacher	Focus	*Now, what's the next thing we need to tell our readers? [pointing at model text]*
Students	Propose	*The **sides**. **Preview***
Teacher	Affirm	*Exactly. A **preview** of the **two sides**.*
	Elaborate	*So we're going to **preview two reasons for** fast food, and **three reasons against**. [pointing at notes on the board]*
Teacher	Prepare	*Let's start by saying many people think. [scribes 'Many people']*
	Focus	*What's two **positive** things they think about fast food?*
Students	Propose	*[reading from notes] Convenient. Cheap.*
Teacher	Affirm	*Right.*
	Focus	*Now let's find another **verb** instead of think. We need one that means it may not be true.*
Students	Propose	*Believe. Reckon. Assume.*
Teacher	Affirm	*[scribing] Brilliant.*
	Elaborate	*We're presenting the **first side**, so these **verbs** suggest that people haven't thought carefully about it. Another one we can use is feel.* *[scribes 'feel that fast food is convenient and cheap.']*

A key device for favouring one side or another in arguments is the choice of reporting verbs. These can be prepared and discussed in commonsense terms as *may not be true*, or *haven't thought carefully*, and organised later in terms of their relative values.

Teacher	Prepare	*Now we need to **preview** the **side** we support.*
	Focus	*First we need a **conjunction** that tells the reader this is the **other** side.*
Student	Propose	*On the other hand.*
Teacher	Affirm	*Brilliant. [scribes 'On the other hand']*
	Focus	*And we can just say others think. But we need a **verb** that means thinking carefully.*
Students	Propose	*Know. Understand. Examine. Analyse.*
Teacher	Affirm	*Great. [scribing notes]*
	Elaborate	*Another **verb** that means thinking carefully is consider [adds to notes]*
	Focus	*So let's say others consider. [pointing at notes] What's our **sentence** going to be? [student name]?*
Student	Propose	*Others consider it is unhealthy, bad for the environment, and manipulates.*
Teacher	Affirm	*Excellent.*
	Elaborate	*Let's say the advertising is manipulative. [scribes 'others consider it to be unhealthy, bad for the environment, and its advertising is manipulative.']*

The exchange to this point would take around five minutes, involving discussion of one paragraph of the Joint Construction. The teacher paces it as fast as necessary to fit within the programming time available, using manual pointing and metalanguage to guide students' proposals, and then making final decisions about what to write and scribing on the board. The teacher consistently uses Focus questions that build on preceding preparations, either here or in earlier discussions, of the topic and elements in the model text. As a result, the class is able to rapidly propose appropriate ideas, which the teacher can affirm, and provide alternatives or rephrases that all students will understand.

This approach to Joint Construction is more supportive than the earlier approach that we illustrated in Chapter 2 (§2.5), because the model text is used more closely to structure the class's choices, with its phases labelled on the projected text. This higher level of support means that students struggle less to propose wordings, so that all students can be more actively involved. The following Joint Construction [4.17] could be written in around 20 minutes in a primary class. It can then be labelled on the board and students' copies.

[4.17] Joint Construction based on Text [4.15]

Issue preview	*Fast food is heavily promoted by the media to young people. Many people feel that fast food is convenient and cheap. On the other hand, others consider it to be unhealthy, bad for the environment, and that its advertising is manipulative.*

Sides	side1 - for
topic	*People are in favour of fast food for a number of reasons. For example, it*
reasons	*saves time, there are outlets everywhere, and does not require shopping for*
	ingredients, so it is convenient. Furthermore, at just a few dollars for a meal it can be a
	cheap alternative for low income families.
	side2 - against
topic	*Conversely, there are many drawbacks to overconsumption of fast food.*
reasons	*Firstly, the evidence shows that fast food contributes to health problems such as*
	obesity. Secondly, its packaging creates environmental problems such as litter.
	Moreover, its constant advertising in the media manipulates young people with images
	of thin happy people having fun.
Resolution	*While fast food may be time saving and relatively low in cost, its advertising*
review	*leads many young people to consume too much, which can affect their health and*
	wellbeing. For these reasons, we consider that the promotion of fast food should be
	more strictly regulated.

As we saw for both stories and factual texts, the Joint Construction tends to be shorter than the model, allowing the task to be completed in the class time available. The purpose is to practise using the structure of the model to scaffold a new text, and to discuss as many relevant language features as possible. When students come to write their own texts, they may of course be longer. Alternatively, the Joint Construction can be planned with the class and then written together as far as time allows, with students completing the task on their own or in groups. This is a realistic option in senior secondary years and tertiary study, where written texts can get very long. As long as the writing has been planned and initiated together, students will be prepared to complete the task individually.

4.5.5   Text responses – evaluating and critiquing

While arguments evaluate issues and points of view, text responses evaluate texts and their moral messages. In §4.2 above we explored the messages in the novel *Follow the Rabbit Proof Fence*, along with the language resources the author uses to engage the reader's interest and empathy. We showed how Preparing for Reading and Detailed Reading can enable all students to read such texts with a depth of engagement and understanding, and to engage actively in class discussions about them.

However, the writing task expected of students after reading and discussion of literary texts is usually not another story but rather a text response. In secondary school the types of text response expected of students are **interpretations**, the functions of which are to evaluate and interpret the messages of a text. Interpretations include three typical stages: an **Evaluation** in which the text and its messages are initially evaluated, a **Synopsis** in which those elements of the story that carry the messages are summarised, and a **Reaffirmation**, in which the text and its messages are finally re-evaluated. An example of a model is the following interpretation [4.18] of Steinbeck's *Of Mice and Men* (adapted from Topham 2010). Three messages are identified in the Evaluation, the settings of these messages in the story are summarised in the Synopsis, and the messages are synthesised in Reaffirmation.

[4.18] Model text response

Evaluation	
message1	John Steinbeck's Of Mice and Men is a moving story of the friendship
friendship	between two men - set against the backdrop of the United States during the
message2	depression of the 1930s. Subtle in its characterization, the book addresses the real
class	hopes and dreams of working-class America. Steinbeck's short novel raises the
	lives of the poor and dispossessed to a higher, symbolic level.
message3	Its powerful ending is climactic and shocking to the extreme. But, we also
tragedy	come to an understanding of the tragedy of life. Regardless of the sufferings of
	those who live it, life goes on.
Synopsis	The novel opens with two workers who are crossing the country on foot
setting of	to find work. George is a cynical, irresolute man. George looks after his companion,
message1	Lennie - treating him like a brother. Lennie is a giant man of incredible strength, but
	has a mental disability that makes him slow-to-learn and almost child-like. George
	and Lennie had to flee the last town because Lennie touched a woman's dress and
	he'd been accused of rape.
setting of	They begin to work at a ranch, and they share their dream: they want to
message2	own their own piece of land and farm for themselves. These people - like them - feel
	dispossessed and unable to control their own lives. The ranch becomes a
	microcosm of the American underclass at that time.
setting of	The climactic moment of the novel revolves around Lennie's love of soft
message3	things. He pets the hair of Curley's wife, but she gets scared. In the resulting
	struggle, Lennie kills her and runs away. The farmhands form a lynch mob to
	punish Lennie, but George finds him first. George understands that Lennie cannot
	live in the world, and he wants to save him the pain and terror of being lynched, so
	he shoots him in the back of the head.
Reaffirmation	The literary power of Of Mice and Men rests firmly on the relationship
reaffirm	between the two central characters, their friendship and their shared dream. These
message1	two men are so very different, but they come together, stay together, and support
	each other in a world full of people who are destitute and alone. Their brotherhood
	and fellowship is an achievement of enormous humanity.
relating	They sincerely believe in their dream. All they want is a small piece of
message1	land that they can call their own. They want to grow their own crops, and they want
and	to breed rabbits. That dream cements their relationship and strikes a chord so
message2	convincingly for the reader. George and Lennie's dream is the American dream.
	Their desires are both very particular to the 1930s but also universal.

This model could be used for a Joint Construction in precisely the way we illustrated for arguments above, substituting evaluations and a synopsis of *Rabbit Proof Fence* for the evaluations and synopsis of *Of Mice and Men*. The class could previously have built up a body of information about *Rabbit Proof Fence* through reading and discussion, as well as text marking and note making, as described above for factual texts and arguments. As a novel, short story, play or poem is read, students can identify and mark key elements in the text. These elements can then be written as notes, along with notes made from oral discussions about the text. These notes can then be drawn on for Joint Construction of a text response.

4.5.6   Detailed Reading and Rewriting – resources for evaluation

From the model text response, one or more paragraphs that deploy the most elaborate resources for evaluation can be selected for Detailed Reading and Rewriting. For example, the Reaffirmation stage of [4.18] is littered with appreciations of the text (*literary power, strikes a chord so convincingly*) and with judgements of the characters (*friendship, shared dream, so very different, destitute and alone, brotherhood and fellowship, achievement of enormous humanity, sincerely believe in their dream*). These and other evaluative resources are shown in bold here.

> The **literary power** of Of Mice and Men **rests firmly** on the relationship between the two central characters, **their friendship** and **their shared dream**. These two men are **so very different**, but they **come together, stay together,** and **support each other** in a **world full of people** who are **destitute and alone**. Their **brotherhood and fellowship** is an **achievement of enormous humanity**.
>
> They **sincerely believe in their dream**. All they want is a **small piece** of land that they **can call their own**. They **want to** grow their own crops, and they **want to** breed rabbits. **That dream cements their relationship** and **strikes a chord so convincingly** for the reader. George and Lennie's dream is the **American dream**. Their desires are both **very particular** to the 1930s but **also universal**.

These resources are used to evaluate messages through contrasts, between *friendship, shared dream, brotherhood and fellowship* versus a *world full of people destitute and alone,* and through the reiterated theme of dreams and desires: *shared dream, sincerely believe their dream, all they want is a small piece, want to grow, want to breed, that dream, their desires.* The themes of friendship and dreams are tied together in the last sentences as the 'American dream' – the universal in the particular. However one considers this interpretation of *Of Mice and Men,* the elaborate patterns through which it is presented are useful for rewriting with the messages of *Rabbit Proof Fence.* Here is one possible Rewrite.

[4.19] Rewrite using appraisal patterns from Text [4.18]

> *The moral impact of Follow the Rabbit Proof Fence flows from the contrast between the Indigenous girls' desire to return to their families, and the white authorities' determination to keep*

them apart. Molly, Gracie and Daisy are so young and vulnerable, but they manage to escape, travel on foot, and survive against every adversity both natural and man-made. Their tenacity and determination are a testament to the power of human devotion.

The girls had an unquenchable love for their families. All they wanted was to return to the land that they knew. They wanted to live in freedom, in the heart of their families. That love embodies their humanity and sparks an intense empathy with the reader. These Indigenous girls' journey is the story of Australia. Their story of injustice and triumph is both particular to the Stolen Generations and emblematic of the struggle for social justice everywhere.

Detailed Reading and Rewriting of these passages could be conducted in similar fashion to that shown for stories and arguments above, with elaborations focusing particularly on the roles and patterns of appraisal. Again, metalanguage can be an invaluable tool for guiding students to identify and propose these elaborate language resources. Repeated practice with different model text responses will expand students' resources for evaluating, and develop their skills in recognising effective devices in their reading and using them in their writing.

4.6 Intensive strategies

The intensive strategies of Sentence Making, Spelling and Sentence Writing can be used to provide a higher level of support for students to practise skills in reading and writing, following Detailed Reading, but before they go on to Rewriting. They are powerful techniques for reinforcing foundation skills, but fully integrated here with reading and writing the curriculum. They are particularly valuable in the primary years, for giving students intensive practice in reading challenging texts, and in spelling and handwriting. They can also be used in the secondary school, particularly for giving students with special needs intensive practice with curriculum texts, including students learning an additional language, but also for giving all students practice with dense technical or abstract sentences. Traditional remedial practices of drilling low level skills on low level texts, or on words, letters and sounds in isolation, can be replaced with Sentence Making, Spelling and Sentence Writing, working on the same challenging texts that the whole class is working on. The place of the intensive strategies in the R2L program is shown in Figure 4.14.

One of the reasons the strategies described in the preceding sections are effective is that they provide learners with sufficient support to do complex tasks in reading and writing in manageable steps. Critically, each step is meaningful within higher levels – as texts are contextualised within their field and genre, each phase contextualised within the text as a whole, each sentence within its phase, each word group within the sentence, and each word within its group. Another factor is the combination of different modalities in Detailed Reading – the teacher prepares orally, then focuses students' attention on the printed words;

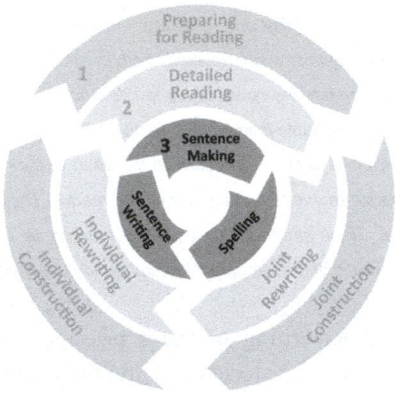

Figure 4.14: Intensive strategies in R2L

the learners then take control as they manually highlight the wordings under focus; and their meanings may be orally elaborated. Another factor is repeated experience of each language feature in different activities – in preparing, reading and discussing the whole text, as it is prepared and elaborated in Detailed Reading, in Joint and Individual Rewriting, and potentially in Joint and Individual Construction as well.

The intensive strategies described in this section extend these principles in three directions: (i) they extend the focus on language features down to the patterns of letters in written words and the sounds that they make as words are spoken, and to the formation of letters in writing; (ii) they strengthen learners' control over the modalities of reading and writing, by cutting up sentences on cardboard strips and writing words and sentences on white or blackboard slates; and (iii) they repeat the experience of each language feature, from Detailed Reading down to these intensive manual activities.

The full sequence of reading activities is correlated with the language model in Figure 4.15. Preparing for Reading first focuses on the context (field and genre), then previews the phases in which the text unfolds, and may be followed with paragraph-by-paragraph reading. In Detailed Reading each sentence is prepared and read, and each word group is identified. Sentence Making and Spelling then extend the focus down to individual words and the syllables, letter patterns and sounds that express them.

4.6.1   Sentence Making

In Sentence Making one or more sentences from the passage used for Detailed Reading are written on cardboard strips by the teacher, who then guides students to cut up the sentences, first into word groups or phrases, and then into individual words. At each step, students mix up the word groups and words, and then re-arrange them into the right sequence (and then variations), re-reading the

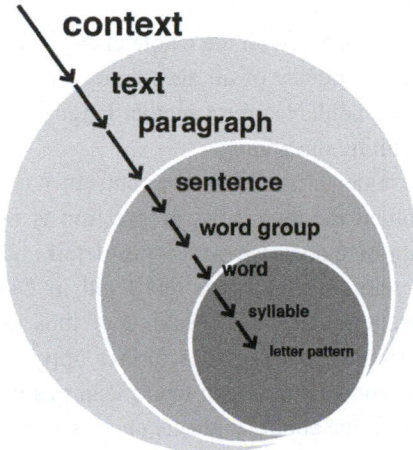

Figure 4.15: Sequence of reading activities

sentence aloud each time. Using sentence strips in this way is a well-known activity for practicing various components of reading. Two key innovations here, which are consistent with our functional model of language in context, are that (i) the sentence is already familiar from a passage that has been read in detail, so that it is contextualised in a whole text, and (ii) the focus is not just on individual words, but on the functions of word groups in the sequence of the sentence, and then on the functions of words in groups. Sentence Making has three broad functions:

*   It extends the discussion of meanings and wordings from Detailed Reading.
*   It enables learners to manipulate wordings to create meaningful sentences without the added load of hand writing.
*   As individual words are cut out they can be used to practise spelling.

Figure 4.16: Sentence Making

Sentence Making can be done with the whole class, in small groups, or in one-on-one support sessions. Students of all ages enjoy the control and success the activity gives them. Even adults learning another language find Sentence Making a powerful aid to controlling the grammar.

The teacher guides students to identify and cut out wordings, using the same discussion as for Detailed Reading. Less preparation is now needed, however, and some elements can be elaborated with more detail and discussion. Elaborations can be used to reinforce meanings discussed in Detailed Reading, or to provide new interpretations. Sentence Making is thus not just a mechanical activity of cutting up words, but provides further opportunities for reinforcing and deepening students' understanding of their meanings in context. It is an ideal place to introduce knowledge about language, once students have a solid grasp of the meanings of the sentences, and are ready to take on more abstract understandings including metalanguage.

4.6.2   Spelling

The R2L approach to word recognition and spelling flows out of students' understanding of meanings in context, which has been guided through Preparing for Reading and Detailed Reading. From the cut up sentences, the teacher can now ask students to hand her individual words that she has previously selected for spelling. In the first instance, this allows the teacher to check that the weakest readers can identify each word within the sentence. (At this point they have the sequence of words in the sentence to support them.) The teacher can now work with a set of 'flashcards' of individual words (Figure 4.17), and can guide students to segment words into their spelling patterns, and then to practise these spelling patterns on individual white or black boards. The individual boards allow students to practise and self-correct using the 'look-cover-write-check' routine, as errors can be easily erased and corrected.

Figure 4.17: Guiding Spelling

Words that students cannot accurately identify are not used for spelling at this point, as they do not have sufficient word recognition to benefit adequately from the spelling activity. Attempting spelling on words that students do not recognise or understand is simply a rote activity that is devoid of meaning. Without an adequate meaning base it is difficult for learners to retain and recall sequences of letters. This is a primary reason why many weaker readers are also weak spellers. Accordingly, it is typically only lexical words that are selected for spelling at this point, as they are meaningful in themselves outside of a sentence, rather than grammatical words, which are meaningful only in relation to other lexical words in a word group or sentence.

This approach to spelling reverses a number of orthodoxies in traditional word recognition and spelling activities. Firstly, word recognition activities traditionally use words in isolation ('sight word' or 'whole word' activities), instead of identifying words in familiar sentences. These activities typically begin with the most common written words, most of which are grammatical words without much lexical content, and therefore meaningless outside of a sentence. Secondly, spelling activities traditionally use word lists that are compiled in isolation, on the basis of their spelling patterns, the topic they belong to, or randomly, instead of using known words from familiar sentences. Thirdly, students are expected to memorise words and their spelling patterns, and then be tested on their memories, instead of first practising to get them correct using individual boards. In one form or another, these traditional activities are very widely practised, whether the classroom is considered more traditional or more progressive. As all teachers know, from these activities some students are better able to retain and recall words and spellings than others, and follow-up testing merely differentiates students according to their aptitude for this task.

There is also a widespread misapprehension that learners must be able to sound out letters and letter patterns in order to read and write words. Experienced readers, however, do not sound out words as they read and write in order to recognise or write words. Spelling and sounding are two alternative ways of expressing words; readers and writers do not undertake 'sound first, write later' routines. Sounding out letters and letter patterns merely adds to the semiotic load of struggling readers, and inhibits their comprehension of what they are reading. The other problem with this strategy is that the sounds that letter patterns make vary with (i) the particular word they are in (*rough/through*), (ii) their position in the syllable (*rough/ghost*), and (iii) their relation to adjacent letter patterns (*rabbit/rabid, rat/rate*). The aim of R2L spelling activities is therefore to guide learners to recognise words from their letter patterns directly, without needing to sound them out as they read. While the words and their letter patterns are repeatedly pronounced during spelling, the focus is on recognising and using spelling patterns, rather than on drilling correspondences between letters and sounds, as phonics programs prescribe.

Words can be chunked into five levels of spelling patterns, shown in Table 4.1.

Examples are shown from Text [4.6], together with other words with similar spelling patterns. Other words can be practised as extension activities, once students can spell the words in the text at hand. The possibilities soon become very large.

Table 4.1: Levels of spelling patterns

Spelling patterns	examples	extensions
Compound words	*night-eyes*	*night-light*
	some-thing	*any-thing*
	moon-light	*day-light*
Suffixes and prefixes	*shin-ing*	*shine*
(word endings and beginnings)	*polish-ed*	*polish*
	stopp-ed	*stop*
	care-ful	*care-less*
	e-special-ly	*special*
Syllables	*sil-ver*	*co-ver*
(multisyllabic words)	*sur-face*	*sur-plus*
	tunn-el	*barr-el*
	in-stant	*in-stance*
	peo-ple	*cou-ple*
Onset and Rhyme	*c-aught*	*dr-aught*
of syllables	*gl-int*	*fl-int*
	br-ight	*fr-ight*
	sm-all	*sm-ell*
	sp-eck	*shr-eck*
	cr-ept	*cr-eep*

The spelling system is large and complex, and there is not the space here to discuss it in any detail. Here are some rules of thumb to start:

1. The spelling system is based on written syllables (which often do not exactly match spoken syllables) (Henderson and Templeton 1986).
2. Each syllable consists of an Onset (initial consonants) and Rhyme (the remainder) (some syllables have no Onset, such as *earth*.)
3. A general rule is to look for groups of letters that are regular common patterns as Onset or Rhyme of syllables, for example, double letters are always kept together.
4. If you are unsure of a spelling pattern, think of other words with the same pattern.

Changes that happen when adding suffixes, such as *stop/stopping*, *shine/shining*, *relate/relation*, can be practised as extension exercises after completing Spelling and Sentence Writing on the actual text. When practising Spelling, words are cut up just as much as needed for students to remember their letter patterns (since patterns can also be pointed out without cutting them). Except with very young children, there is usually no need to break up Rhymes into smaller parts. For example, 'ough' is a regular Rhyme pattern, so there is usually no need to cut it into 'ou' and 'gh', although these letter combinations can be pointed out.

4.6.3   Sentence Writing

Once all learners can automatically spell most of the words in the paragraph, they can practise writing the original sentences from memory on their individual boards (Figure 4.18). The purpose of Sentence Writing is for students to practise fluently writing stretches of meaningful text, without the load of inventing a story for themselves, planning how to write it, thinking of the words to use, and knowing how to spell them. At the same time they practise writing the words they have spelt in context, which is the most effective way to remember them, and they practise spelling the words that were not practised in the Spelling activity.

To begin with, some memory games can be used to help students remember the sequence of words in the sentences. For example, the sentence strips can be displayed on a sentence maker[5] or electronic smartboard, and words can be turned over as the class reads them, eventually leaving just a few grammatical words displayed as a skeletal framework to remember the sequence of the sentences. As the quicker students write independently, the teacher can support weaker students to write the sentences, by reminding them of the sequence. If needed, the teacher can support by telling some words, or even writing some words, and let the student write the rest.

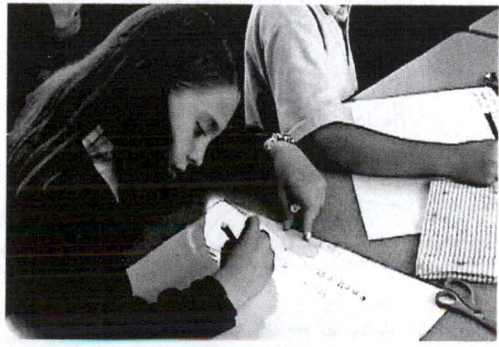

Figure 4.18: Sentence Writing

---

[5] A sentence maker is a device for displaying sentences written on cardboard or paper strips. Plastic sentence makers can be purchased from education suppliers, or they can be made simply by gluing plastic joining strips (to hold the cardboard) onto a 600 × 900mm sheet of light particle board, that can be purchased from a hardware store.

Although these intensive strategies are only used on a few sentences of text at a time, the practice gives students insights into general patterns of language, which they can immediately transfer to the rest of the Detailed Reading passage, thus supporting them to read the whole passage with comprehension and fluency. Likewise the practice with the Detailed Reading passage soon enables students to read the rest of a longer text with comprehension and fluency. And practice reading one text, after Detailed Reading, soon enables them to independently read other similar texts.

4.7   Beginning reading and writing in the early years

4.7.1   The problem of unequal learning rates

Given what we know of the complexity of the spoken-language learning task, we might expect that any child who has mastered their mother tongue by the time they start school should be able to learn to read and write without too much trouble. And this is often the case for children who arrive at school with the rich experience of parent-child reading that we discussed in §4.2 above. But for children who start school with less experience of written ways of meaning and talk-around-text, their literacy development can be much slower. Text [4.20] shows a typical example of a child with a less enabling orientation to literacy after a full year of school, with the teacher's corrections and translation. The writer is a six-year-old child in a rural community.

[4.20] Year 1 writing and illustration (after one year)

Children such as this writer will continue to be affirmed and valued by their early years teachers, despite continual assessments that measure the widening gap between them and more successful students within and beyond their class. These assessments of their learning abilities will then be passed on to their middle primary classes, where they will find themselves inadequately prepared to access the curriculum through reading and writing, and will fall further behind each year. Text [2.2] in Chapter 2 above showed a common standard for many children in Year 3, as does [2.3] for Year 5, and [2.4] for junior secondary school.

As far as we can see, the hierarchy of success and failure that ultimately results in unequal school outcomes begins with unequal rates of literacy learning in the early years of school. If children are not independently reading with confidence and comprehension by the end of Year 2, they will not be ready for learning from reading in the middle to upper primary years, and will be unable to cope with the demands of independent study in the secondary school (Rose 2004, 2005, 2007). The explanation for this inequality lies not with the quasi-biological notion of innate ability, but with differences in children's experience with parent-child reading in the home, and associated orientations to meaning (Hasan 2009, Williams 1999b, 2005b). Current literacy practices in the early years of school are clearly not adequate for overcoming these differences (shown in Charts 6.10 and 6.11 below).

In this section we outline strategies that are designed to break this cycle, by explicitly teaching children each level of the language learning task in context, from genre down to letter formation. Like those we described in the previous sections, these strategies are designed for the whole class to develop skills at the same pace. The change this approach can produce is illustrated in Text [4.21], independently written by the author of [4.20] just two months later, using the R2L strategies described below.

[4.21] Year 1 writing and illustration (2 months later)

This six-year-old has written a detailed, coherent and legible description on a topic she has studied, has self-corrected while drafting it, and has incorporated key elements in her illustration, including the mother seal, the hole in the ice with a line for the direction of her dive, and the storm gathering in the sky above. Under normal circumstances this child may have taken another three to four years before writing at this standard and perhaps stalling there as far as literacy development is concerned. Instead, she will be thoroughly prepared by the end of Year 2 for learning the primary curriculum through reading and writing.

4.7.2 Integrating skills in reading

Williams 1995 shows that non-middle-class parents often read to their children as frequently as middle-class parents, but that there may be less interactive discussion of inferential and interpretive meanings. All the parents and children in his study discussed the events in story books. In Williams' terms the key difference with middle-class families is:

> that the child learns to explicate bases of judgement as well as to understand the plot relations. Such an orientation to ways of meaning is clearly evident … [the child] has no problem with understanding the narrative development. But, crucially, she has to say how she knows (1995: 147).

In the terms we are using here, middle-class parents guide children not only to comprehend the plot literally, but to interpret events. This type of orientation was illustrated in exchange [4.5] in which the mother asks a series of interpretive questions: *Do you think there was really truly a lion? Why do you think so? How do you know he's not dreaming?* Exchange [4.4] around *The Three Little Pigs* showed how children are prepared for this from an early age. Williams also shows that reading activities in the first year of school tend to follow similar kinds of interaction as in middle-class parent-child reading, so that children from other backgrounds may be less well prepared, engaged and affirmed by these activities. In particular, the widespread practice of continually asking interpretive questions of the class reveals the gap between children who are more or less likely to respond with successful interpretations. A glance at virtually any transcript of early years classes shows this pervasive phenomenon. Here is the example we first presented in Chapter 1 from Williams (1995: 501).

[1.1'] Typical exchange in Shared Book Reading

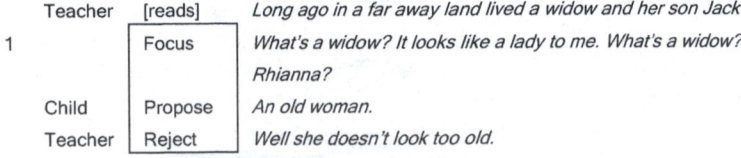

Teacher	[reads]	*Long ago in a far away land lived a widow and her son Jack.*
1	Focus	*What's a widow? It looks like a lady to me. What's a widow? Rhianna?*
Child	Propose	*An old woman.*
Teacher	Reject	*Well she doesn't look too old.*

		Focus	*Is there a daddy there?*
	Children	Propose	*No.*
2	Child		*Looks like …*
	Teacher	Focus	*What do you think has happened to the daddy?*
	Child	Propose	*… a cow.*
	Teacher	Focus	*David?*
	Child	Propose	*It's it's it's a little cow.*
	Teacher	Reject	*No no.*
3		Focus	*When there's a widow, something's happened to daddy.*
	Child	Propose	*He died? Miss, he died?*
	Teacher	Affirm	*Yes that's right.*
		Elaborate	*A widow means that her husband has died.*
4		[reads]	*They only had a cow. They sold the cow's milk …*
		Focus	*… to buy …? What were they …?*
	Child	Propose	*Money and … food.*
	Teacher	Focus	*Would you need to buy money?*
	Children	Reject	*No.*
	Teacher	Focus	*What would you need to buy, Lucy?*
	Child	Propose	*Food.*
	Teacher	Affirm	*Food. Yes food.*

In contrast to the designed interactions illustrated in §§4.3-6 above, the teacher in this interaction reads the sentence without preparation, and then asks the class to interpret the word *widow* from their own knowledge (1). Instead, Rhianna proposes a literal response from the picture on the page *an old woman*, which the teacher rejects. In response to this failure, the teacher starts to provide criteria for children to give the answer she wants, in the form of further Focus questions: *Is there a daddy there? What do you think has happened to the daddy?* Unfortunately, focusing on the picture prompts David to propose what he literally sees in the picture, *a little cow* (2), which the teacher also rejects with *No, no.* She then narrows the criteria again *When there's a widow, something's happened to daddy* (3), so that one child at least can give a response she can affirm, *he died?*, and elaborate with a definition: *A widow means that her husband has died.* After this apparently successful cycle, the teacher starts reading again and asks another interpretive question: *to buy …?* (4). She then enjoins the class to reject one child's response, *money*, before affirming another child, *Lucy*.

This is not an example of particularly poor teaching. On the contrary, it is quite representative of classroom exchanges in the activity commonly known as Shared Book Reading. Early years teachers are generally trained not to use explicit instruction but to encourage children to 'infer' or 'interpret' for themselves, by questioning rather than telling them. One inevitable consequence is illustrated in this class of 20 or more children, in which three have been explicitly rejected, and just two affirmed, out of the small minority that responded at all. This type of exchange is repeated day after day, year after year, in the typical early years classroom, and beyond. For children who arrive at school without the orientation to written ways of meaning and talk-around-text provided by parent-child reading in middle-class homes, this kind of classroom discourse can have significant consequences, not only for their engagement in reading, but for their identities as successful or failing learners (Rose 2004, 2007, 2011a).

At the opposite end of language from interpretive comprehension, it is widely assumed that children must first be able to decode letter patterns, in order to independently access written meanings at any level. Let us reconsider this assumption here, with reference to a well-known English text, written here in a 'wingding' font.

◀▷↓↔ㅈↄ⇥ ◀▷↓↔ㅈↄ⇥ ↄ↓◀◀ↄ⇥ ▽◀ↄ△
↑◊▷ ⇉ ▷◊↔⇦⇦△ ▷↑⇦◀ ◢◊▶ ⇦△⇥
▶▲ ⇦⇦◊◁⇦ ◀↑⇥ ▷◊△ↄ⇥ ▽◊ ↑↓→↑
ↄ↓ㅈ⇥ ⇦ ⇦↓⇦ϟ◊↔⇦ ↓↔ ◀↑⇥ ▽ㅈ▲
◀▷↓↔ㅈↄ⇥ ◀▷↓↔ㅈↄ⇥ ↄ↓◀◀ↄ⇥ ▽◀ↄ△
↑◊▷ ⇉ ▷◊↔⇦⇦△ ▷↑⇦◀ ◢◊▶ ⇦△⇥

For children first learning to read, this is what a written text looks like – if they do not know the text, the graphic symbols are meaningless. However, if they are familiar with the spoken text, they can be guided to recognise correspondences between the spoken words they know and the written words on the page, and can soon learn to read the written version, word-for-word. This can be shown if we tell you this text's genre and field, when it suddenly becomes readable. It is a nursery rhyme, about a star in the sky. Take a moment to look at the text with this knowledge.

As you may have guessed, the first line is *twinkle twinkle little star*, and no doubt you are able to read the rest, and even to translate the wingding symbols into English letters and sounds. This is possible because the text is familiar in the oral mode. So we read it first from above, from meaning in context, and this enables us to decode the graphic symbols. Likewise, once children can recognise each written word in a familiar text, they can be easily guided to decode the patterns of letters that make up the words they know. It is relatively easy for them to recognise the patterns of letters because they have become meaningful – meaningful in that they are expressing meanings that the children are already familiar with.

There is no need to spend the first months of children's schooling drilling them in the letters of the alphabet and the sounds they make, before they can start reading and writing actual texts. This venerable practice supports children with the right orientation to literacy from parent-child reading to start decoding the meanings they already understand in books; on the other hand, children without this meaning base can take much longer to start reading. This practice functions to institutionalise different rates of learning from the very beginning of school. It makes these different learning rates appear to be intrinsic in the children, when in fact they are produced by the school practice itself.

A more effective and equitable practice is to teach letters and sounds in the context of meaningful engaging books. One ideal starting point is the popular picture book *Rosie's Walk* (Hutchins 1968), which consists of one sentence spread over 28 pages. The story consists of just one activity, *Rosie the hen went for a walk*, and each double page in the book illustrates a series of locations where she walked around her farm. In this one sentence of 32 words, *Rosie's Walk* uses 22 of the 26 letters in the alphabet, most of them repeated several times in different words. In addition to single letters, it also uses about 30 different letter combinations as the Onset or Rhyme of syllables [4.22].[6]

[4.22] Rosie's Walk analysed in letter patterns

> *Ros - ie the h - en w - ent for a w - alk*
> *a - cr - oss the y - ard*
> *a - r - ou-nd the p - ond*
> *ov - er the h - ay - c - ock*
> *p - ast the m - ill*
> *thr - ou-gh the f - ence*
> *und - er the b - ee - h - ive - s*
> *and g - ot b - ack in t - ime for d - inn - er.*

Because they are meaningful in the context of familiar words in a simple shared story, children can be taught to recognise, say, read and write all these letters and letter patterns in a few weeks of consistent practice at the very start of school.

4.7.3   Shared Book Reading

The starting point is to make the words of a story familiar for children, using the strategy of Shared Book Reading, but redesigning it along the lines of Preparing for Reading described in §4.3.1 above. Shared Book Reading is perhaps the most important single literacy activity in the early years, because it gives all children an orientation to reading as a meaningful shared activity. To be most effective for all students, it needs to be planned and implemented along the lines of effective parent-child reading. As we saw in §4.2, parents start reading with children by telling them what a story is about, by talking through the pictures. Children's picture books are designed for this activity; they use repeated patterns and funny stories that parents usually have to explain to children. If children enjoy the story, parents will read and discuss it over and over again.

---

[6] Complex Rhymes can also be split into common digraphs 'ou-nd', 'ou-gh' for young children.

Shared Book Reading in Australia is typically conducted with the children seated on the floor around the teacher. Ideally the book is in big book format, sitting on a low easel so the teacher can turn and point at the pages, and children can see easily and come forward to point at pictures (see Figure 4.23 below). The exchange we show below starts with the cover, which the teacher interactively explains to the children. This contrasts with the widely used practice of asking children to guess what a book is about from its cover. In fact the plot, events, settings and characters of any book worth reading with children is normally well outside their realm of experience, particularly of children with less experience of parent-child reading. So this kind of guessing competition merely differentiates children on their home experience, engaging some but invalidating others.

For example, *Rosie's Walk* is designed to introduce young children to the common literary phenomenon of a story with two fields (Rothery and Stenglin 1997). On one level it is a simple recount of Rosie the hen walking around the farm, but there is a second plot in which a fox repeatedly tries to jump on Rosie, but is thwarted each time. On this level it is a narrative consisting of a series of problems and solutions, but this plot is realised only through the images, which requires the parent/teacher to verbalise it for children. The key elements are presented on the cover (Figure 4.19).

Figure 4.19: Cover of *Rosie's Walk* by Pat Hutchins (published by The Bodley Head, reprinted by permission of The Random House Group Limited)

The children's tasks, as the book is discussed, are to attend to the elements of the picture that the teacher focuses on, and to say some words. This prepares them to recognise these elements and say the words in the next pages. In the following transcript the children's parts in the exchange are largely invisible, as they are simply attending to the images.

Exchange in Shared Book Reading

Teacher	Prepare	*This book is about a hen named Rosie.*
	Focus	*Here she is. [points]*
Students	Attend	
Teacher	Direct	*Everyone say Rosie.*
Students		*Rosie!*
Teacher	Affirm	*Beautiful*
	Prepare	*She lives on a farm in a little house.*
	Focus	*Can you see her little house here? [points]*
Students	Attend	
Teacher	Prepare	*Rosie is going for a walk around the farm. But there's a fox who wants to catch Rosie.*
	Focus	*Can you see the fox?*
Students	Attend	

On the next page (Figure 4.20) the teacher repeats some elements and asks the children to repeat others.

Figure 4.20: *Rosie's Walk*, pp. 1-2 (by permission of The Random House Group Limited)

Teacher	Focus	*Here's Rosie. [points]*
		What's her name?
Students	Identify	*Rosie!*
Teacher	Affirm	*Beautiful*
	Focus	*What's she doing? [points]*
Students	Identify	*Walking!*
Teacher	Affirm	*That's right.*
	Elaborate	*She's going for a walk.*
	Focus	*And who's hiding under Rosie's house?*
Students	Identify	*Fox!*
Teacher	Affirm	*Yes.*

	Elaborate	*He's looking at Rosie.*
	Focus	*Can you see his tongue poking out? [points]*
Students	Attend	
Teacher	Elaborate	*That's because he's hungry and he wants to catch Rosie for his dinner.*
	Focus	*What's going to happen? Let's find out. [turns page]*

Pages 3-4 present the first problem (Figure 4.21). By this time all the children can respond immediately to some questions.

Figure 4.21: *Rosie's Walk*, pp. 3-4 (by permission of The Random House Group Limited)

Teacher	Focus	*Who's this? [points]*
Students	Identify	*Rosie!*
Teacher	Affirm	*Exactly*
	Elaborate	*She's still walking.*
	Focus	*And who's this? [points]*
Students	Identify	*Fox!*
Teacher	Affirm	*Right.*
	Focus	*Look the fox is going to jump on Rosie! [points]*
	Focus	*But what's that on the ground?*
Student	Identify	*Rake.*
Teacher	Affirm	*That's right. It's a rake.*
	Elaborate	*For raking up leaves and grass.*
	Focus	*Do you think the fox is going to catch Rosie?*
Students	Propose	*No ... Yes ...*
Teacher	Focus	*Let's find out. [turns page]*

Pages 5-6 solve the problem (Figure 4.22).

Figure 4.22: ***Rosie's Walk***, **pp. 5-6 (by permission of**
The Random House Group Limited)

Teacher	Focus	*Who's this? [points]*
Students	Identify	*Fox!*
Teacher	Affirm	*It is.*
	Elaborate	*Look he fell on the rake. And the rake jumped up and hit him on the nose.*
Teacher	Focus	*Who's that? [points]*
Students	Identify	*Rosie!*
Teacher	Affirm	*Yep.*
	Focus	*What's she doing? [points]*
Students	Identify	*Walking!*
Teacher	Affirm	*That's right.*
	Elaborate	*She's still walking.*
	Focus	*Did the fox catch Rosie?*
Students	Identify	*No!*
Teacher	Affirm	*No he didn't catch her this time.*
Teacher	Focus	*What's going to happen next? Let's find out. [turns page]*

The same pattern is repeated through five similar episodes on the following pages, until the final Resolution when Rosie 'got back in time for dinner' to her little house. As each episode is discussed, the children can say more and more of what is going on. They typically also start to point out marginal elements of the pictures, such as birds and animals, which the teacher can affirm and elaborate. After talking through the pictures once, the teacher can now come back to the beginning and start reading the words, along with discussing the pictures again. Each time the children contribute more shared knowledge about the text, at literal, inferential and interpretive levels, in contrast to the standard practice of testing children's knowledge, illustrated in exchange [1.1'] above.

4.7.4   One-for-one word recognition

Ideally *Rosie's Walk* could be read like this two to three times a day for several days, repeating and deepening the discussion, with the students taking over more control, until the whole class can say all the words of the story along with the teacher, and understand what they mean. At this point they can be guided to read the words themselves. This is done by writing the first part of the sentence on a cardboard strip and showing the children how to point at each word as they say it, shown in Figure 4.23.

Figure 4.23: Pointing and saying words

As they point and say, they learn to distinguish each written word, as they can already distinguish the spoken words, and are starting to recognise differences between each word in the sentence. A crucial support for word recognition at this stage is the sequence of words in the sentence. This support is missing from traditional 'sight word' or 'whole word' practices that require children to memorise individual words out of context, without the sequence or the contrasts between words in a sentence.

4.7.5 Sentence making

Once all children can say and point to each word accurately, they are ready to start cutting words out of the sentence and re-ordering them, to reinforce their word recognition. At this point they are not merely saying the words in sequence, but pointing out individual words, although still with the support of the sequence. The words chosen to cut off are those that will be practised spelling later. These will usually be lexical words. The manual practice is a powerful tool for young children to reinforce language learning. It puts them in control of their own physical activity, and simultaneously of their mental activity.

At this point children are able to recognise words intuitively by visual cues, without formally spelling them, as they have seen and said them so many times, and are thoroughly familiar with their meanings. It is hardly surprising that they can do so, as they can recognise any object or image without being explicitly taught any formal criteria for identifying them. The assumption that children must first be taught the formal criteria of letters and sounds in order to recognise words is mistaken, as both experience and logic tells us. If they know the words orally, they can easily be guided to recognise them visually.

4.7.6 Spelling

Only after children can recognise words in and out of the sentence, are they ready to start spelling them. As well as spelling patterns, this activity teaches sound-letter correspondences, in the context of words that children can already recognise, know the meanings of, and can say fluently. As with the teaching sequence as whole, spelling begins not with individual letters, but with the patterns of which they are part. And the starting point is not with the simplest word, such as 'hen', but with the word that is most interesting to the children, in this case *Rosie*.

This approach guides children to deconstruct whole words that they understand and can clearly articulate into their component phonemes, expressed by letter patterns. It is directly opposite to the approach of phonics and 'phonemic awareness' programs that start with decontextualised sounds and letter patterns, and expect children to construct meaningful words out of them. It still astounds us that children who can articulate words clearly in Shared Book Reading are frequently diagnosed as lacking 'phonemic awareness' if they cannot pronounce decontextualised phonemes in formal tests, and that this is seriously claimed by 'experts' to be the reason they cannot read independently.

4.7.7 Forming letters

Once children recognise the components of a word, the teacher can guide them to write each syllable on individual boards, one letter at a time. The teacher writes the first letter on a board and says it as the children all watch, showing how to start at the top and keep the pen or chalk on the board. In addition, the teacher can recount the movements as the letter is written, such as 'down-up-and-around' or 'around-up-and-down'. This demonstration may be repeated several times as children watch, before asking them to do the same on their own boards. As they attempt it themselves, the teacher watches and guides them again as needed.

Crucially, the activity is not copying letters from a model that is printed or written on the class board, as is a common practice in letter formation activities. This ancient practice institutionalises the activity of copying that bleaches the social meaning out of learning, particularly for weaker students. Here instead the children follow the actions that the teacher demonstrates, which supports them to mirror the movements of the teacher (Figure 4.24). Demonstration and guided practice are normal modes of teaching manual skills in many contexts (e.g. learning to tie shoe laces, bowl a cricket ball, 'bend it like Beckham'), and all children are familiar with them.

Figure 4.24: Demonstrating letter formation

4.7.8   Sentence Writing

Once children can spell the lexical words in the sentence, they can be guided to write the whole sentence, again by the teacher demonstrating as the children watch. The first time this is done the teacher can demonstrate one word at a time, including the words that the children have practised spelling. This shows them how to organise their sentence on their boards, to space the words, and to write the grammatical words that were not previously spelt. This is the context in which the children learn how to spell these grammatical words and form their letters. After it is written, the children can read their own sentences aloud.

Ideally each child should have their own copy of the book being studied (in this case *Rosie's Walk*), so they can now read it on their own or in groups together. At the same time, other books are being read in Shared Book Reading to keep building their experience of reading, including books that may be selected for the next series of reading and writing lessons.

In the first few weeks of school, these activities can be repeated again and again each day, until all the children can write the sentence fluently. The strategies can then be extended to the following pages in the book, until they can write several episodes of the story. In the case of *Rosie's Walk* each episode is just a location – *across the yard*, *around the pond*, *through the fence*. Again the teacher provides children with whatever support they need to complete the task. This may include prompting their memories, or writing some words for them, or the beginning of words, which enables them to write the remainder.

4.7.9   Rewriting

Once all children can confidently read, write and illustrate their first reading book, they may be ready for Joint Rewriting of the story, or part of it. The starting point for this activity, as described for *Fantastic Mr Fox* in §4.3.3 above, is to brainstorm new characters, events and settings for the story, which will fit into the patterns of the shared reading story. Once the characters, events and settings have been chosen, the teacher guides children to write the new sentences on the board. Some of these words will have been listed during brainstorming, so the children need only copy them. The teacher can write words they do not know, to practise spelling later. As the class writes, they can keep generating new elements to fit into the patterns of the shared reading story. Here is one example of a Rewrite from *Rosie's Walk*.

[4.23] Rewrite from *Rosie's Walk*

> *Billy the rabbit went for a hop*
> *across the field*
> *around the dam*
> *through the gate*
> *under the bushes*
> *and got back in time for lunch.*

Rewriting may be practised again and again before expecting children to write independently. They need to work gradually towards independent writing, with continual teacher support to build up written language resources through the modelled and guided activities described above. The activities outlined here for starting with *Rosie's Walk* may take the first four to six weeks or more of school. Other books can be read and discussed in this period, but all the language work is flowing from this one book.

Through the first year of school, these strategies can be practised with increasingly longer and more complex texts. The patterns of repeated episodes persist through picture books that are more challenging than *Rosie's Walk*, but the episodes grow to whole sentences and then whole paragraphs to each page. These can be ideal for Detailed Reading and Rewriting, building children's language repertoires at the levels of words, word groups, sentences and phases.

4.8   Pedagogic theory and practice

The large body of knowledge about pedagogy accumulated in the *Reading to Learn* program has been presented in this chapter as far as possible through demonstration in context. This was a deliberate choice, not only to make the methodology more accessible, but to reduce the insulation between theory and classroom practice that is often a problem for teacher education (Nuthall 2004, 2005). This does not make the methodology any less theoretical, but rather makes the theory more functional. The pedagogic theory and its classroom practice have developed in dialogue with each other. Parameters of the program's theory and practice include:

- nine sets of teaching strategies, providing three levels of support for reading and writing, diagrammed in Figure 4.5;
- sequencing of strategies from the level of social context, through patterns meaning in whole texts, to patterns of wordings in sentences, and patterns of spelling in words;
- a model of reading behaviours correlated with strata of language in context, from interpretive comprehension of relations to social contexts, through inferential comprehension of relations across texts, to literal comprehension of wordings in sentences, and decoding of letter patterns in words;
- variations in the strategies according to the genre and field being explored, including (i) children's fiction, (ii) adult literature, (iii) technical texts in the sciences, (iv) abstract texts in humanities, (v) arguments and (vi) text responses;
- variations in the strategies with respect to a developmental sequence, from learning to read and write in the first months of school, through learning from reading in primary school, to studying academic disciplines in secondary and further education;
- a model of learning activities centred on the learner's task, preceded by a task focus and followed by evaluation, and potentially extended by preparing first and elaborating afterwards;
- detailed analysis and re-design of teacher/student interactions using this model, which prepare all students to access meanings in texts and then elaborate their understanding towards curriculum goals;
- design of learning activities and classroom interactions aimed at engaging all students equally, and so overcoming inequalities in educational outcomes.

Rich as they may be, these pedagogic parameters are only one dimension of the program; another is the knowledge about language that underpins all these activities, outlined in Chapter 5 below; and a third is the professional learning program that makes this knowledge about pedagogy and language available to the teacher, outlined in Chapter 6.

5 Knowledge about language (KAL)

> This chapter builds up a metalanguage that teachers can use for analysing texts, planning and teaching lessons, and assessment. The first section explores patterns of meaning in grammar, and the second section explores patterns of meaning in discourse, both from the perspective of their usefulness in teaching. The discussion is designed to build up knowledge about language in steps, modelling the sequence that can be followed in teacher education and in the classroom.

5.1 A pedagogic metalanguage

We said in Chapter 1 that language is the most complex system we know of, and each subsequent chapter has helped to demonstrate this. Teachers and even their youngest students possess a colossal body of knowledge about language, but most of it is unconscious or intuitive. Yet everyday speech contains a great many words for talking about language, from *tell me a story* to *how do you say that word*. In Chapter 1 we quoted Clare Painter's conversation with her son about the terms *question* and *order* (1999: 124).

[1.3'] age 4;6

Stephen	*Mummy, is a **question** that you don't eat porridge with your fingers? [pause] It's a **question** that you don't eat porridge with your fingers.*
Mother	*That's not a **question** it's an **order**.*
Stephen	*What's an **order**?*
Mother	*It's something that you tell somebody and they have to do.*
Stephen	*I meant an **order**.*

When they get to school, children encounter a great many more such terms, which teachers use to talk about reading, writing and curriculum subjects, from *full stops* through *sentences* and *paragraphs* all the way up to *novels* and *textbooks*. Discussing language is always a blend of words that explicitly refer to aspects of language, like *word, story, say, tell, question, order, full stop, capital letter*, alongside our intuitive knowledge as speakers. Teaching language explicitly means bringing unconscious knowledge about language to consciousness. To do this, teachers and students need to be able to name what they are talking about, and this involves a systematic understanding of how language works. We introduced such a framework in Chapter 1, with the functional model of language as text-in-context, and have referred to it constantly throughout the following chapters. The model included three levels: discourse, grammar and phonology/graphology, and a contrast between language systems and the texts that are instances of these systems. In this chapter we will discuss language systems in more detail, beginning with patterns of meaning within sentences, or grammar, followed by patterns of meaning across whole texts, or discourse.[1] These two levels of meaning are shown in the systemic functional linguistic (SFL) model in Figure 5.1.

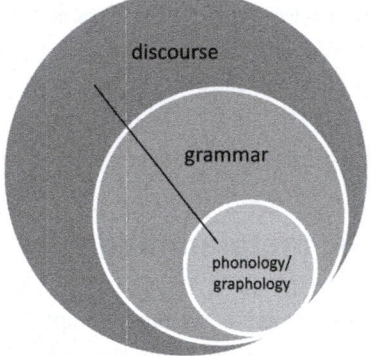

Figure 5.1: Meaning as grammar and discourse

The purpose of this chapter is to build up a metalanguage[2] that teachers can use to select and analyse texts in their curriculum, plan their lessons, teach in the classroom, and assess their students' progress. These are four different tasks, which require different tools. Selecting and analysing texts involves knowledge

---

[1] In SFL theory, grammar is referred to as **lexicogrammar**, as it includes both words and grammatical structures, and the technical term for discourse is **discourse semantics**. However, the familiar terms **grammar** and **discourse** are sufficient for the pedagogic metalanguage we are building here.

[2] The metalanguage has been adapted from Halliday 1994 (for grammar), Martin and Rose 2003/2007 and Martin and White 2005 (for discourse) and Martin and Rose 2008 (for register and genre).

about genres and their structures in different subject areas, discussed in Chapters 2, 3 and 4. But it also involves the more detailed knowledge about language that we present in this chapter. This knowledge about genres and their language features is also useful for assessing students' development, particularly their writing, which we will touch on in Chapter 6 below. Planning lessons involves knowledge about both the language of written texts and the learning interactions that we discussed in Chapter 4.

Teaching these lessons in the classroom, however, is a different matter, because the metalanguage that students need for learning about reading and writing is not the same as the metalanguage that teachers need for all their professional activities. Teachers have a double job with metalanguage: (i) applying what they know to selecting, analysing, planning and assessing, and (ii) recontextualising what they know for discussion in the classroom. A common issue with language courses in teacher education is that they present language as theory describes it, which teachers are then left to recontextualise for themselves, both for preparing and for delivering lessons. A common outcome is that few teachers are able to do so as well or as consistently as theorists, teacher educators or syllabus writers may expect.

In this chapter we present a metalanguage that is grounded in theory, so that it is systematic and consistent, but is recontextualised on two levels: (i) as metalanguage that can be used in teacher education, and by teachers in lesson preparation, and (ii) as metalanguage that can be used in the classroom to talk about reading and writing. In Bernstein's terms we are proposing a linguistic description that has been recontextualised for teaching – a pedagogic metalanguage. The theory is of course SFL, but the angle we take on it comes from many years working with teachers on the most effective ways to use it in their practice, and the most effective ways in which teachers can learn it themselves.

Unlike a typical linguistics course, the sequence in which knowledge about language (KAL) is introduced is not determined by the organisation of the theory, but by the ease with which learners can master it, and its usefulness in teaching. The sequence and the learning activities through which we introduce KAL here are intended to model the sequences and activities in which it can be presented to (trainee or practising) teachers, and in which teachers can present it to their students. The basic strategy for each learning activity in this chapter applies the model outlined in Chapter 1. The reader's task at each step here is to read one or more texts that display a particular language feature. Sometimes the task is not to read an actual text, but a list of examples taken from texts, each displaying the language feature under focus. The task is prepared with a basic outline of the language feature, and it is then elaborated with more detail. The affirmation comes from the reader's own success in mastering each task.

At each step we discuss the functions of each element of KAL in language learning and classroom teaching. Our first step is to consider what happens when children start school.

5.2 Grammar: words and structures

Long before they get to school, young children know that language is made up of words, and they know that each word has a specific meaning. They most likely also know the words *word* and *mean* and can use them to ask adults the meanings of words they hear, and to ask for words to express the meanings they want to say, as Painter's work shows (e.g. 1996, 1999). As they first learn to read in school, children discover that words are written with spaces between them, and that there are many more words than they knew about, or had thought of as words before. Another thing they discover through written language is that it is also made up of sentences, which are written with a capital letter and a full stop (period).

As words express meanings, so too do sentences, but it is hard to explain to young children what kind of meaning a sentence expresses; teachers often use glosses such as 'an idea' or 'an action'. As it is not possible to define exactly what goes into a sentence, it is actually left to children's intuitions to recognise much of it for themselves. In the absence of precise criteria, one strategy that teachers can always rely on is repeated practice. If children do not use capitals and full stops where their sentences should begin and end, the teacher keeps pointing it out to them until they can intuitively recognise it for themselves.

5.2.1 Word groups and clauses

Three things that children do know are that (i) sentences are about people and things, (ii) people do things, and things happen, and (iii) they happen in various places and times. When they discuss these meanings with others, including teachers, they can use words like *who* for people, *what* for things, *where* for places, *when* for times, *what's happening* or *what [someone's] doing* for processes, and *how* or *what like* for qualities. All languages we know of have words like this, which stand for a small set of general meanings: people, things, places, times, processes and qualities. In English they are known as 'wh' words, for obvious reasons. Some languages have a wider set than English, such as words that mean 'whatting' instead of English's *what [is someone] doing*.

In all languages these general types of meanings are expressed by groups of words in each sentence. Although these word groups are not usually marked by punctuation, young children and their teachers understand them intuitively. They can have meaningful discussions about them using wh-words, e.g. *can you see who this sentence is about?, what's he doing?*, without naming them explicitly. So the first step we will take here, in making intuitive knowledge about language conscious, is to give names to each of these types of meanings in sentences. To begin, we will use just six names:

name	wh-word
people	*who*
thing	*what*
process	*what doing/happening*
place	*where*
time	*when/how long*
quality	*how/what like*

To show how this works, we can apply these six terms to a few sentences from a familiar text [5.1], in this case *Follow the Rabbit Proof Fence*, discussed in Chapter 4. The principle here is the same as outlined in §4.7 for beginning reading: using a familiar text for learning something new, whether this is learning to read, to write, or do linguistic analysis. In the following five sentences, each group of words that expresses these kinds of meanings is marked with a slash /, and the type of meaning is labelled below it. If you are not sure why we have used a particular label for a word group, try asking the relevant wh-question about it.

[5.1] Word groups and their meanings

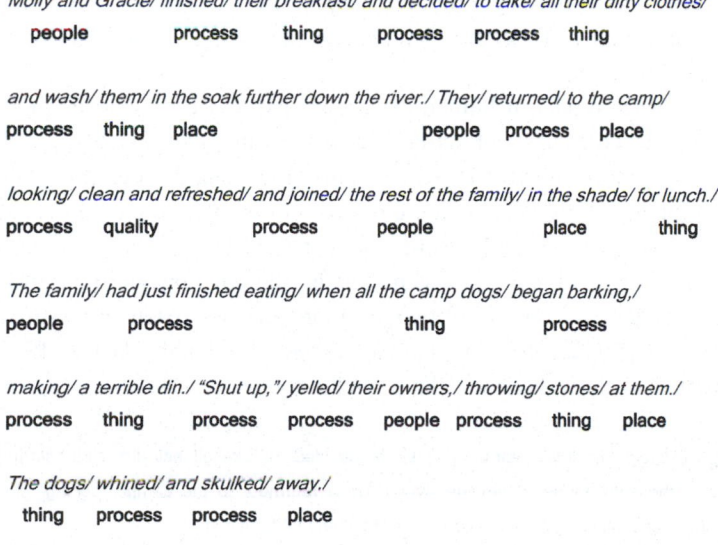

Molly and Gracie/ finished/ their breakfast/ and decided/ to take/ all their dirty clothes/
people   process   thing   process   process   thing

and wash/ them/ in the soak further down the river./ They/ returned/ to the camp/
process   thing   place   people   process   place

looking/ clean and refreshed/ and joined/ the rest of the family/ in the shade/ for lunch./
process   quality   process   people   place   thing

The family/ had just finished eating/ when all the camp dogs/ began barking,/
people   process   thing   process

making/ a terrible din./ "Shut up,"/ yelled/ their owners,/ throwing/ stones/ at them./
process   thing   process   process   people process   thing   place

The dogs/ whined/ and skulked/ away./
thing   process   process   place

One thing we can note at this stage is that some of these meanings are expressed by single words, especially the processes – *finished, decided, wash, returned, looking, making, yelled, throwing, whined, skulked* – but that most of these meanings are expressed by groups of words. We are not ready to discuss all the functions of these words, but we can mention the **conjunctions**, since conjunction is a familiar term – ***and*** *decided,* ***and*** *wash,* ***and*** *joined,* ***when*** *all the* *camp dogs began barking,* **and** *skulked.* These conjunctions are linking together the parts of sentences known as **clauses**.

Although the term **conjunction** is widely used by teachers, the term **clause** is not, despite the fact that the clause is a pivotal grammatical structure in any language.[3] From the early years of school, teachers often use the terms **simple** and **complex** sentences, without defining the concept of a clause. The sentences in [5.1] are all complex, but some of their clauses could function as simple sentences, with the addition of a full stop:

> *Molly and Gracie/ finished/ their breakfast./*
>   **people**   **process**   **thing**
> *They/ returned/ to the camp./*
> **people** **process**   **place**
> *The family/ had just finished eating./*
> **people**   **process**
> *The dogs/ whined./*
>   **thing**   **process**

What makes these sentences simple is that they include just one process each. In other words, a simple sentence is a single clause, and each clause includes one process. Each process may also involve people, things, places, times and qualities. Thus the meaning of a clause is a process, involving people, things, places, times and qualities.

This is the basic model of human experience expressed by clauses in all languages – experience consists of series of processes involving people and things, associated with places, times and qualities. This fundamental pattern of meaning is understood intuitively by very young children, but is often not acknowledged in traditional school grammars, which are more concerned with rules than meanings. For our purposes here, it is the first step in understanding how grammar means.

Complex sentences consist of two or more clauses, each consisting of a process. Here is [5.1] again, with clauses marked by a double slash //. Processes are highlighted, to show that each clause includes one process.

> Molly and Gracie/ **finished**/ their breakfast// and **decided**// to **take**/ all their dirty clothes// and **wash**/ them/ in the soak further down the river.// They/ **returned**/ to the camp// **looking**/ clean and refreshed// and **joined**/ the rest of the family/ in the shade/ for lunch.//

> The family/ **had just finished eating**// when all the camp dogs/ **began barking**,// **making**/ a terrible din.// '**Shut up**,'// **yelled**/ their owners,// **throwing**/ stones/ at them.// The dogs/ **whined**// and **skulked**/ away.//

---

[3] One reason teachers do not use the term clause is that its traditional definition is even harder to explain and not very useful, e.g. 'a clause is a pair or group of words that consists of a subject and a predicate'.

From the perspective of writing, these two paragraphs consist of five sentences separated by full stops. But from the perspective of grammar, they consist of a series of clauses. One thing that stands out here is that almost all the clauses are either marked by punctuation (commas, full stops, speech marks), or joined by conjunctions (*and*, *when*). Here it is again, with each clause on a separate line, to show these patterns more clearly.

> Molly and Gracie finished their breakfast
> **and** decided
> to take all their dirty clothes
> **and** wash them in the soak further down the river.
> They returned to the camp
> looking clean and refreshed
> **and** joined the rest of the family in the shade for lunch.
> The family had just finished eating
> **when** all the camp dogs began barking,
> making a terrible din.
> 'Shut up,'
> yelled their owners,
> throwing stones at them.
> The dogs whined
> **and** skulked away.

Each sentence consists of a series of clauses, called a **clause complex**. That is, the definition of a sentence is a clause complex. To sum up so far, we have identified:

1. **Word groups** in each sentence expressing six types of meanings. To identify the meaning expressed by each word group we can ask a wh-question – *who or what it's about, what they are doing/did, where, when, how*. Word groups can be marked with a slash /.
2. **Clauses**, by first finding each process, and the people, things and other elements involved in each process. Clauses may also be marked by punctuation and joined by conjunctions. Boundaries between clauses can be marked with a double slash //.

This analysis is easy to do with a little practice, and easy to show students. One technique is to enlarge and copy a passage of text, for students to mark and label as we have done in [5.1]. Another is to write sentences on cardboard or paper strips, for students to cut up the word groups (as in Sentence Making) and label them on the back.

We also presented each clause in [5.1] on a separate line, which makes it easier to see many of the patterns in language, such as conjunctions linking clauses in a clause complex. Another thing we mentioned is that some clauses in a clause complex could stand on their own as simple sentences. Here is the passage again, with these clauses underlined.

<u>Molly and Gracie finished their breakfast</u>
and decided
to take all their dirty clothes
and wash them in the soak further down the river.
<u>They returned to the camp</u>
looking clean and refreshed
and joined the rest of the family in the shade for lunch.
<u>The family had just finished eating</u>
when all the camp dogs began barking,
making a terrible din.
<u>"Shut up,"</u>
 yelled their owners,
throwing stones at them.
<u>The dogs whined</u>
and skulked away.

We will refer to these clauses as the **primary clauses** in a clause complex, and the others as **secondary clauses**. Traditional school grammars also make a distinction between complex sentences and compound sentences. In a complex sentence the relation between clauses is unequal, and one clause is dependent on the other. The dependent clause can come before or after the primary clause:

They returned to the camp // looking clean and refreshed.
Looking clean and refreshed // they returned to the camp.

In a compound sentence, the relation between clauses is equal, and the order may not be reversible:

The dogs whined // and skulked away.
[not *and skulked away // the dogs whined]

In actual texts there are often sentences that include both equal and unequal relations between clauses. These are traditionally known as complex/compound sentences:

They returned to the camp // [unequal] looking clean and refreshed // [equal] and joined the rest of the family in the shade for lunch.

For the sake of simplicity it may be sufficient for teachers to just use the terms simple and complex sentences, as it seems many teachers already do with their classes. A complex sentence is thus a clause complex; one clause is primary and the other clauses are secondary.

One useful activity to explore in more detail with primary and secondary clauses (without piling on more detailed terminology)[4] is simply to practise rephrasing secondary clauses in a text as simple sentences, and discussing what has changed (e.g. *Molly and Gracie returned to the camp. They looked clean and refreshed. They joined the rest of the family in the shade for lunch.*) One thing that has changed in these examples is that the missing people have been rendered with *They*. In the original clause complex these identities were presumed from the primary clause (see Identificaton §5.3.3 below).

5.2.2   Types of word groups

Our next step for KAL is towards a little more detail – distinguishing three main types of word groups, and two others. Despite the decline of grammatical training in schools and teacher education in recent decades, it seems that most teachers use the terms **verb** and **noun** with their students. We can draw on this existing metalanguage and relate it to the semantic metalanguage we are building up here, since **verbs** express the meaning of a process and **nouns** express the meaning of people or things. But as we have seen, these meanings are not always expressed by single words, but very often by groups of words. So types of meanings within clauses are expressed by different types of word groups.

> Processes are expressed by one or more verbs, or **verbal groups**.
>
> People and things are expressed by word groups around a noun, or **nominal groups**.[5]

The third main type of word group expresses the meaning of places and times, of which there are a few in our passage. Their distinctive feature is that they start with a **preposition** (in bold below).

> **in** the soak
>
> **further down** the river
>
> **to** the camp
>
> **in** the shade

---

[4] Primary clauses are also known as *independent, main, free, dominant, initiating*. Other terms for secondary clauses include *dependent, subordinate, coordinate, continuing*. This is more detail than we need at this point.

[5] Teachers often simply use 'verb group' and 'noun group' with their students, but it is not hard to explain that **nominal** is the adjectival form of noun (the etymology of both is related to 'name'). One reason for using these terms is that these groups do not just consist of verbs and nouns (e.g. verbal group *be able to go*, nominal group *new running shoes*).

When we ask even young children *where Molly and Gracie washed their clothes*, *where the soak was*, *where they returned*, or *where the family sat*, what children notice intuitively is the preposition: *in*, *down*, *to*, which they associate with the meaning 'place'. This type of meaning is expressed by a nominal group preceded by a preposition. Teachers can use a simple definition.

> Places are expressed by noun groups that are introduced by a preposition, or **prepositional phrases**.

The term **phrase** is used here to make a clear distinction from nominal **groups**. While places are by far the most common meanings expressed by prepositional phrases, there are a number of others, which even our struggling writers in Chapter 2 know. Table 5.1 shows a few, with their functional names to the right, and the wh-words that can be used to identify and discuss them.

Table 5.1: Some meanings expressed by prepositional phrases

*On the holiday I went to my dads **for 3 weeks***	when, how long	Time
*an we went to ante Jhins house **for crismuse***	why, what for	Reason
*Aboriginals hunt goannas **for food***	why, what for	Purpose
*and the fat inside the goannas are used **for medicine***	why, what for	Purpose
*They camouflage their self **with the area***	how, what with	Means
*their colour looks **like yellowish-brown***	what like	Comparison
On the weekend I Play footyball	when	Time
*Then I went **to the river***	where to	Place
*my cousin Jack Jumpet **out of the tree***	where from	Place
*I was worr[ied] **about my cousin***	what about	Matter
*When I was walking **up to Ms Cox room***	where to	Place
I seen a suitcase. and a slimy thing hanging out		
*and it looked **like a baby octopus.***	what like	Comparison
*it was a cat playin **with a baby toy***	what with	Accompaniment
*I laughed **at myself***	what at	Target
*shes a princess **in a cuddly sort of way***	how, in what way	Quality
*A shark is shaped **like a torpedo***	what like	Comparison
*Earth started **as a ball of fire.***	what as	Role
*But it was still too hot **for Life.***	why, what for	Purpose
*There's nothing in the meadow **except grass and trees***	except for what	Condition

Note that the same preposition can have different meanings in different types of phrases, e.g. *for* (Time, Reason, Purpose), *with* (Means, Accompaniment), *at* (Place, Target). In order to explain prepositional phrases, teachers need to define 'preposition', which is easy to do with examples of prepositional phrases in actual texts. They are a small set of small words that usually come before a noun group, which is also the etymology of *preposition* – 'positioned in front'.

Because these types of meanings are elements in functional grammar, initial capitals are used to distinguish them from ordinary semantic labels. Halliday (2004) groups these meanings together as types of **circumstance**. A clause consists of three main elements expressed by word groups: (1) a process, (2) people and things that participate in the process, and (3) circumstances associated with it. The process is the core element of the clause; the process and its participants (people and things) form the nucleus of the clause; the circumstances are more marginal elements. This nuclear perspective on the meaning of a clause is diagrammed in Figure 5.2.

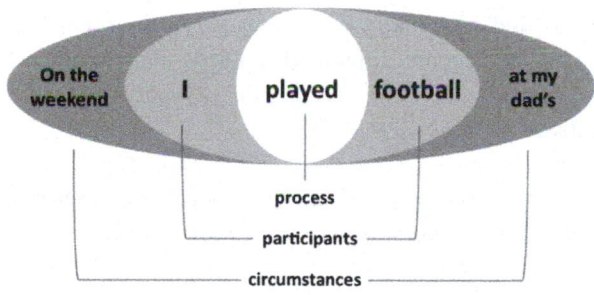

Figure 5.2: Orbital view of the clause

A diagram like this can be useful for clarifying the elements of a clause with students, but it may not always be necessary in the classroom to add the technical terms 'participant' for people and things, and 'circumstance' for places and times. We can use them here in order to take two more steps in the KAL we are building for teachers. The first step is that circumstances can also be expressed by **adverbs** or **adverbial groups**.

> **Slowly** water formed and then the first signs of life
> Every sea creature sees my shark **differently**

These adverbs express the meaning of **qualities** that modify the process: *slowly formed, sees differently*. One of the things about qualities is that they can be intensified: ***very slowly*** *water formed, every sea creature sees my shark **completely differently***. These circumstances have now been expanded into adverbial groups.

Some clauses ascribe qualities to people and things.

Molly and Gracie looked **clean and refreshed**

I was **very happy**

the Octopus thinks shes **funny**

It's **crazy** though

Mr stingray thinks shes **precious and adorable**

I think shes **the coolest**

Earth's core is **as hot as the furthest outer layer of the sun**

soon the gurgling sound got **farther**

then it was **gone**

at first I was **scared**

but when I look it wasn't **that scary**.

In these cases the qualities are expressed by **adjectives**: *clean, refreshed, happy, funny, crazy, precious, adorable, coolest, hot, farther, gone, scared, scary*. These can also be intensified – ***very** happy*, ***as** hot **as** the furthest outer layer of the sun*, ***that** scary* – and so become **adjectival groups**, along with adding qualities together: *precious **and** adorable, clean **and** refreshed*. Adverbs are used to intensify adjectives.

totally freaked out, **especially** upset, **mortally** wounded, **nearly** perfect, **intensely** religious, **determinedly** innocent, **nearly** dark, **relatively** safe, **perfectly** obvious ...

To sum up at this point, we have shown how each chunk of meaning in a clause is expressed by different **classes of words** or **word groups**, in Table 5.2.

Table 5.2: Classes of words and word groups

meaning	word class	word group	simple definition
process	verb	verbal group	*one or more verbs*
thing/person	noun	nominal group	*group of words around a noun*
place/time	preposition	prepositional phrase	*noun group introduced by a preposition*
quality (of process)	adverb	adverbial group	*one or more adverbs*
quality (of thing)	adjective	adjectival group	*one or more adjectives*

Other terms we have used include **intensify** for words that intensify the strength of qualities, and **express** for the relation between meanings and wordings.[6] These

---

[6] The technical term for the relation between meanings and wordings is **realisation**, but *express* is so widely used and understood for this relation that we can retain it for the classroom.

are commonsense terms, but teachers can also use them systematically in the same way. We have also just used the term **wording** to contrast with **meaning**. The term 'wording' can be used to cover any grammatical item from a word, to a word group, to a clause and a sentence. **Grammatical items** or **structures** are more technical terms for wordings.

Let us now explore what goes on within word groups – what are the functions of the various other words that we have not yet focused on?

5.2.3   Nominal groups

Nominal groups tend to be fairly simple in speaking, but a lot of meaning gets packed into nominal groups in writing, so they are worth looking at closely. To show the full potential of nominal groups we will use examples from well-written texts like *Fantastic Mr Fox* and *Follow the Rabbit Proof Fence*.

The simplest nominal groups consist of single elements that refer to a person or thing. These include **pronouns** (*I, we, you, it*) and **proper names** for people and places (*Mollie, Gracie, Earth, Sydney*). Proper names can also consist of two or more words, such as *Gracie Fields, Mr Fox, Constable Riggs, Amazon River, Planet Earth*. As these refer to specific people or things, the pronoun or name may be all the information we need to identify them. We call this central element of the nominal group the **Thing** (using an initial capital for this functional element).

Thing
Mr Fox

On the other hand, words like *shark, breakfast, dogs, girl* refer to whole classes of things, so we often need more information about them. This may simply involve indicating which thing we are talking about. Nominal groups often start with a word that does this, which we will call the **Pointer**. Some common Pointers are *a* (which usually indicates you do not know it yet), *the* (which indicates you do know it), *this, that, these, those* (indicating which thing), *my, their* (indicating whose thing) or *same, other* (comparing one thing with another).

Pointer	Thing
a	shark
the	dogs
my	shark
their	breakfast
this	reaction
the other	girls

Things can also be counted, ordered or measured with a **Number** that comes after the Pointer and before the Thing. There can be more than one Number.

Pointer	Number	Thing
	thirty	miles
	twenty-five	seconds
the	first	rays
a	few	miles
the last	two or three	generations

Things can be described with respect to their qualities, such as size, shape, colour and our attitude to them. We will call this element the **Describer**, which comes after the Pointer and before the Thing. There can also be more than one Describer.

Pointer	Describer	Thing
the	dark	tunnel
his	long handsome	face
his	black	nose
a	tiny	noise
a	soft rustling	sound
a	long	time
some other	small	animal

As well as describing the qualities of things, they can also be classified as one or another kind. Qualities can be intensified, but classes cannot – a thing is either one class or another. The **Classifier** comes after the Describer but before the Thing.

Pointer	Describer	Classifier	Thing
		native	animals
every		sea	creature
the	cool	night	air
a		field	mouse
his	sharp	night	eyes
all the		camp	dogs
a	tall, rugged	white	man

These Classifiers cannot be intensified, but the Describers can. We could say *acutely sharp* eyes, but not *very night eyes, very sea creatures*.

Each of these elements – Pointer, Number, Describer, Classifier – comes before the Thing. But Things can also be modified after, with prepositional phrases and clauses. These elements are called Qualifiers, because they qualify the Thing in some way.

Pointer	Describer	Thing	Qualifier
The		smoke	[from the three guns]
		miles	[out of his way]
		what	[you need]
a	long	way	[to go yet]
the	fateful	day	[they had been dreading]
the		man	[who was taking their daughters away]
The		cries	[of agonised mothers]
the	deep	sobs	[of grandfathers, uncles and cousins]
This		reaction	[to their children's abduction]

These phrases and clauses are part of the nominal group. They are said to be 'embedded' in the nominal group, so square brackets are used to show they are embedded and not separate clauses or separate elements of clauses.[7] This is helpful when Qualifiers get embedded within Qualifiers, which is common in writing, forming very long nominal groups that students often find hard to understand.

Another place we find embedded word groups is at the front of the nominal group. The Pointer can be an embedded nominal group that identifies whose Thing it is.

Pointer	Thing
[a fox]'s	tail
[Aunty Joan]'s	house
[her life]'s	work

Embedded word groups can also come before the Pointer, starting with some perspective on the Thing – a part, facet, measure, type or group. Since it is concerned with perspective we will call this the **Focus** of the nominal group. The Focus is linked to the nominal group with 'of'.

Focus	Pointer	Describer	Thing
[the mouth] of	his		hole
[the front half] of	his		body
[the barrel] of	a		gun
[the scent] of			danger
[a small silver speck] of			moonlight
[a glint] of			something
[a patch] of		dry	leaves
[one] of			them

---

[7] Technically, double brackets are used for embedded clauses, but this can add clutter to text analyses, and our focus here is simply to mark embedding.

Common meanings of a Focus are **parts** or **facets** of things (the mouth of, the front of, the barrel of, the rest of, the scent of, the meaning of), **measures** (a small speck of, a glint of, a patch of, one of, lots of, two litres of), **types** (a make of, species of, kind of) and **groups** (a mob of, herd of, gaggle of), often called 'collective nouns'. We should note here that 'of' has at least two functions in nominal groups. Here it links the Focus to the Thing. But it can also link the Qualifier to the Thing, as shown above [**of** agonised mothers…], [**of** grand-fathers…], and these are sometimes hard to distinguish.

The elements of nominal groups are certainly useful terms to share with students. They can be practised by labelling nominal groups on enlarged copies, as we described above for word groups in clauses. Nominal groups can also be written on cardboard or paper strips, and their elements cut up and labelled on the back. The elements we have discussed are summed up in Table 5.3, along with the wh-words that can be used to discuss each element.

Table 5.3: Elements of nominal groups

element	wh-word	function
Focus	*what part, group …*	perspective on the Thing
Pointer	*which*	indicates which or whose Thing
Number	*how many/much*	counts, orders, measures
Describer	*what like*	describes qualities (can be intensified)
Classifier	*what kind*	classifies what kind (cannot intensify)
Thing	*what*	person, thing or place
Qualifier	*what like/which*	qualifies the thing with prep. phrase or clause

The technical terms for Pointer, Number and Describer are the Greek and Latin *Deictic*, *Numerative* and *Epithet* respectively. We have followed sugges-tions by Rothery here (e.g. 1989), using Pointer, Number and Describer because they are more transparent for English-speaking teachers and students. Teachers often use the term 'describing word', so Describer will make sense for many. Less familiar are the different functions of Describer and Classifier, as well as the functions of Focus and Qualifier; but these are indispensable terms for talking about written meanings with students.

5.2.3   Verbal groups

English has a complex system for verbal groups that is quite different from many other languages. Many students have difficulties with aspects of verbal groups, especially if English is another language for them, or they speak another dialect such as Aboriginal English. With this in mind we can have a brief look at the meanings in verbal groups. They express the meaning of a process, but this meaning can be expanded in several ways, including the time of the process (**tense**), how likely the process is (**modality**), whether it is **negative**, and whether it is **passive**.

Most of the processes in our text examples were expressed by single verbs that are either **present** or **past tense**. Stories are mostly **simple past**, and descriptions and reports are mostly **simple present**. Some of the processes in dependent clauses have no tense, because it is presumed from the clause they depend on; and simple commands also have no tense.

simple past	simple present	no tense
finished	is, are	looking
decided	live	making
returned	eat	throwing
joined	have	hanging out
yelled	lay	laughing
whined	sees	playing
skulked	thinks	'Shut up'
appeared	cracks up	
rowed	tries	
came	love	

In these examples of simple past and present tense, the meaning of the process is combined with the meaning of time, sometimes using endings -ed or -s. Here are some ways this can be expanded, using the verbs 'be', 'have' and 'do'. These are often known as **auxiliary verbs**.

1. Simple past and present tense can also be expressed, more emphatically, by 'do'.

   did finish, *did* decide, *did* return; *does* see, *does* think, *do* love, *do* have.

2. More complicated past, present and future tenses can be expressed by 'be', 'have' and 'go'.

   I am walking, *was* walking, *had* walked, *will* walk, *am going to* walk, *will be* walking.

3. If the auxiliary comes before a nominal group it makes a question.

   did they finish? *do* you think?

4. Auxiliary verbs can be contracted

   I'd walked, *I'm* walking, *I'll* walk

5. The process can be made **negative**, with 'not', or by contracting *not* (as *n't*) with the auxiliary.

   didn't finish, *doesn't* see, *don't* love.

6. English tenses can also be expanded two, three or more times, to express very precise times.

   I had been walking, *I will have been* walking, *I'm going to be* walking, *I won't have been going to* walk.

As well as tense, verbal groups can express five kinds of **modality**: how likely (probability), how often (usuality), how obliged (obligation), how inclined (inclination) and how able (ability). Except for ability, each of these can be adjusted in degrees between 'yes' and 'no'. These meanings can be expressed by **modal verbs**, shown in Table 5.4.

Table 5.4: Examples of modality

	probability/usuality	obligation	inclination
'yes'	*it is*	*Do it!*	*I'll do it*
high	*it **must** be*	*you **must** do*	*I **must** do*
median	*it **will** be*	*you **should** do*	*I **should** do*
low	*it **may** be*	*you **may** do*	*I **may** do*
'no'	*it isn't*	*Don't do it!*	*I won't do it*

Modality can also be expressed by adverbs or adjectives (that are not part of the verbal group):

	adverbs	adjectives
probability	*possibly/probably/certainly*	*It's possiible/likely/sure*
usuality	*sometimes/usually/always*	*It's rare/common/typical*
inclination/obligation	*reluctantly/willingly/gladly*	*I'm reluctant/willing/anxious*

Verbal groups can also be expanded with a secondary process that adds some meaning, including modality:

phase	*start/continue/cease to do/doing*
success	*try/fail/learn/manage to do*
desire	*like/want/hate/ to do*
obligation	*have to/need to/like to do*
quality	*tend/venture/hesitate to do*
locution	*ask/agree/promise to do*

Finally verbal groups can be made passive, using the auxiliary verbs *be* or *get*:

active	passive
He asked to go	*and he'll be sent soon*
I've warned you	*so you've been told*
Did he jump	*or did he get pushed?*

Technically, the lexical verb in a verbal group is known as the **Event**. Tense, modal and passive verbs come before the Event. The structure of verbal groups can be built up as a series working back from the Event, to demonstrate appropriate structures in English, as in Figure 5.3.

These are perhaps the main aspects of verbal groups that teachers need to be aware of when reading, writing and speaking with their students. Most teachers probably use the terms **tense, past, present** and **future**. Some useful terms to add include **simple** (*walks, does walk; walked, did walk; will walk*), **continuous** (*is walking, was walking, will be walking*) and **completed** (*had walked* – also known as 'past perfect').

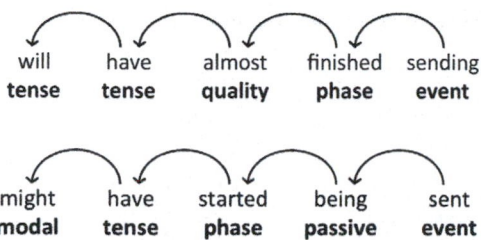

Figure 5.3: Serial structure of verbal groups

The term auxiliary verb could be useful when discussing these options. Alternatively they could be named as **tense**, **modal** and **passive** verbs. These each add something to the meaning of the process, but the event itself is expressed by a **lexical** verb. Lexical words are often called 'content' words, because they express specific meanings of processes, people, things, places, times and qualities. A simple strategy to show students the difference between lexical verbs and other elements is to find verbal groups with two or more verbs, and guide students to highlight the lexical verb in each group. With young children, teachers often use terms such as 'content' and 'helper' to distinguish lexical and auxiliary verbs.

As with all these language systems, modality is something that can be discussed in context as the need arises in joint reading and writing, and built up over time, using commonsense terms: *how **likely**, how **often**, how **obliged**, how **inclined**,* as well as *how **strong*** for the degrees between yes and no. When students are thoroughly familiar with these kinds of meanings, after reading, writing and discussing instances in a series of texts, they may be consolidated in tables like 5.4, with exercises. The same applies to **passive** and **active** forms. These also need to be encountered repeatedly in texts, so students thoroughly understand their functions, before using grammar exercises, such as the popular activity of changing active to passive.

5.2.4   Word classes and functions

Lexical words include **lexical verbs, nouns, proper names, numerals, adverbs** and **adjectives**. These are word classes with a lot of members in any dictionary or thesaurus. In contrast, word classes with just a few members include **modal** and **auxiliary verbs, articles, pronouns, prepositions** and **conjunctions**.[8] These are often called 'grammatical words', 'structure words' or 'function words'.

There is no one-to-one correspondence between word classes and the meanings they express. Table 5.5 compares the elements of nominal groups with a range of word classes that can be used to express them.

---

[8] Technically, articles, demonstratives and comparatives are classed together as determiners.

Table 5.5: Word classes that express nominal group elements

element	class	examples
Focus	[nominal group] ^of	*[the front half] of*
Pointer	article	*a, the, some*
	demonstrative	*this, that, these, those*
	comparative	*other, same, more, fewer*
	adjective	*usual, typical, identical*
	possessive	*my, our, their*
	[nominal group] ^'s	*[Aunty Joan]'s*
Number	cardinal (count) numeral	*3, xiv, forty-four*
	ordinal (order) numeral	*sixth, 21st*
	measure adjective	*few, several, many*
Describer	descriptive adjective	*clean, refreshed, soft, dark*
	attitudinal adjective	*happy, scary, perfect, major*
	verb	*rustling sound, tattered remains*
	intensifying adverb	*very scary, deliriously happy*
Classifier	noun	*sea creature, night eyes*
	verb	*walking stick, ground pepper*
	adjective	*blue whale, snowy owl*
	numeral	*2006 vintage, third prize*
Thing	noun	*animal, shark, man*
	pronoun	*he, you, they …*
	proper name	*Mr Fox, Australia, Google*
Qualifier	[prepositional phrase]	*smoke [from the three guns]*
	[clause]	*the man [who took their children]*

5.2.5 Expanding meanings in writing

One of the differences between speaking and writing is the degree to which meanings are expanded upon. In the following extract from *Fantastic Mr Fox* that we discussed in Chapter 4, wordings that expand meanings are in bold.

[4.6′] Extract from *Fantastic Mr Fox*

He crept **a little further** out of the hole … **then further still. He was almost right out in the open now.** He took a **last careful** look around. The wood was murky **and very still. Somewhere in the sky** the moon was shining.

Just then, **his sharp night-eyes caught a glint of** something **bright** behind a tree **not far away.** It was a **small silver** speck **of** moonlight shining **on a polished surface.** Mr Fox lay still, **watching it. What on earth was it?**

Now it was moving. **It was coming up and up … Great heavens!** It was the barrel of a gun!

Quick as a whip, Mr Fox jumped **back** into his hole and **at that same instant** the **entire** wood seemed to explode **around him. Bang-bang! Bang-bang! Bang-bang!**

Here is the passage again minus these expansions.

> He crept out of the hole. He took a look around. The wood was murky. The moon was shining. Then he saw something behind a tree. It was a speck shining. Mr Fox lay still. It was moving. It was the barrel of a gun. Mr Fox jumped into his hole and the wood exploded.

The unexpanded version is more like the relatively unadorned character of much of everyday speaking. Not surprisingly, it is also reminiscent of story writing by students with relatively little experience of reading in the home (Van Leeuwen 2008, Williams 1995, 2005b). This simple comparison is a strong argument in itself for abandoning the wide-spread school practice of writing from personal experience (also known as process writing or journal writing) in favour of using texts by accomplished authors for Detailed Reading and Rewriting.

But the comparison is also very useful in teaching, as it can show students the contribution that each expansion makes to the meaning of a text. An effective strategy for this is to use a sentence maker or electronic smartboard, turn over or mask the expanding wordings, show them again, and discuss their functions. This activity is an ideal context to introduce and reinforce metalanguage, as each function is discussed. It should follow Detailed Reading, so that all students fully comprehend the text before discussing its linguistics.

The expansions of meaning are at multiple levels.

words within groups	*a **little further**, a **last careful** look, **Just** then, his **sharp night**-eyes, a **small silver** speck **of moonlight**, jumped **back**, the **entire** wood, **seemed to** explode*
groups within clauses	*... then further still, Somewhere in the sky, and very still, not far away, on a polished surface, Now, Quick as a whip, at that same instant, around him*
clauses and sentences	*He was almost right out in the open now; his sharp night-eyes caught a glint; watching it; What on earth was it?; It was coming up and up ...; Great heavens!; Bang-bang! Bang-bang! Bang-bang!*
phases within stages	[problem1] *something bright behind a tree ...*
	[reaction] *Mr Fox lay still ...*
	[problem2] *Now it was moving ...*
	[reaction] *Great heavens! ...*
	[problem3] *the entire wood seemed to explode ...*

The terms we have introduced so far in this chapter can be used to discuss each of these expansions, including the classes and functions of words that expand nominal and verbal groups, and the meanings of circumstances that expand clauses (such as place, time and quality), and their expression as prepositional phrases or adverbial groups. Terms for phases within text stages were introduced in Chapters 2, 3 and 4, for stories, factual texts and arguments.

Beyond the level of phases, the whole novel *Fantastic Mr Fox* is a serial narrative, in which the story is expanded with a series of Complications and temporary Resolutions. Similarly, the description of cells in the science textbook [4.9] was expanded with a series of compositional and classifying reports, and the Description stages in each of these reports were expanded with phases describing the structures and functions of cells. Novels and textbooks are examples of macrogenres, as are chapters and sections within textbooks.

A common way of expanding meanings at all these levels is to repeat a pattern two, three or more times. We saw this in *Rosie's Walk* in Chapter 4, in which the places that Rosie walked were expanded with a series of prepositional phrases: *across the yard, around the pond, over the haycock, past the mill, through the fence, under the beehives*. The meaning of place is repeated but the specific places vary. More complex picture books for children also use repetition, but at the scale of episodes and their elements, which each follow similar structures with changing content. A similar syndrome can be seen in texts for older children and adults, with series of Complications in stories, series of descriptions in reports, series of factors in explanations, or series of supporting arguments in expositions.

At the grammatical level, such repetitions are also very common in all genres. For example, in [4.6], the meaning of **extent** or how far Mr Fox crept out of his hole is expanded three times across two sentences: *a little further ... then further still ... almost right out in the open*; the night's **qualities** are expanded twice: *murky* and *very still*; the **location** of *something bright* is expanded twice: *behind a tree not far away*; its **movement** is expanded twice: *it was moving. It was coming up and up*; and the **sound** of the farmers' shotguns is repeated three times: *Bang-bang! Bang-bang! Bang-bang!* In Rabbit Proof Fence we saw similar expansions through repetition: of **qualities**, *clean and refreshed*, and **processes**, *the dogs whined and skulked*. In the factorial explanation [4.12], two **factors** are presented with the same sentence structure of cause-and-effect.

> The government's policies of repression had bred anger and fear.
>
> Its policies of reform had given rise to expectations ... of changes

These two sentences are similar because they share the same function as factors in the explanation, but the policies and their effects are contrasting. Students' attention can be drawn to these kinds of repeated patterns in Detailed Reading, by preparing with the number of repetitions, e.g. *it tells how far Mr Fox crept out three times*, and asking students to identify them one at a time. Elaborations can then discuss the functions of both the grammatical feature and its expansion by repetition.

5.2.6   Lexical metaphor

Another way to expand meaning is with metaphor, adding a layer of inferred meaning that can be quite different from the literal meaning of the lexical words themselves. A significant contrast between *Fantastic Mr Fox*, which is aimed at young children, and *Follow the Rabbit Proof Fence*, which was written for adults, is that lexical metaphor is used extensively in *Rabbit Proof Fence* to enhance imagery, but *Fantastic Mr Fox* has relatively little, despite its literary qualities. One reason for this is that metaphors involve two layers of meaning: the literal meaning of the lexical words, and the inferred meaning[9] of the metaphor. These two layers of meaning are in tension, but must be read simultaneously to comprehend the metaphor. Until the age of nine or ten it can be difficult for children to manage such multi-layered reading, but for adults the tension between layers of meaning sparks the imagination and enhances the pleasure of reading.

The events in *Rabbit Proof Fence* start off fairly literally – the family eating, dogs barking, owners yelling and throwing stones. But when the author wants to raise the stakes to describe the white man and the family's reaction she uses metaphor – *all eyes turned, fear and anxiety swept over them.*

> The family had just finished eating when all the camp dogs began barking, making a terrible din. 'Shut up,' yelled their owners, throwing stones at them. The dogs whined and skulked away.
>
> Then all eyes turned to the cause of the commotion. A tall, rugged white man stood on the bank above them. He could easily have been mistaken for a pastoralist or a grazier with his tanned complexion except that he was wearing khaki clothing.
>
> Fear and anxiety swept over them when they realised that the fateful day they had been dreading had come at last. They always knew that it would only be a matter of time before the government would track them down.

Literally, *all eyes turned* means just their eyes turned, which cannot simply be read literally in the context. The inferred meaning is that 'everyone turned to look at the same time', diagrammed in Figure 5.4. Likewise, *fear and anxiety swept over them* literally means these emotions quickly covered everyone, which is again far less than is meant here. The inferred meaning is that their feelings were so strong they could not control them, as if they were being swept over by a wave or flood. Note that these metaphors are not just word groups, but involve whole **figures** (process + participants).

---

[9] Technically, the inferred meaning of a metaphor is known as the **transferred** meaning, but we are minimising such technical terms that need defining.

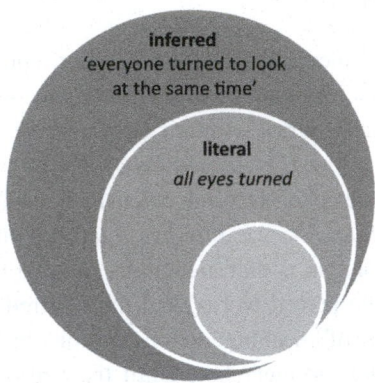

Figure 5.4: Literal and inferred meanings of lexical metaphor

In §4.3.5 we suggested a way to support students to read lexical metaphors by preparing them with the inferred meaning, which they then apply to identify the metaphorical wording in the text. This is possible for them because metaphor is actually a common part of everyday discourse, which most (but not all) students are familiar with – *pull your socks up*, *keep your eye on the ball* and so on. So with guidance they can intuitively recognise the connection between the inferred meaning and the metaphorical wording. The elaboration then makes this relation explicit, first by pointing out the inadequacy of a literal reading – *Was it just their eyes that moved?* – and then giving the inferred meaning more precisely. In fact the inferred meaning is often both **inferential**, because it must be read with the co-text to make sense, and **interpretive**, because the precise meaning can often only be interpreted from experience related to the metaphor. For example, we may need experience of the metaphor *all eyes turned* to know it means 'they turned around *at the same time*', as this is not recoverable from the text itself.

In addition to these lexical metaphors, the description and reaction paragraphs above include several other figures of speech: *could easily have been mistaken*, *the fateful day*, *a matter of time*, *track them down*. Expressions like this often seem so ordinary that they scarcely need commenting on, but to students who are not familiar with written ways of meaning, or certain dialects of English, they may be opaque. For example, they may assume that someone really was mistaken, or wonder what kind of day is *fateful*, or what is the matter with time, or what *track down* means.

These kinds of wordings are often referred to as **idioms**. Idioms are defined by the Macquarie Dictionary as 'a form of expression peculiar to a language, especially one having a significance other than its literal one' (2011). We could refine this as 'an expression peculiar to a particular register or dialect, whose meaning is not directly composed by the actual words involved'. Some of these are 'frozen metaphors', that is, metaphors that have become such common usage that they no longer seem metaphorical (e.g. *kick the bucket, out of the blue, fit as* *a fiddle*). It is important that teachers watch out for all these types of wordings and support students to read them using the same strategy as for metaphors, by preparing with their inferred meaning and elaborating with a precise definition.

5.2.7   Grammatical metaphor

Like lexical metaphors, grammatical metaphor involves two layers of meaning that must be read simultaneously to comprehend. But the tension is not between the literal and inferred meanings of the figure, but between meanings of grammatical structures and their discourse functions.

In Chapter 3 (§3.6), we showed how the whistleblower Ridenhour used grammatical metaphor to grade his attitudes, by expressing qualities and events as nouns instead of adjectives and verbs (*a very substantial amount of **truth**, slaughter, murder, barbarism*). We also saw how historical recounts often code events as nominal groups, to package them up in phases of time (*the **fall** of Dien Bien Phu, the **surrender** of the Japanese*). We saw how historical accounts and explanations frequently express cause/effect relations within clauses, with the causal relation often expressed as a verbal group (*the Vietnam conflict gave rise to social division, It also produced ... a siege mentality*). And we saw how technicality and explanations are constructed in science by coding events as nominal groups, and causal relations as verbal groups (*charges are driven apart by as-yet uncertain processes, Charge separation appears to require strong updrafts*).

Grammatical metaphor has evolved in writing as the key semiotic resource for constructing academic discourses in the humanities, science and social sciences. As such, understanding grammatical metaphor is the gateway to school knowledge. It starts to appear in factual texts in the middle primary years, and becomes common across subject areas in the upper primary. In the secondary it is endemic in texts across the curriculum. However, a large proportion of students of all ages cannot read grammatical metaphor with adequate comprehension, and certainly cannot use it to write coherently. For these students it is not the gateway but the barrier to school knowledge, so it is imperative for teachers to understand how grammatical metaphor works and how to teach it.

In Chapter 4 (§4.4.5), we showed how grammatical metaphor can be unpacked when preparing a highly abstract text before reading it to the class.

> *The particular time we're going to look at is this one here, the mid-1980s, so it's 1984, 1985, 1986. Now this is when the next student uprising started in townships like Sobantu. This little part of the textbook is about why the violence started in the townships at that time.*
>
> *But it starts off telling us that people were rebelling in the black townships, and there were three reasons for this. Because the government, on one side they had a policy to keep the people down, to repress the people with the police and the army. And of course this made the people very angry and frightened.*

So they had this policy on one side of keeping people down, but on the other side, and they didn't.

The third reason was that all the parties fighting apartheid joined together to make it very difficult for the government.

In this spoken version, various activities are expressed as clauses involving people and things in places and times: *people were rebelling in the black townships*, *the government had a policy to repress the people*; *all the parties fighting apartheid joined together.* Here events are expressed by verbal groups and entities by nominal groups. Qualities are also expressed by adjectives: *this made the people very **angry and frightened***; *people expected things to get **better**.* And causal relations between events are expressed by conjunctions: *people were rebelling in the black townships ... **Because** the government had a policy to keep the people down*; *they promised to make things better ... **So** people expected things to get better.*

In the written version [4.12'] these events and qualities are expressed as nominal groups: *a rebellion, policies of repression, anger and fear, the various forces of resistance*; and causal relations are expressed as verbal groups: *had bred, had given rise to, had been unable to meet, combined to create.*

[4.12'] Historical explanation showing abstraction

In the mid-1980s **South African politics**[10] erupted in a **rebellion** in black townships ...

The government's **policies of repression** had bred **anger and fear**.

Its **policies of reform** had given rise to **expectations** amongst black people of **changes** which the government had been unable to meet.

The **various forces of resistance** now combined to create a **major challenge** for the government.

When we read the written version we recognise that lexical words like *rebellion*, *repression* and *expectations* express the meaning of events that inherently involve people, but at the same time their grammatical class as nouns construes the meaning of entities. These kinds of words are traditionally known as 'abstract nouns', but we can extend this to 'abstract nominal groups', since they involve groups of words. There are thus two layers of meaning involved. From the perspective of grammar, these abstract nominal groups mean an **entity**, but from the perspective of discourse they mean a **figure** (event + entities). These two layers are diagrammed in Figure 5.5.

---

[10] Politics is an abstract noun, but not a grammatical metaphor – it does not stand for a figure.

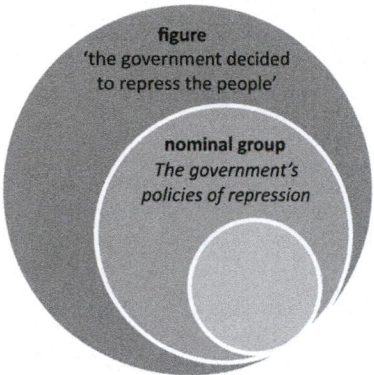

Figure 5.5: Grammatical metaphor – figure expressed as nominal group

Seen as a semiotic process, grammatical metaphor turns figures into abstract nominal groups that can be evaluated and organised as chunks of information in Themes and News.

Themes	News
In the mid-1980s South African politics	erupted in a **rebellion in black townships.**
The **government's policies of repression**	had bred **anger and fear.**
Its **policies of reform**	had given rise to **expectations of changes**
The **various forces of resistance**	now combined
	to create **a major challenge for the government.**

Alongside these abstract nominal groups, each of the clauses in [4.12] expresses a sequence of cause and effect as a relation between two abstract nominal groups. The verbal groups in each clause construe this relation as a process. As we read each clause, we recognise that it is expressing a causal sequence of events: 'the government repressed the people **so** they became angry and frightened', 'they promised reforms **so** the people expected changes'; but at the same time their grammatical realisation as a single clause literally expresses the meaning of a single figure (event + entities). Again there are two layers of meaning involved. As we said earlier, the meaning of a clause is a process, so from the perspective of grammar these clauses mean a **single process**, but from the perspective of discourse they mean a **sequence**. These two layers are diagrammed in Figure 5.6. These two layers of meaning turn sequences of events into **abstract clauses** that can be evaluated and organised to meet the rhetorical purposes of the text (in this case as a series of factors in the explanation).

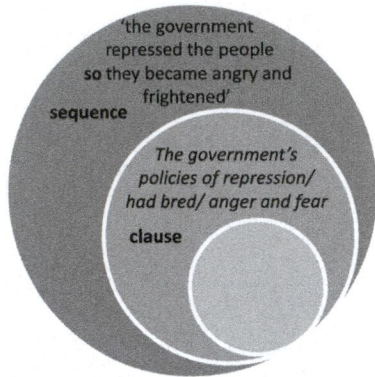

Figure 5.6: Grammatical metaphor – sequence expressed as clause

Realising cause as a process opens up a much wider range of causal relations than conjunctions can express. In [4.12] the evaluation of the events is carried in the processes. Instead of simply 'caused', ***erupted*** suggests pressure building up to explode; ***bred*** *anger and fear* suggests contagion like breeding disease; ***create*** *a major challenge* suggests constructive agency on the part of the forces of resistance.

Other ways of realising causal relations within clauses include prepositional phrases, **because of** the government's repression the people became angry and frightened, and nominal groups, **the consequences** of the government's repression were anger and fear (for more examples see Table 3.3 in Chapter 3).

For the sake of consistency we will refer to the grammatical meanings of grammatical metaphors as **literal** (what the grammatical structure literally means) and their discourse meanings as **inferred**. As we showed in Chapter 4 (§4.4.5), teachers can guide students to read grammatical metaphor by preparing with the inferred meaning, and then elaborating by unpacking the metaphor. The inferred meaning may be prepared with a familiar synonym, e.g. *a word that means rebellion*, or by unpacking the figure *a policy that repressed people*.

By unpacking, we mean turning an abstract nominal group back into a process, and putting the participants back in, or turning an abstract clause back into a sequence of clauses. This can be done interactively in elaborations, such as this discussion of 'uprising' during Detailed Reading.

	Prepare	*You know why it's called an uprising?*
	Focus	*Because what did the people do?*
Students	Propose	*Rise up.*
Teacher	Affirm	*The people rise up, yes.*
	Focus	*And who were they rising up against?*
Students	Propose	*The government.*
Teacher	Affirm	*The government, that's right*

Or if the wording is judged too difficult, the teacher can simply define it, e.g. *repression means keeping the people down, repressing them.* When it comes to Joint Rewriting from notes, abstract nominal groups and clauses can be unpacked to figures expressed by clauses, and sequences expressed by clause complexes, with causal relations expressed by conjunctions.

> *Because the government repressed the people, they were frustrated and frightened.*
> *Because the government promised changes, the people expected things to get better.*

However, students also need to learn how to package up figures and sequences as grammatical metaphors. Again we showed in §4.4.5 how teachers can guide students to do so by following the sentence patterns of a Detailed Reading passage such as [4.12] with a new field. Events and qualities can be packaged as nominal groups, organised as Themes and News (in bold), and related by verbal groups (underlined).[11]

[4.14'] Rewrite using sentence patterns from Text [4.12]

By the late 1980s, the apartheid system	*was **under siege** on many fronts.*
International economic sanctions	*were crippling the economy.*
The internal movement for change	*had gathered **strength and legitimacy***
which the government	*was no longer able to counter.*
Political, military and economic factors	*were overwhelming the government*
	*and forcing it to negotiate **transfer of power**.*

To facilitate this type of guidance through interaction, the metalanguage shared by teachers and students could include the following.

meaning	class
sequence	clause complex, conjunction
figure (event + entities)	clause
event	verb/verbal group
entity (people/things)	noun/nominal group
circumstance (place/time/...)	preposition/prepositional phrase
quality	adjective/adverb
literal/inferred	
lexical/grammatical	
abstract nominal group/abstract clause	
Theme/New	

Packaging and unpacking grammatical metaphor often requires a further step,

---

[11] Not all the abstract nominal groups in 4.14 are grammatical metaphors; *apartheid system, economic sanctions, economy* and *government* are technical entities, rather than metaphors.

because the elements of figures are reconstrued as the elements of nominal groups.

[The government]'s	policies	[of repression]	had bred	anger and fear.
Pointer	Thing	Qualifier	Process	Thing

If we unpack this abstract clause to a sequence of clauses, we can show the processes of grammatical metaphor – building tensions between grammar and the underlying discourse meaning, as in Figure 5.7.

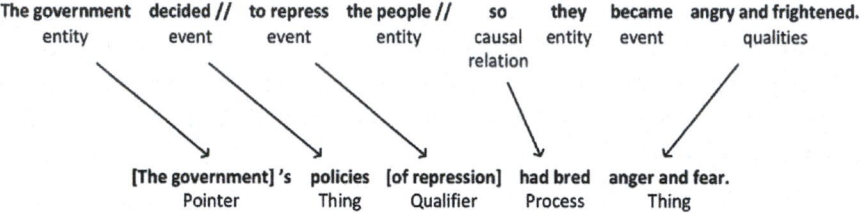

Figure 5.7: Processes of grammatical metaphor

When processes become nominalised as Things, the entities that participate in them are often elided (just as *the people* disappear in the abstract clause here), or they are downgraded as a Pointer (*[the government]'s policies*), or as a Classifier (*government policies*) or Qualifier (*policies [of the government]*). Whether students are being guided to unpack or package up grammatical metaphor, it is clearly useful to have these terms for nominal group elements, to discuss how the meanings are expressed. Constructing a diagram like 5.7 on the whiteboard is a useful strategy to support this.

5.2.8 Mood and Theme

Two of the meaning expansions in text [4.6'] that we did not discuss were Mr Fox's question *What on earth was it?* and exclamation *Great heavens!*

One factor that shapes the structure of a clause is its function in giving information or asking for it. In statements, a participant comes before the auxiliary verb: *the soldiers **were** marching*; but in a yes-no question, the order is reversed and the auxiliary verb comes before the participant: ***were** the soldiers marching?* Technically, this hinge participant is the **Subject** of the clause, and the hinge verb that expresses tense or modality is the **Finite** (short for Finite operator).

Questions can also be asked about particular elements of information using wh-words: *how/why/when/where **were** the soldiers marching?* (with the Finite before the Subject[12]). Exclamations can also be expressed with wh-words: *How well the soldiers marched!* (with the Subject before the Finite). Commands on the other hand typically have just the lexical verb without tense or modality: *Quick march!*

Grammatically, the differences between these clauses structures are known as **mood**. Mood is concerned with the **interpersonal** function of the clause, as an exchange between speakers, discussed below in §5.3.6. The basic mood system is set out in Table 5.6.

Table 5.6: Basic mood options in English

speech function	example	structure	mood type
statement	*the soldiers were marching*	Subject^Finite	declarative
yes-no question	*were the soldiers marching?*	Finite^Subject	polar interrogative
wh-question	*where were the soldiers marching?*	wh-word; Fin^Sub	wh interrogative
exclamation	*how the soldiers marched!*	wh-word; Fin^Sub	exclamative
command	*quick march!*	lexical verb only	imperative

For the classroom, the main metalanguage needed here are just the names for speech functions – **statement**, **question**, **exclamation**, **command** – which are already part of everyday metalanguage, except for the distinction between **yes-no** and **wh-questions**.

However, these are just the bare outlines of the systems of mood and speech function. In discourse, the potential for meaning can be expanded by expressing speech functions through alternative mood choices. For example, in the following passage of teacher talk in a kindergarten class [5.2] (from Williams 1995: 370), the teacher expresses a series of commands and questions by various means. The alternative mood choices are in bold.

[5.2] Interpersonal metaphor in teacher talk

		speech function	mood
1	*Now before we start//could you two boys come over here?*	command	**interrogative**
2	*Richard and ah Robert right over here.*	command	**minor**
3	*Stand up Robert.*	command	imperative
4	*Quickly.*	command	**minor**
5	*Don't roly poly on the way.*	command	imperative

---

[12] The exception to this interrogative sequence is wh- question about the Subject, e.g. *Who marched?*

6	*Er sit down Jessy on your on your bottom.*	command	imperative
7	*Robert, there's a space there.*	statement	declarative
8	*I'd love you in there.*	command	**declarative**
9	*Let's have a look at this here.*	command	**suggestive**
10	*I'm going to read you a sad story.*	statement	declarative
11	*Everyone look sad.*	command	imperative
12	*Have a look over here at this picture*	command	imperative
13	*Put your hand up//*	command	imperative
	if you can tell me//why you think//this story might be sad//	question	**declarative**
	by looking at the front cover ...		
14	*I wonder why//he's sad*	question	**declarative**

The alternative expressions are grammatical metaphors of the interpersonal type. Like the ideational grammatical metaphors we discussed above, their literal wording is in tension with their inferred discourse meaning. In line 1, the teacher clearly intends a command but expresses it with interrogative mood. Lines 2 and 4 are **minor** clauses, lacking any explicit mood. Line 8 is a declarative clause expressing a command, in which *I'd love you to* emphasises the obligation and makes it explicitly subjective, with the teacher *I* as Subject. Line 9 expresses a command with the sub-type of imperative known as **suggestive**, in which *let's* includes the speaker and addressee. Line 13 asks a question 'why is this story sad?' with a series of verbal and mental processes *you can **tell** me why you **think** this story might be* ... Line 14 also asks a question with declarative mood, with the teacher as Subject, *I wonder*. One child recognises this as a question and answers in line 15 below.

Student	15	*I know. He's lost the mum and dad.*
Teacher	16	*He might have lost his mummy and daddy.*
	17	*Do you think//that might be why he's sad?*

The teacher affirms in line 16, and asks another question in 17. But she also adds modality *might have*, *might be*. Modality can also be made explicitly subjective by expressing it as a mental process with the speaker or addressee as Subject. For example, *I'd love you to* expresses high obligation with the speaker *I* as Subject. *Do you think* expresses low probability with the addressee *you* as Subject. In contrast to these subjective expressions, modality can also be expressed objectively, with 'it' as Subject (*it's possible/likely/certain; it's suggested/expected/required*). Objective expressions such as these, among others, are common choices in academic writing (e.g. *it is widely acknowledged*). Interpersonal grammatical metaphors enable speakers and writers to subtly adjust the tenor of a text.

Another function that shapes the structure of clauses, which we have touched on several times, is the organisation of information as **Theme** and **New**.[13] For example, a key resource for expanding clauses in Text [4.6′] were prepositional phrases expressing circumstances. Circumstances usually come at the end of clauses, as New information, but some occur at the start of clauses as Theme (underlined).

> He crept <u>a little further out of the hole … then further still</u>.
>
> He was <u>almost right out in the open now</u>.
>
> He took a last careful look <u>around</u>.
>
> <u>Somewhere in the sky</u> the moon was shining.
>
> Just then, his sharp night-eyes caught a glint of something bright <u>behind a tree not far away</u>.
>
> It was a small silver speck of moonlight shining <u>on a polished surface</u>.
>
> It was coming <u>up and up</u> …
>
> <u>Quick as a whip</u>, Mr Fox jumped <u>back into his hole</u>
>
> <u>and at that same instant</u> the entire wood seemed to explode <u>around him</u>.

Because the usual placement of such circumstances is at the end of a clause, when a circumstance occurs as Theme it marks the clause as especially significant in some way. The functions of such **marked Themes** in organising texts is discussed below in §5.3.1. Theme and New are parts of the **textual** function of the clause, as a unit of information or message.

5.2.9   Types of processes

Our last step as far as knowledge about grammar is concerned is that there are three main types of processes. At the start of our discussion of grammar, we said that clauses express an underlying model of human experience – as processes involving people and things, with places, times and qualities. If we look a little more closely we find that this model divides experience into three general process types – doing/happening, saying/sensing, and being/having. Here again we can draw on teachers' existing metalanguage of nouns and verbs, and relate it to the semantic metalanguage we are building up. Teachers often define the term **verb** as a 'doing word' or 'action word'. This is quite true for most verbs: *finish, take, wash, return, eat, make, throw, whine, skulk* are all material actions – what the people and their dogs *did*.

But some verbs in the passage [5.1] are not material actions. For example, *deciding* is a mental process – a type of thinking – and people can decide to do a material action: *they **decided** to **take** all their dirty clothes/they decided that they*

---

[13] Technically theme and information are separate systems in the grammar. It is simpler when discussing writing to treat them as a single structure with two elements – Theme and New information.

would take their clothes. Material doing processes cannot do this: you cannot *throw to take your clothes* or *eat that you will take them*. Furthermore, 'yelling' is a verbal process – a type of saying – and verbal processes can say another process: '**Shut up,**' *yelled their owners*. Likewise, doing processes cannot do this: you can *tell someone to* shut up, but you cannot *throw shut up* or *eat shut up*.

So another group of processes aside from material 'doing' includes **verbal processes** or types of saying, and **mental processes** or types of sensing (thinking, feeling, seeing, hearing). Mental processes can think, see, hear and feel '**ideas**' (what is sensed): *they decided 'to take all their dirty clothes'*; *they realised 'that the fateful day had come'*. Verbal processes can say '**locutions**' (what is said): '*Shut up,' yelled their owners*. Locutions and ideas can be whole clauses, which we can mark with 'quote marks'.

Halliday (2004) generalises saying and sensing as **projecting**. That is, processes of saying and sensing can *project* locutions or ideas. Projection is represented by speech bubbles and thought bubbles in comic books – speech bubbles = locutions, thought bubbles = ideas (Figure 5.8).

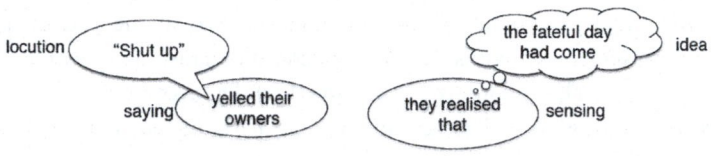

Figure 5.8: Projection represented by speech bubbles and thought bubbles

In Chapter 2, the description Text [2.5] described 'The Coolest Shark in the World', and each description was projected by a mental process.

> The penguins **think** 'she is The brother'.
> The great white shark **thinks** 'shes a princess but in a cuddly sort of way'.
> The crab next door **thinks** 'shes smart'
> mr stingray **thinks** 'shes precious and adorable'

The projected clauses here are not 'doing' processes either; they are 'being' processes: *she is smart, she is precious and adorable, she is the brother, she is a princess*. Processes of being relate people and things to their qualities (*smart, precious, adorable*) and to their identities (*the brother, a princess*). For this reason they are known as **relational** processes. Not all relational processes use the verb 'be', though it is very common; for example, we can say *Molly and Gracie looked clean and refreshed*. The verb *look* can also refer to an action (*the family looked at Molly and Gracie*), but in this case its meaning is quite different; here it relates Molly and Gracie to their qualities – *clean and refreshed*. It is expressing a kind of 'being'.

Because they relate people and things to their qualities and identities, relational processes are particularly common in descriptions and reports. For example, the shark report [2.6] used the verb *be* to classify sharks.

> A shark **is** a type of species that lives in the sea.
>
> A shark **is** one of the largest sea creatures.
>
> There **are** 350 type of shark.

The Komodo dragons report [4.1] used *be* to classify Komodo dragons, but it also used *have* to describe the species, by relating the whole dragon to the parts of its body.

> The largest of all lizards would **be** the Komodo Dragon
>
> which **has** a strong body also long tail.
>
> The Komodo Dragon **has** scales all over its body
>
> The Komodo Dragon **has** very visible earhole
>
> The Komodo Dragon **has** the same tongue like the goanna in Australia
>
> The Komodo Dragon **has** teeth, less than an inch long

Processes of 'having' are thus another type of relational process – they relate people and things to their parts and possessions, e.g. *Mary **had** a little lamb*. (One thing to watch out for is that verbs like *is/are/was/were* and *has/have/had* can function either as distinct relational processes of being or having, or as auxiliary verbs in verbal groups.)

So another basic feature of language that our students know intuitively but which we are bringing to consciousness here is that it divides experience into three general types of processes.

> **material** processes   doing/happening
>
> **mental** and **verbal** processes   saying/sensing
>
> **relational** processes   being/having

This distinction between types of processes does not have to be drilled into students, but it can often be useful to point it out when we are exploring a written text or writing a new one. Either the technical terms can be used, **material**, **mental**, **verbal**, **relational**, or the more commonsense *doing/happening*, *saying/sensing*, *being/having*, or both. Naming process types can be particularly useful when discussing the punctuation used for verbal and mental projection, or when discussing the types of processes used to express relations in science and other factual texts. So this element of KAL is useful for teachers to be aware of, when they are analysing texts to plan lessons, and exploring them with students.

5.3   Discourse: meaning beyond the clause

To this point we have explored patterns of meaning within and between clauses, or grammar. Beyond clauses, patterns of meaning that unfold across whole texts are known as **discourse**. In this section we will explore six systems of meaning at the level of discourse: periodicity, identification, conjunction, ideation, appraisal and negotiation. Most of these systems were first introduced in Chapter 2, to describe differences between two students' description and report about sharks, and were touched on in Chapters 3 and 4.

Periodicity is the flow of information in a text, particularly as starting and end points of clauses, paragraphs and texts. Information patterns at the level of the clause include Themes and News, as we have discussed already. At the level of the paragraph they include topic sentences, and at the level of whole texts they include introductions and conclusions.

Conjunction is the logical relations between clauses, sentences and phases. Logical relations include addition (*and/or*), comparison (*like/unlike*), time (*then/ before*) and consequence (*so/because*).

Identification includes the words that identify people, places and things, and keep track of them from sentence to sentence, such as articles (*a, the*), demonstratives (*this, these, those*), comparatives (*each, other, more, less*) and pronouns (*he, she, it, they, you, me*).

Ideation includes the lexical words that express the meanings of processes, people, things, places and qualities, as well as the relations between lexical words from sentence to sentence, such as repetitions, similarities and contrasts. These are known as lexical relations.

Appraisal includes the words we use for evaluating feelings, people and things. Appraisals can be positive or negative: *happy/sad, good/evil, beautiful/ ugly*. They can also be amplified: *happy/joyous/ecstatic*. And they can be sourced to the writer, *I believe that* …, or to others *It is widely acknowledged that* …

Negotiation is the resources that speakers use to interact with each other, including speech functions like question, statement, command, but also the responses to each of these moves in an exchange between speakers.

Because they are concerned with interacting and evaluating feelings, the functions of negotiation and appraisal are **interpersonal**. As ideation and conjunction are concerned with people, things, processes and relations, their functions are **ideational**. Periodicity and identification are concerned with organising discourse so it is meaningful in context, so their function is **textual** (Figure 5.9).

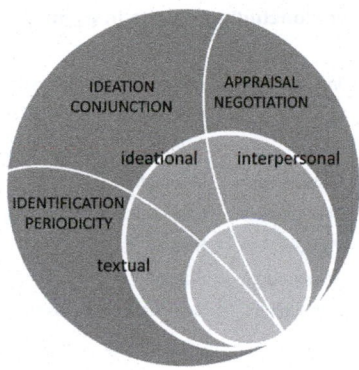

Figure 5.9: Discourse systems and functions of language

5.3.1   Periodicity – information flow

The term **periodicity** refers to the wave-like patterns of information flow in texts. Starting points and end points form the peaks of each wave, at the levels of texts, paragraphs and clauses. This kind of wave-like structure was illustrated graphically with text [3.30′].

[3.30′] Text level and paragraph level information peaks

The Vietnam war, which is the main topic of this chapter, also had a major impact on the twentieth century national history of the USA and was one of the defining events of the Cold War.

> Professor David Kennedy of Stanford University has argued that the cost and trauma of the Vietnam War produced a 'crisis of confidence' in the USA.

>> Until the Vietnam War, Americans had generally felt confident in their ability to mould events through the exercise of their ingenuity, energy and vast economic resources. Vietnam proved to be a problem that they couldn't manage.

> The Vietnam conflict gave rise to social division and distrust of government in the US.

>> It ended the political career of President Lyndon Johnson and his dreams of major social reform. It also produced, in the case of Richard Nixon's presidency, a siege mentality that contributed directly to the infamous Watergate Scandal (1973-74) and the resignation, in disgrace, of Nixon. Because of the Vietnam War, as part of the wider conflict in Indochina, a generation of Americans identified with anti-conscription and anti-war protest movements. Many of the social and political effects evident in the US were also present in Australia.

The introductory paragraph is the text level peak, introducing the field of the text. The topic sentences of each paragraph are secondary peaks, introducing the field of each paragraph. Most texts preview their field with an introduction, but the type of introduction varies with the genre, and only argument genres necessarily review the arguments in a conclusion. Here are some examples in Table 5.7.

Table 5.7: Introductory and concluding stages in genres

genre	'introduction'	'body'	'conclusion'
exposition	Thesis	Arguments	Restatement
discussion	Issue	Sides	Resolution
report	Classification	Description	
explanation	Phenomenon	Explanation	
procedure	Purpose/Aim	Steps	
historical recount	Background	Stages	
narrative	Orientation	Complication + Resolution	

In Chapter 2, we expanded the stages of an exposition in Figure 2.5, with the phases **position**, **preview**, **topic**, **elaboration**, **review** and **restate**.

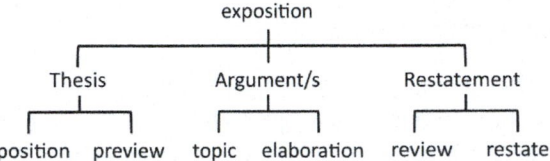

Figure 2.5': Stages and phases of an exposition

In Chapter 4 we applied these terms for argument phases to a model discussion [4.15].

[4.15'] Model discussion

Issue	Whenever we turn on the TV or radio, we are dazzled by sports heroes
preview	celebrating their victory by drinking alcohol or smoking tobacco. At first, we may think it is entertaining and harmless, but if we examine the issue more closely, questions arise in our minds about the effect these advertisements have on people.
Sides	
topic	There are several reasons why sporting heroes should promote alcohol and tobacco products ...
topic	On the other hand, there are many reasons why sporting heroes should not promote tobacco and alcohol products ...
Resolution	Even though there seem to be reasonable arguments for sporting heroes
review	promoting such products, the advertising of these products may be bad for the health and well-being of young Australians. Therefore it has more disadvantages than advantages.

The first sentence in the Issue stage presents the issue, and the remainder previews the sides to come. The Resolution stage begins by reviewing the sides, and the last sentence resolves the discussion. Preview and review are not identical: whereas the preview predicts what each following argument (or sides in a discussion) will be about, the review distils the points that the writer has made.

The technical terms for information peaks are:

	starting point	end point
clause	Theme	New
paragraph	hyperTheme	hyperNew
text	macroTheme	macroNew

We can use these terms where necessary for our discussion here, but in the classroom the terms **topic** for hyperTheme and **point** for hyperNew are sufficient. For macroTheme and macroNew, the terms 'introduction' and 'conclusion' can be used simply as a bridge to the specific names for genre stages in Table 5.7. With respect to writing, students are expected to scaffold their arguments for the reader, so preview, review, topic and point are crucial terms.

These are not only useful categories for scaffolding writing, but also for reading. MacroThemes are intended to provide a preview for readers, much as orally preparing for reading does in the R2L methodology; and hyperThemes preview paragraphs, which is also done orally in R2L paragraph-by-paragraph reading (§4.4.1, §4.4.3). Recognising the functions of macroThemes and hyperThemes supports the reader to predict the field that follows. Furthermore, familiarity with hyperThemes and hyperNews helps readers to identify key information as they read texts, and to make notes. Paragraph-by-paragraph reading and text marking guides students to develop these skills. Some general guidelines are as follows.

Most paragraphs begin with a topic that is located towards the end of the first or second sentence, i.e. as News in the sentence. (The first sentence may be a linking or literary device, so that the topic is presented in the second sentence.) Many paragraphs also come to a point, towards the end of the paragraph (although this is less common). The first paragraph in Text [3.30'] is arguably of this type. Its topic and point are highlighted here.

> Professor David Kennedy of Stanford University has argued that the cost and trauma of the Vietnam War produced a 'crisis of confidence' in the USA.
>> Until the Vietnam War, Americans had generally felt confident in their ability to mould events through the exercise of their ingenuity, energy and vast economic resources. Vietnam proved to be a problem that they couldn't manage.

Note that the relevant information is at the end of each sentence as New. The information in the topic and point may be sufficient to summarise what the paragraph is about. The rest of its sentences may elaborate on this key information with examples and further explanation. This detail may not be required for summarising.

Some paragraphs do not come to a point, but consist of an explanation or argument sequence. In this case each main step in the explanation or argument may need highlighting. The second paragraph in text [3.30'] is of this type, with a series of examples of the topic, each of which is highlighted. Again the key information is presented as News in each sentence.

> The Vietnam conflict gave rise to social division and distrust of government in the US. It ended the political career of President Lyndon Johnson and his dreams of major social reform. It also produced, in the case of Richard Nixon's presidency, a siege mentality that contributed directly to the infamous Watergate Scandal (1973-74) and the resignation, in disgrace, of Nixon. Because of the Vietnam War, as part of the wider conflict in Indochina, a generation of Americans identified with anti-conscription and anti-war protest movements. Many of the social and political effects evident in the US were also present in Australia.

Another way of scaffolding waves of information is by using a circumstance of time or place to signal a shift of gears. In the following narrative [5.3] (from Janke 2002), the Orientation builds through a series of problems that foreshadow the Complication, when baby Shane disappears. Each problem is signalled by starting the sentence with a time or place (in bold here). The Complication is signalled more strongly with both time and place.

[5.3] Narrative extract from *Butterfly Song* by Terry Janke

Orientation	
setting	I can see the beach [where we used to go swimming as kids, in the colder months, before the stingers came out].
	I remember how my blue swimming togs always held a pile of sand in the crotch.
problem	**Somewhere in the dunes** I lost my red bucket.
problem	**It was the day** we deliberately left Nobby at the beach.
reaction	The three of us kids cried a lot.
description	Nobby was a stray mongrel dog that had moved into our house.
	Clarissa, Shane and I wanted to keep him.
	Dad said he was a bad dog
	because he jumped up and grabbed clothing, like Dad's work socks, off the clothesline.
	Nobby also chased cars
	and gave the postman on his bicycle a hard time.
problem	**So that day**, we left the beach without him.
problem	**The next weekend**, when we went back for a swim,
	Nobby was still there, hanging around the car park.
	He looked very sad and dejected.

<u>Dad</u> made us act as if we couldn't see him. 'Pretend he's invisible.'

Complication

setting	**Later, on the beach**, <u>we</u> set up our picnic.
problems[14]	<u>Shane</u> had just learnt to walk -
	<u>well, really he</u> went straight to running.
	<u>Dad</u> was having a swim
	<u>and my mother</u> was making sandwiches
	<u>when Shane</u> disappeared.
	<u>We</u> searched the beach and the car park
	<u>and</u> could not find him.
reaction	<u>Nobby</u> was still there,
	<u>so my frantic mother</u> said to him, 'Shane, help us find Shane.'
	<u>She</u> had watched too many Lassie movies.

Resolution

solution	<u>Nobby</u> barked and headed towards the estuary.
	<u>Sure enough, Shane</u> was there, within metres of the deep water.
	'<u>We</u> have to take the dog,' my mother insisted.
comment	<u>That's</u> how Nobby won his place in our family.
	<u>To think that</u> was around twenty years ago -
	<u>but the beach</u> looks just the same.

While these **marked Themes** of time or place serve to signal shifts from phase to phase of the text, the unmarked Themes (underlined above) are concerned with tracking and switching identities of people and things through the discourse.

I, I, I, we, The three of us kids, Nobby, Clarissa, Shane and I, Dad, he, Nobby, we, we, Nobby, He, Dad, We, Shane, he, Dad, my mother, Shane, We, Nobby, my frantic mother, She, Nobby, Shane, We, That, that, the beach

The Theme of a clause includes everything up to and including the first participant, including conjunctions and circumstances. Sometimes this participant is implicit, such as *We searched the beach <u>and (we)</u> could not find him*. In these cases the Theme is presumed from the preceding clause.[15]

Against the background continuity of identities, marked Themes punctuate the discourse, organising it into identifiable phases. Historical texts use this resource more formally to organise recounts into biographical or historical stages, such as Text [3.27] reproduced below.

---

[14] Note the common pattern of worsening problems in the Complication: *straight to running, disappeared, could not find him.*

[15] Embedded clauses (as in the first sentence in [5.3]) and projected clauses (as in what Dad said) are not included in the Theme analysis as they do not contribute to the flow of information in the text.

[3.27'] Historical recount

> <u>In August 1945</u> the French colony of Indo-China (Vietnam, Laos and Cambodia, now called Kampuchea) was occupied by British and Nationalist Chinese troops after the surrender of the Japanese who had seized it in 1941.
>
> <u>In October 1945</u> the French returned determined to re-establish their control, especially in Vietnam. French forces easily re-occupied the southern portion of Vietnam, but were faced in the north with a new communist regime which had been established in their absence by the communist leader Ho Chi Minh.
>
> <u>During the war</u> Ho had led the resistance to the Japanese occupation of Vietnam, and after the war led a communist-dominated organisation which represented Vietnamese nationalist aspirations. Ho's organisation was known as the Viet-Minh. The French were determined to retake northern Vietnam and <u>in 1946</u> began military operations against the Viet-Minh, thus triggering the first Indo-China War.

While marked Themes are a resource in both speaking and writing for signalling phase shifts, paragraphing has evolved in writing to serve a similar function. However, there is often no one-to-one match between paragraphs and text phases, illustrated by the inclusion of two stages in the last paragraph in [3.27']. Such mismatches between graphology and periodicity are also something to watch out for when identifying the topic and point of paragraphs, since writers sometimes finish a paragraph with the topic of the next paragraph.

Alongside these functions of clause Themes in information flow, the end of each clause builds New information about the field. In the classifying report [3.12] reproduced below, Themes are underlined and News are in bold.

[3.12'] Classifying report

Classification	<u>As far as the ability to carry electricity is concerned, we</u> can place most substances into **one of two groups**.
Description	
type 1	<u>The first group</u> contains materials with **many electrons that are free to move**.
	<u>These materials</u> are called **conductors**
	<u>because they</u> readily **carry or conduct electric currents**.
	<u>Conductors</u> are **mostly metals but also include graphite**.
type 2	<u>The second group</u> contains materials with **very few electrons that are free to move**.
	<u>These materials</u> are called **nonconductors**
	<u>and</u> are **very poor conductors of electricity**.
	<u>Nonconductors</u> can be used to **prevent charge from going where it is not wanted**.
	<u>Hence they</u> are also called **insulators**.
	<u>Some common insulators</u> are **glass, rubber, plastic and air**.

type 3	There are a few materials, such as **germanium and silicon, called semiconductors**. Their ability to conduct electricity is **intermediate between conductors and insulators**. Semiconductors have played **an important role in modern electronics**.

The first sentence in [3.12'] uses a marked Theme to signal that this is a new text within the macrogenre of the textbook, and then presents the classification in *two groups* as New. The two sub-types are then signalled by paragraphing and naming them as *The first group* and *The second group*, and their features, members and technical names are News in each clause. The intermediate type 3 is presented by an **existential** clause. This clause type begins with *there*, which is not actually a participant or circumstance. Its function is rather to announce that something exists; thus existential clauses are also often used to signal phase shifts in texts, as in [3.12'] here.

This text is a technical one, but is relatively non-metaphorical. Grammatical metaphor is, however, used twice, firstly to announce the overall criterion for classification in the first sentence *the ability to carry electricity*, and finally to specify the criterion for semiconductors *Their ability to conduct electricity is intermediate*. In the rest of the text, ability is expressed congruently as 'can do' (*free to move, readily carry or conduct, can be used*) or 'can't do' (*very few electrons that are free to move*). Expressing these modal meanings as an abstract thing *ability* enables its presentation as Theme with an abstract quality *intermediate* as New. As we saw in the factorial explanation [4.12] above, grammatical metaphor is a crucial resource for organising information into Themes and News in technical and abstract discourse.

5.3.2   Conjunction

Conjunction covers the logical relations linking clauses, sentences and phases in a text. There are four main types of logical relations:

- addition *and/or*
- comparison *like/unlike*
- time *then/while*
- consequence *so/by/if ... then/in order to*

These logical relations are often expressed by an explicit conjunction, but they can also be left implicit, for the reader to infer. Conjunction can be used to construct a sequence of events, as in a story or explanation; or it can be used to organise the unfolding development of a text, such as a series of arguments in an exposition. Conjunctions that construe series of events are known as **external**; conjunctions that organise a text are known as **internal**.

Some general options for conjunctions are set out in Table 5.8. For each type of logical relation there are two or more options, and each option may be external or internal. A helpful way to read the table is to look at the examples and compare them with the names for each type.

Table 5.8: Conjunction in brief

		external (connecting events)		internal (organising text)	
addition	additive	*and, besides*	written	*in addition, further*	
	alternative	*or*	spoken	*well, okay, anyway*	
comparison	similar	*like, as if*	similar	*similarly, for example*	
	different	*instead of, whereas*	different	*by contrast, rather*	
time	successive	*then, after, before*	successive	*first, secondly, finally*	
	simultaneous	*while, as, when*	simultaneous	*at the same time, still*	
consequence	cause	*because, so*	concluding	*thus, consequently*	
	means	*by, thus*	countering	*nevertheless, however*	
	condition	*if ... then*			
	purpose	*so that, in order to*			

The examples of external conjunction are the kinds that are familiar in everyday discourse, which students tend to know from spoken language. The internal examples are mostly the kinds that students need to learn to control written discourse. The exceptions are spoken internal addition, *well, okay, anyway*, which function in everyday interactions and classroom teacher talk to stage spoken discourse.

Patterns of conjunction vary widely with the type of text. Stories and procedures tend to be organised by time and addition, whereas explanations feature time and cause. Arguments and text responses tend to be organised by internal conjunctions of addition, time and consequence. Reports tend to have few conjunctions as they are about entities rather than sequences of events, explanations or arguments (e.g. [3.12] above).

As the default logical relation in stories is succession in time, there is usually no need to make it explicit in writing with *then, when, after, before*. Instead, events are typically linked by *and*, or simply by the sequence of sentences, without any conjunctions. One payoff is that explicit conjunctions can be used judiciously to signal significant events. In the following extract from Text [4.6'], implicit conjunctions are rendered in brackets and explicit conjunctions in bold.

[4.6′] Extract from *Fantastic Mr Fox*

Mr Fox crept up the dark tunnel to the mouth of his hole.

(then) He poked his long handsome face out into the night air

and sniffed once.

(then) He moved an inch or two forward

and stopped.

(then) He sniffed again.

(then) He inched forward a little more.

The front half of his body was **now** in the open.

(then) His black nose twitched from side to side,

sniffing and sniffing for the scent of danger.

(then) He found none,

and he was just about to go trotting forward into the wood

when he heard or thought he heard a tiny noise, a soft rustling sound,

as though someone had moved a foot ever so gently through a patch of dry leaves.

(so) Mr Fox flattened his body against the ground

and lay very still, his ears pricked.

(then) He waited a long time,

but he heard nothing more.

Against the background of *and*'s and implicit conjunction, the explicit conjunctions *when* and *as though* stand out to signal the problem of the *tiny noise*, and the explicit *but* signals its solution. Implicit conjunction is also the norm in explanations, as we discussed in Chapter 3 for Text [3.24].

[3.24′] Explanation of lightning

Warm air rises in hot clouds

and (then) encounters cold air,

(then) charging the particles in the cloud

(then) making them both positive and negative ...

When enough positive and negative charges occur,

(then) they build up too much energy

and (then) explode in a flash of light ...

(then) This flash of light helps balance out the number of negative and positive charges in the atmosphere.

The only explicit conjunction *when* is used here to signal the phase shift from charging particles to releasing charges as lightning. We also pointed out that this is not just a temporal sequence, because the relations between events are implicitly conditional '**if** this happens, **then** this ensues' (*if warm air rises in hot clouds **then** it will encounter cold air*).

Another key resource we discussed in relation to Text [3.24'] was cause-in-the-clause, expressing causal relations as nouns:

Cause		Effect
The movement between the	is	**the reason** [[that tall objects on earth like trees
atmosphere and the ground		are struck by lightning]]

This figure could be unpacked to a sequence 'the electric energy moves between the atmosphere and the ground **so** tall objects are struck by lightning'. And cause was also expressed by a prepositional phrase *because of this*, where *this* referred to the preceding cause:

> Light travels faster than sound,
> and **because of this**, we see the flash of lighting
> before we hear the clap of thunder.

Again this prepositional phrase could be unpacked with the conjunction 'so'. These logical grammatical metaphors can be unpacked when preparing in Detailed Reading, and in Rewriting. And they can be used to package sequences into figures in Rewriting as we described in §4.4.5 above.

Another feature we discussed in relation to Text [3.24'] was the use of *thus* to link the explanation sequence to the writer's conclusion.

> There is **thus** a direct relationship between thunder and lightning;
> they are not separate phenomena.

The conjunction *thus* refers here to the scientific reasoning involved, rather than to cause-and-effect relations between the events. The explanation sequence becomes the grounds for drawing a conclusion that thunder and lightning are not separate phenomena. The conjunction *thus* signals this conclusion. In other words *thus* realises the rhetoric of the text rather than the sequence of events. We can paraphrase the conjunction with a verbal process like *explain*, using this 'speech act' verb to refer to the preceding explanation sequence.

> Light travels faster than sound,
> and because of this, we see the flash of lighting
> before we hear the clap of thunder.
> This **explains** the direct relationship between thunder and lightning;
> they are not separate phenomena.

This is an example of the text organising function of internal conjunctions. While

external consequence construes sequences of cause-and-effect, **internal consequence** draws conclusions with *thus/therefore*, or counters expectations with *however/nevertheless*. Internal addition and time are often used to scaffold a sequence of arguments. Here is Lyndon Johnson's address [3.32] again, with each new argument signalled by **internal time** and **addition** (in place of 'also' which he used in his speech).

[3.32'] Johnson's exposition with internal conjunction added

	... Why are these realities our concern? Why are we in South Vietnam?
argument1	**Firstly** we are there because we have a promise to keep. Since 1954 every
grounds	American President has offered support to the people of South Vietnam. We have
	helped to build, and we have helped to defend. **Thus**, over many years, we have
conclusion	made a national pledge to help South Vietnam defend its independence. And I
	intend to keep our promise. To dishonor that pledge, to abandon this small and
	brave nation to its enemy, and to the terror that must follow, would be an
	unforgivable wrong.
argument2	**Furthermore** we are there to strengthen world order. Around the globe, from
grounds	Berlin to Thailand, are people whose well-being rests, in part, on the belief that they
	can count on us if they are attacked. **Therefore** to leave Vietnam to its fate would
conclusion	shake the confidence of all these people in the value of American commitment, the
	value of America's word. The result would be increased unrest and instability, and
	even wider war.
argument3	**Finally** we are there because there are great stakes in the balance. Let no
grounds	one think for a moment that retreat from Vietnam would bring an end to conflict. The
	battle would be renewed in one country and then another. The central lesson of our
	time is that the appetite of aggression is never satisfied. To withdraw from one
conclusion	battlefield means only to prepare for the next. **Hence** we must stay in Southeast
	Asia, as we did in Europe, in the words of the Bible: 'Hitherto shalt thou come, but
	no further.' ...

In addition, the phases within each of Johnson's arguments consist of the **grounds** for the argument, and a **conclusion**. Johnson signalled his first conclusion with *Thus*; we have also added *Therefore* and *Hence* to the second and third conclusions in order to draw attention to his rhetoric. These conjunctions imply that the conclusion is expected – that it flows naturally from the evidence presented as grounds for the argument.

Another genre that is organised rhetorically rather than temporally is factorial explanations. We pointed out in §4.4.5 that the logical relations in explanation [4.12] were implicit, and needed to be made clear for students. Here it is again, explicitly scaffolded with internal comparison and time.

[4.12'] Factorial explanation with internal conjunction added

In the mid-1980s South African politics erupted in a rebellion in black townships throughout the country. There were **three reasons** for this.

For one thing the government's policies of repression had bred anger and fear.

In addition its policies of reform had given rise to expectations amongst black people of changes which the government had been unable to meet.

As well the various forces of resistance now combined to create a major challenge for the government.

Internal comparison, time and **addition** were also used in the model discussion [4.15′] above, with *On the other hand* signalling the opposing side 2, and each supporting reason signalled by *Firstly*, *Secondly* and *Finally*. Another resource used for countering side 1 in the preview and review phases were the concessive *but* and *even though*. The meaning of *but* is basically 'not what was expected', technically known as **concession**.

Perhaps the most useful thing we can offer the reader at this point is the following Table 5.9, which assembles conjunctions that can be used in the classroom – as a ready reckoner for resources in writing, or for analysing texts and preparing lessons. Most of the categories have been discussed or are self-explanatory. Noteworthy are the **expectant** and **concessive** options for each type of external consequence, in contrast to the **concluding** or **countering** options for internal consequence. **Continuatives** are a small set of resources for conjunction that are associated with the verbal group, rather than clause as a whole.

Table 5.9: Conjunctions in full

External conjunctions (connecting events)		
Addition	add	*and, besides, both ... and*
	subtract	*nor, neither ... nor*
	alternative	*or, either ... or, if not ... then*
Comparison	similar	*like, as if*
	different	*whereas, while, instead of, in place of, rather than, except that, other than, apart from*
Time	successive	*after, since, now that; before, once, as soon as; until*
	simultaneous	*as, while, when*
Cause	expectant	*because, so, therefore*
	concessive	*although, even though, but, however*
Means	expectant	*by, thus*
	concessive	*even by, but*
Condition	expectant	*if, then, provided that, as long as*
	concessive	*even if, even then, unless*
Purpose	expectant	*so that, in order to, in case*
	concessive	*even so, without, lest, for fear of*

Internal conjunctions (organising text)

Addition	written	*further, furthermore, moreover, in addition, as well, besides, additionally; alternatively*
	spoken	*now, well, alright, okay, anyway, anyhow, by the way*
Comparison	similar	*similarly, again; that is, i.e., for example, for instance, e.g.; in general, in particular, in short*
	different	*in fact, indeed, at least; rather, by contrast; on the other hand, conversely*
Time	successive	*first, secondly, third, next, previously, finally, lastly*
	simultaneous	*at the same time, still*
Consequence	concluding	*thus, hence, accordingly, in conclusion, consequently, after all, therefore*
	countering	*anyway, anyhow, in any case, at any rate, nevertheless, nonetheless, still, admittedly, of course, needless to say*

Continuatives

Addition		*too, also, as well, so (did he)*
Comparison	less than expected	*only, just*
	more than expected	*even*
Time	sooner than expected	*finally, at last*
	longer than expected	*still*
	persistent	*again*
	repetitive	*already*

5.3.3   Identification

Identification introduces people, things and places into a text, and keeps track of their identities from sentence to sentence, so readers can tell who, what or where is being referred to. In our discussion of nominal groups above (§5.3.3), we saw that people, things and places can be identified by a noun (*farmers*), proper name (*Mr Fox*) or personal pronoun (*he*), which each function as the Thing. Alternatively they can be identified by a Pointer, such as articles (*a, the*), demonstratives (*this, that*), possessives (*his, their*) or comparatives (*other, more*). Some basic resources for presenting and presuming identities are set out in Table 5.10. Identification either **presents** people, things and places as if for the first time, or **presumes** that we already know them.

Table 5.10: Basic resources for identification

Presenting

	indefinite	*a, an, one; someone, anyone, some, any;*
	comparative	*every, all, another, some other*

Presuming

definite	*the*
demonstrative	*this, that; these, those*
possessive	*his, hers, theirs, Molly's*
comparative	*same, similar, other, another, different, else ...,*
	such goodness, so good, as good as ...,
	first, second, third; next, last;
	preceding, subsequent, former, latter ...,
	more, fewer, less ...;
	better, best; richer, richest ...
	each, both; neither, either
pronoun	*I, me, you, she, he, it; we, us, they, them,*
	here, therewith
text reference	*this, that, it, this book, a letter, the story's*

Because it contains dialogue, Text [5.3] (from Lobel 1980) illustrates some complex identification patterns. Identities are highlighted with shading, with their reference words in bold, and in the first episode arrows show how they track identities.

[5.3] The Frogs at the Rainbow's End

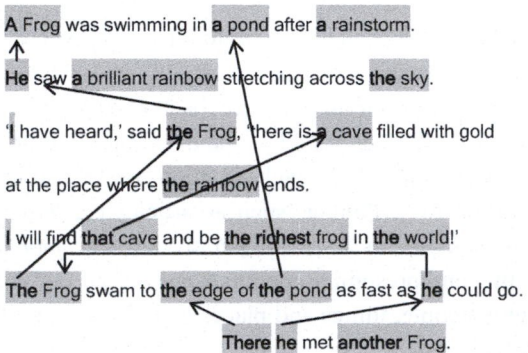

A **Frog** was swimming in a pond after a rainstorm.

He saw a brilliant rainbow stretching across the sky.

'**I** have heard,' said **the** Frog, 'there is a cave filled with gold at the place where the rainbow ends.

I will find **that** cave and be **the richest** frog in **the** world!'

The Frog swam to **the** edge of **the** pond as fast as **he** could go.

There he met **another** Frog.

'Where are **you** rushing to?' asked **the second** Frog.
'**I** am rushing to **the** place where **the** rainbow ends,' said **the first** Frog.
'There is a rumour,' said **the second** Frog, 'that there is a cave filled with gold and diamonds at **that** place.'
'Then come with **me**,' said **the first** Frog. 'We will be **the two richest** frogs in the world!'
The two Frogs jumped out of the pond and ran through **the** meadow. **There they** met **another** Frog.

'What is the hurry?' asked the third Frog.

'We are running to the place where the rainbow ends,' said the two Frogs.

'I have been told,' said the third Frog, 'there is a cave filled with gold and diamonds and pearls at that place.'

'Then come with us,' said the two Frogs. 'We will be the three richest frogs in the world!'

The three Frogs ran for miles.

Finally they came to the rainbow's end. There they saw a dark cave in the side of a hill.

'Gold! Diamonds! Pearls!' cried the Frogs, as they leaped into the cave.

A Snake lived inside. He was hungry and had been thinking about his supper. He swallowed the three Frogs in one quick gulp.

The first sentence presents *A frog*, *a pond* and *a rainstorm*. In the following sentences the frog is referred to as *he*, *I*, *the Frog*, *I*, *the richest frog in the world*, and *the Frog* again. He meets *another Frog* who is then presumed as *the second Frog*, in contrast to *the first Frog*. The second Frog addresses him as *you*, the first Frog calls himself *me*, and then includes both of them as *we* and *the two richest frogs in the world*. Cardinal numbers also contribute to tracking *the two frogs* and *the three frogs*. Three places are presented and referred to again: *a pond* becomes *the edge of the pond*, which is referred to as *There*; *a cave* becomes *that cave*; and *the place where the rainbow ends* becomes *that place*.

Another point to mention is that although *the sky*, *the world* and *the place where the rainbow ends* are presumed with 'the', they have not been previously presented. Rather they are presumed from readers' cultural knowledge, as things we all know of.

Table 5.11 gives some examples of identification resources in Text [5.3]. The first frog is presented with the indefinite *a frog*, who is then presumed either with pronouns or Pointers in nominal groups. These Pointers are either definite articles *the*, possessive *his*, or demonstrative *that*. The other frogs are presented with comparative Pointers (*another*), and they are all presumed comparatively with superlatives: *the richest*, *the first*.

Table 5.11: Identification in Text [5.3]

presenting	article	*a frog, a pond, a brilliant rainbow, a cave, a dark cave in the side of a hill, a snake, one quick gulp*
	comparative	*another frog*
	mass noun	*gold*
	plural	*diamonds, pearls*
presuming	pronoun	*he saw, I will find, there he met, where are you, come with me, we will be, there they met, come with us, they came, they leapt, he swallowed*
	article	*the frog, the pond, the world, the meadow, the cave*
	+ numeral	*the two frogs, the three frogs*
	possessive	*his supper, the rainbow's end*

demonstrative	*that place, that cave*
comparative	*the first frog, the richest frog*
+ numeral	*the two richest frogs, the three richest frogs*

In addition, we can note that mass nouns (*gold*) and plurals (*diamonds*, *pearls*) can be presented without a Pointer. A Focus is specified by the following Thing, so its Pointer is often definite 'the': *[the edge] of the pond, [the side] of a hill.* And a Thing may be specified by its Qualifier so its Pointer is definite: *the place [where the rainbow ends].*

Another point to note here is that indefinite reference is normally used to present new identities (*a frog*, *a pond*) and definite reference to presume them (*the frog*, *the pond*). But in factual texts, both definite and indefinite reference are often used to refer to **general classes**. Examples in text [3.12] above are underlined, including the plural indefinite *conductors … Conductors*, and *non-conductors … Nonconductors*. Technical terms are often repeated rather than referred to. The young writer of the shark report [2.6] uses both singular and plural indefinites in this way.

> **A shark** *is a type of species that lives in the sea.* **A shark** *is one of the largest sea creatures. There are 350 type of shark* **A shark** *is shaped like a torpedo …*
> **Sharks** *live in Oceans.* **Sharks** *have to swim but if they don't swim they will sink or suffocate.*
> **Harmless sharks** *eat Plants but* **harmful sharks** *eat live meat.* **Sharks** *have up to forty two pups.*
> **Some sharks** *lay eggs and some have them live.* **Some sharks** *have to defend the pups.*

Another feature of factual texts is the use of comparative reference to imply sub-classes. For example, *some sharks* implies other species that do not lay eggs or defend their pups. These are important signals for students to recognise when reading and writing technical texts.

As well as people, things and places, it is also possible to refer to what was said using text reference, as we saw above for the lightning explanation text [3.24], where *this* refers back to the preceding event.

> Light travels faster than sound,
> and because of **this**, we see the flash of lighting
> before we hear the clap of thunder.

In the narrative [5.3] *that* refers back to the solution of Nobby saving Shane, and then to the whole story.

> **That's** how Nobby won his place in our family.
> To think **that** was around twenty years ago -
> but the beach looks just the same.

As we are discussing discourse here, we use text reference constantly (e.g. the word *here* here). Text reference is very common and varied in texts that discuss other texts, such as reviews and analyses of all kinds.

5.3.4   Ideation

Ideation covers resources for building the field of a text, as the text unfolds. It includes the lexical words in a text, and relations between them from sentence to sentence, known as lexical relations. There are five types of lexical relation:

- **repetitions**, where the same word is repeated;
- **synonyms**, where a similar meaning is repeated in different words;
- **contrasts**, where words have the opposite meaning;
- **whole–part** relations, where one word represents a whole, such as *body*, and another word represents a part of that whole, such as *hands*;
- **class–member** relations, where one word is a class of things, such as *mammal*, and another word is a member of that class, such as *kangaroo*.

Repetition is a resource for keeping track of participants through a text, as we saw for the conductors and shark reports above. It is often used in very complex texts to maintain a constant thread of meaning, while the other meanings proliferate around it. For example, the word *conduct* is repeated in some form in almost every sentence of Text [3.12] above. For the same reason, repetition is used in texts for beginning readers, so they do not have to continually struggle to recognise new words. This allows them to attend to the other things that are happening in the text. For example, we have seen that Text [5.3] *The Frogs at the Rainbow's End* involves a lot of complexity, but is simplified by repeating words like *frog*, *pond*, *rainbow*, *cave*, *world*, *place*, *richest*, *gold*, *diamonds*, *pearls*, as well as repeated episode patterns.

In literary texts, on the other hand, too much repetition may give an impression that the text is not going anywhere, so writers often use synonyms instead. However, synonyms are by no means the main lexical resource for building the field of stories; part–whole and class–member relations are often more significant. In [4.6], reproduced below, Mr Fox's activities are underlined and his parts are in bold. Elements of the environment are in italics.

[4.6'] Some lexical relations in *Fantastic Mr Fox*

Mr Fox <u>crept</u> up *the dark tunnel* to *the mouth of his hole*.

He <u>poked</u> **his long handsome face** out into *the night air*

and <u>sniffed</u> once.

He <u>moved</u> an inch or two forward

and <u>stopped</u>.

He <u>sniffed</u> again.

He was always especially careful

when coming out from *his hole*.

He inched forward a little more.

The front half of his body was now in *the open.*

His black nose twitched from side to side,

sniffing and sniffing for the scent of danger.

He found none,

and he was just about to go trotting forward into *the wood*

when he heard or thought he heard a tiny noise, a soft rustling sound,

as though someone had moved a foot ever so gently through *a patch of dry leaves.*

Mr Fox flattened **his body** against *the ground*

and lay very still, **his ears** pricked.

He waited a long time,

but he heard nothing more.

'It must have been *a field-mouse*,' he told himself, 'or some other *small animal*.'

He crept a little further out of *the hole* ... then further still.

He was almost right out in *the open* now.

He took a last careful look around.

The wood was murky and very still.

Somewhere in *the sky the moon* was shining.

Just then, **his sharp night-eyes** caught a glint of something bright behind *a tree* not far away.

The field unfolds through 11 parts of the environment, 6 parts of Mr Fox and 18 types of his activities (mostly types of movement). The few synonyms here include *noise-sound* and *speck-glint*, as well as *inched forward-crept further*; and there are many repetitions of *hole* and *sniffing*. The field of stories like this is construed mainly through parts of the setting and characters, and types of processes.

However, these parts and types of lexical items are only one side of the story's field; the other is the sequence of activities that constitutes the plot. We saw in §5.3.3 above that there are few conjunctions constructing this activity sequence; rather it is the series of processes that does so, together with circumstances. Here is the passage again, showing just the processes and circumstances.

crept up the dark tunnel to the mouth of his hole

poked out into the night air

sniffed once

moved an inch or two forward

stopped

sniffed again

inched forward a little more

was now in the open

twitched from side to side

sniffing and sniffing for the scent of danger

found none

just about to go trotting forward into the wood

heard a tiny noise

flattened against the ground

lay very still

waited a long time

heard nothing more

told himself

crept a little further out of the hole … then further still

was almost right out in the open

took a last careful **look** around

caught a glint of something bright behind a tree not far away

So lexical relations interact with activity sequences to build the field of texts that are focused on activities, such as stories or explanations. On the other hand, parts and types are critical lexical resources for building the field in texts that are focused on entities. For example, the classifying report on conductors [3.12] builds a classification taxonomy of materials shown in Figure 5.10.

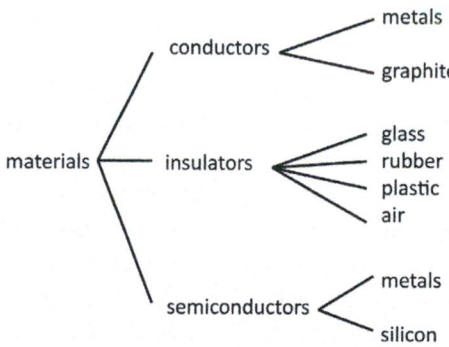

Figure 5.10: Classification taxonomy construed by classifying report [3.12]

We have seen how this taxonomy is scaffolded through identification and repetition: *one of two groups, The first group, The second group*. But another key resource is lexical contrasts, between **things** (*conductors, nonconductors, semi-conductors*) and **qualities** (*readily carry or conduct, very poor conductors, intermediate between insulators and conductors*). Taxonomies such as these can be used both for preparing for reading and elaborating after reading by jointly constructing them.

Contrasts include the well-known term **antonyms** (*success/failure*) but also

converse roles (*teacher/student*), **series** (*hot-warm-tepid-cool-cold*) and **cycles** (*summer-autumn-winter-spring*).

To sum up, ideation construes fields in terms of (1) wholes and their parts, (2) classes and their members and (3) sequences of activities. The technical terms for parts of wholes are **meronyms**, and members of classes are **hyponyms**. The lexical relations that are used to build a field thus include **repetition**, **synonymy**, **contrast**, **meronymy** and **hyponymy**. We can see each of these at work in the lightning explanation [3.24]. Parts of the atmosphere are in bold, types of energy are in italics, and activities are underlined.

[3.24'] Explanation of lightning

> **Warm air** <u>rises</u> in **hot clouds**
> and <u>encounters</u> **cold air**,
> <u>charging</u> the **particles in the cloud**
> <u>making</u> them both *positive and negative*...
> When enough *positive and negative charges* <u>occur</u>,
> they <u>build up</u> too much *energy*
> and <u>explode</u> in a *flash of light*...
> This *flash of light* <u>helps balance out</u> the number of *negative and positive charges* in **the atmosphere**.

The contrasts between *warm air*, *hot clouds* and *cold air* leads to *charging particles*, which is repeated as *charges* and classified as *energy*. The contrast between *positive and negative charges* leads to a *flash of light*, a synonym for lightning. Implicit here is the theory of electromagnetism, which explains relations between heat energy, mechanical energy, electrical energy and light. The activity sequence explains how this all occurs, inferring an implication sequence, in which each event is both an effect of the preceding event, and a condition for the next event. These are the kinds of inferential connections that need careful elaborating in Detailed Reading and Rewriting.

5.3.5   Appraisal

While lexical relations construe the field of a text, appraisal evaluates it. Appraisal expresses people's attitudes, including emotions, judgements of people, and appreciations of things. Attitudes can be positive or negative, and they can be graded (amplified or diminished). The source of the attitude can come from the writer, the characters in a story, other people, and can include the reader. Table 5.12 sets out the basic system.

Table 5.12: Basic options in appraisal

attitudes	emotions	*happy/sad*
	judging people	*kind/cruel*
	appreciating things	*interesting/boring*
graduation		*happy/joyous/ecstatic*
		down/sad/miserable
source		*I think (self)*
		it is well known (other)

In stories, authors use appraisals extensively to engage the reader by expressing emotions, judging characters' behaviour, and appreciating things and places in descriptions. In arguments and text responses, appraisal is used for judgements of people or institutions, and appreciations of events, ideas and texts. In factual texts, appraisals contribute to classifying and explaining phenomena.

Emotions are used in this familiar extract from *Rabbit Proof Fence* [4.8′] to engage readers' empathy with the family, but the contrast between their feelings and those of Constable Riggs also carries a key message of the novel. Explicit attitudes are in bold, graduation underlined, and implicit attitudes in italics.

[4.8′] Extract from *Follow the Rabbit Proof Fence*

When Constable Riggs, Protector of Aborigines, finally spoke his voice was <u>full of</u> **authority and purpose**. They knew <u>without a doubt</u> that he was *the one who took children in broad daylight* - not like the **evil** spirits who came into their camps at night. 'I've come to take Molly, Gracie and Daisy, the three half-caste girls, with me to Moore Rive Native Settlement,' he informed the family.

The old man nodded to show that he understood what Riggs was saying. The rest of the family *just hung their heads, refusing to face the man who was taking their daughters away from them*. <u>Silent</u> **tears** <u>welled in their eyes</u> and <u>trickled down their cheeks</u>.

… 'Where's the other one, Daisy?' he asked **anxiously** … 'Hurry up then, I want to get started,' he said, handing the reins over to Molly. Riggs was **annoyed** that he had to go **miles out of his way** to find these girls.

Molly and Gracie *sat silently* on the horse, **tears** <u>streaming down their cheeks</u> as Constable Riggs turned the big bay stallion and led the way back to the depot. A <u>high pitched</u> **wail** <u>broke out</u>. The **cries** of **agonised** mothers and the women, and the <u>deep</u> **sobs** of grandfathers, uncles and cousins <u>filled the air</u>.

The explicit positive judgement of Riggs with *authority and purpose* contrasts with his implicit negative judgement as *the one who took children in broad daylight*. Likewise, his *anxiety* and *annoyance* at having to go *miles out of his way* contrasts with the building prosody of grief as the family reacts. It is through contrasting appraisals such as this that the social messages of stories are highlighted for readers to infer. In this case the messages are the brutality of the colonial policy of Indigenous child removal, and the apparent heartlessness of the agents who carried it out, in contrast to the powerlessness and grief of the Indigenous children and their families.

The technical term for emotions is **affect**, and explicit attitudes are said to be **inscribed** in the words, whereas implicit attitudes are **invoked** by them. Table 5.13 sets out inscribed and invoked attitudes and graduations in the passage.

Table 5.13: Appraisals in Text [4.8']

	inscribed	invoked
affect	*tears, anxiously, annoyed, tears, wail, cries, agonised, sobs, sorrow*	*hung their heads, refusing to face, sat silently*
judgement	*authority and purpose*	*the one who took children, the man who was taking their daughters away*
appreciation		*miles out of his way*
graduation	*full of, without a doubt, silent, welled in their eyes and trickled down their cheeks, streaming down their cheeks, high pitched, deep, filled the air*	

In arguments, graduation and sourcing become very significant (Hood 2010). This can be seen in the discussion rewrite [4.26] from Chapter 4. Attitudes are in italics, graduation in bold and sourcing is underlined (*carefully* is tenacity).

[4.16'] Discussion showing appraisals

> **Every time** young people access the media, they are exposed to images of *happy healthy* families *enjoying quality time* by eating fast food and drinking fizzy drinks. On one hand, **many** people believe fast food is *nutritious and delicious*. However, if we study the research *carefully*, the evidence **suggests** that promotion of fast food **may** have *detrimental* effects on the health of young people.

Sourcing is a way of introducing other voices into the discourse. Three types of resource enable this: projection, modality and concession. Projection directly introduces what people say and think (*many people believe, the evidence suggests*). Concessive conjunctions counter alternative points of view (*however*), and comparative conjunctions signal alternative voices (*on one hand*). Modality implies alternative possibilities: if *fast food may have detrimental effects*, it also *may not* do. Stronger modality closes down other options, weaker modality opens them up. Graduation in general can be used to this end: *many* people *believe* implies some who do not; *evidence* **suggests** implies it may be wrong.

However, it is not just the resources themselves, but the ways they are deployed that negotiates the discussion with the reader. Without the circumstance *every time* in [4.16'], the first sentence would just be a statement of fact – amplifying makes it an issue worth discussing. The writer then engages the reader with a prosody of positive attitudes *happy, healthy, enjoying, quality time, nutritious and delicious*, and concedes that **many** *people* hold this view. But the projecting verb *believe* implies the possibility of delusion, made more explicit by the contrast with *study the research carefully* and *evidence*. At this point the reader is included as *we* who study the research, but rather than closing down discussion, it is opened up by diminishing the evidence with *suggests* and *may*, which also diminishes the negative impact of *detrimental effects*. The complexity of these appraisal patterns makes it clear why Detailed Reading and Joint Rewriting is useful to guide students to effectively manage evaluation in arguments and text responses, as we showed in Chapter 4 (§4.5.5). Resources like graduation and sourcing are arguably harder to bring to consciousness than meanings of other kinds and thus have a tendency to be overlooked without explicit scaffolding; in fact, they are a crucial dimension of any successful writer's maturing repertoire.

By Year 12, a few students have mastered these kinds of appraisal sufficiently to successfully control evaluation in history, as we illustrated with the exposition [3.33] in Chapter 3. This young writer also controls the interplay of appraisal with periodicity – limiting inscribed evaluations to the macroTheme, hyper-Themes and macroNew, from where they scope forward and back over the 'hard' evidence presented in the body of the essay. Again, attitudes are in italics, graduations in bold, and sourcing underlined.

[3.33] Student's exposition

Thesis preview	It was *inevitable* that the USA and the Republic of Vietnam would be defeated in the Second Indochina war of 1965-1973 because of the *effective* strategies used by the North, with the use of Guerrilla warfare and the Ho Chin Minh trail. The south was defeated because their tactics like using conventional ground warfare and air warfare and their Pacification Campaigns were **totally** *inappropriate* for the war in Vietnam ...
Arguments [topics only]	The US tactics were *wrong* ... The goal of the NVA and VC was to unify North and South as one nation by defeating the US and their allies. <u>This cause</u> became an **all consuming** one ... The US and SV were **very** *disadvantaged* ... But the **main** reason, and **most** *effective* part of the VC's strategy was that they had <u>a cause</u> ... The US and RoV Social <u>policies</u> were also a *failure*, and a **major part** to the **inevitability** of their loss ...
Restatement review	It was *inevitable* that the US and RoV were to be defeated in the Second Indochina war. What attributed to this defeat were <u>not only</u> *the strengths* of the North's strategy of guerrilla warfare and the **vital** *success* of the Ho Chi Minh Trail in supplying the troops. The strategy of the US and the South was *hopeless* **in all senses** for this type of war. Their use of conventional techniques and Pacification programs in the end pushed <u>the people to believe</u> they are <u>in fact</u> the *enemy*. <u>The fact that</u> the North has

> an *emotional* cause appealing to the whole of the people and the **all-round**
> *inappropriate* strategy of the south and US it was *inevitable* from the start that the
> South would be defeated.

The word *inevitable* strongly counters any alternative view that the USA and RoV could have succeeded. Otherwise, appraisal is relatively muted in the Thesis paragraph, as it should be to display objectivity, only appreciating *effective strategies* against *totally inappropriate* ones in previewing the arguments (*totally* appears overstated here). Appraisal is then gradually built up through the ensuing topic sentences, focusing around the NVA and VC's *cause* and the US and RoV's *policies*. These are metaphorical projections of what the Vietnamese people 'believed' and the US and RoV 'decided', which is why we have under-lined them as sources.

In the Restatement stage, judgements and appreciations are reviewed, and the effect of the North's *cause* is then amplified by synonyms (*the people believe, cause appealing to the people*), with concession and judgement (*in fact the enemy*), with affect (*emotional cause*), and graduation (*the whole of the people*), before restating the writer's position that defeat was inevitable. These kinds of text-level patterns of appraisal, in macroTheme, hyperThemes and macroNew, can be negotiated with students in Joint Construction, particularly in the secondary school, using accomplished models such as this.

In technical texts there tends to be little attitude, but graduation can be used extensively for explaining and classifying. It is deployed to explain lightning in [3.24].

> When **enough** positive and negative charges occur,
> they build up **too much** energy
> and **explode** in a flash of light ...
> This flash of light **helps** balance out the number of negative and positive charges in the
> atmosphere.

Energy is graded here from *enough* to *too much* to *exploded*, to explain how electrical energy is transferred to light energy. The secondary verb *helps* implies that lightning is only one of the factors that balance out charges in the atmos-phere. This classifying function of graduation is expressed by *sometimes* in the next phase of the explanation, to classify two types of lightning.

> **Sometimes** the flash of light is movement within the cloud
> and **sometimes** it is movement between the atmosphere and the ground.

In the next phase, *thus* implies that the writer's conclusion flows naturally from the explanation, and **negation** is used to counter an alternative view.

> Light travels faster than sound, and because of this, we see the flash of lighting before we hear the clap of thunder. There is **thus** a direct relationship between thunder and lightning; they are **not** separate phenomena.

As we showed in Table 5.4 above, negation is the outer limit of modality, and thus of sourcing; saying something is **not** true implies that someone thinks it **could be**. In the last phase, graduation is used to explain the duration in time of lightning.

> Thunder and lightning lasts **only as long as is necessary** to get **all** the electrical charges in the atmosphere back in balance.

So as we can see, factual writing of this kind is far from purely 'objective'. The interpersonal resource of appraisal is used in science in the service of ideational functions, to classify and explain natural phenomena, as well as to counter alternatives. These are crucial matters for elaborating in Detailed Reading and Rewriting of science texts, as students learn to control scientific discourse.

5.3.6   Negotiation

We have shown above how evaluation is negotiated in written texts through appraisal. In spoken interactions, social relations are additionally negotiated through exchanges between speakers. The aim of this section is to give teachers and teacher educators a set of tools for analysing their own classroom discourse, in order to redesign it more effectively.[16] To this end we will build up these tools in a series of steps.

In §5.2.8 above, we introduced some basic types of **speech function** (statement, question, command) in relation to the different mood structures of clauses that express these meanings. Table 5.14 expands these basic speech functions in three directions: (i) what is being exchanged (information or goods-and-services), (ii) whether the speaker is giving or demanding, and (iii) whether the move is initiating an exchange or responding.

Table 5.14: Basic speech functions

	initiating	responding to
demanding information	question	answer
giving information	statement	acknowledgement
demanding goods-and-services	command	compliance
giving goods-and-services	offer	acceptance

---

[16] For a more technical detailed account, see Martin 2007a, Martin and Rose 2005, 2007.

Compliance to a command means providing goods or service. The person who provides the goods or service is the actor in the exchange, whom we will refer to as A1 (following Berry 1981; cf. Ventola 1987). The person who demands the goods or service, or accepts an offer is A2. For example, in the following exchange the teacher demands and the students act:

Teacher	A2	*Everyone highlight 'a little further'.*
Students	A1	*[all highlight their texts]*

Non-verbal actions in exchanges are generally stated in square brackets like this *[all highlight their texts]*. Note that A2 is the person in an exchange with authority or familiarity to demand a service, in this case the teacher.

Conversely, the person with the authority to give **information** is the primary knower in an exchange, or K1. In pedagogic interactions this is usually the parent or teacher, and the learner is the secondary knower or K2. This can be easily seen in early parent–child exchanges, in which the parent gives information, the child repeats it, and the parent affirms.

Mother	K1	*[points to the wolf] Oh oh, I see that wolf.*
Child	K2	*[turns to page 4 and points to wolf] Oh oh.*
Mother	K1	*Oh oh.*

When it comes to classroom exchanges, the teacher is usually the one who asks questions, demanding information from learners. The teacher is still the primary knower or K1 because the teacher has the ultimate authority to evaluate students' responses. Even as they give information in response, the students are still secondary knowers or K2. Thus in any pedagogic exchange, the teacher's evaluation is obligatory (as we showed in Chapters 1 and 4). In a sense it is delayed by first asking a question so that students can respond and be evaluated. So we can label the teacher's question as **delayed K1**, or **dK1**. Evaluations can be positive or negative.

Teacher	dK1	*What's a widow? Rhianna?*
Student	K2	*An old woman.*
Teacher	K1	*Well she doesn't look too old.*

Teacher	dK1	*So if Mr Fox is almost right out, what part of him might still be in the hole?*
Student	K2	*His tail.*
Teacher	K1	*That's exactly right.*

The difference between these two examples is that the first teacher's question does not provide adequate criteria for Rhianna to respond successfully, so she is rejected, whereas the second teacher's question does provide sufficient information for a successful response, which is affirmed. This kind of exchange structure correlates with the nucleus of a pedagogic exchange that we outlined in Chapter 4, correlated in Figure 5.11 (the carets ^ mean 'followed by').

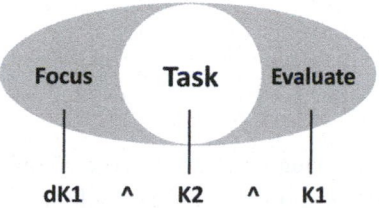

Figure 5.11: Nucleus of learning activity and exchange structure

This nucleus of exchange structure can be expanded both before and afterwards. Firstly, the teacher may include more than one dK1 question in the Focus. The second dK1 expands the first, indicated by '='.

Teacher	dK1	*Can you see the word that tells us South African politics blew up?*	Focus
	=dK1	*South African politics … ?*	
Student	K2	*Erupted.*	Identify
Teacher	K1	*Erupted!*	Affirm

The dK1 move is expanded here to make the task easier, by reading up to the word to identify. Such a sequence of dK1 moves is known as a **move complex** (as a clause complex consists of a sequence of clauses). Secondly, the teacher may give information in a statement before the Focus, in the K1 move we call **Prepare**.

Teacher	K1	*Then it tells us that South African politics blew up.*	Prepare
Teacher	dK1	*Can you see the word that tells us South African politics blew up?*	Focus
	=dK1	*South African politics … ?*	
Student	K2	*Erupted.*	Identify
Teacher	K1	*Erupted!*	Affirm

The K1 Prepare move is outside the nucleus of the exchange, indicated by the underline. After the students' response, the teacher may ask for clarification. These are called **tracking** moves, labelled **tr**. Students' **responses to tracking** moves are labelled **rtr**. In the next part of the exchange a tracking move is used to involve the whole class in affirming the response.

Teacher	K1	*Then it tells us that South African politics blew up.*	Prepare
Teacher	dK1	*Can you see the word that tells us South African politics blew up?*	Focus
	=dK1	*South African politics ... ?*	
Student	K2	*Erupted.*	Identify
Teacher	K1	*Erupted!*	Affirm
	tr	*Is he right?*	
Students	rtr	*Yes.*	

Again, the sequence of tracking moves is a move complex, which makes up the Affirm phase in the exchange. In the next example from a Year 5 maths lesson, the teacher expands the dK1 question simply by repeating it until the student responds, and then tracks his response by asking him to repeat it.

Teacher	K1	*So B will go right in the middle there, won't it Hasan? B.*	Prepare
	=dK1	*Do you see why it will go in the middle there?*	Focus
	=dK1	*Do you see why it will go in there?*	
Teacher	=dK1	*Can you explain why?*	
Student	K2	*It's got five faces.*	Propose
Teacher	tr	*Pardon?*	
Student	rtr	*[louder] It's got five faces.*	
Teacher	K1	*Good, it's got five faces.*	Affirm

Although this teacher has prepared with literal information in the diagram they are studying, the dK1 Focus question then demands an interpretive response, from the student's own knowledge. As this is a struggling student, his response takes too long, so the teacher repeats the question, which is too mumbled, and so it must be repeated.

Without adequate preparation in either the Prepare or Focus moves, students may be unable to respond at all. In this case, teachers typically give the class more criteria. The following Year 5 class is constructing a graph using data about weather.

Teacher	dK1	*So what we going to do now?*	Focus
	=dK1	*How are we going to show the weather on Monday of last week?*	
	-	*[no response]*	
Teacher	K1	*Well it was sunny.*	Prepare
	dK1	*What could you do to show that?*	Focus
Student	K2	*Put it in a colour ... of the sun. Put yellow.*	Propose
Teacher	K1	*Good idea.*	Affirm

More often, students give answers the teacher does not want, which the teacher usually evaluates and then provides more criteria. In the Year 1 exchange [1.1] we saw in Chapters 1 and 4, the teacher narrows the criteria through four Focus questions before getting the desired response.

1	Teacher	dK1	*What's a widow?*	Focus
		=dK1	*It looks like a lady to me.*	
		=dK1	*What's a widow? Rhianna?*	
	Student	K2	*An old woman.*	Propose
	Teacher	K1	*Well she doesn't look too old.*	Reject
2	Teacher	dK1	*Is there a daddy there?*	Focus
	Students	K2	*No.*	Propose
3	Teacher	dK1	*What do you think has happened to the daddy?*	Focus
	Student	K2	*Looks like ... a cow.*	Propose
	Teacher	tr	*David?*	
	Student	rtr	*It's it's it's a little cow.*	
	Teacher	K1	*No no.*	Reject
4	Teacher	dK1	*When there's a widow, something's happened to daddy.*	Focus
	Student	K2	*He died? Miss, he died?*	Propose
	Teacher	K1	*Yes that's right.*	Affirm

This is an exchange complex, consisting of a series of four exchanges. Extended interactions often consist of such exchange complexes.

One consequence of the hierarchy created by ordinary classroom interactions is that students who are rarely affirmed either eventually withdraw or resist. As we pointed out in Chapter 4, the withdrawal option does not show up in lesson transcripts, because only those students who are still engaged respond to teacher questions, except when the teacher purposely targets weaker students, as with Hasan above. A favourite student tactic of resistance is to ridicule teachers' questions. This type of move is a **challenge**, which we label as **ch**. A common teacher tactic is to ignore unwanted responses, including challenges. The following Year 8 class has been reading a novel and is discussing the characters.

Teacher	dK1	*What kind of a man is Abel?*	Focus
Student	**ch**	*A man.*	Propose
Teacher	dK1	*Think of the kinds of things he did.*	Focus
Student	K2	*He had the fantasy of the ocean.*	Propose
Teacher	tr	*What? Repeat that.*	
Student	rtr	*Dreamed about the ocean.*	
Teacher	K1	*Thank you June. [writes on the board]*	Affirm

The resistant student subverts the classification the teacher is asking the class to construct. However, the aim of challenging is not to be ignored, but to get attention, if not from the teacher then from the class of peers. So another student further subverts the teacher's classification, and the teacher is forced to respond (labelled **rch**).

Teacher	dK1	*What sort of man was Mad Macka?*	Focus
Student	ch	*A dog.*	Propose
Teacher	**rch**	*Ben, we won't have stupid answers.*	Reject
		[students start calling out answers]	

The point of asking questions and evaluating students' responses should not be simply to create a hierarchy among students, but to elaborate on students' responses building towards the lesson's learning goals. Elaborations can consist of a single K1 move that follows the Evaluation. Here is the Year 5 graph lesson again.

Teacher	dK1	*How would we represent that sort of information?*	Focus
	=dK1	*All that information on one graph?*	
Student	K2	*You could put them ... like the Monday, underneath it like that.*	Propose
Teacher	K1	*You could.*	Affirm
	K1	*You could put Monday, Tuesday, Wednesday, Thursday, Friday at the bottom of your graph.*	Elaborate

All teachers depend on students like this one to provide responses that can be used for elaborating. As Focus questions often do not provide sufficient information for many students to confidently respond, a minority of students consistently do so in any class. In this case the student's response comes from his knowledge of the graph genre, and the teacher's Elaboration builds on it with more detail. Like Prepare moves, the Elaboration is outside the nucleus of the exchange, indicated by the line above it.

Elaborations can also be negotiated as an exchange. This is used, for example, in Detailed Reading to unpack lexical and grammatical metaphors, such as the following, about Text [4.12].

Teacher	dK1	*You know why it's called an uprising?*	Focus
	=dK1	*Because what did the people do?*	
Students	K2	*Rise up.*	Propose
Teacher	K1	*The people rise up, yes.*	Affirm
	dK1	*And who were they rising up against?*	Focus
Students	K2	*The government.*	Propose
Teacher	K1	*The government, that's right*	Affirm
	K1	*So it was an uprising.*	Elaborate

This exchange complex works smoothly because the students respond to the semantic categories given in the Focus questions (*What did the **people do**? **Who were they rising up against**?*), in order to jointly re-express the grammatical metaphor as a process involving people and things. Finally, the teacher elaborates by restating the nominal expression (*it was an uprising*). At this point the teacher could also have further elaborated by naming it as a thing that stands for a process – a metaphor.

These options for pedagogic exchanges are correlated with the orbital model of learning activities in Figure 5.12. As we have seen, each move in the nucleus (dK1, K2, K1) can be expanded as a move complex. The Prepare and Elaborate phases consist of further K1 moves than can be expanded as exchanges. They are related to the nucleus as an exchange complex, indicated here by double slashes // (as clauses are indicated in a clause complex).

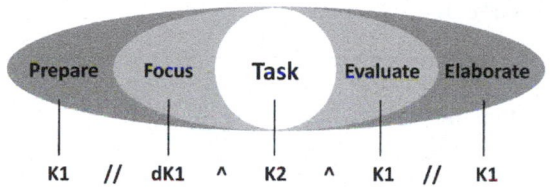

Figure 5.12: Pedagogic exchanges and learning activities

Options for each phase of an exchange complex are expanded in Tables 5.15-18 below. Examples are taken from the exchanges above, so that the contexts can be easily recovered. Possibilities for initiating, responding and evaluating depend on the level of guidance. The purpose is to show contrasts between exchanges where teachers provide a high level of support to students and where inadequate support is provided. To this end, examples of high level support are taken from the Detailed Reading exchange about Text [4.12].

Table 5.15: Initiating options

	K1		dK1			=dk1	
low support	no preparation	-	Focus	no criteria	Do you see why it will go in the middle there?	repeat question	Do you see why it will go in there? Can you explain why?
high support	**Prepare**	Then it tells us that South African politics blew up	**Focus**	provide criteria	Can you see the word that tells us South African politics blew up?	extend criteria	South African politics … ?

Table 5.16: Responding options

	K2			tr		rtr	
low support	**Propose**	from experience	*He had the fantasy of the ocean*	track response	*What? Repeat that*	repeat response	*Dreamed about the ocean*
high support	**Identify**	from text	*Erupted*	track evaluation	*Is he right?*	affirm	*Yes*
	Propose	from Prepare and Focus cues	*Volcanoes*				

Table 5.17: Evaluating options

	dK1	K2	K1	
low support	*What kind of a man is Abel?*	*A man* [challenge]	**Reject** ignore	–
	What's a widow?	*An old woman*	qualify	*Well she doesn't look too old*
	What's a widow?	*It's it's it's a little cow*	negate	*No no*
	What sort of man was Mad Macka?	*A dog*	admonish	*Ben, we won't have stupid answers*
high support	*What did the people do?*	*Rise up*	**Affirm**	*The people rise up, yes.*

Table 5.18: Elaborating options

monologic elaboration			dialogic elaboration		
K2		*You could put them … like the Monday, underneath it like that*	K2		*Rise up*
K1		*You could*	K1		*The people rise up, yes*
			dK1	Focus	*And who were they rising up against?*
			K2	Propose	*The government*
			K1	Affirm	*The government, that's right*
K1	Elaborate	*You could put Monday, Tuesday, Wednesday, Thursday, Friday at the bottom of your graph*	K1	Elaborate	*So it was an uprising*

In many instances, elaborations are necessarily monologic, as the teacher must give students new information, such as definitions and explanations. Many examples are shown in Chapter 4 above. However, a common problem to guard against is for monologic elaborations to go on too long, and give too much information that many students cannot follow or retain.

Not included in Tables 5.15-18 is the A2 move in which teachers direct students to highlight wordings they have identified. Naturally, there are also many other contexts in which teachers direct students, particularly in exchanges concerned with classroom routines and students' behaviour, illustrated by exchange [5.2] in §5.2.8 above. In Detailed Reading, the Direct move is used to ensure that all students know exactly which words to highlight.

This outline of resources for negotiation, in the context of classroom discourse, is intended to give teachers, teacher educators and reseachers a systematic set of tools to interpret learning interactions. For educational researchers, these tools can help to inform interpretations that are currently often more commentaries on lessons than rigorous analyses. For teacher educators they can help to inform a more rigorous approach to apprenticing trainee teachers, in place of such ill-defined notions as 'teacher-centred/learner-centred' or 'open/closed questioning'. For teachers, they can provide powerful insights into the nature of their own discourse, and the means to consciously design it to more effectively reach all their students.

6 Knowledge about pedagogy

In this chapter we review the knowledge about pedagogy that has been accumulated through the Sydney School research project and outlined in the chapters of this book. We begin with the strategies that have been designed for teaching reading and writing in the classroom, and conclude with an outline of the teacher professional learning program that has evolved to apprentice teachers into the knowledge about pedagogy and language.

6.1 The curriculum genre: a theory of teaching and learning

The analysis and design of pedagogic practice described in Chapters 1–5 can be aligned in three broad categories in terms of tenor, field and mode: (i) pedagogic relations between teachers and students, (ii) pedagogic activities and sequences of activities, and (iii) pedagogic modalities, including spoken, written visual and manual practice. In this section we summarise our analyses and designs through a series of visual images, culminating in a model that integrates them towards a language-based theory of teaching and learning (Halliday 1993, Rose 2007, 2011b).

6.1.1 Pedagogic relations

We began this book with what we see as the central problem for education: inequality between students with respect to participation in the learning activities of the school, including both classroom learning and individual learning from reading. We suggested that this inequality originates with differing experiences of parent-child reading in the home and associated orientations to meaning (Adams 1990, Williams 1995, Hasan 2009), rather than from in-born learning capacities, and is compounded over the years of schooling by the ineffectiveness of teaching practices to neutralise these differences (Hattie 2009). The inequality of participation creates hierarchies of success and failure (Bernstein 1990, 1996/2000) and circles of inclusion and exclusion (Nuthall 2005), in the school and each classroom; these construct children's identities as more or less successful learners, as diagrammed in Figure 6.1.

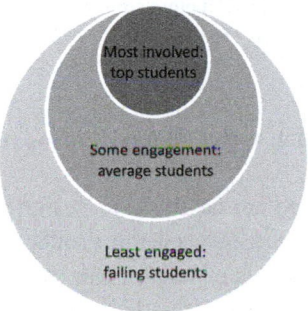

Figure 6.1: Hierarchies of success and failure, inclusion and exclusion

In Bernstein's view, students' internalisation of the hierarchy serves to naturalise the gross inequality of school outcomes, as 'failure is attributed to inborn facilities (cognitive, affective) or to the cultural deficits relayed by the family' (1996/2000: 5). This inequality of outcomes has become dysfunctional in a changing socio-economic order, creating pressure on schools and teachers to improve literacy teaching.

6.1.2   Pedagogic activities

In our view, inequality of outcomes is sustained by failing to explicitly teach all students the skills they need to independently read and write the curriculum at each stage of school. Instead, successful students tacitly acquire skills at each stage that will prepare them for the next stage. Rather than explicitly teaching skills needed in each stage, students are evaluated on skills they may have tacitly acquired in preceding stages, beginning with parent-child reading and associated orientations to meaning in the home (Hasan 2009, Williams 1995, 1999b, 2001). This sequence of tacit preparation and evaluation is diagrammed in Figure 6.2 (see Rose 2004, 2007 for further discussion).

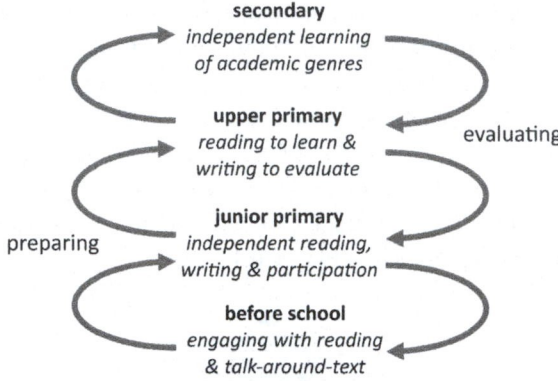

Figure 6.2: Tacit learning sequence in school

Our approach to the problem has been to design teaching activities that can provide all students with the skills needed for success and can be integrated with curriculum teaching at all levels of school. Our starting point was an analysis of learning activities that positioned the learner's task as the central element, initiated by a task focus and followed by evaluation. The task focus may or may not provide all students with sufficient support to succeed with the task. For example, students may be given a model or simply be directed to write on a topic. Some students may have sufficient experience of the expected genre, field and language resources to create successful texts, while others do not. Evaluation thus ranks students on the previous experience they bring to the task. Inequality can be reduced by adequately preparing all students for each learning task. Success with a learning task then provides a basis for an elaborating step in the learning activity, which may involve deeper understanding. This nuclear model of learning tasks is diagrammed in Figure 6.3.

Figure 6.3: Five phases of a learning activity

The nuclear model of learning activities is applied to analyse and design activities at the levels of curriculum units, of each activity in a lesson, and of classroom interactions. The five phases are also interpreted as a cycle, in which each elaboration phase provides a basis for preparing the next task, as in Figure 6.4.

Figure 6.4: Learning activity as a cycle

As each learning activity cycle builds on preceding cycles, teaching sequences take the form of a spiral curriculum. Each task is more challenging than the last, as students' skills and knowledge accumulate (Figure 6.5).

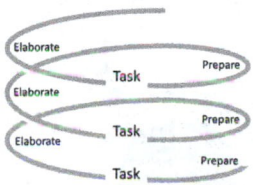

Figure 6.5: Spiral curriculum of learning cycles

To design effective preparations for the language learning task, we took the concept of 'guidance through interaction in the context of shared experience' from Halliday's and Painter's observations of language learning in the home. Guidance through interaction enables learners to do tasks that may be well beyond their independent competence. Guided repetition of high-level tasks enables learners to develop skills more effectively than individual practice of lower-level tasks. Well-designed preparations enable all students in a class to do the same high-level tasks, through guided joint practice, despite different initial skill levels. Over time, repeated joint practice reduces the inequality between students, shown in Figure 6.6.

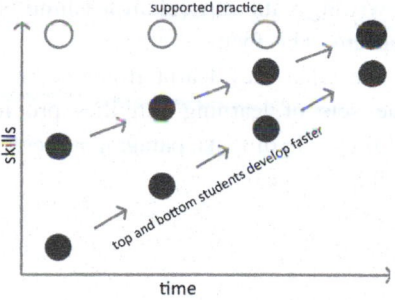

Figure 6.6: Narrowing the gap with guided repetition

In the Sydney School project's first two phases (*Language and Social Power* and *Write it Right*), a teaching/learning cycle (TLC) was designed and refined for teachers to guide students to successfully write the genres of schooling. In this cycle, the students' final task is Independent Construction of the genre under focus. Preparation was designed in two stages, including Deconstruction of a model text, and Joint Construction of a new text by the class, both guided by the teacher in interaction with students. The *Write it Right* version of the cycle was diagrammed in Figure 6.7.

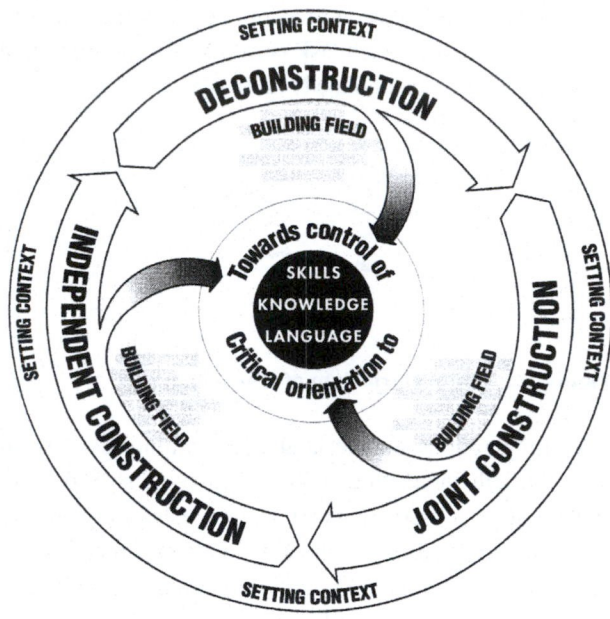

Figure 6.7: Teaching/learning cycle for genre writing

In the project's most recent phase, the writing pedagogy was extended to integrate reading and writing with curriculum teaching at all year levels in the *Reading to Learn* program. The focus is on preparing all students to read curriculum texts and to use what they learnt from reading in their writing. The program includes nine sets of learning activities providing three degrees of scaffolding support, at the scale of texts, paragraphs, sentences, word groups and words – as consolidated in Figure 6.8.

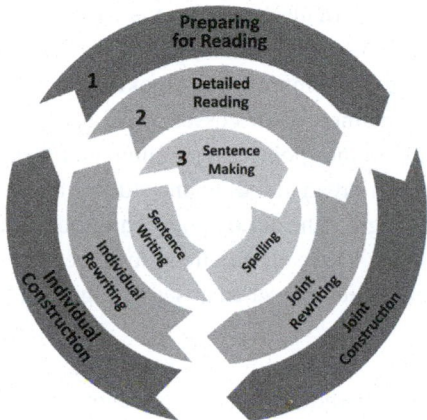

Figure 6.8: Nine sets of learning activities in *Reading to Learn*

6.1.3   Pedagogic modalities

Genre pedagogy deploys relations between pedagogic modalities – spoken, written, visual and manual – in order to maximise the effectiveness of learning activities. The spoken discourse of the classroom is carefully designed to engage all students successfully in the tasks of reading and writing. The starting point is with spoken preparation for reading, followed by reading aloud, and then spoken discussion of meanings in the text. Reading and discussion of texts then leads to writing activities, in which students are guided to use the language resources they have learnt from reading, through further discussion. This designed talk-around-text also involves reading visual images and their relation to written text, exemplified for science texts in §4.4.1 and children's picture books in §4.7.2. Manual activity is also deployed to give students greater control over reading and writing, using highlighters, cardboard and scissors, and whiteboards, marker pens and erasers.

The integration of these modalities is most closely designed in Detailed Reading, in which the teacher (i) orally prepares and (ii) focuses students' visual attention on the words, (iii) the students identify the written words and (iv) manually highlight them, and (v) the teacher and students orally elaborate their meanings. These five moves between spoken, written, visual and manual modalities are shown in Figure 6.9.

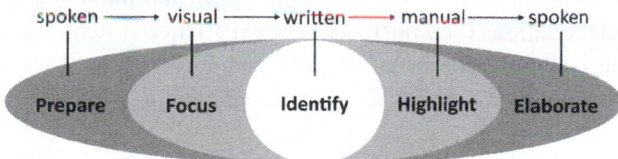

Figure 6.9: Pedagogic modalities in Detailed Reading cycles

The spoken preparation provides access to the written meaning by generalising or paraphrasing it in commonsense terms; that is, less meaning is committed. In contrast, more meaning is committed in spoken elaborations, as the written meaning is defined, explained or discussed (Liu 2010).[1] Students' attention is initially directed aurally to the spoken preparation, and then visually to the words on the page. The words are read aloud by one student and restated by the teacher in the direction to highlight. The act of highlighting enhances students' perception of the words, so they are ready to attend to the elaboration. These relations between pedagogic modalities are schematised in Figure 6.10.

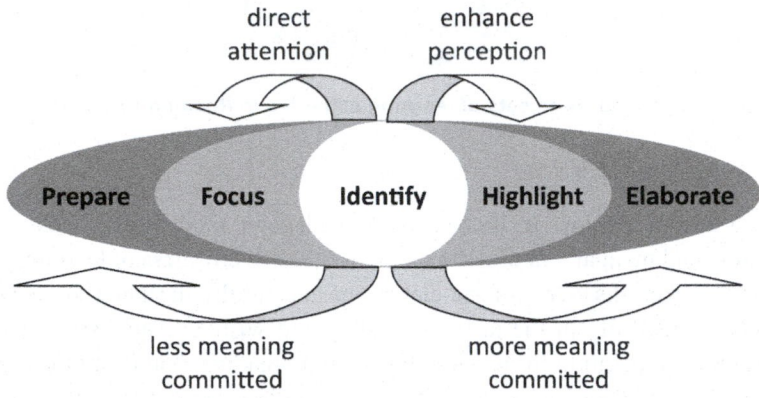

Figure 6.10: Functions of pedagogic modalities in Detailed Reading cycles

6.1.4 Knowledge about language (KAL)

The goal of the pedagogic practices reviewed above is to give all students access to the same level of curriculum knowledge. In the process, students acquire knowledge about language, at the levels of genre, register, discourse, grammar and graphology/phonology. KAL at each of these levels is made explicit by means of a pedagogic metalanguage that is systematic and consistent, and is introduced in the process of jointly reading and writing texts.

The metalanguage is based on the SFL model of language in social contexts, including three types of meaning or metafunctions, interpersonal, ideational and textual, realised as patterns of discourse, grammar and phonology/graphology, that enact social relations (or tenor), construe experience as activities, people and things (or field), and present meanings as text-in-context (or mode). These three dimensions of register are woven together in each genre, which we defined as a

---

[1] Commitment refers to the degree of specificity of the meaning instantiated in a text; this has to do with how many optional choices for meaning are taken up and how generally the choices a text subscribes to are instantiated (Martin 2010).

'staged, goal-oriented social process', modelled in Figure 6.11.

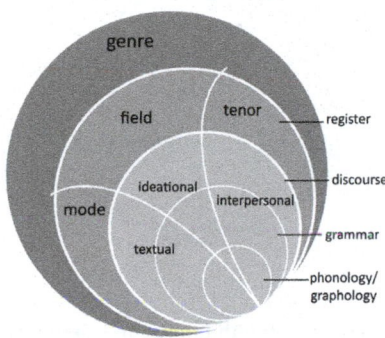

Figure 6.11: Language in social contexts

Using this approach to discourse analysis, a set of genres was identified in the project's first phase, which students were expected to write in the primary school; and their purposes, stages and key language features were described. The key genres and their purposes are distilled in Table 6.1.

Table 6.1: Basic genres in the primary school

	genre	purpose
stories	**recount**	recounting events
	narrative	resolving a complication
	anecdote	sharing an emotional reaction
	exemplum	judging character or behaviour
factual	**description**	describing specific things
	report	classifying & describing general things
	explanation	explaining sequences of events
	procedure	how to do an activity
	protocol	what to do and not to do
arguments	**exposition**	arguing for a point of view
	discussion	discussing two or more points of view

Genres were modelled as patterns of language patterns – genres consist of meanings and meanings construe the genre, as in Figure 6.12.

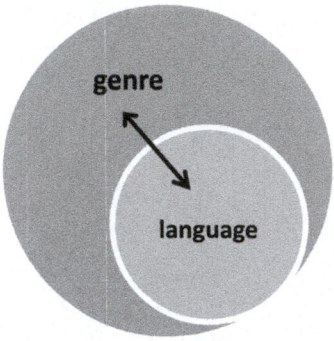

Figure 6.12: Genre realised through language – language construing genre

In the project's second phase *Write it Right*, analysis of learning tasks was extended to the types of knowledge that students are expected to acquire in the school curriculum. Genres that students read and write in each secondary school subject area were identified along with their purposes, stages and language features. The key genres were classified as a typology in Figure 6.13.

Figure 6.13: Map of genres in school

A focus of *Write it Right* was on resources for interpreting and contesting knowledge as well as describing and explaining the natural and social worlds. This perspective was presented as a topology of tendencies in Figure 6.14.

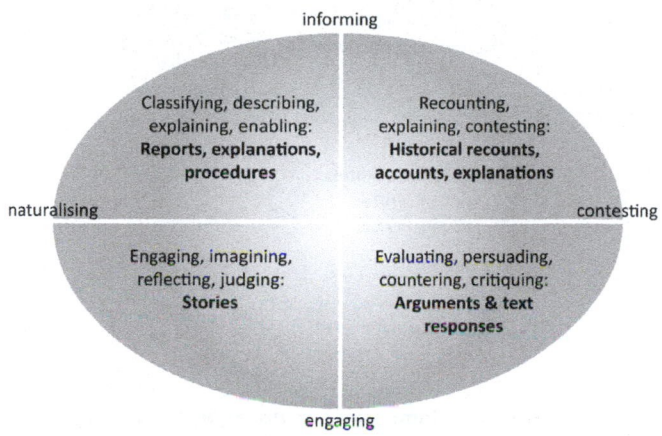

Figure 6.14: Genres and types of knowledge in the school curriculum

As the project developed, a pedagogic metalanguage was designed for teachers to analyse texts, plan lessons and share with students in the classroom. At the level of grammar, this metalanguage includes knowledge about the structures and functions of clauses, word groups and words, expansions of meaning in writing, and lexical and grammatical metaphor. At the level of discourse, it includes knowledge about systems of interpersonal, ideational and textual meanings that organise written texts and enact exchanges in the classroom.

6.1.5   Integrating pedagogic practice

In sum, the three dimensions of pedagogic practice described in the Sydney School research are (i) pedagogic relations between teachers and students and between students, (ii) pedagogic activities and sequences of activities, at the levels of curriculum programs, lesson activities and classroom interactions, and (iii) pedagogic modalities, including speaking, reading, writing, viewing images and manual practice. These three dimensions correlate with the tenor (relations), field (activities) and mode (modalities) of the contexts of schooling (Figure 6.15).

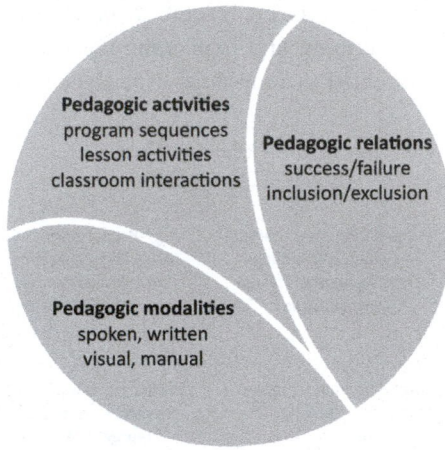

Figure 6.15: Dimensions of pedagogic practice

The goal of the pedagogic practices of the school is to shape the consciousness of students, in terms of both the knowledge they acquire and their social identities as learners, workers and citizens (Bernstein 1996/2000, Christie 1999). Knowledge and identities are brought into being by the activities, relations and modalities of pedagogic practice. Together, pedagogic practices and the knowledge and identities they produce constitute the contexts of schooling that we have referred to as the curriculum genre (Christie 1999, 2002, Martin 2007c, Martin and Rose 2008), schematised in Figure 6.16.

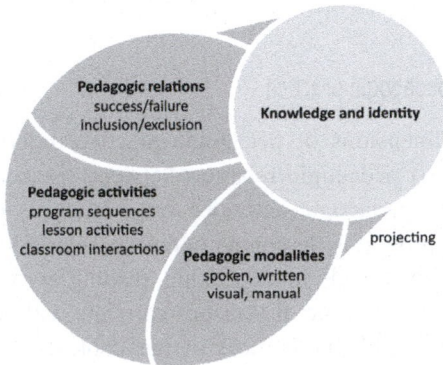

Figure 6.16: Knowledge and identity in relation to pedagogic practice

In this model, the relation between pedagogic practice, knowledge and identity is a projecting relation: pedagogic practice **projects** knowledge and identities, as processes of saying and thinking **project** locutions and ideas (§5.1.9 above); knowledge is manifested as teachers and learners say, write, read and practise it. The analysis is applicable to any pedagogic situation in and out of school, since any pedagogic practice includes relations between learners and teachers, and activities that involve speaking, reading, writing, viewing or doing; and any pedagogic practice has implications for both knowledge and identity. The analysis illuminates Bernstein's point that 'skills' and 'values' are produced by the same pedagogic practice.

> Often people in schools and in classrooms make a distinction between what they call the transmission of skills and the transmission of values. These are always kept apart as if there were a conspiracy to disguise the fact that there is only one discourse. In my opinion there is only one discourse, not two, because the secret voice of this discourse is to disguise the fact that there is only one (Bernstein 1996: 46-7).

Bernstein is referring here to the distinction he makes in pedagogic practice between an **instructional** function, which creates 'specialised skills and their relationship to each other', and a **regulative** function, which creates 'order, relations and identity' (1996: 46). In the preceding quote, Bernstein's point is that instructional ('skills') and regulative ('values') are dimensions of the one practice.[2]

Classroom discourse is sometimes analysed as though its instructional functions are realised by the ideational content of the lesson, and its regulative functions are realised by teacher evaluations and instructions to students. This is an example of the artificial distinction that Bernstein is critiquing. In fact, it is the whole configuration of pedagogic activities, relations and modalities that serves both instructional and regulative functions at the same time. Bernstein elaborates that 'the instructional discourse is embedded in the regulative discourse, and the regulative discourse is the dominant discourse' (1996: 46). In our terms, the whole of pedagogic practice is shaped by its regulative function, to create 'order, relations, identity'. If the social order, relations and identities are unequal, then pedagogic activities, relations and modalities will be shaped to create and maintain inequality. In other words, the inequality of social relations beyond the school is recontextualised in the pedagogic practices of the school. The result is that one and the same pedagogic practice produces grossly unequal outcomes in students' knowledge and identities.

For example, the interactional and reading practices of middle-class families are recontextualised in early years school as practices that enable the children of

---

[2] In SFL terms, Bernstein's use of the term **discourse** refers to fields of social activity, coloured by tenor. The term is also used similarly by critical theorists and discourse analysts such as Gee (e.g. 2005). We have paraphrased it here simply as 'practice'.

these families to successfully participate in classroom interactions and rapidly learn to read independently, but simultaneously constrain the reading development and successful participation of children from other types of families (Hasan 2009, Williams 1995, 1999b, 2001). In an upper primary classroom, the same activity may enable some students to write successful texts or solve maths problems successfully, while other students remain unable to do so. In the secondary school, these groups of students will be streamed into different classes studying different levels of curriculum (Figure 6.17).

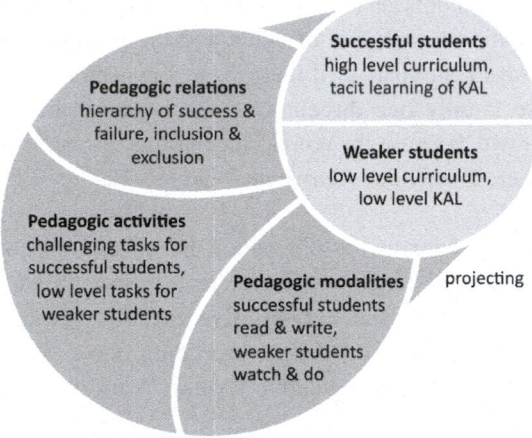

Figure 6.17: Ordinary pedagogic practices project unequal knowledge and identities

Our response has been to carefully analyse and redesign each dimension of pedagogic practice, using our knowledge about language, starting with the learning tasks of reading, writing and speaking in classroom interactions. We have analysed the structures and complexities of these learning tasks, as the genres and fields of schooling, and designed learning activities in which teachers can prepare all students to do each task successfully. We have closely analysed the structures of classroom interactions to show how teachers' initiating moves consistently enable some students to respond successfully but constrain others, and have redesigned exchanges to ensure that all students are able to successfully respond and benefit equally from elaborations. We have designed a metalanguage that can be built up through elaborations at the levels of classroom exchanges, lesson activities and programs. This knowledge about language thus becomes an explicit dimension of the knowledge projected by the school's pedagogic practice, replacing tacit learning of language by intuition (Figure 6.18).

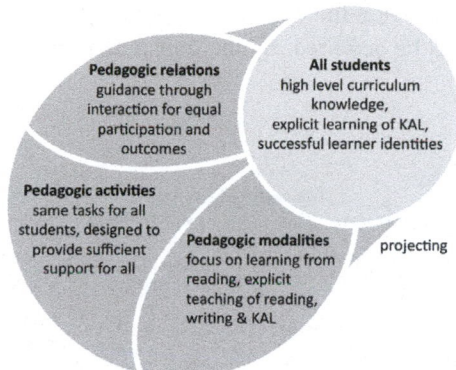

Figure 6.18: Genre pedagogy projects equality of knowledge and identities

Each dimension of design – of activities, relations, modalities and the knowledge they project – is informed by knowledge about language. Furthermore this KAL is provided to teachers as tools for designing both their own practice and the knowledge they provide to students. The outcomes for all students in Figure 6.18 – *high level curriculum knowledge and KAL, successful learner identities* – are not merely wishful thinking, they are consistent outcomes of genre pedagogy, illustrated by the data in Figures 6.21–6.22 below.

6.1.5   From theory to meta-theory

Taking a step up from theory to meta-theory, we can position the Sydney School literacy project in relation to alternative positions on pedagogic discourse, using Bernstein's analysis.[3] Bernstein compares pedagogic theories in a topology that we have adapted as Figure 6.19 below. He outlines the axes in the diagram as follows:

> The vertical dimension would indicate whether the theory of instruction privileged relations internal to the individual, where the focus would be *intra-individual*, or ... relations *between* social groups (inter-group). In the first case ... the theory would be concerned to explain the conditions for changes within the individual, whereas in the second the theory would be concerned to explain the conditions for changes in the relation between social groups. The horizontal dimension would indicate whether the theory articulated a pedagogic practice emphasising a logic of acquisition or ... a logic of transmission. In the case of a logic of acquisition ... the

---

[3] Cf. Alexander 2000 for an informative world tour of culture and pedagogy.

acquirer is active in regulating an *implicit* facilitating practice. In the case of a logic of transmission the emphasis is upon *explicit* effective ordering of the discourse to be acquired, by the transmitter (Bernstein 1990: 213-14).

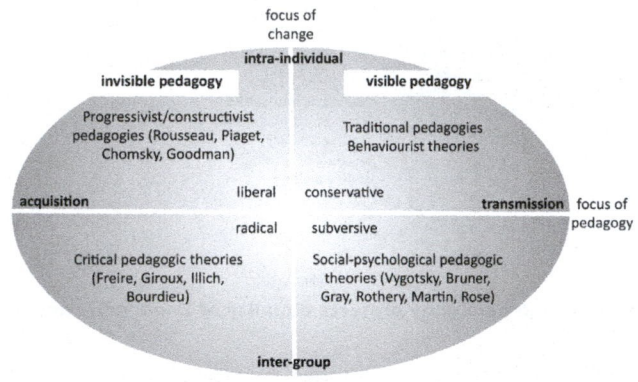

Figure 6.19: Types of pedagogy

Bernstein also comments,

It is a matter of interest that this top right-hand quadrant is regarded as conservative but has often produced very innovative and radical acquirers. The bottom right-hand quadrant shows a radical realization of an apparently conservative pedagogic practice ... each theory will carry its own conditions of contestation, 'resistance', subversion (1990: 73).[4]

As the matrix implies, our approach in the lower right-hand quadrant has always been both visible and interventionist, with a strong focus on the explicit transmission of knowledge about language with the aim of empowering otherwise disenfranchised groups.

Despite this pedagogic focus on transmission, our focus on guidance through interaction and our social semiotic perspective contrasts with the individual focus and cognitivist perspective of traditional and behaviourist pedagogies. Where critical pedagogic theories consider that empowerment lies with critiquing hegemonic discourses, our aim is rather to redistribute semiotic resources through literacy education. Our experience over the years with the consequences

---

[4] At the time of writing this comment, Bernstein was unaware of the Sydney School work; developing acquaintance is documented in Christie 1999. Alexander 2008 comments insightfully on the polarisation of pedagogies across the top half of the topology, especially in the English-speaking world.

for the most disadvantaged students of progressivist/constructivist pedagogies has led us to regard these approaches as socially irresponsible at best. Our observations and those of the teachers we have worked with are born out by Hattie's 2009 large scale meta-analysis of the outcomes of literacy teaching approaches. He found that 'The least effective methods [for teaching reading] are whole language' (2009: 140), and delivers a withering critique of constructivism's tenets.

> Constructivism too often is seen in terms of student-centred inquiry learning, problem based learning, and task-based learning and common jargon words include 'authentic', 'discovery' and 'intrinsically motivated learning'. The role of the constructivist teacher is claimed to be more of facilitation to provide opportunities for individual students to acquire knowledge and construct meaning through their own activities, and through discussion, reflection and the sharing of ideas with other learners with minimal corrective intervention (Cambourne 2003, Daniels 2001). These kinds of statements are almost directly opposite to the successful recipe of teaching and learning (2009: 26).

In contrast, Hattie's meta-analyses found that transmission-focused pedagogies are far more effective. The most effective methodology he identified includes seven key features:[5]

1. learning intentions … what specifically should the student be able to do, understand, care about;
2. success criteria of performance;
3. commitment and engagement in the learning task;
4. guides to how the teacher should present the lesson;
5. the notion of guided practice;
6. closure involves clarifying key points of a lesson, tying them together into a coherent whole;
7. independent practice once students have mastered the content or skill (2009: 205).

These criteria could equally well apply to the genre pedagogy we have described in this book, although without the knowledge about language that underpins genre pedagogy.

---

[5] This program *Direct Instruction* or *DISTAR* (Adams and Engelmann 1996), originated around the same time as genre writing pedagogy. Hattie did not include genre pedagogy in his meta-analysis.

Our focus on empowerment through guidance resonates with the position articulated by Mercer and his colleagues in Britain (1995, 2000), and Wells' neo-Vygotskyan perspective in the US (1999, 2002). However, these theories construe the problem differently in two respects. Firstly, their focus on classroom talk as the primary mode of learning backgrounds what we see as the central role of learning from reading in the school, and the role of writing in demonstrating what has been learnt. Secondly, they see the dominant role of the teacher as the significant problem with classroom discourse, for which the solution is to empower students to take more initiative, particularly by means of group discussion or so-called 'peer scaffolding' (a term we regard as oxymoronic). In his 1999 social constructivist manifesto, Wells completely elides the role of the teacher. In this respect, Wells' views appear to align more closely with the top-left quadrant in Bernstein's analysis.[6]

Bernstein (1990, 1996/2000) offers a sociological interpretation of the tensions between the positions in Figure 6.19. He associates traditional/behaviourist pedagogies with what he calls 'agents of production', that is, members of the old middle class whose economic base rests upon 'ownership/control over special-ized physical resources, although it would also include entrepreneurial profes-sional occupations such as lawyers, medical consultants, solicitors, accountants' (1990: 19). On the other hand, progressivist/constructivist pedagogies are asso-ciated with 'agents of symbolic control', members of the new middle class whose economic base lies in symbolic occupations such as administration, education, the arts and media. These fractions of the western middle class are in conflict over the control of education. With respect to school outcomes, the interests of the old middle class and working classes partly coincide in that the former want an educated workforce and the latter want better opportunities for their children. On the other hand, it is not necessarily in the interests of the new middle class to make their symbolic resources freely available to the whole of society – their children cannot, after all, directly inherit their power, but have to be apprenticed into the means to acquire it through education. Significantly, the economic interests of this fraction of the middle class are masked in a rhetoric of individual freedom and creativity. This is not a conscious conspiracy, but a product of a different form of consciousness associated with a different socioeconomic position. Accordingly, constructivism does not need evidence of effective outcomes to make its case; its visceral appeal lies in the rhetoric that Hattie cites above.

---

[6] To be fair, there are many places in Wells 1999 and 2002 where teacher-centred activities are acknowledged. Brophy 2002 provides a balanced overview of social constructivist teaching initiatives. Muller 2000 critiques the very disturbing supposedly 'progressive' implementation of social constructivist principles in South Africa after apartheid (see also Taylor et al. 2003).

6.2   Recontextualisation: a note on teacher education

6.2.1   Designing metapedagogy

Designing an effective classroom pedagogy is of little benefit unless there is a means of making it available to teachers. Genre pedagogy has evolved in partnership with teachers and teacher educators, in the context of continual professional learning programs. The pedagogy we have described in this book is a consequence of this partnership and is designed to be used in teacher professional learning, whether in pre-service training or in-service programs.

In this respect, genre pedagogy differs from many other learning theories, in that it is not merely *about* learning, but incorporates a detailed set of procedures for teaching. Where other theories expect teacher educators to recontextualise theory for teacher training, and then expect teachers to recontextualise it for their students, genre pedagogy involves both a theory and its recontextualisation as practice. This characteristic of the theory is a consequence of its purpose. It is not designed merely as a theory for describing educational practice, or for prescribing what should and should not be done in schools. Rather, its purpose is to effect change for social justice, and that change can only be achieved by teachers.

In this concluding section, we present a brief overview of the strategies for teacher education that have evolved in tandem with genre pedagogy. The first principle is that training is delivered in tandem with classroom practice. This is critical, as the methodology only really makes sense to teachers when they deliver it in the classroom. The body of new knowledge about pedagogy and language in the program is simply more than trainee teachers can be expected to comprehend, interpret, remember and apply months or years after being exposed to it in a pre-service training program.

This is, of course, a general issue for pre-service teacher education. In our work with practising teachers, we are often told that they learnt most of their practice on the job, and that most of what they learnt in training was not relevant to the issues they face in the classroom. The distance between the academic lecture hall and the school classroom is one drawback of the professionalisation of teaching that we touched on in Chapter 1. Nuthall confirms this experience with large-scale data on teachers' practice:

> Compelling evidence indicates a continuing gap between research on effective teaching and the practice of teaching ... Research is often seen by teachers as too theoretical, too idealistic, or too general to relate directly to the practical realities of classroom life ... They evaluate research by finding out if its recommendations can be effectively adapted to their own classrooms ... Most teachers are convinced that they develop their teaching skill or craft knowledge through their experiences in the

classroom … The dominant influences during their early development as teachers are the practices they see other teachers using or that they experienced themselves as students … (2004: 273-4).

6.2.2   Four phases of professional learning

For these reasons, one of the aims of genre pedagogy is to integrate academic learning of pedagogic and linguistic theory with the classroom practice through which it is applied. To this end, four elements of the R2L teacher professional learning program are (i) knowledge about language and pedagogy, (ii) lesson planning, (iii) classroom implementation, and (iv) assessment of students' growth. Knowledge about pedagogy and language are built up in steps, with each step followed by application in the classroom and student assessment (Figure 6.20).

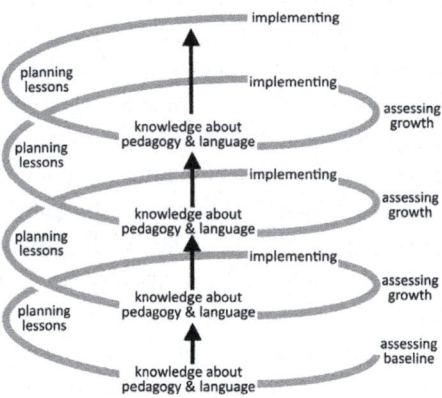

Figure 6.20: Spiral curriculum of teacher training in genre pedagogy

In the first phase of the professional learning program, seven elements of the methodology are introduced in the following sequence:

1. the model of pedagogy, including the principle of supporting all students to do high-level tasks by means of guidance through interaction, and the model of learning activities as cycles of Prepare-Task-Elaborate;
2. the model of language as a hierarchy of patterns, from the context to the text, paragraphs, sentences, word groups, words and sound/letter patterns, and the principle of teaching the language task in an integrated sequence from the context down;

3. the three levels of support provided by (i) Preparing for Reading and Joint Construction, (ii) Detailed Reading and Rewriting, (iii) Sentence Making, Spelling and Sentence Writing;
4. the set of genres students learn to read and write in school, their purposes, stages and phases;
5. the level of texts that students should be reading at each year level;
6. principles of text selection, analysis and lesson planning to integrate reading and writing with curriculum teaching;
7. the writing assessment tool for assessing students' growth.

Teachers are guided to practise Preparing for Reading and Joint Construction using model texts, including stories and factual texts, along the lines described in Chapters 2 and 4 above. They are then guided to identify examples of each of the genres presented in Figure 6.13 above, and to analyse their stages and phases. They apply these analyses to texts of their own that they have selected from their teaching programs, and write lesson plans including the genre, purpose, year level, preparation for reading, and sample comprehension questions at literal, inferential and interpretive levels.

The final step in this phase of the program is the writing assessment tool. The R2L assessment is designed to identify the language resources that students bring to each writing task, and measure them against expected writing standards at each school year level. It includes 14 criteria, with teacher questions summarised in Table 6.2.

Table 6.2: Writing assessment criteria

CONTEXT	[Quick judgements are made about these context criteria.]
Purpose	*How appropriate and well-developed is the genre for the writing purpose?*
Staging	*Does it go through appropriate stages, and how well is each stage developed?*
Phases	*How well organised is the sequence of phases in the text?*
Field	*How well does the writer understand and explain the field in factual texts, construct the plot, settings and characters in stories, or describe the issues in arguments?*
Tenor	*How well does the writer engage the reader in stories, persuade in arguments, or objectively inform in factual texts?*
Mode	*How highly written is the language for the school stage? Is it too spoken?*
DISCOURSE	[Discourse criteria are marked in the text, to give an accurate measure.]
Ideation	*What are the writer's lexical resources? How well is lexis used to construct the field?*
Appraisal	*What are the writer's appraisal resources? How well is appraisal used to engage, persuade, evaluate?*
Conjunction	*Is there a clear logical relation between all sentences?*
Identification	*Is it clear who or what is referred to in each sentence?*

GRAMMAR AND GRAPHIC FEATURES [Grammar features are judged overall rather than one-by-one.]

Grammar *Is there an appropriate variety of sentence and word group structures for the school stage? Are the grammatical conventions of written English used accurately?*

Spelling *How accurately spelt are core words and non-core words?*

Punctuation *How appropriately and accurately is punctuation used?*

Presentation *Are paragraphs used? How legible is the writing? Is the layout clear? Are illustrations/diagrams used appropriately?*

Students' writing samples are compared with analysed writing exemplars at each school year level, and each criterion is given a score from 0 to 3 against the standard in the exemplar. For example, the following Year 6 science report [6.1] is assessed with teachers' comments in Table 6.3. Its total score of 37 out of a possible 42 places this student at the top standard for upper primary.

[6.1] Year 6 science report

How do we breath

The respiritory system is made up of three importants organs that are the nose, trachea and lungs. The exchange of gases (oxygen and carbon dioxide), wich are nesessary for us to survive are enabled by this system.

Breathing is controlled by the brain. It provides messages by transmiting them through the nerves in the spinal cord to the intercostal muscles they are located between the ribs and the diaphramm please finish.

Air is first brought into the body by the nose or mouth. It then goes in the throat (The pharnx) then through to the voice box (The larynx). The voice box has a cover called the epiglottis.

When a breath is taken the cover opens food is keep out but/ air can go down to the trachia.

After the air passes down the trachea it goes into the lungs down either side of the bronchus, passing by the bronchus and then into small air sacs. They are called alveoli. These air sacs are covered in blood vessels which are called capillaries. From here the oxygen is finally taken into the blood stream and carbon dioxide comes back to the lungs.

Your intercostal muscles push the rib cage inward. So then your pressure rises pushing forces your carbon dioxide out the lungs.

Table 6.3: Assessment of science report [6.1]

PURPOSE	explain breathing - good explanation	3
STAGING	detailed Explanation but no statement of Phenomenon to be explained	2
PHASES	clear logical sequence of phases, marked by paragraphs	3
FIELD	detailed technical knowledge of breathing for this stage	3
TENOR	objective, with some personal *your intercostal muscles*, *your pressure*	2
MODE	highly technical	3
LEXIS	excellent technical lexis for this stage, with nominalisations *The exchange of gases*	3
APPRAISAL	objective, with some scientific appraisal *important*, *necessary*	3
CONJUNCTION	clear logical sequences, with varieties of causal verbs *enabled*, *controlled*, *provides*, *located*, *transmitting*	3
REFERENCE	clear reference with scientific reference *the brain*, *the nerves*, *the spinal cord*	3
GRAMMAR	no grammar problems, manages grammatical metaphor	3
SPELLING	accurate spelling with some problems	2
PUNCTUATION	a few punctuation problems	2
PRESENTATION	paragraphing, weak handwriting	2
Total		37

Language resources in other students' writing in this school stage can be measured against this standard. Assessments are conducted each term (four times a year), which gives teachers a very accurate picture of each students' growth through the year, overall and in terms of each language criterion in the assessment. Applied to the whole class, it also gives teachers an accurate picture of their own success in narrowing the gap between top and bottom students in the class.

A further benefit of introducing the writing assessment in the first phase of professional training is that it enables teachers to practise analysing texts using the discourse analysis tools we have described in this book. At this stage, their application of these tools is rudimentary, but for many teachers it is the first time they have ever analysed language, and the first time for virtually all teachers using the SFL model of text-in-context. Applying it to their own students' writing, and seeing the clear picture of students' language resources that it illuminates, is a powerful entry point to the metalanguage built up in the program. Text [6.2] is a sample teachers' analysis of a student narrative, with lexical and appraisal words underlined, and conjunctions and reference words circled.

[6.2] Teacher's analysis of student writing

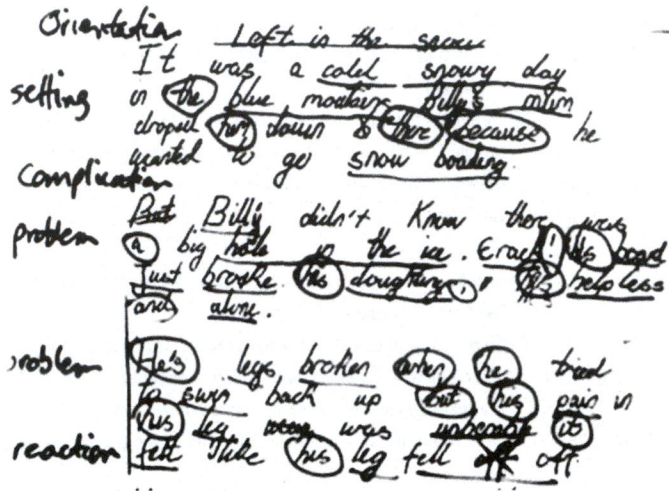

In addition to the benefits for individual teachers and students, applying this assessment across classes and schools gives education systems an accurate measure of their students' growth. The quantitative scoring affords comparison of growth rates using genre pedagogy, with standard average growth rates. For example, the charts in Figures 6.21 and 6.22 compare assessment scores before and after teachers were trained in R2L in 80 NSW schools in 2010 (Rose 2011c).[7] The charts show the gap between low, middle and high achieving student groups in Kindergarten and in junior, middle and upper primary and junior secondary school stages. Figure 6.21 shows the average 'Pre' scores for each student group and school stage in Term 1, before R2L teaching. Figure 6.21 shows the average 'Post' scores for each student group and school stage, after three terms of R2L teaching.

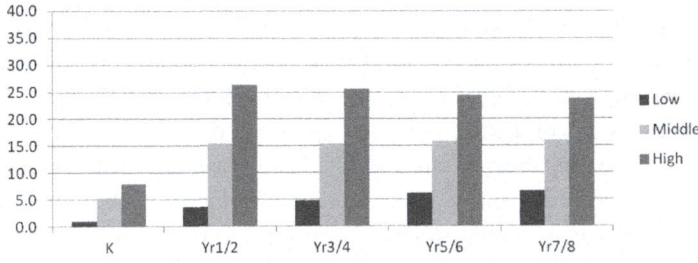

Figure 6.21: Pre scores before R2L teaching

---

[7] The assessments were from a cohort of around 400 teachers, representing 8–12,000 students.

In Pre scores, the gap between low and high achieving students at the start of Kindergarten is 16% of the total possible score (i.e. 42). By the start of Yr1/2, average scores have risen by 25% of the total, but the gap between low and high students has tripled to over 50% – the high group has gone up but the low group is still near zero. This gap then continues throughout the years, decreasing slowly. The low group improves very slowly from Yr1/2 to Yr7/8, the middle group remains steady, and the high group falls slightly.

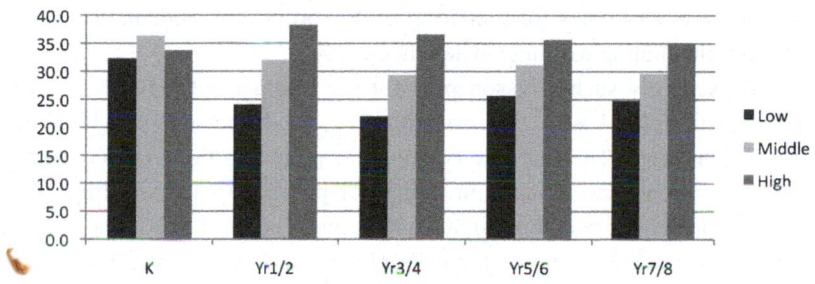

Figure 6.22: Post scores after R2L teaching

In Post scores, average growth in Kindergarten is 70% above Pre scores, and the gap between low and high achieving groups is reduced to 9%.[8] In the other year levels, growth is 30–40% above the Pre scores (double the standard growth rate), and the gap is reduced to 20–30%. These results are consistent with a series of published evaluations over the years, which show growth of all students from all backgrounds and ability levels, at an average double to four times standard growth rates (Culican 2006, McCrae et al. 2000, Rose et al. 2008). For teachers, schools and students these results are a powerful motivator for sustaining the changes in practice wrought by genre pedagogy.

Following this first phase of training, teachers implement the strategies of Preparing for Reading and Joint Construction in their classes and assess their students' writing growth. Their experience with analysing texts for lesson planning, and with using guided interaction to teach reading and writing, as well as improvements in students' results, prepares teachers for the next phase of training focused on Detailed Reading and Rewriting. These strategies are more challenging for teachers, as they involve significant changes in the way they interact with their classes, using very detailed lesson plans. The starting point is to analyse samples of classroom discourse, using the categories described in Chapters 4 and 5. These analyses bring teachers' intuitive classroom practice to

---

[8] That the gap in Kindergarten is halved with R2L, but tripled with standard early years practices, supports Bernstein's (1996) and Nuthall's (2005) assertions that failure is more a consequence of ineffective teaching than anything innate within children.

consciousness, enabling them to see and name their components in detail, as a basis for redesigning their practice.

Detailed Reading lesson plans are written on short passages of text, of the kinds illustrated in Chapter 4. Teachers first select text passages that display features which they want their students to read with detailed comprehension, and which they can use in their writing tasks. The lesson plans include five elements: (i) an analysis of the phases the passage goes through, (ii) the wordings marked that students will identify in the lesson, (iii) notes for preparing each sentence before reading it, (iv) notes for preparing each wording for students to identify, (v) notes for elaborating wordings where necessary.

We can exemplify such a lesson plan for the fragment of Detailed Reading illustrated in Chapter 4 with *Fantastic Mr Fox*. In the lesson plan [6.3] each sentence is numbered. The first line is a note for preparing the sentence, with its number. The second line is notes in italics for preparing each wording. These notes are written above each highlighting wording. The third line is the sentence itself. Under the sentence, notes for elaborating wordings are written with dot points. Question marks indicate opportunities for elaborating discussion.

[6.3] Detailed Reading lesson plan for *Fantastic Mr Fox*

setting - Mr Fox comes out of his hole	
1 how carefully Mr Fox came out of his hole	- Sentence preparation
how moved how far three little dots - kept going	- Preparations for wordings
1 He crept a little further out of the hole . . . then further still.	- Sentence (wordings highlighted)
• *creeping = very slowly, keeping low*	- Elaborations
• *further still = crept even more, dots = time passing*	
2 almost right out of his hole	- Sentence preparation
how far out outside	- Preparations for wordings
2 He was almost right out in the open now.	- Sentence
• *what part still in the hole?*	- Elaborations
• *open = outdoors, nowhere to hide, how would he feel?*	
3 checks for danger	- Sentence preparation
kind of look	- Preparations for wordings
3 He took a last careful look around.	- Sentence
• *Why a last look?*	- Elaborations
4-5 what he sees	- Sentence preparation
two qualities of the wood	- Preparations for wordings
4 The wood was murky and very still.	- Sentence
• *murky = dark, see a little but not much*	- Elaborations
5 there was some light from the moon	- Sentence preparation
where shining what doing	- Preparations for wordings
5 Somewhere in the sky the moon was shining.	- Sentence
• *somewhere in the sky = couldn't see it*	- Elaborations
• *how would he know the moon was shining?*	

In the actual lesson, these brief notes expand into the kinds of complex exchanges illustrated in Chapter 4. Such detailed lesson planning involves very careful reading of the text, to identify wordings that need highlighting and discussing, and their relation to the contexts of the sentence and the text. Each of these elements must also be thought through in relation to the learning needs of the students, and how they will be discussed in the Detailed Reading lesson. Lesson planning proceeds by (i) identifying the wordings for students to identify, followed by (ii) decisions about appropriate preparation cues that will enable them to identify each wording, and (iii) elaborations that are required to deepen their comprehension of the wording, the context or the type of language feature. This close reading of the sentence enables teachers to see just what the sentence means in its context, and so to (iv) write a note for sentence preparation. (This planning sequence is not the same as the sequence in which the lesson is delivered.)

This kind of analysis gives teachers instant insight into the complexity and language demands of texts their students are expected to read, and the need for meticulous guidance for students to comprehend and use this language effectively. As the planning and use of such detailed plans for classroom exchanges is so different from ordinary teaching practice, teachers are guided in the training to practise with a shared text, before writing and practising on their own texts with partners. Furthermore, as Rewriting after Detailed Reading is also a complex activity in the classroom, teachers practice Joint Rewriting with guidance on the shared text, and then on their own texts.

Also in this second phase of training, teachers plan and practise Sentence Making, Spelling and Sentence Writing. They are first guided to make cardboard sentence strips, and cut them up using planned preparation cues, then to select words for spelling and cut them up into their letter patterns. They are then guided to practise these activities with one or two children each in a primary school classroom. All teachers report that guiding children through these intensive strategies, until they can read, spell and write the sentences successfully, is one of the most powerful experiences of the whole training program. The insight it gives them into the learning processes of individual children has a profound influence on their practice with their whole classes.

Following this phase of training, teachers plan and implement Detailed Reading and Rewriting on a series of texts in their curriculum programs, along with Preparing for Reading and Joint Construction, plus the intensive strategies in the primary school. A planning proforma is negotiated, which in the primary school includes a Joint Construction each week, which prepares students for an independent writing task every two to three weeks. Each day, a text is prepared and read with the class, and a short passage selected for Detailed Reading and Rewriting, and then one or more sentences for the intensive strategies. This daily detailed work develops a bank of language resources and information that feeds into the weekly Joint Construction, and then into students' independent writing tasks. In secondary school subjects, with much less available class time, teachers plan a Joint Construction every three to four weeks, with Detailed Reading and Rewriting once or twice a week. In the first year of school, teachers focus on Shared Book Reading, and Sentence Making, Spelling and Sentence Writing, in order to build up children's foundation literacy skills. They may plan to do a Joint Rewrite once a week, leading up to children doing Individual Rewrites every two to three weeks, until they are have enough language resources and experience to tackle larger texts in Joint Construction.

These lesson sequences are presented as a set of sequencing options in Figure 6.23. Within each cycle there is a sequence of activities, and arrows show options for programming sequences from level to level. However, Preparing for Reading is always the starting point, and the goal is Joint and Individual Construction, leading to independent writing. (Note that the direction of the middle cycle is reversed in order to simplify the diagram sequence from level to level.)

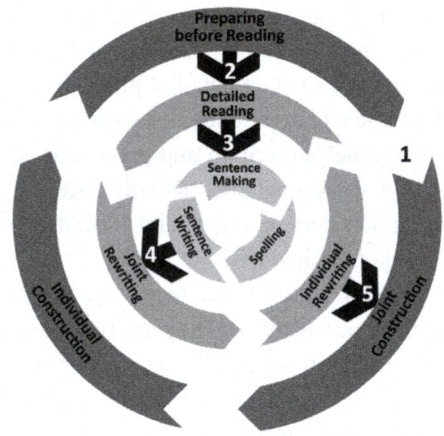

Figure 6.23: Sequencing options for teaching-learning cycles

Analysing, planning and implementing a series of reading and writing lessons with this degree of detail gives teachers a strong foundation for the third phase of training, in which detailed knowledge about language is introduced, starting with grammar. Teachers are guided through the series of analysis activities that we presented in §5.2. Each activity involves a brief preparation of the grammar system under focus, followed by guided and independent analysis of text examples, which is then elaborated with further discussion about the grammar system. This approach is an ideal illustration of the spiral curriculum approach, as each cycle of Prepare-Task-Elaborate builds on preceding cycles, towards full control of the pedagogic metalanguage. The end point is for teachers to understand the processes of grammatical metaphor and conceptualise how they can teach it in their classrooms, along with the other grammar systems that have been built up through the training session. Teachers then apply what they have learnt about grammar to analysing texts of their own, and then plan further Detailed Reading lessons that incorporate this knowledge about language. The fourth phase of training then repeats these activities with the discourse systems laid out in §5.3.

Each phase of training revisits activities with text analysis, lesson planning and writing assessment, as teachers apply their classroom experience and the new resources that are added in each training phase. The principle of guided repetition is thus applied in the teacher education program as it is in the classroom methodology. In each revisiting, learners apply their growing competence to new texts, new teaching strategies and language systems.

6.3   Envoi

One of the ideas we have returned to several times through this book is the concept of a macrogenre, including complexes of genres such as textbooks, novels or websites, and the sequences of lessons that Christie (1999, 2002) describes as a curriculum macrogenre. Such longer texts have complex social purposes, within an overall goal that takes multiple genres to accomplish. Of course, this book is also a macrogenre, and our purposes have been no less complex. We wanted to frame the Sydney School research in the social context of its development, so we began with historical recounts in Chapters 1, 2, 3 and 4. We wanted to describe the knowledge about language in school that has emerged from the research, so we included a series of reports that classified and described the written genres of school (Chapter 2), the language of disciplines (Chapter 3), and systems of grammar and discourse for teachers' KAL (Chapter 5). We wanted to provide a guide for teachers and teacher educators to use the knowledge about pedagogy accumulated in the research, so we recounted procedures for writing genres (Chapter 2), for reading and writing different genres at each stage of school (Chapter 4), and for training teachers in the pedagogy (Chapter 6). And we wanted to distil this accumulated knowledge about language and pedagogy within a theoretical framework, so we summarised it as a multimodal report describing the components of pedagogic practice, in §6.1 above.

But our overarching purpose is neither history, description nor procedure; it is justice. Each component of this book, and of the Sydney School project it outlines, is aimed towards this goal, so the genre we conclude with is an argument. To begin we will let Bernstein state the Thesis, with more wisdom and eloquence than we can claim:

> Education is central to the knowledge base of society, groups and individuals. Yet education also, like health, is a public institution, central to the production and reproduction of distributive injustices. Biases in the

form, content, access and opportunities of education have consequences not only for the economy; these biases can reach down to drain the very springs of affirmation, motivation and imagination. In this way such biases can become, and often are, an economic and cultural threat to democracy. Education can have a crucial role in creating tomorrow's optimism in the context of today's pessimism. But if it is to do this then we must have an analysis of the social biases in education. These biases lie deep within the very structure of the educational system's processes of transmission and acquisition and their social assumptions (Bernstein 1996: 5).

Our commitment and belief in the potential of education for achieving social justice flows not only from our ideals, but from our work and personal relations with those who live the consequences of education's social biases, including families, their children and teachers. To imagine schools that give every child the same opportunities instead of reproducing the inequalities of the past, we have had to penetrate deep into their processes of transmission and acquisition, to give teachers the resources to redesign their practice. Bernstein goes on to propose 'three interrelated rights' that we need to institutionalise in schools if we are serious about democracy, culture and education:

The first right is the right to individual enhancement. I want to suggest that this right is the condition for *confidence* ... and operates at an individual level. The second right is the right to be included, socially, intellectually, culturally and personally ... Inclusion is a condition for *communitas* and this right operates at the level of the social. The third right is the right to participate ... Participation is the condition for *civic practice*, and operates at the level of politics (1996: 5).

We have tried to show how genre pedagogy can raise the confidence of each student by enhancing their skills in reading and writing, and thus their capacity for learning in school, at least to the standard expected of their school stage. In doing so the pedagogy carefully and deliberately reconfigures the community of the classroom so that every student is equally included in the learning conversation, and not in groups of high or low achievement. Belonging equally in the school's community of learners is a necessary foundation for participation in the civic practice of the school, as we illustrated with the primary students' civic campaigns in Chapter 2. But beyond the school, it is the knowledge and identity as successful learners, which genre pedagogy affords to each student, that we hope will give them the resources to participate on a more equal footing in the society we would like to imagine for the future.

References

Acevedo, C. 2010 *Will the Implementation of Reading to Learn in Stockholm Schools Accelerate Literacy Learning for Disadvantaged Students and Close the Achievement Gap?* Stockholm: Multilingual Research Institute

Adams, M. J. 1990 *Beginning to Read: Thinking and Learning about Print: A Summary*. Urbana-Champaign: University of Illinois

Adams, G. L. and S. Engelmann 1996 *Research on Direct Instruction: 20 Years beyond DISTAR*. Seattle, WA: Educational Achievement Systems.

Alexander, R. 2000 *Culture and Pedagogy: International Comparisons in Primary Education*. Oxford: Blackwell

Alexander, R. 2008 Beyond dichotomous teaching. In R. Alexander *Essays on Pedagogy*. London: Routledge, 72-91.

Applebee, A. M. and J. Langer 1983 Instructional scaffolding: reading and writing as natural language activities. *Language Arts* 60.2: 168-75.

Australian Bureau of Statistics 1994, 2004. *Australian Social Trends 1994 and 2004: Education – National summary tables*. Canberra: Australian Bureau of Statistics, www.abs.gov.au/ausstats.

Axford, B., P. Harders and F. Wise 2009 *Scaffolding Literacy: An Integrated and Sequential Approach to Teaching Reading, Spelling and Writing*. Camberwell, Victoria: ACER.

Bakhtin, M. M. 1986 The problem of speech genres. In M. M. Bakhtin *Speech Genres and Other Late Essays* [translated by V McGee]. Austin: University of Texas Press, 60-102.

Bernstein, B. 1971 *Class, Codes and Control*. I. *Theoretical Studies towards a Sociology of Language*. London: Routledge and Kegan Paul (Primary Socialisation, Language and Education) [republished with an Appendix added by Palladin, 1974].

Bernstein, B. (ed.) 1973 *Class, Codes and Control*. II. *Applied Studies towards a Sociology of Language*. London: Routledge and Kegan Paul (Primary Socialisation, Language and Education).

Bernstein, B. 1975 *Class, Codes and Control*. III. *Towards a Theory of Educational Transmissions*. London: Routledge and Kegan Paul (Primary Socialisation, Language and Education).

Bernstein, B. 1979 The new pedagogy: sequencing. In J. Manning-Keepes and B. D. Keepes (eds.) *Language in Education: The LDP Phase 1*. Canberra: Curriculum Development Centre, 293-302.

Bernstein, B. 1990 *Class, Codes and Control*. IV. *The Structuring of Pedagogic Discourse*. London: Routledge.

Bernstein, B. 1996 *Pedagogy, Symbolic Control and Identity: Theory, Research, Critique*. London: Taylor and Francis [rev. edn 2000].

Berry, M. 1981 Systemic linguistics and discourse analysis: a multi-layered approach to exchange structure. In M. Coultard and M. Montgomery (eds.) *Studies in Discourse Analysis*. London: Routledge and Kegan Paul, 120-45.

Britton, J. 1970 *Language and Learning*. London: Pelican.

Brophy, J. (ed.) 2002 *Social Constructivist Teaching: Affordances and Constraints*. London: Elsevier (JAI: Advances in Research on Teaching 9).

Bruner, J. S. 1986 *Actual Minds, Possible Worlds*. Cambridge, MA: Harvard University Press.

Callow, J. 1996 *The Action Pack: Environment (Activities for Teaching Factual Writing)*. Sydney: Metropolitan East DSP (Language and Social Power Project).

Callow, J. (ed.) 1999 *Image Matters: Visual Texts in the Classroom*. Marrickville, NSW: Primary English Teaching Association.

Cambourne, B. 2003 Taking a naturalistic viewpoint in early childhood literacy research. In N. Hall, J. Larson and J. Marsh (eds.) *Handbook of Early Child Literacy*. London: Sage, 411-23.

Chen, J. 2010 *Sydney School Genre-based Literacy Approach to EAP Writing in China*. PhD Thesis, Department of Lingusitics, University of Sydney and School of Foreign languages, Sun Yat Sen University.

Childs, M. 2008 *A Reading Based Theory of Teaching Appropriate for the South African Context*. PhD Thesis, Nelson Mandela Metropolitan University, Port Elizabeth, South Africa

Christie, F. 1993 The 'received tradition' of English teaching: the decline of rhetoric and the corruption of grammar. In Bill Green (ed.) *The Insistence of the Letter: Literary Studies and Curriculum Theorizing*. London: Falmer Press, 75-106.

Christie, F. 1995 Pedagogic discourse in the primary school. *Linguistics and Education* 3.7: 221-42.

Christie, F. (ed.) 1999 *Pedagogy and the Shaping of Consciousness: Linguistic and Social Processes*. London: Cassell (Open Linguistics Series).

Christie, F. 2002 *Classroom Discourse Analysis*. London: Continuum.

Christie, F., B. Gray, P. Gray, M. Macken, J. R. Martin and J. Rothery 1992 *Exploring Explanations: Teachers Book (Levels 1–4)*. Sydney: Harcourt Brace Jovanovich (HBJ Language: a resource for meaning).

Christie, F. and M. Macken-Horarik 2007 School English: what kind of knowledge? In F. Christie and J. R. Martin (eds.) *Language, Knowledge And Pedagogy: Functional Linguistic and Sociological Perspectives*. London: Continuum, 156-83.

Christie, F. and M. Macken-Horarik (2011) Disciplinarity and the case of school subject English. In F. Christie and K. Maton (eds.) *Disciplinarity: Functional Linguistic and Sociological Perspectives*. London: Continuum, 175-96.

Christie, F. and J. R. Martin (eds.) 1997 *Genre and Institutions: Social Processes in the Workplace and School*. London: Cassell.

Christie, F. and J. R. Martin (eds.) 2007 *Language, Knowledge and Pedagogy: Functional Linguistic and Sociological Perspectives*. London: Cassell.

Coe, R., L. Lingard and T. Teslenko (eds.) 2002 *The Rhetoric and Ideology of Genre: Strategies for Stability and Change*. Cresskill, NJ: Hampton Press.

Coffin, C. 1996 *Exploring Literacy in School History*. Sydney: Metropolitan East Disadvantaged Schools Program.

Coffin, C. 1997 Constructing and giving value to the past: an investigation into secondary school history. In F. Christie and J. R. Martin (eds.) *Language, Knowledge and Pedagogy: Functional Linguistic and Sociological Perspectives*. London: Cassell, 196-230.

Coffin, C. 2000 Defending and challenging interpretations of the past. *Revista Canaria de Estudios Ingleses* 40: 135-54.

Coffin, C. 2003 Reconstruals of the past – settlement or invasion? The role of judgment analysis. In J. R. Martin and R. Wodak (eds.) *Re/Reading the Past: Critical and Functional Perspectives on Discourses of History*. Amsterdam: Benjamins, 219-46.

Coffin, C. 2006 *Historical Discourse: The Language of Time, Cause and Evaluation*. London: Continuum.

Coffin, C., J. Donohue and S. North 2009 *Exploring English Grammar: From Formal to Functional*. London: Routledge.

Coffin, C., A. Hewings and K. O'Halloran (eds.) 2004 *Applying English Grammar: Functional and Corpus Approaches*. London: Arnold.

Colombi, C. and M. Schleppegrell (eds.) 2002 *Developing Advanced Literacy in First and Second Languages*. Mahwah, NJ: Erlbaum, 87-118.

Condon, C. 1987 *The Making of the Modern World*. South Melbourne: Macmillan.

Cope, W. and M. Kalantzis (eds.) 1993 *The Powers of Literacy: A Genre Approach to Teaching Literacy*. London: Falmer (Critical Perspectives on Literacy and Education) and Pittsburg: University of Pittsburg Press (Pittsburg Series in Composition, Literacy, and Culture).

Cranny-Francis, A. and J. R. Martin 1993 Making new meanings: literary and linguistic perspectives on the function of genre in textual practice. *English in Australia* 105: 30-44.

Cranny-Francis, A. and J. R. Martin 1994 In/visible education: class, gender and pedagogy in Educating Rita and Dead Poets Society. *Interpretations: Journal of the English Teachers' Association of Western Australia* 27.1: 28-57.

Cranny-Francis, A. and J. R. Martin 1995 Writings/readings: how to know a genre. *Interpretations: Journal of the English Teachers' Association of Western Australia* 28.3: 1-32.

Culican, S. 2006 Learning to read: *Reading to Learn*, a middle years literacy intervention research project, final report 2003-4. Catholic Education Office, Melbourne. http://www.cecv.melb.catholic.edu.au/ResearchandSeminarPapers

Culican, S. 2007 *Scaffolding Pedagogic Change in Middle Years Literacy*. PhD Thesis, Deakin University, Melbourne.

Dahl, R. 2007. *Fantastic Mr Fox*. London: Puffin Books.

Dennett, B. and S. Dixon 2003 *Key Features of Modern History* (2nd edn). Melbourne: Oxford University Press.

Derewianka, B. 1991 *Exploring How Texts Work*. Sydney: Primary English Teaching Association.

Disadvantaged Schools Program 1988 *Teaching Factual Writing: A Genre Based Approach*. Sydney: Disadvantaged Schools Program.

Disadvantaged Schools Program 1989 *The Report Genre*. Sydney: Disadvantaged Schools Program.

Eggins, S., J. R. Martin and P. Wignell 1993 The discourse of history: distancing the recoverable past. In M. Ghadessy (ed.) *Register Analysis: Theory and Practice*. London: Pinter (Open Linguistics Series), 75-109.

Fairclough, N. (ed.) 1992 *Critical Language Awareness*. London: Longman (Real Language Series).

Folds, R. 1987 *Whitefella School: Education and Aboriginal Resistance*. Sydney: Allen and Unwin

Freebody, P., and A. Luke 1990 Literacies programs: debates and demands in cultural context. *Prospect: Australian Journal of TESOL* 5.7: 7-16.

Freedman, A. and P. Medway (eds.) 1994a *Learning and Teaching Genre*. Portsmouth, NH: Boynton/Cook.

Freedman, A. and P. Medway (eds.) 1994b *Genre and the New Rhetoric*. London: Taylor and Francis (Critical Perspectives on Literacy and Education).

Gee, J. 2005 *An Introduction to Discourse Analysis*. London: Routledge.

Gibbons, P. 2002 *Scaffolding Language, Scaffolding Learning: Teaching Second Language Learners in the Mainstream Classroom*. Portsmouth, NH: Heinemann.

Gibbons, P. 2006 *Bridging Discourse in the ESL Classroom: Students, Teachers and Researchers*. London: Continuum.

Gibbons, P. 2009 *English Learners Academic Literacy and Thinking: Learning in the Challenge Zone*. Portsmouth, NH: Heinemann.

Glendinning, E. H. 1980 *English in Electrical Engineering and Electronics*. London: Oxford University Press (English in Focus).

Goodman, K. 1986 *What's Whole in Whole Language*. Portsmouth, NH: Heinemann.

Graves, D. 1983 *Writing: Teachers and Children at Work*. London: Heinemann.

Gray, B. 1986 Aboriginal education: some implications of genre for literacy development. In C. Painter and J. R. Martin (eds.) *Writing to Mean: Teaching Genres across the Curriculum*. Applied Linguistics Association of Australia (Occasional Papers 9): 188-208.

Gray, B. 1987 How natural is 'natural' language teaching: employing wholistic methodology in the classroom. *Australian Journal of Early Childhood* 12.4: 3-19.

Gray, B. 1990 Natural language learning in Aboriginal classrooms: reflections on teaching and learning. In C. Walton and W. Eggington (eds.) *Language: Maintenance, Power and Education in Australian Aboriginal Contexts*. Darwin: Northern Territory University Press, 105-39.

Gray, B., D. Rose and W. Cowey 1998 *Project Report for Scaffolding Reading and Writing for Indigenous Children in School, December 1998*. Canberra: DEST Indigenous Education Branch and University of Canberra.

Green, B. and A. Lee 1994 Writing geography lessons: literacy, identity and schooling. In A. Freedman and P. Medway (eds.) *Learning and Teaching Genre*. Portsmouth, NH: Boynton/Cook, 207-24.

Gregory, M. 1967 Aspects of varieties differentiation. *Journal of Linguistics* 3: 177-98.

Gregory, M. and S. Carroll 1978 *Language and Situation: Language Varieties and their Social Contexts*. London: Routledge and Kegan Paul.

Haire, M., E. Kennedy, G. Lofts and M. J. Evergreen 2004 *Core Science*. I. *Stage 4*. Sydney: Jacaranda.

Halliday, M. A. K. 1975 *Learning how to Mean: Explorations in the Development of Language*. London: Edward Arnold (Explorations in Language Study).

Halliday, M. A. K. 1977 Ideas about language. In M. A. K. Halliday *Aims and Perspectives in Linguistics*. Applied Linguistics Association of Australia (Occasional Papers 1): 32-49 [reprinted in J. Webster (ed.) *The Collected Works of M. A. K. Halliday*. III. *On Language and Linguistics*. London: Continuum, 2003: 92-115].

Halliday, M. A. K. 1978 *Language as a Social Semiotic: The Social Interpretation of Language and Meaning*. London: Edward Arnold.

Halliday, M. A. K. 1993 Towards a language-based theory of learning. *Linguistics and Education* 5.2: 93-116 [reprinted in Halliday 2003: 327-52].

Halliday, M. A. K. 1994 *An Introduction to Functional Grammar* (2nd edn). London: Edward Arnold [1st edn 1985, 3rd edn with C. M. I. M. Matthiessen 2004].

Halliday, M. A. K. 2003 *The Collected Works of M. A. K. Halliday*. IV. *The Language of Early Childhood*. London: Continuum.

Halliday, M. A. K. 2004 *The Collected Works of M. A. K. Halliday*. V. *The Language of Science* (ed. J. Webster). London: Continuum.

Halliday, M. A. K. and W. S. Greaves 2008 *Intonation in the Grammar of English*. London: Equinox.

Halliday M. A. K. and R. Hasan 1976 *Cohesion in English*. London: Longman (English Language Series 9).

Halliday, M. A. K. and J. R. Martin 1993 *Writing Science: Literacy and Discursive Power*. London: Falmer (Critical Perspectives on Literacy and Education).

Hammond, J. (ed.) 2001 *Scaffolding: Teaching and Learning in Language and Literacy Education*. Sydney: Primary English teaching Association (PETA).

Hasan, R. 2005 *The Collected Works of Ruqaiya Hasan*. I. *Language, Society and Consciousness* (ed. Jonathon Webster). London: Equinox.

Hasan, R. 2009 *The Collected Works of Ruqaiya Hasan*. II. *Semantic Variation: Meaning in Society and Sociolinguistics* (ed. Jonathon Webster). London: Equinox.

Hasan, R. and J. R. Martin (eds.) 1989 *Language Development: Learning Language, Learning Culture*. Norwood, NJ: Ablex.

Hasan, R., C. M. I. M. Matthiessen and J. Webster (eds.) 2005 *Continuing Discourse on Language: A Functional Perspective*. Vol. 1. London: Equinox.

Hasan, R. and G. Williams (eds.) 1996 *Literacy in Society*. London: Longman.

Hattie, J. A. C. 2009 *Visible Learning: A Synthesis of over 800 Meta-Analyses Relating to Achievement*. London: Routledge.

Heffernan, D. A. and M. S. Learmonth 1983 *The World of Science – Book 4*. Melbourne: Longman Cheshire

Henderson, E. H. and Templeton S. 1986 A developmental perspective of formal spelling instruction through alphabet, pattern, and meaning. *The Elementary School Journal* 86.3: 304-16.

Hoepper, B., D. Henderson, J. Hennessey, D. Hutton and S. Mitchell 1996 *Inquiry 2: A Source-Based Approach to Modern History*. Milton: Jacaranda

Hood, S. 2010 *Appraising Research: Evaluation in Academic Writing*. London: Palgrave.

Humphrey, S. 1996 *Exploring Literacy in School Geography*. Sydney: Metropolitan East Disadvantaged Schools Program.

Hutchins, P. 1968 *Rosie's Walk*. New York: The Bodley Head

Hyon, S. 1996 Genre in three traditions: implications for ESL. *TESOL Quarterly* 30.4: 693-722.

Iedema, R. 1995. *Literacy of Administration (Write it Right Literacy in Industry Research Project – Stage 3)*. Sydney: Metropolitan East Disadvantaged Schools Program.

Iedema, R 1997a The language of administration: organizing human activity in formal institutions. In F. Christie and J. R. Martin (eds.) *Genre and Institutions: Social Processes in the Workplace and School*. London: Cassell, 73-100.

Iedema, R 1997b The history of the accident news story. *Australian Review of Applied Linguistics* 20.2: 95-119.

Iedema, R. 2003 *Discourses of Post-Bureaucratic Organization*. Amsterdam: Benjamins.

Iedema, R., S. Feez and P. White 1994 *Media Literacy (Write it Right Literacy in Industry Research Project – Stage 2)*. Sydney: Metropolitan East Disadvantaged Schools Program [reprinted Sydney: NSW AMES, 2008].

Jabangardi Poulson, C. 1988 The school curriculum I would like for my children. *Curriculum Perspectives* 8.2: 68-9.

Janke, T. 2002 *Butterfly Song*. Sydney: Penguin

Jenneson, J. R. 1980. *Electrical Principles for the Electrical Trades*. Sydney: McGraw Hill.

Johns, A. M. (ed.) 2002 *Genre in the Classroom: Applying Theory and Research to Practice*. Mahwah, NJ: Lawrence Erlbaum.

Jones, J. 2007 Multiliteracies for academic purposes: multimodality in textbook and computer-based learning materials in science at university. In McCabe et al. 2007: 103-21.

Jones, J. 2008 Multiliteracies for academic purposes: a metafunctional exploration of intersemiosis and multimodality in university textbook and computer-based learning resources in science. PhD Thesis: University of Sydney. http://ses.library.usyd.edu.au/handle/2123/2259.

Koop, C. and D. Rose 2008 Reading to learn in Murdi Paaki: changing outcomes for indigenous students. *Literacy Learning: the Middle Years* 16.1: 41-6, http://www.alea.edu.au/

Labov, W. and J. Waletzky 1967 Narrative analysis. In J. Helm (ed.) *Essays on the Verbal and Visual Arts* (Proceedings of the 1966 Spring Meeting of the American Ethnological Society). Seattle: University of Washington Press, 12-44 [reprinted in *Journal of Narrative and Life History* 7.1-4].

Lee, A. 1996 *Gender, Literacy, Curriculum: Re-Writing School Geography*. London: Taylor and Francis (Critical perspectives on Literacy and Education).

Lemke, J. L. 1990. *Talking Science: Language, Learning and Values*. Norwood, NJ: Ablex (Language and Educational Processes).

Lester, Y. 1993 *Yami: The Autobiography of Yami Lester*. Alice Springs: Institute for Aboriginal Development.

Liu, Y. 2010. *Commitment Resources as Scaffolding Strategies in the Reading to Learn Program*. PhD Thesis, University of Sydney, Sun Yat Sen University.

Lobel, A. 1980 *Fables*. New York: HarperCollins.

Luke, A. 1996 Genres of power? Literacy education and the production of capital. In R. Hasan and G. Williams (eds.) *Literacy in Society*. London: Longman, 308-38.

Macken-Horarik, M. 1997 Relativism in the politics of discourse: response to James Paul Gee. In S. Muspratt, A. Luke and P. Freebody (eds.) *Constructing Critical Literacies: Teaching and Learning Textual Practice*. Sydney: Allen and Unwin, 303-14.

Macken-Horarik, M. 1998 Exploring the requirements of critical school literacy: a view from two classrooms. In F. Christie and R. Misson (eds.) *Literacy and Schooling*. London: Routledge, 74-103.

Macken-Horarik, M., J. R. Martin, G. Kress, M. Kalantzis, J. Rothery, W. Cope 1989 *An Approach to Writing K-12: Vol. 1–4*. Sydney: Literacy and Education Research Network and Directorate of Studies, NSW Department of Education.

Malcolm, I. 1991 'All right then, if you don't want to do that…': strategy and counter-strategy in classroom discourse management. *Guidelines* 13.2: 11-17.

Martin, J. R. 1985 *Factual Writing: Exploring and Challenging Social Reality*. Geelong: Deakin University Press [republished by Oxford University Press 1989].

Martin, J. R. 1990a Language and control: fighting with words. In C. Walton and W. Eggington (eds.) *Language: Maintenance, Power and Education in Australian Aboriginal Contexts*. Darwin: Northern Territory University Press, 12-43.

Martin, J. R. 1990b Literacy in science: learning to handle text as technology. In F. Christie (ed.) *Literacy for a Changing World*. Melbourne: Australian Council for Educational Research (Fresh Look at the Basics), 79-117. [republished in M. A. K. Halliday and J. R. Martin, *Writing Science: Literacy and Discursive Power*. London: Falmer (Critical Perspectives on Literacy and Education) 1993: 166-202].

Martin, J. R. 1991 Critical literacy: the role of a functional model of language. *Australian Journal of Reading* 14.2: 117-32.

Martin, J. R. 1992 *English Text: System and Structure*. Amsterdam: Benjamins.

Martin, J. R. 1993a Technology, bureaucracy and schooling: discursive resources and control. *Cultural Dynamics* 6.1: 84-130.

Martin, J. R. 1993b Life as a noun. In M. A. K. Halliday and J. R. Martin, *Writing Science: Literacy and Discursive Power*. London: Falmer (Critical Perspectives on Literacy and Education), 221-67.

Martin, J. R. 1996 Evaluating disruption: symbolising theme in junior secondary narrative. In R. Hasan and G. Williams (eds.) *Literacy in Society*. London: Longman, 124-71.

Martin, J. R. 1999a Mentoring semogenesis: 'genre-based' literacy pedagogy. In F. Christie (ed.) *Pedagogy and the Shaping of Consciousness: Linguistic and Social Processes*. London: Cassell (Open Linguistics Series), 123-55.

Martin, J. R. 1999b Linguistics and the consumer: theory in practice. *Linguistics and Education* 9.3: 409-46.

Martin, J. R. 2000a Design and practice: enacting functional linguistics in Australia. *Annual Review of Applied Linguistics* 20 (20th Anniversary Volume 'Applied Linguistics as an Emerging Discipline'): 116-26.

Martin, J. R. 2000b Grammar meets genre – reflections on the 'Sydney School'. *Arts: The Journal of the Sydney University Arts Association* 22: 47-95 [reprinted in *Educational Research on Foreign Languages and Arts* Sun Yat Sen University, Guangzhou (Special issue on Functional Linguistics and Applied Linguistics) 2 (2006): 28-54].

Martin, J. R. 2000c Close reading: functional linguistics as a tool for critical analysis. In L. Unsworth (ed.) *Researching Language in Schools and Communities: Functional Linguistics Approaches*. London: Cassell, 275-303.

Martin, J. R. 2002a From little things big things grow: ecogenesis in school geography. In R. Coe, L. Lingard and T. Teslenko (eds.) *The Rhetoric and Ideology of Genre: Strategies for Stability and Change*. Cresskill, NJ: Hampton Press, 243-71.

Martin, J. R. 2002b Writing history: construing time and value in discourses of the past. Colombi and Schleppergrell 2002: 87-118.

Martin, J. R. 2003 Making history: grammar for explanation. In J. R. Martin and R. Wodak (eds.) *Re/Reading the Past: Critical and Functional Perspectives on Discourses of History*. Amsterdam: Benjamins, 19-57.

Martin, J. R. 2004 Grammatical structure: what do we mean? In C. Coffin, A. Hewings and K. O'Halloran (eds.) *Applying English Grammar: Functional and Corpus Approaches*. London: Arnold, 57-76.

Martin, J. R. 2007a Construing knowledge: a functional linguistic perspective. In F. Christie, and J. R. Martin (eds.) *Language, Knowledge and Pedagogy: Functional Linguistic and Sociological Perspectives*. London: Cassell, 34-64.

Martin, J. R. 2007b Genre and field: social processes and knowledge structures in systemic functional semiotics. In L. Barbara and T. Berber Sardinha (eds.) *Proceedings of the 33rd International Systemic Functional Congress*. São Paulo: PUCSP. Online publication available at http://www.pucsp.br/isfc.

Martin, J. R. 2007c Metadiscourse: designing interaction in genre-based literacy programs. In R. Whittaker, M. O'Donnell and A. McCabe (eds.) *Language and Literacy: Functional Approaches*. London: Continuum, 95-122.

Martin, J. R. 2010 Semantic variation: modelling realisation, instantiation and individu-
ation in social semiosis. In M. Bednarek and J. R. Martin (eds.) *New Discourse on
Language: Functional Perspectives on Multimodality, Identity and Affiliation*.
London: Continuum.

Martin, J. R., K. Maton and E. Matruglio 2010 Historical cosmologies: epistemology and
axiology in Australian secondary school history *Revista Signos* 43.74: 433-63.

Martin, J. R. and R. McCormack 2000 Mapping meaning: profiling with integrity in a
post-modern world. *Applied Language Studies* 1.1: 6-18.

Martin, J. R. and G. Plum 1997 Construing experience: some story genres. *Journal of
Narrative and Life History* 7.1-4: 299-308.

Martin, J. R. and D. Rose 2003 *Working with Discourse: Meaning beyond the Clause*.
London: Continuum [2nd rev. edn 2007].

Martin, J. R. and D. Rose 2005 Designing literacy pedagogy: scaffolding asymmetries. In
R. Hasan, C. M. I. M. Matthiessen and J. Webster (eds.) *Continuing Discourse on
Language*. London: Equinox, 251-80.

Martin, J. R. and D. Rose 2007 Interacting with text: the role of dialogue in learning to
read and write. *Foreign Languages in China* 4.5: 66-80.

Martin, J. R. and D. Rose 2008 *Genre Relations: Mapping Culture*. London: Equinox.

Martin, J. R. and R. Veel (eds.) 1998 *Reading Science: Critical and Functional Perspectives on Discourses of Science*. London: Routledge.

Martin, J. R. and P. R. R. White 2005 *The Language of Evaluation: Appraisal in English*.
London: Palgrave.

Martin, J. R., P. Wignell, S. Eggins and J. Rothery 1988 Secret English: discourse tech-
nology in a junior secondary school. In L. Gerot, J. Oldenberg and T. Van Leeuwen
(eds.) *Language and Socialisation: Home and School*. Sydney: School of English and
Linguistics, Macquarie University (Report of the 1986 Working Conference on
Language in Education), 143-73 [republished in B. Cope and M. Kalantzis (eds.)
Genre Approaches to Literacy: Theories and Practices (Papers from the 1991 LERN
Conference, University of Technology, Sydney, 23–24 November 1991). Sydney:
Common Ground, 1993: 43-76].

Martin, J. R. and R. Wodak (eds.) 2003 *Re/Reading the Past: Critical and Functional
Perspectives on Discourses of History*. Amsterdam: Benjamins.

McCabe, A., M. O'Donnell and R. Whittaker (eds.) 2007 *Advances in Language and
Education*. London: Continuum.

McGee, L. M. 1998. How do we teach literature to young children? In S. B. Neuman and
K. A. Roskos (eds.) *Children Achieving: Best Practices in Early Literacy*. Newark:
Newark International Reading Association, 162-79.

McRae, D., G. Ainsworth, J. Cumming, P. Hughes, T. Mackay, K. Price, M. Rowland,
J. Warhurst, D. Woods and V. Zbar 2000 *What has Worked, and Will Again: The
IESIP Strategic Results Projects*. Canberra: Australian Curriculum Studies Associ-
ation.

Mehan, H. 1979 *Learning Lessons: Social Organization in the Classroom*. Cambridge,
MA: Harvard University Press.

Mercer, N. 1995 *The Guided Construction of Knowledge: Talk amongst Teachers and Learners*. Clevedon: Multilingual Matters.

Mercer, N. 2000 *Words and Minds: How we Use Language to Work Together*. London: Routledge.

Muller, J. 2000 *Reclaiming Knowledge: Social Theory, Curriculum and Education Policy*. London: Routledge (Knowledge, Identity and School Life Series 8).

Murray, N. and K. Zammit 1992 *The Action Pack: Animals (Activities for Teaching Factual Writing)*. Sydney: Metropolitan East DSP (Language and Social Power Project).

Nassaji, H. and G. Wells 2000 What's the use of 'Triadic Dialogue'?: an investigation of teacher–student interaction. *Applied Linguistics* 21.3: 376-406.

New London Group 1996 A pedagogy of multiliteracies: designing social futures. *Harvard Educational Review* 66.1: 60-92.

Nuttall T., J. Wright, J. Hoffman, N. Sishi and S. Khandlhela 1998 *From Apartheid to Democracy: South Africa 1948–1994*. Pietermaritzburg: Shuter & Shooter.

Nuthall, G. 2004 Relating classroom teaching to student learning: a critical analysis of why research has failed to bridge the theory-practice gap. *Harvard Educational Review* 74.3: 273-306.

Nuthall, G. A. 2005 The cultural myths and realities of classroom teaching and learning: a personal journey. *Teachers College Record* 107.5: 895-934.

Ng, J., J. Powditch, L. Abeni and J. Callow 1999 'Vote for Me!' The art of persuasion. In J. Callow (ed.) *Image Matters: Visual Texts in the Classroom*. Marrickville, NSW: Primary English Teaching Association, 65-74.

Oakes, J., K. H. Quartz, J. Gong, G. Guiton and M. Lipton 1993 Creating middle schools: technical, normative and political considerations. *The Elementary School Journal* 93.5: 461-80.

O'Halloran, K. L. 2005 *Mathematical Discourse: Language, Symbolism and Visual Images*. London: Continuum.

Painter, C. 1984 *Into the Mother Tongue: A Case Study of Early Language Development*. London: Pinter.

Painter, C. 1986 The role of interaction in learning to speak and learning to write. In C. Painter and J. R. Martin (eds.) *Writing to Mean: Teaching Genres across the Curriculum*. Applied Linguistics Association of Australia (Occasional Papers 9), 62-97.

Painter, C. 1991 *Learning the Mother Tongue* (2nd edn). Geelong, Vic.: Deakin University Press.

Painter, C. 1996 The development of language as a resource for thinking: a linguistic view of learning. In R. Hasan and G. Williams (eds.) *Literacy in Society*. London: Longman, 50-85.

Painter, C. 1999 *Learning through Language in Early Childhood*. London: Cassell.

Painter, C. and J. R. Martin (eds.) 1986 *Writing to Mean: Teaching Genres across the Curriculum*. Applied Linguistics Association of Australia (Occasional Papers 9).

Pilkington, D. 1996. *Follow the Rabbit-Proof Fence*. St Lucia: University of Queensland Press.

Reid, I. (ed.) 1987 *The Place of Genre in Learning.* Geelong, Vic.: Centre for Studies in Literary Education, Deakin University (Typereader Publications 1).

Rose, D. 1992 Protection, self-determination and language learning in Aboriginal early childhood education: review of Aboriginal language education policy statements. *Education Australia* Spring: 5-6.

Rose, D. 1997 Science, technology and technical literacies. In F. Christie and J. R. Martin (eds.) *Genre and Institutions: Social Processes in the Workplace and School.* London: Cassell, 40-72.

Rose, D. 1998 Science discourse and industrial hierarchy. In J. R. Martin and R. Veel (eds.) *Reading Science: Critical and Functional Perspectives on Discourses of Science.* London: Routledge, 236-65.

Rose, D. 1999 Culture, competence and schooling: approaches to literacy teaching in Indigenous school education. In F. Christie (ed.) *Pedagogy and the Shaping of Consciousness: Linguistic and Social Processes.* London: Cassell (Open Linguistics Series), 217-45.

Rose, D. 2004 Sequencing and pacing of the hidden curriculum: how Indigenous children are left out of the chain. In J. Muller, A. Morais and B. Davies (eds.) *Reading Bernstein, Researching Bernstein.* London: RoutledgeFalmer, 91-107.

Rose, D. 2005 Democratising the classroom: a literacy pedagogy for the new generation. *Journal of Education* 37: 127-64, http://www.ukzn.ac.za/joe/joe_issues.htm

Rose, D. 2006a Reading genre: a new wave of analysis. *Linguistics and the Human Sciences* 2.2: 185-204.

Rose, D. 2006b Literacy and equality. In A. Simpson (ed.) *Proceedings of Future Directions in Literacy Conference.* University of Sydney, 188-203. http://www.proflearn.edsw.usyd.edu.au/resources/2006_papers.shtml

Rose, D. 2007 Towards a reading based theory of teaching. Plenary paper in *Proceedings 33rd International Systemic Functional Congress 2006.* São Paulo: PUCSP. http://www.pucsp.br/isfc

Rose, D. 2008a Writing as linguistic mastery: the development of genre-based literacy pedagogy. In R. Beard, D. Myhill, J. Riley and M. Nystrand (eds.) *Handbook of Writing Development.* London: Sage, 151-66.

Rose, D. 2008b Redesigning Foundations: integrating academic skills with academic learning. Keynote for *Conversations about Foundations Conference*, Cape Peninsula University of Technology, Cape Town, October 2007. http://associated.sun.ac.za/heltasa/foundationprogram.html

Rose, D. 2010a Meaning beyond the margins: learning to interact with books. In J. Martin, S. Hood and S. Dreyfus (ed.) *Semiotic Margins: Reclaiming Meaning.* London: Continuum, 177-208.

Rose, D. 2010b Learning in linguistic contexts: integrating SFL theory with literacy teaching. In Y. Fang and C. Wu (eds.) *Challenges to Systemic Functional Linguistics: Theory and Practice. Proceedings of the 36th International Systemic Functional Congress, Beijing July 2009.* Beijing: Tsinghua University, Sydney: Macquarie University, 258-63.

Rose, D. 2011a *Reading to Learn: Accelerating Learning and Closing the Gap*. Teacher training books and DVD. Sydney: Reading to Learn. http://www.readingtolearn.com.au.

Rose, D. 2011b Beyond literacy: building an integrated pedagogic genre. *Australian Journal of Language and Literacy* 34.1: 81-97 (also in Proceedings of ASFLA Conference, Brisbane, October 2009 www.asfla.org.au).

Rose, D. 2011c *Implementation and Outcomes of the Professional Learning Program, 2010: Report for Western NSW Region, NSW Department of Education and Childrens Services*. Sydney: Reading to Learn. http://www.readingtolearn.com.au.

Rose, D. 2011d Beating educational inequality with an integrated reading pedagogy. In F. Christie and A. Simpson (eds.) *Literacy and Social Responsibility: Multiple Perspectives*. London: Equinox, 101-15.

Rose, D. 2011e Genre in the Sydney School. In J. Gee and M. Handford (eds.) *The Routledge Handbook of Discourse Analysis*. London: Routledge, 209-25.

Rose, D. and C. Acevedo 2006 Closing the gap and accelerating learning in the middle years of schooling. *Australian Journal of Language and Literacy* 14.2: 32-45. http://www.alea.edu.au/llmy0606.htm

Rose, D., B. Gray and W. Cowey 1999 Scaffolding reading and writing for indigenous children in school. In P Wignell (ed.) *Double Power: English Literacy and Indigenous Education*. Melbourne: National Language and Literacy Institute of Australia (NLLIA), 23-60.

Rose, D., D. McInnes and H. Korner 1992 *Scientific Literacy (Write it Right Literacy in Industry Research Project – Stage 1)*. Sydney: Metropolitan East Disadvantaged Schools Program [reprinted Sydney: NSW AMES, 2007].

Rose, D., L. Lui-Chivizhe, A. McKnight and A. Smith 2004 Scaffolding academic reading and writing at the Koori Centre. *Australian Journal of Indigenous Education* 30th Anniversary Edition: 41-9. http://www.atsis.uq.edu.au/ajie

Rose, D., M. Rose, S. Farrington and S. Page 2008 Scaffolding literacy for Indigenous health sciences students. *Journal of English for Academic Purposes* 7.3: 166-80.

Rothery, J. 1989 Learning about language. In R. Hasan and J. R. Martin (eds.) *Language Development: Learning Language, Learning Culture*. Norwood, NJ: Ablex, 199-256.

Rothery, J. 1994 *Exploring Literacy in School English (Write it Right Resources for Literacy and Learning)*. Sydney: Metropolitan East Disadvantaged Schools Program.

Rothery, J. 1996 Making changes: developing an educational linguistics. In R. Hasan and G. Williams (eds.) *Literacy in Society*. London: Longman, 86-123.

Rothery, J. and M. Stenglin 1997 Entertaining and instructing: exploring experience through story. In F. Christie and J. R. Martin (eds.) *Genre and Institutions: Social Processes in the Workplace and School*. London: Cassell, 231-63.

Rothery, J. and M. Stenglin 2000 Interpreting literature: the role of appraisal. In L. Unsworth (ed.) *Researching Language in Schools and Communities: Functional Linguistics Approaches*. London: Cassell, 222-44.

Schleppegrell, M. J. 2004 *The Language of Schooling: A Functional Linguistic Perspective*. Mahwah, NJ: Erlbaum.

Scott, D. 1983 *A Manual for the Writing Teacher*. Bundoora: Centre for Study of Urban Education, La Trobe University.

Sinclair, J. and R. Coulthard 1975 *Towards an Analysis of Discourse: The English Used by Teachers and Pupils*. London: Oxford University Press.

Swales, J. M. 1990 *Genre Analysis: English in Academic and Research Settings*. Cambridge: Cambridge University Press (Cambridge Applied Linguistics Series).

Swales, J. 2004 *Research Genres: Explorations and Applications*. Cambridge: Cambridge University Press.

Taylor, N., J. Muller and P. Vinjevold 2003 *Getting School Working: Research and Systemic School Reform in South Africa*. Cape Town: Pearson Education.

Tjungutu Uwankaraku 1985 *Amata: Social Crisis and Substance Abuse*, Report for the SA Minister of Health. Adelaide: SA Health. http://www.readingtolearn.com.au/

Topham, J. 2010 Review of Steinbeck's 'Of Mice and Men', http://classiclit.about.com/od/ofmiceandmensteinbeck/fr/aa_ofmice.htm

Turbill, J. 1983 *Now we Want to Write*. Sydney: Primary English Teaching Association.

UNESCO 2010 UNESCO Constitution. http://www.unesco.org/

Unsworth, L. 1997a Scaffolding reading of science explanations: accessing the grammatical and visual forms of specialised knowledge. *Reading* 31.3: 30-42.

Unsworth, L. 1997b Explaining explanations: enhancing scientific learning and literacy development. *Australian Science Teachers Journal* 43.1: 34-49.

Unsworth, L. 1997c 'Sound' explanations in school science: a functional linguistic perspective on effective apprenticing texts. *Linguistics and Education* 9.2: 199-226.

Unsworth, L. 1999a Developing critical understanding of the specialised language of school science and history: a functional grammatical perspective. *Journal of Adolescent and Adult Literacy* 42.7: 508-27.

Unsworth, L. 1999b Explaining school science in book and CD Rom formats: using semiotic analyses to compare the textual construction of knowledge. *International Journal of Instructional Media* 26.2: 159-79.

Unsworth, L. 2001a Evaluating the language of different types of explanations in junior high school science texts. *International Journal of Science Education* 23.6: 585-609.

Unsworth, L. 2001b *Teaching Multiliteracies across the Curriculum: Changing Contexts of Text and Image in Classroom Practice*. Buckingham: Open University Press.

Unsworth, L. 2008 *New Literacies and the English Curriculum: Multimodal Perspectives*. London: Continuum.

Van Leeuwen, T. 2008 *Discourse and Practice: New Tools for Critical Analysis*. Oxford: Oxford University Press.

Veel, R. 1992 Engaging with scientific language: a functional approach to the language of school science. *Australian Science Teachers Journal* 38.4: 31-5.

Veel, R. 1995 Making informed choices or jumping through hoops? The role of functional linguistics in an Outcomes-based curriculum. *Interpretations* 28.3: 62-76.

Veel, R. 1997 Learning how to mean – scientifically speaking: apprenticeship into scientific discourse in the secondary school. In F. Christie and J. R. Martin (eds.) *Genre and Institutions: Social Processes in the Workplace and School*. London: Cassell, 161-95.

Veel, R. 1998 The greening of school science: ecogenesis in secondary classrooms. In J. R. Martin and R. Veel (eds.) *Reading Science: Critical and Functional Perspectives on Discourses of Science*. London: Routledge, 114-51.

Veel, R. 1999 Language, knowledge and authority in school mathematics. In F. Christie, (ed.) *Pedagogy and the Shaping of Consciousness: Linguistic and Social Processes*. London: Cassell (Open Linguistics Series), 185-216.

Veel, R. 2006 The 'Write it Right' project. In R. Whittaker, M. O'Donnell and A. McCabe (eds.) *Language and Literacy: Functional Approaches*. London: Continuum, 66-92.

Veel, R. and C. Coffin 1996 Learning to think like an historian: the language of secondary school history. In R. Hasan and G. Williams (eds.) *Literacy in Society*. London: Longman, 191-231.

Ventola, E. 1987 *The Structure of Social Interaction*. London: Pinter.

Vygotsky, L. S. 1962 *Thought and Language*. Cambridge, MA: MIT Press.

Vygotsky, L. S. 1978 *Mind in Society: The Development of Higher Psychological Processes* (ed. M. Cole, V. John Steiner, S. Scribner and E. Souberman). Cambridge, MA: Harvard University Press.

Walshe, R. D. (ed.) 1981 *Donald Graves in Australia*. Sydney: Primary English Teaching Association.

Wells, G. 1999 *Dialogic Inquiry: Toward a Sociocultural Practice and Theory of Education*. Cambridge: Cambridge University Press (Learning in Doing: Social Cognitive and Computational Perspectives).

Wells, G. 2002 Learning and teaching for understanding: the key role of collaborative knowledge building. In J. Brophy (ed.) *Social Constructivist Teaching: Affordances and Constraints*. London: Elsevier (JAI: Advances in Research on Teaching 9), 1-41.

White, P. 1997 Death, disruption and the moral order: the narrative impulse in mass 'hard news' reporting. In F. Christie and J. R. Martin (eds.) *Genre and Institutions: Social Processes in the Workplace and School*. London: Cassell, 101-33.

White, P. 1998 Extended reality, proto-nouns and the vernacular: distinguishing the technological from the scientific. In J. R. Martin and R. Veel (eds.) *Reading Science: Critical and Functional Perspectives on Discourses of Science*. London: Routledge, 266-96.

White, P. R. R. 2000 Dialogue and inter-subjectivity: reinterpreting the semantics of modality and hedging. In M. Coulthard, J. Cotterill and F. Rock (eds.) *Working with Dialogue*. Tübingen: Neimeyer, 67-80.

Wignell, P. 1994 Genre across the curriculum. *Linguistics and Education* 6: 355-72.

Wignell, P., J. R. Martin and S. Eggins 1989 The discourse of geography: ordering and explaining the experiential world. *Linguistics and Education* 1.4: 359-92.

Williams, G. 1995 Joint book-reading and literacy pedagogy: a socio-semantic examination. Volume 1. CORE. 19(3). Fiche 2 B01- Fiche 6 B01.

Williams, G. 1999a Grammar as a metasemiotic tool in child literacy development. In C. Ward and W. Renandya (eds.) *Language Teaching: New Insights for the Language Teacher*. Singapore: Regional English Language Centre (RELC)/SEAMIO, 89-124.

Williams, G. 1999b The pedagogic device and the production of discourse: a case example in early literacy education. In F. Christie, (ed.) *Pedagogy and the Shaping of Consciousness: Linguistic and Social Processes*. London: Cassell (Open Linguistics Series), 88-122.

Williams, G. 2001 Literacy pedagogy prior to schooling: relations between social positioning and semantic variation. In A. Morais, I. Neves, B. Davies and H. Daniels (eds.) *Towards a Sociology of Pedagogy: The Contribution of Basil Bernstein in Research*. New York and Washington: Peter Lang, 17-46.

Williams, G. 2004 Ontogenesis and grammatics: functions of metalanguage in pedagogical discourse. Williams and Lukin 2004: 241-67.

Williams, G. 2005a Grammatics in schools. In R. Hasan, C. M. I. M. Matthiessen and J. Webster (eds.) *Continuing Discourse on Language: A Functional Perspective*. London: Equinox, 281-310.

Williams, G. 2005b Semantic variation. Hasan et al. 2005: 457-80.

Williams, G. and A. Lukin (eds.) 2004 *The Development of Language: Functional Perspectives on Species and Individuals*. London: Continuum (Open Linguistics Series).

Wood, D., J. Bruner and G. Ross 1976 The role of tutoring in problem solving. *Journal of Child Psychology and Psychiatry* 17: 89-100.

Index

Lightning Source UK Ltd.
Milton Keynes UK
UKOW04f1050131216

289884UK00001B/10/P

9 781845 531447